Business Networking

Springer
*Berlin
Heidelberg
New York
Barcelona
Hong Kong
London
Milan
Paris
Singapore
Tokyo*

Hubert Österle · Elgar Fleisch
Rainer Alt

Business Networking

Shaping Collaboration Between Enterprises

Second, Revised and Extended Edition

With 120 Figures
and 40 Tables

With Contributions by
Volker Bach, Vladimir Barak, Robert Betts, Ralph Dolmetsch,
Karl Maria Grünauer, Thomas Huber, Norbert Kaltenmorgen,
Roland Klüber, Günter Lehmann, Andreas Pfadenhauer, Sven Pohland,
Thomas Puschmann, Christian Reichmayr, Thomas Reiss,
Karl-Heinz Schelhas, Jens Schulze, Frederic Thiesse, Rudolf Zurmühlen

 Springer

Professor Dr. Hubert Österle
Dr. Elgar Fleisch
Dr. Rainer Alt

Institute of Information Management
University of St. Gallen
Müller-Friedberg-Strasse 8
9000 St. Gallen
Switzerland
E-mail: <firstname.lastname@unisg.ch>
WWW: http://www.iwi.unisg.ch

ISBN 3-540-41351-0 Springer-Verlag Berlin Heidelberg New York

Library of Congress Cataloging-in-Publication Data
Die Deutsche Bibliothek – CIP-Einheitsaufnahme
Business networking: collaborative processes at work; with 40 tables / Hubert Österle ... With
contributions by Volker Bach ... – 2., rev. and extended ed. – Berlin; Heidelberg; New York;
Barcelona; Hong Kong; London; Milan; Paris; Singapore; Tokyo: Springer, 2001
    ISBN 3-540-41351-0

Springer-Verlag Berlin Heidelberg New York
a member of BertelsmannSpringer Science+Business Media GmbH

© Springer-Verlag Berlin · Heidelberg 2000, 2001
Printed in Germany

SPIN 10789973   43/2202-5 4 3 2 1 0 – Printed on acid-free paper

Preface

Since the first edition of Business Networking was published in late 1999, a profound development has taken place in the business-to-business area. Portals and electronic marketplaces have been established at a fast pace – [Keenan Research 2000] for example reports that between November 1999 and April 2000 a total of 620 Internet exchanges were founded. Some 4,000 were forecasted for 2004. Today, the smoke over the water is becoming clearer and we see the first B2B sites and exchanges being acquired or exiting the market [cf. e.g. Ante/Weintraub 2000]. The obvious conclusion is that there will be only two or three winners in each market segment.

In our opinion, this development shows that shaping relationships among businesses, an area we termed 'Business Networking', is only a technological game to a limited degree. Links to strategy and business processes are vital, and strategies for EC need to be planned jointly with supply chain or customer relationship strategies. Therefore, the mission of Business Networking, i.e. to provide an integrated process-oriented concept for all areas of eBusiness, remains more critical than ever.

This second edition differs quite substantially from the first. We not only corrected spelling and wording, improved and expanded definitions of key terms (e.g. Chapter 1, *Introduction*), and updated company-specific data in Chapters 9, Overview on *Supply Chain Management Systems* and 10, *Electronic Commerce in the Procurement of Indirect Goods*. We also completely revised Chapters 3, *The Networked Enterprise* and 14, *Towards a Method for Business Networking*, added Chapters 12, *eServices for Integrating eMarkets* and 15, *Application of the Business Networking Method at SAP*, and last but not least made it easier to access data contained in the book by means of a new comprehensive index.

The publication of this book has been made possible largely thanks to the support of three groups of people: (a) the partner companies of the Competence Centers in Business Networking (cf. Chap. 1.3.3), (b) the Board of the 'Business Engineering HSG' research program, and (c) the people who dealt with the nuts and bolts of the book itself.

Some fifteen executives from large Swiss and German enterprises together with the three Professors from IWI-HSG form the Board of the 'Business Engineering HSG' research program. The Board helps to collect and prioritize research topics and perform reality checks on the results achieved. The topic of Business Networking was derived from the ongoing cooperation between research and practice. This book is just one result of the open and cooperative culture which exists between industry and research as well as between different research chairs, namely those of Prof. Andrea Back and Prof. Robert Winter at the IWI-HSG.

Sybille Lötscher, junior research assistant at the IWI-HSG, and Thomas Pusch-mann, senior research assistant at the IWI-HSG, were responsible for the organ-izational side of compiling this book. They succeeded in perfectly balancing the multiple goals, enablers and restrictions of authors, editors, publisher, standards and Microsoft Office. Melanie Fletcher and Eduard Alt helped us to translate German thought into English word.

We hope you will enjoy reading this second edition and find it helpful in your daily work. Needless to say, any feedback that contributes to further improve-ments in Business Networking is most welcome.

Hubert Österle

Elgar Fleisch

Rainer Alt

Overview of Contents

1 Introduction – Chances and Challenges in Business
   Networking 1

Part 1: Building the Foundation.. 15

2 Enterprise in the Information Age 17

3 The Networked Enterprise 55

Part 2: Business Concepts 87

4 Strategies for Business Networking 89

5 Business Networking Lessons Learned: Supply Chain
   Management at Riverwood International 111

6 Electronic Commerce and Supply Chain Management at
   'The Swatch Group' 121

7 Knowledge Enabled Customer Relationship Management 135

Part 3: Information System Concepts.. 153

8 Future Application Architecture for the Pharmaceutical
   Industry... 155

9 Overview on Supply Chain Management Systems 175

10 Electronic Commerce in the Procurement of Indirect Goods. 193

11 Templates: Standardization for Business Networking 211

12 eServices for Integrating eMarkets.. 229

Part 4: Key Success Factors... 247

13 Key Success Factors for Business Networking Systems........ 249

14 Towards a Method for Business Networking 265

15   Application of the Business Networking Method at SAP 289

16   Architecture Planning for Global Networked Enterprises...... 305

17   Business Networking - Summary and Outlook 323

List of Abbreviations 331

Glossary 335

References.. 345

Index 379

Authors 395

Questionnaire for Networkability Assessment 397

Table of Contents

1   **Introduction – Chances and Challenges in Business Networking** 1

   1.1 Networked Enterprise: The Vision 2
      1.1.1 Business Networking and the New Economy 2
      1.1.2 Five Phases Towards Business Networking 2

   1.2 Networking the Enterprise: The Transformation 4
      1.2.1 Closing the Gap Between Strategy and Reality 4
      1.2.2 Achieving Networkability 5
      1.2.3 Part One: Building the Foundation 6
      1.2.4 Part Two: Business Concepts 7
      1.2.5 Part Three: Information System Concepts 8
      1.2.6 Part Four: Key Success Factors 8

   1.3 Research Approach 9
      1.3.1 Applied Research: Providing Practical Guidelines 9
      1.3.2 Action Research: Balancing Rigor and Relevance 10
      1.3.3 Competence Centers in Business Networking 11

Part 1: Building the Foundation 15

2   **Enterprise in the Information Age** 17

   2.1 Challenge of the Information Age 18

   2.2 Imperatives of Business in the Internet Age 19
      2.2.1 Coverage 20
      2.2.2 Partnering 20
      2.2.3 Critical Mass of Customers and Suppliers 20
      2.2.4 Position in the Business Network 21
      2.2.5 Focusing 21
      2.2.6 Process Efficiency 22
      2.2.7 Networkability 22
      2.2.8 Change Management 23

   2.3 Seven Trends 23
      2.3.1 Enterprise Resource Planning 24
      2.3.2 Knowledge Management 28
      2.3.3 Smart Appliances 32
      2.3.4 Business Networking 36
      2.3.5 Electronic Services 43
      2.3.6 Customer Process Support 45
      2.3.7 Value Management 51

3   The Networked Enterprise 55

3.1 Introduction 56

3.2 Business Networking Case Examples 57
    3.2.1 Dell: Supply Chain Management and Customer
        Relationship Management 57
    3.2.2 Amazon.com: Supply Chain Management and Customer
        Relationship Management 59
    3.2.3 Avnet Marshall: Supply Chain Management and
        Customer Relationship Management 61
    3.2.4 SAP: Customer Relationship Management 62
    3.2.5 MarketSite.net: Procurement and Sales 63
    3.2.6 UBS: Procurement 65
    3.2.7 Migros Cooperative: Development 66
    3.2.8 Commtech: Procurement, Finance, Real Estate and Taxes 67

3.3 Networked Business Processes 69
    3.3.1 Networking Through Coordination 70
    3.3.2 Collaborative Processes 71

3.4 Model of a Networked Enterprise 75
    3.4.1 eServices 75
    3.4.2 Standards 76
    3.4.3 Model 76

3.5 Networkability as a Competitive Factor 77
    3.5.1 Concept and Design Objects of Networkability 78
    3.5.2 Approaches to Measuring Networkability 79

3.6 Consequences for Management: Design for Networkability 81

3.7 Conclusions 84

Part 2: Business Concepts 87

4   Strategies for Business Networking 89

4.1 Introduction 90
    4.1.1 Strategic Relevance of Business Networking 90
    4.1.2 Overview of Strategies 91

4.2 Organization Strategies 92
    4.2.1 Outsourcing – Externalizing Non-core Competencies 93
    4.2.2 Insourcing – Strengthening Existing Competencies 94
    4.2.3 Virtual Organizing – New Segments with Cooperation
        Partners 95
    4.2.4 Developing New Business Segments 96
    4.2.5 Summary of Organization Strategies 98

4.3   Networking Strategies 99
      4.3.1   Electronic Commerce – Transaction Perspective....................101
      4.3.2   Supply Chain Management – Flow Perspective 104
      4.3.3   Customer Relationship Management – Relationship
              Perspective 107
      4.3.4   Summary of Networking Strategies 108

4.4   Interaction of Business Networking Strategies 109

4.5   Conclusions..110

**5   Business Networking Lessons Learned: Supply Chain
      Management at Riverwood International 111**

5.1   Business Networking Is Customer and Supplier Integration...............112

5.2   Establishing the Business Networking Vision 113

5.3   Implementing the Business Networking Vision....................................114

5.4   As the Tide Comes In All Boats Go Up..115

5.5   Shaping Competitive Advantage..116

5.6   Creating the Coordination Backbone 117

5.7   Becoming Part of the Business Networking Infrastructure 118

**6   Electronic Commerce and Supply Chain Management
      at 'The Swatch Group'.. 121**

6.1   Introduction..122

6.2   Comparison of Concepts 122

6.3   Case Study: EC and SCM at ETA SA...124
      6.3.1   Goals of EC and SCM at ETA SA...124
      6.3.2   Initial Problems at ETA SA 124
      6.3.3   Phase I: Re-engineering the Supply Chain...............................125
      6.3.4   Phase II: Introduction of a EC Solution 126
      6.3.5   Complementarity of Concepts and Implementation..................128

6.4   Critical Success Factors at ETA SA...129
      6.4.1   Master Data Management as 'Hidden Success Factor'............129
      6.4.2   Strategic Alignment with Marketing Strategy 130
      6.4.3   Reciprocity of Benefits 130
      6.4.4   Common Basis for Communication..131
      6.4.5   Method for Structured Procedure..132

6.5   Conclusions and Next Steps...133

**7   Knowledge Enabled Customer Relationship
      Management 135**

   7.1   Introduction 136
      7.1.1   Business Trend: Customer Centricity 136
      7.1.2   Technology Trend: Tools for Marketing, Sales and
            Service Automation 137

   7.2   Case Study: LGT Bank 139

   7.3   Managing Customer Knowledge 141
      7.3.1   Knowledge Management 141
      7.3.2   Relationship Marketing 142
      7.3.3   Knowledge Enabled Customer Relationship Management 143

   7.4   Towards a CRM Reference Model 144
      7.4.1   Business Processes 145
      7.4.2   Knowledge Structure 148
      7.4.3   Knowledge Infrastructure 150
      7.4.4   Knowledge Measurements 151

   7.5   Knowledge in Business Networks 152

Part 3: Information System Concepts 153

**8   Future Application Architecture for the Pharmaceutical
      Industry 155**

   8.1   Introduction – New Business Models Are Emerging 156

   8.2   From Business Model to Application Architecture 157

   8.3   Future Business in the Pharmaceutical Industry 159
      8.3.1   Elements of the Business Model 160
      8.3.2   Relevance of the Seven Trends for the Pharmaceutical
            Industry 162

   8.4   Application Architecture of the Information Age 164
      8.4.1   Flexibility 165
      8.4.2   Networking - Capability of Integration 165
      8.4.3   Standardization 166

   8.5   Components of the Application Architecture 166
      8.5.1   Future Application Architecture Areas 166
      8.5.2   'Extended' Make-or-Buy Decision 168
      8.5.3   Application Architecture Components 170

   8.6   Summary and Outlook 173

9   Overview on Supply Chain Management Systems............ 175

9.1 Introduction...176
      9.1.1 Objectives 176
      9.1.2 Supply Chain Pyramid 177

9.2 Planning Processes and Planning Horizons.......................................179

9.3 Software Concepts for Supply Chain Management 180
      9.3.1 Transaction and Planning Systems.......................................180
      9.3.2 Material Requirements Planning (MRP I) 181
      9.3.3 Manufacturing Resource Planning (MRP II) 181
      9.3.4 Advanced Planning Systems 183

9.4 Brief Overview on Advanced Planning Systems 185
      9.4.1 Functionality and Modules..185
      9.4.2 Rhythm Solutions of i2 Technologies....................................188
      9.4.3 Manugistics6 of Manugistics 189
      9.4.4 APO of SAP...189
      9.4.5 Numetrix of J.D. Edwards...190

9.5 Conclusions..190

10   Electronic Commerce in the Procurement of Indirect
     Goods 193

10.1 Challenge in Indirect / MRO Procurement.......................................194
      10.1.1 Introduction..194
      10.1.2 Current Procurement Scenarios 195
      10.1.3 Relevance of Indirect / MRO Procurement...........................197

10.2 Vendors of Desktop Purchasing Systems..198
      10.2.1 Ariba Operating Resources Management System...................198
      10.2.2 Commerce One BuySite / MarketSite.....................................199
      10.2.3 iPlanet BuyerXpert / ECXpert 199

10.3 Overview of System Components and Functionality 200

10.4 Process and Workflow Functionality 201
      10.4.1 Catalog and Sourcing Services 201
      10.4.2 Purchase Requisition and Order Placement 202
      10.4.3 Delivery and Receipt...203
      10.4.4 Payment and Booking 204
      10.4.5 Process Management 204

10.5 Content Management 204
      10.5.1 Content Classification...205
      10.5.2 Content Aggregation...205
      10.5.3 Content Personalization 206

10.6 System Administration...207

10.7 Integration with Legacy / ERP Systems.................................207

10.8 Potential Savings of Desktop Purchasing Systems 208

11   Templates: Standardization for Business Networking 211

11.1 Introduction...212

11.2 Definition and Approaches to Standardization......................213
    11.2.1 Definition and Dimensions of Standardization 213
    11.2.2 Requirements of Inter-process Integration...............................214
    11.2.3 Approaches to Close the 'Organization Gap' 215

11.3 Template Handbook 216
    11.3.1 Idea of a Template Handbook...217
    11.3.2 Components of a Template Handbook..217
    11.3.3 Activities in Template Design and Roll-out..............................218
    11.3.4 Who Should Design and Use a Template Handbook?.............219

11.4 Template Handbook at the Robert Bosch Group 220
    11.4.1 Development of the Template Handbook 220
    11.4.2 Overview and Experiences..221
    11.4.3 Example Documents 223

11.5 Benefits of Templates in a Pharmaceutical Company...........225

11.6 Conclusions...227

12   eServices for Integrating eMarkets..................................... 229

12.1 Business Networking and ERP Integration 230

12.2 eMarkets and eServices in Business Networking...................231
    12.2.1 Evolution and Market Potential 231
    12.2.2 Benefits of eMarkets 231
    12.2.3 Benefits of Process Integration 232
    12.2.4 Integration Requirements..232

12.3 eServices for Integration - Case of Triaton 234
    12.3.1 newtron and Triaton – eMarket and System Supplier..............234
    12.3.2 Considerations on eMarket Integration Potential.....................235
    12.3.3 Triaton eService 'A2A e-Link for eMarkets'............................236
    12.3.4 Cooperation newtron and Triaton 237
    12.3.5 Business Process Support and Benefits.....................................239

12.4 Implementation and Architecture of A2A e-Link for
    eMarkets...240

12.5 Digression: Solution Enhancement Potentials with IBM
    tpaML...243

12.6 Conclusions and Outlook 246

Part 4: Key Success Factors.. 247

13 Key Success Factors for Business Networking Systems.... 249

13.1 Challenges in Designing Business Networking Systems 250
    13.1.1 Adoption-lag of Interorganizational Systems 250
    13.1.2 Gap Between Business and IT Issues.....................................251

13.2 Characterization of Business Networking Systems...........................252
    13.2.1 Types of Transaction-oriented Business Networking
           Systems 252
    13.2.2 Specifics of Business Networking Systems 253

13.3 Key Success Factors in Designing Business Networking
    Systems 255
    13.3.1 Cases for Business Networking Systems 255
    13.3.2 Setting-up Partner Profiles...257
    13.3.3 Reciprocity: Creating Win-Win Situations 260
    13.3.4 Networking Projects are Business Projects............................261
    13.3.5 Nucleus and Rapid Diffusion: 'Grow by Chunking' 261
    13.3.6 Standards and System Integration as a 'Conditio Sine Qua
           Non'...262

13.4 Conclusions...263

14 Towards a Method for Business Networking...................... 265

14.1 Challenges of Making Business Networking Happen.........................266
    14.1.1 Relevance of a Method for Business Networking...................266
    14.1.2 Existing Approaches and Requirements 266
    14.1.3 Benefits of an Engineering Approach....................................268
    14.1.4 Focus and Procedure Model of the Method 270

14.2 Case I: eProcurement at Deutsche Telekom AG................................272
    14.2.1 Business Context of Deutsche Telekom AG............................272
    14.2.2 Options for Organizing Procurement.....................................272
    14.2.3 Steps Undertaken at Deutsche Telekom 274

14.3 Case II: Supply Chain Management at Riverwood
    International 275
    14.3.1 Supply Chain Scenario at Riverwood International.................275
    14.3.2 Steps Undertaken at Riverwood International 277

14.4 Towards a Method for Business Networking 280
        14.4.1 Design Areas of a Method for Business Networking 281
        14.4.2 Meta Model 282
        14.4.3 Role Model 283
        14.4.4 Procedure Model and Techniques 283

    14.5 Conclusions and Outlook 286

15 Application of the Business Networking Method at SAP . 289

    15.1 Distinction Between Business Networking Strategies 290
        15.1.1 Overview 290
        15.1.2 Interaction of Strategies From the Customer Perspective 290

    15.2 A Method for Implementing Supply Chain Modules 292
        15.2.1 Goals of the Method 292
        15.2.2 Business Networking Systems and Methods of SAP 292
        15.2.3 Accelerated SAP (ASAP) Roadmap 293
        15.2.4 Strategic Blueprint of ASAP for APO 2.0a 294

    15.3 Reference Case for the Strategic Blueprint: Woodbridge, Int. 295

    15.4 Conclusions and Next Steps 302

**16 Architecture Planning for Global Networked
    Enterprises 305**

    16.1 Introduction 306
        16.1.1 Challenge of Architecture Planning 306
        16.1.2 Goals of Architecture Planning 307

    16.2 Business Architecture 309
        16.2.1 Organization Profile 309
        16.2.2 Process Architecture 311

    16.3 Application Architecture 313
        16.3.1 Distribution Concepts in Packaged Software 313
        16.3.2 Integration Areas at the Application Level 313
        16.3.3 Structure of Application Architecture 314

    16.4 Methodological Procedure 316
        16.4.1 Existing Approaches 316
        16.4.2 Deficits of Existing Methods 318
        16.4.3 Proposed Method 318

    16.5 Conclusions and Outlook 321

17   Business Networking - Summary and Outlook................**323**

    17.1 Bottom Line of Business Networking.................................324
        17.1.1 Improving Business Efficiency and Creating New
             Opportunities 324
        17.1.2 Goals of Business Networking.................................325
        17.1.3 Changing Face of Business Networking Systems....................326
        17.1.4 Model of Business Networking.................................327

    17.2 Next Steps in Business Networking 328
        17.2.1 Advent of Process Portals and eServices 328
        17.2.2 Networking Smart Appliances and Real-Life Assets...............330

List of Abbreviations **331**

Glossary **335**

References..**345**

Index...**379**

Authors **395**

Questionnaire for Networkability Assessment..........................**397**

1 Introduction – Chances and Challenges in Business Networking

Rainer Alt, Elgar Fleisch, Hubert Österle

1.1 Networked Enterprise: The Vision..2
   1.1.1 Business Networking and the New Economy 2
   1.1.2 Five Phases Towards Business Networking..................................2

1.2 Networking the Enterprise: The Transformation 4
   1.2.1 Closing the Gap Between Strategy and Reality 4
   1.2.2 Achieving Networkability...5
   1.2.3 Part One: Building the Foundation 6
   1.2.4 Part Two: Business Concepts..7
   1.2.5 Part Three: Information System Concepts 8
   1.2.6 Part Four: Key Success Factors 8

1.3 Research Approach 9
   1.3.1 Applied Research: Providing Practical Guidelines 9
   1.3.2 Action Research: Balancing Rigor and Relevance 10
   1.3.3 Competence Centers in Business Networking 11

1.1   Networked Enterprise: The Vision

1.1.1   Business Networking and the New Economy

We see that many businesses today are hoping to find the rules which govern the new economy [cf. Kelly 1998], also referred to as the digital economy (cf. [Negroponte 1995], [Tapscott 1995]), the networked economy [cf. Shaprio/Varian 1999], the information economy [cf. Varian 1994], the Internet economy [cf. Zerdick et al. 1999] or the information age [cf. Lane 1998]. Information and communication technology (IT)[1] enables and shapes the new economy in the same way that steam, gas, and electricity transformed the agricultural economy into the industrial economy a hundred years ago.

Business Networking is not the only feature of enterprises in the information age, but certainly the most important. In the past, Business Networking was the basis for the division of labor in agricultural as well as in industrial society, and a prerequisite for increasing prosperity. As already stated by [Smith 1776], the division of labor is limited by the geographical reach of the market. Before the emergence of local farming markets, every farmer produced everything he or she needed to live. With the introduction of new transportation technologies, the market span grew and consequently led to the specialization of the industrial economy. In our time, IT is pushing the physical disintegration of markets and enterprises to its global limits and thus enabling the maximal specialization of enterprises.

Business Networking in the new economy can be seen as the coordination of processes within and across companies. More precisely, we define Business Networking as the management of IT-enabled relationships between internal and external business partners. So far, there has been no clear vision of the business units and processes nor of the coordination mechanisms that Business Networking has in store for the economy. Disintegration, specialization, reintegration, centralization, etc. are certainly among the current trends that present a growing challenge for business management and science.

1.1.2   Five Phases Towards Business Networking

Looking back, the importance of Business Networking grew with the integrated support of business processes. In the early phase, the integration area[2] was rather

---

[1]   Due to the convergence of information processing and communication, we will refer to the combination of information and communication technologies as IT.

[2]   The integration area describes the number of tasks of an enterprise implemented in an integrated information system [Österle et al. 1993].

small. As technology developed, the integration area grew. In this development, we distinguish five phases (see Figure 1-1).[3]

Phase 1 (1970s): The aim of *computerizing single 'island' functions* was to automate individual business functions, such as invoicing. Manual operations were generally transferred to the computer without any modification [cf. Alpar et al. 1998, 29]. This led to isolated solutions which efficiently supported individual operations.

Phase 2 (1980s): The *computerization of functional areas,* such as production, financial accounting or distribution, achieved integration within the most important business function areas [cf. Raffeé 1993] and improved the efficiency of whole departments. For the first time, IT made it possible to apply new methods, such as production or financial planning, which transform business processes and present new challenges for employees.

Phase 3 (1990s): The development of systems for enterprise resource planning (ERP) enabled companies to implement *integrated processes* across various departments and/or functions. Hence it was possible to set up pervasive processes (e.g. order processing) from the customer (e.g. sales, order receipt) to the customer (e.g. distribution, invoices, payment receipt). ERP systems (cf. Chap. 2.3.1) soon became the nerve center of enterprises since they guarantee that every (authorized) employee has real-time access to all operational information.

Phase 4 (1990s): Concurrently with the implementation of ERP systems, some enterprises went for link-ups with their customers or suppliers. For instance, they would use electronic data interchange (EDI) systems in order to handle high-volume transactions efficiently. However, what they did was merely to set up rather expensive 1:1 or 1:n relationships. This was one important reason why a broad diffusion of EDI was not taking place as anticipated.[4]

Phase 5 (ca. 1990-2005): Here we see a new stage in customer orientation. Following Reverse Engineering ideas, companies will adapt and be built to suit customer needs and processes. Standardized systems for supply chain management (SCM) and electronic commerce (EC) enable quick and efficient linkages among business partners. The Internet plays a key role in improving these n:m networking capabilities, since it provides a standardized technological infrastructure. Taking the analogy of the road network, we can look forward to the growth of this networking infrastructure in the years to come, with all its standards (e.g. road width, signs, traffic regulations), coordination technologies and systems (e.g. traffic lights, GPS systems) and services (e.g. police, highway maintenance, fees,

---

[3]   For further models (cf. [Venkatraman 1991], [Lane 1998], [Clark 1999] or [Nolan/Croson 1995]). For the technical development of informatization from mainframe computing in the 1960s to today's electronic business [cf. Schnedl/Schweizer 1999].

[4]   For reasons to explain the disappointing diffusion of EDI (cf. [Kalakota/Whinston 1997], [Christiaanse et al. 1996] and [Alt/Klein 1999]).

tolls, automobile clubs). Various initiatives (e.g. Bolero, Uddi) are underway to establish this standardized networking infrastructure which we refer to as the 'business bus' (cf. Chap. 2.3.4). It forms the core of the business collaboration infrastructure which eventually will evolve from marketplaces.

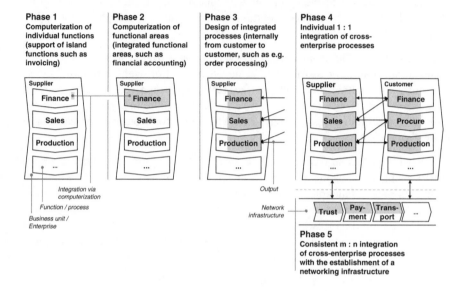

Figure 1-1: Development of Business Networking

1.2   Networking the Enterprise: The Transformation

1.2.1   Closing the Gap Between Strategy and Reality

Today, researchers and managers are overwhelmed by the large number of publications on the new economy. Most authors delve into the economic aspects and arrive at a highly aggregated view. Important scientific contributions have come from transaction cost theory [cf. Williamson 1989], organizational theory (cf. [Sydow 1992], [Snow et al. 1992], [Müller-Stewens 1997], [Ruigrok et al. 1999]), institutional economy [cf. Williamson 1991], coordination theory [cf. Malone/Crowston 1994], business networks and information management (cf. [Malone et al. 1987], [Klein 1996], [Wigand et al. 1997]) and economics [cf. Varian 1994]. Together with anecdotal management literature, these provide valuable insights at a rather strategic level. For instance, they help to set up strategic partnerships between enterprises, to position an enterprise within a supply chain, or to understand the long-term impact of IT on organizational structures.

However, what companies are regularly faced with is the challenge of actually implementing Business Networking strategies. It is our research partners in industry - about ten globally active enterprises – to whom we are indebted for in-depth information on the less frequently discussed hurdles encountered in trying to translate Business Networking strategies into practice.

This book is designed to supply some 'building blocks' to close the gap between networking strategies and the nuts and bolts of, say, an up-and-running EC or SCM system. On the one hand, our intention is to help translate strategies into business process networks that can be implemented by IT means. On the other hand, it is hoped that we shall assist users in finding new processes and strategies based on new IT.

We propose to close the gap by introducing a *business process* view on Business Networking. We conceive of Business Networking as the logical result of a consistent process orientation. Business process redesign represents an enterprise-internal focus on processes. However, processes start and end with customers. While enterprise borders are alien to processes, the business network provides processes with a playground [cf. Venkatraman 1991].

1.2.2   Achieving Networkability

The main goal of the book is to show how enterprises can achieve networkability[5]. We define networkability as the ability to cooperate internally as well as externally [Wigand et al. 1997, 11]. Networkability refers to (a) resources, such as employees, managers and information systems, (b) business processes, e.g. the sales process, and (c) business units, e.g. an enterprise in a supply chain. Networkability describes the ability to rapidly establish an efficient business relationship.

[Klein 1996] presents an extensive framework along which he discussed multiple aspects of Business Networking. The fact that our focus is on processes as well as information and communication technology compels us to ignore many of these important aspects here. In discussing networkability, we will concentrate instead on the processes around the supply chain, electronic commerce and relationship management, and on transaction-oriented information systems. For content-oriented Business Networking literature see ([Bach/Österle 2000], [Bach et al. 2000]).

This book is intended to address two main audiences: the scientific community and the business community. It is divided into four parts. Part 1 builds the foun-

---

[5]   Also referred to as 'Net Readiness' [cf. Hartman et al. 2000].

dation for the book and thus provides the reader with our process-oriented framework for Business Networking. Part 2 discusses business concepts in Business Networking, Part 3 deals with IT issues and Part 4 collates the experiences reported in order to deduce the critical success factors and management techniques (see Figure 1-2).

Chapter 1:   Introduction - Chances and Challenges in Business Networking

Part One:	Building the Foundation
Chapter 2:	Enterprise in the Information Age
Chapter 3:	The Networked Enterprise

Part Two:	Business Concepts	Part Three:	Information System Concepts
Chapter 4:	Strategies for Business Networking	Chapter 8:	Future Application Architecture for the Pharmaceutical Industry
Chapter 5:	Business Networking Lessons Learned: Supply Chain Management at Riverwood International	Chapter 9:	Overview on Supply Chain Management Systems
Chapter 6:	Electronic Commerce and Supply Chain Management at 'The Swatch Group'	Chapter 10:	Electronic Commerce in the Procurement of Indirect Goods
Chapter 7:	Knowledge-enabled Customer Relationship Management	Chapter 11:	Templates: Standardization for Business Networking
		Chapter 12:	eServices for Integrating eMarkets

Part Four:	Key Success Factors
Chapter 13:	Key Success Factors for Business Networking Systems
Chapter 14:	Towards a Method for Business Networking
Chapter 15:	Application of the Business Networking Method at SAP
Chapter 16:	Architecture Planning for Global Networked Enterprises

Chapter 17:   Business Networking - Summary and Outlook

Figure 1-2: Content Structure

1.2.3   Part One: Building the Foundation

In Chapter 2, *Enterprise in the Information Age,* Business Networking is seen as one of seven trends that will ultimately lead to the enterprise of the new economy. With Business Networking viewed within a broader perspective, Chapter 2 establishes a rich context for evaluating findings that are specific to Business Networking. The other trends discussed are enterprise relationship management, knowledge management, smart appliances, electronic services, customer processes and value management.

Chapter 3, *The Networked Enterprise*, details the trend of Business Networking to the level of business processes and provides a process-oriented framework as an aid to understanding and managing the diversity of Business Networking. With reference to several disparate practical cases, different forms of networking are discussed and the tools of coordination theory applied to derive a generic model of a networked enterprise. According to this model, every networked enterprise is part of multiple internal and external networks and called upon to manage networking scenarios, in some cases simultaneously, such as supply chain management, relationship management, innovation, enterprise infrastructure and organizational development. The concept of networkability is introduced to support *'classical'* companies to transform into networked companies.

1.2.4   Part Two: Business Concepts

Part 2 concentrates on the business-oriented aspects of Business Networking. Chapter 4, *Strategies for Business Networking,* describes how Business Networking can link up to corporate strategy and how it can sustain core competencies and future market segments. Three organizational strategies (outsourcing, insourcing and virtual organizing) are distinguished. Implementation and process-orientation are introduced with three networking strategies (electronic commerce, supply chain management and customer relationship management). Based on numerous practical cases, Chapter 4 provides some insights into how it is feasible to influence market position through Business Networking.

Chapter 5, *Business Networking Lessons Learned: Supply Chain Management at Riverwood International*, concentrates on the Business Networking strategy for supply chain management. In the style of a management paper, it presents the challenges, benefits and conclusions drawn from Riverwood International's 'Strategic Enterprise Partnership' project. The lessons learned then serve as the basis for Part 4.

In Chapter 6, *Electronic Commerce and Supply Chain Management at 'The Swatch Group'*, the complementarity of supply chain management and electronic commerce is discussed. Whereas some authors view electronic commerce as part of the implementation of supply chain management (cf. Chap. 2), this Chapter takes a closer look at the interrelationships of both concepts. A case study from 'The Swatch Group' is used to illustrate the results and the benefits of an integrated strategy. Again, the lessons learned serve as the basis for Part 4.

Although this book concentrates on transaction-oriented processes and information systems in Business Networking, Chapter 7 looks into aspects of *Knowledge-enabled Customer Relationship Management*. It shows that cross-enterprise processes, such as customer relationship management, may depend heavily on unstructured data or, more precisely, unstructured knowledge. Electronic commerce is often described as covering the transactional part of customer relationships. Since knowledge management covers the non-transactional part, customer relationship management requires both concepts, i.e. electronic commerce and knowledge management. Chapter 7 links knowledge-enabled customer relationship management with Business Networking and comes up with a process-oriented customer relationship management reference model.

1.2.5   Part Three: Information System Concepts

Part 3 balances business requirements with the potentials and restrictions of information systems. Chapter 8 *Future Application Architecture for the Pharmaceutical Industry* translates the seven trends and the Business Networking model (cf. Chaps. 2 and 3) into an application architecture for a pharmaceutical company. It discusses processes to be supported, deduces requirements to be fulfilled, structures future software components and combines processes and components into an application architecture of the information age.

Chapter 9, *Information Systems for Supply Chain Management: An Overview*, focuses on the software components for supply chain management. Business goals and processes to be supported by the components are discussed and an overview is given of some classes of systems, such as MRP I, MRP II or APS. Finally, the class of APS systems is discussed in greater detail and some insights provided into the most important functions, vendors and products.

Chapter 10, *Electronic Commerce in the Procurement of Indirect Goods*, concentrates on software components for the procurement of indirect goods. We believe that these so-called desktop purchasing systems have the potential to become a killer application in Business Networking. On the basis of a business process model for the procurement of indirect goods, the authors look into the potentials of and ideas behind desktop purchasing systems. Again, a brief overview is given of the most important functions, vendors and products.

Chapter 11, *Templates: Achieving Standardization for Business Networking*, shows that achieving standardization is the key challenge for Business Networking. Chapter 11 presents some definitions and dimensions of standardization and then focuses on templates as a technique for standardization. The authors develop a template handbook and demonstrate its successful application within the Robert Bosch Group to achieve networkability.

Chapter 12, *eServices for Integrating ERP and eMarkets*, focuses on the cross enterprise integration of business processes, another key challenge of Business Networking. For linking (external) eMarkets with (internal) enterprise resource planning (ERP) systems, it discusses the concept, architecture, and implementation of external integration services along the real live case study Triaton.

1.2.6   Part Four: Key Success Factors

Part 4 translates the lessons learned from Chapters 2 through 12 into management guidelines. Chapter 13, *Key Success Factors for Business Networking Systems*, analyses what are considered to be the key success factors in implementing Business Networking systems on the basis of three different cases. Two techniques are then developed (partner profiling and creation of win-win situations) which helped enterprises to manage the key success factors.

Chapter 14, *Towards a Method for Business Networking,* translates the key success factors of Chapter 13 into a robust method which guides managers in designing and implementing cooperation-intensive business networks. The proposed method covers aspects from strategy to implementation, takes into account the new business logic as outlined in Chapter 2, and follows the principles of method engineering. Cases in eProcurement and supply chain management illustrate the method in practice.

Chapter 15, *Application of the Business Networking Method,* applies the method proposed in the previous chapter to an fictitious case with many real world nuts and bolts. It shows that implementing networking strategies such as EC, CRM, or SCM, may lead to significant interdependencies on process and IT level. In this Chapter we also show how SAP incorporates the Business Networking method into its method framework (so-called Accelerated SAP).

Chapter 16, *Architecture Planning for Global Networked Companies,* directs attention to the information system level. The authors show how to deduce an application architecture from a business architecture by introducing a methodology for architecture planning, referred to as PROMET eBN.

Finally, Chapter 17, *Business Networking - Summary and Outlook,* summarizes the findings of the book and outlines the next steps proposed in Business Networking research. Future work in the field of Business Networking is certain to include such topics as the advent of numerous electronic services and networked real-life assets.

1.3   Research Approach

1.3.1   Applied Research: Providing Practical Guidelines

Our research approach to Business Networking combines insights from practice and theory. The applicability of these findings in practice is our primary research goal. Four aspects can be mentioned to describe what distinguishes our approach to Business Networking from others.

- *Practice relevance.* The goal of this book is to ensure the applicability of findings, concepts and methods in practice. Action research principles based on established literature are used. Case studies have been undertaken at ETA SA, Riverwood International, Deutsche Telekom, Robert Bosch Group, newtron/Triaton, Commtech and others to elaborate and explain Business Networking.

- *Engineering perspective*. We believe that Business Networking concepts have to provide management support in strategic as well as technological areas. To ensure this holistic management approach, we follow the systematic principles of method engineering (cf. Chap. 14.1.3) which provide a structured framework for developing information age strategies. This engineering approach clearly differentiates Business Networking from models that focus on unspecific high-level advice, and is valuable in transferring knowledge from previous projects.

- *Process orientation*. This book presents a process-oriented view of networking that sees cooperation between business partners as networks of processes. We follow coordination theory to present a model of networked processes which embrace resources shared between two (or more) processes (cf. Chap. 3.3.1). We will apply and test this model in cases throughout the book. Process orientation not only reflects the fact that Business Networking solutions need to have close links with business processes, but also that they have to establish a very specific starting point for shaping underlying applications.

- *Single enterprise view*. Finally, it should be noted that we see Business Networking from the point of view of an individual company. Contrary to existing networking literature which focuses on the network per se as the design object, the underlying theorem of this book is that all decisions that lead to action have to be performed by a specific actor, i.e. a company.

1.3.2   Action Research: Balancing Rigor and Relevance

To study the time-dependent, complex and social phenomena of Business Networking, we designed our research process in accordance with the *action research* guidelines proposed by Checkland.[6] Within the action research process, the researcher becomes part of the experiment, and thus the mental models or, as [Checkland/Holwell 1998] puts it, the 'Weltanschauung' of the researcher colors the results. Evidently, every researcher in the same research situation would produce different results that would not be reproducible elsewhere since it is unlikely that any two researchers would apply exactly the same mental models.

Results will only be truly scientific if different individuals can successfully apply them in different situations. Scientific results have to be *reproducible*. And scientific results must differ from anecdotal story-telling which often produces not reproducible but merely *plausible* results.

---

[6]   A good overview on action research is provided by ([Checkland 1991], [Checkland 1997] and [Checkland/Holwell 1998]).

To design action research processes which lead to reproducible as well as more than plausible results, [Checkland 1997] introduced the criterion of recoverability. Recoverability postulates that a research process should enable a reasonably educated person to reproduce or *recover* results achieved elsewhere. If recoverability is to be maintained, researchers must declare their research themes, their research methods and their areas of concern ex ante. Research themes in action research correspond to hypotheses in the natural sciences.

Our book reflects major results from the Competence Centers for electronic Business Networking (CC eBN) and inter-Business Networking (CC iBN). Team members participated in the projects undertaken by the partner companies of CC eBN and conducted regular workshops and steering committee meetings. The team was and still is aware of the benefits and drawbacks of action research. By carefully managing the recoverability of its results, we try to maximize both rigor and relevance: Today, the main results of both research projects, the methodologies PROMET eBN and iBN are being used in companies to solve different problems. Parts of the methodologies are incorporated in other methodologies, the eBN method (cf. Chap. 16) in SAP's Global ASAP [SAP 1999b] and the iBN method (cf. Chap. 14) in SAP's ASAP for APO 2.0a.

1.3.3   Competence Centers in Business Networking

The Competence Center for eBN (March 1996 until March 1998) was funded by and operated in collaboration with four partner companies (see Table 1.2). One of the goals of CC eBN was to develop a robust methodology for distributing processes and information systems within an enterprise. The Competence Center for iBN (March 1998 until February 2000) concentrated on the extended supply chain and the management of customer / supplier relationships and shifted the focus from ERP to SCM and EC systems. Our partner companies are shown in Table 1.2. In parallel with the Competence Centers, the project Business Network Redesign (BNR)[7] was conducted, which focuses on similar aspects to those of CC iBN. Following successful conclusion of the CC iBN, the work has been continued in the Competence Center for Business Networking (March 2000 until March 2002) which focuses on developing an architecture and method for new approaches in Business Networking, such as eServices, eMarkets and portals.

All projects are part of the 'Business Engineering HSG' research program. This program relies on teamwork and field research rather than on typical academic, single-person desk research. In every project, a research team covering the roles of (a) project leader, (b) steering committee and (c) work group members design and execute research plans. Four to six doctoral students from the Institute of Infor-

---

[7]   This project was supported by the Swiss National Fund for the Promotion of Scientific Research (Project No. 5003-045377).

mation Management at the University of St. Gallen (IWI-HSG) and six to twelve managers from the partner companies form the work group. The project is led by an experienced post-doc (Rainer Alt/Elgar Fleisch) who regularly reports the work group results to the steering committee. This consists of the professor in charge of the project (Hubert Österle), a senior executive from each partner company and the project leader. For a list of steering committee members and work group members of CC eBN, CC iBN, CC BN and the BNR project see Table 1-1.

Partner Company	Steering Committee Member	Work Group Members
Competence Center electronic Business Networking (CC eBN)		
Deutsche Telekom AG Bonn, Germany	Karl-Heinz Schelhas	Klaus Basten Wolfgang Kilian
Henkel KgaA Düsseldorf, Germany	Eckhard Dieckmann	Jens Kalke Franz-Josef Thissen
Hewlett Packard GmbH Böblingen, Germany	Georg Illert	Armin Schneider Ulrich Modler
SAP AG Walldorf, Germany	Heinz-Ulrich Roggenkemper	Cay Rademann
Competence Center inter-Business Networking (CC iBN)		
Bayer AG Leverkusen, Germany	Andreas Klosson	Rolf Guntermann Gisela Schmitz
Deutsche Telekom AG Bonn, Germany	Karl-Heinz Schelhas	Jörg Fuhr
ETA SA Fabriques d'Ebauches Grenchen, Switzerland	Ernst Martin	Rudolf Zurmühlen
F. Hoffmann-La Roche Ltd., Basel, Switzerland	Vladimir Barak	Martin Wyss
HiServ GmbH Frankfurt, Germany	Norbert Kaltenmorgen	Mark Pietzner
Riverwood International Corporation Atlanta, USA	Robert Betts	Chuck Lawrence Jim Vrieling
Robert Bosch GmbH Stuttgart, Germany	Günter Lehmann	Martin von Ehr Sandra Hausmann
SAP AG Walldorf, Germany	Thomas Reiss	Andreas Pfadenhauer

Competence Center Business Networking (CC BN)		
DaimlerChrysler AG, Stuttgart, Germany	Frank Appenzeller	Günter Kapusta Erich Haase
Deutsche Telekom AG Bonn, Germany	Karsten Schweichart Torsten Minkwitz	Axel Meckenstock Rainer Scheibehenne Karl-Heinz Schelhas
emagine GmbH, Eschborn, Germany	Roland Härtner	Elmar Sänger Werner Sobek
ETA SA Fabriques d'Ebauches Grenchen, Switzerland	Kaspar Glatthard	Thomas Bühler Rudolf Zurmühlen
F. Hoffmann-La Roche Ltd., Basel, Switzerland	Vladimir Barak	Thomas Huber
Hewlett-Packard GmbH, Switzerland	Hans-Peter Furrer Mark Gasteen	Michel Benard Mark Gasteen
HiServ GmbH, Frankfurt, Germany	Norbert Kaltenmorgen	Oliver Adamczak Moni Meltke
Robert Bosch GmbH Stuttgart, Germany	Günter Lehmann	Christine Bondel Dirk Sassmannshausen
SAP AG Walldorf, Germany	Thomas Reiss	Axel Luther

Table 1-1: Research Projects and Partners

It should be noted that this book presents only a fraction of the work undertaken and the results recorded by the Competence Centers. Further information can be obtained by visiting www.iwi.unisg.ch.

Part 1

Building the Foundation

Part One: **Building the Foundation**
Chapter 2: Enterprise in the Information Age
Chapter 3: The Networked Enterprise

Part Two: **Business Concepts**
Chapter 4: Strategies for Business Networking
Chapter 5: Business Networking Lessons Learned: Supply Chain Management at Riverwood International
Chapter 6: Electronic Commerce and Supply Chain Management at 'The Swatch Group'
Chapter 7: Knowledge-enabled Customer Relationship Management

Part Three: **Information System Concepts**
Chapter 8: Future Application Architecture for the Pharmaceutical Industry
Chapter 9: Overview on Supply Chain Management Systems
Chapter 10: Electronic Commerce in the Procurement of Indirect Goods
Chapter 11: Templates: Standardization for Business Networking
Chapter 12: eServices for Integrating eMarkets

Part Four: **Key Success Factors**
Chapter 13: Key Success Factors for Business Networking Systems
Chapter 14: Towards a Method for Business Networking
Chapter 15: Application of the Business Networking Method at SAP
Chapter 16: Architecture Planning for Global Networked Enterprises

2 Enterprise in the Information Age

Hubert Österle

2.1 Challenge of the Information Age..18

2.2 Imperatives of Business in the Internet Age...19
    2.2.1 Coverage...20
    2.2.2 Partnering..20
    2.2.3 Critical Mass of Customers and Suppliers..................................20
    2.2.4 Position in the Business Network 21
    2.2.5 Focusing..21
    2.2.6 Process Efficiency...22
    2.2.7 Networkability 22
    2.2.8 Change Management 23

2.3 Seven Trends...23
    2.3.1 Enterprise Resource Planning 24
    2.3.2 Knowledge Management 28
    2.3.3 Smart Appliances...32
    2.3.4 Business Networking 36
    2.3.5 Electronic Services..43
    2.3.6 Customer Process Support 45
    2.3.7 Value Management 51

2.1   Challenge of the Information Age

Business is undergoing a transformation from the industrial to the information age. Information technology (IT) opens up possibilities for new business solutions; it offers exceptional opportunities for fast innovators and harbors fundamental risks for laggards.

This transformation poses a gigantic challenge for both business and society. Success stories alternate with news of project failures. New companies, such as Amazon, Siebel or Yahoo!, have been growing at rates of 100 percent a year and more and achieve quite incredible levels of market capitalization within a few years of their existence while others, such as banks or travel agencies, introduce drastic cutbacks in staff every year or disappear from the market.

Enterprises and individuals are under great pressure to act. At the same time, the feeling of uncertainty has never been as great as it is now. The high volatility of shares in innovative companies is indicative of this mood. Sensational success stories in management journals, recipes for success from IT prophets, buzz-words, such as virtualization, and finally the abundant superlatives employed in announcing new IT products, provide a confusing picture of the information age, while many companies already have their hands full dealing with restructuring, mergers and acquisitions, globalization, Y2K, the Euro, technically outdated applications and other operative problems.

Information technology makes new business solutions possible. This might mean new or improved products and services (e.g. automobile and navigation), additional sales channels (e.g. Internet banking), more efficient forms of procurement (e.g. global procurement by means of electronic markets), new ways in which suppliers and customers can cooperate (e.g. collaborative planning), new services (e.g. virtual communities), more effective management (e.g. through the automatic measurement of key performance indicators) or new information services (e.g. product catalogs).

Transformation means innovation in existing enterprises (e.g. direct selling by an insurance company), but above all the establishment of new enterprises. Start-ups include software houses, such as iXOS, consultancy firms, such as Cambridge Technology Partners, industry analysts, such as Ovum, network providers, such as Tobit, providers of Internet services, such as Yahoo!, outsourcers, such as Debis, information services, such as all-hotels.com and market services, such as Harbinger.

Changes are becoming increasingly more radical. Corporations are being broken down into components and reassembled along different lines. New business ideas are being tried out in start-ups and where successful frequently rolled out globally by large corporations with a suitable customer base.

The ability to identify chances at an early stage and see them through to implementation is opening up a world of opportunities akin to an industrial revolution. Entrepreneurs are looking for a business model of the information age which will allow them to identify real options and to assess the consequences of their decisions. The Institute of Information Management at the University of St. Gallen is working on a business model of this kind within the framework of a research program entitled 'Business Engineering HSG' (BE HSG) in collaboration with representatives from the business world with the objective of

- Identifying new IT based business solutions at an early stage,

- Understanding the rules of business in the information age and,

- Formulating procedures to ensure a successful transformation.

Some of the results of this work are presented here in order to provide a holistic picture of Business Networking from the entrepreneur's point of view.

2.2 Imperatives of Business in the Internet Age

Imagine a scenario in which every employee, every customer, every business partner, every appliance and every computer has immediate access to each other's data at any time. That is exactly what the Internet is about to make possible within a few years. What will your business be like by then?

We summarize the most important rules within the framework of the business model of the information age and explain them with the aid of the example of the process car ownership in Figure 2-1.

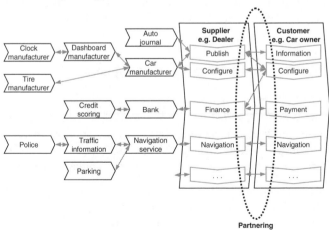

Figure 2-1: Enterprise in Business Networks

2.2.1   Coverage

Networking makes it possible to offer all products and services for a customer process on a coordinated basis and from a single source. It is not the customer but the supplier who is the specialist in the process car ownership. The car dealer takes on the task of helping the customer with car selection, obtaining the test reports, financing, navigation, resale, etc. This applies equally to the stages upstream of the car dealer, e.g. completeness of a car journal's services, perhaps including online research in earlier issues or access to sources. The credit scoring institute provides not only the customer's credit rating but also concrete information on delays in payment or loan insurance, the tire dealer supplies not only the tires but also the CAD data (computer aided design) and test reports as well as batch quality data, etc.

2.2.2   Partnering

Cooperation is not limited to a shopping relationship but becomes true collaboration, i.e. the processes work together. Customers give the car dealer data on vehicle use (e.g. garage bills), data from the on-board computer and of course the ongoing communication data on their interests, their purchasing behavior and their preferences. The supplier develops detailed customer profiles which allow him to give customers targeted information in the sense of one-to-one marketing, to remind customers when a service is due, etc. The bank, on the other hand, can give the car owners credit software which enables them to consider the credit for the car as an integral part of their overall financial planning. The car dealer will try to tie in his financing service. Partnering can lead to customer lock-in and thus create a high entrance barrier for competitors. The result is a customer support process which is closely meshed with the customer's car ownership process.

2.2.3   Critical Mass of Customers and Suppliers

In view of the fact that there will be competition by services, the costs of establishing and marketing integrated customer solutions will be enormous. As the solutions will require little manual intervention, the costs of the individual transactions will be virtually negligible. The objective will therefore be to allocate the development costs to as many transactions and thus customers as possible.

In the example of the car dealer, he will try to gain a maximum market share. For this purpose he will form alliances with car magazines, insurance companies, etc. He will also endeavor to globalize his offering as the Net will drastically reduce the marginal costs for entering new markets. Furthermore, he will try to have his services incorporated in those of other suppliers, such as used car dealers or insurance companies.

Customers prefer car dealers who can offer, on the one hand, the most comprehensive range of products and services and, on the other, the biggest selection of suppliers for each category of product and service.

Suppliers, i.e. car journals, car manufacturers and navigation services, will concentrate on car dealers who can provide them access to the largest number of customers, particularly in the case of exclusive agreements or adherence to specific standards.

Every additional supplier, every additional service and every additional customer strengthens the position and the profitability of the car dealer. Therefore some speak of the law of increasing revenues. As a result of the economies of scale, the benefits for the customer and last but not least branding, the above mentioned developments are conducive to the establishment of entrance barriers and/or monopoly-like positions.

2.2.4 Position in the Business Network

Like the car dealer, all the suppliers in the network, from the bank to the tire manufacturer, must find their position in the business network (supply chain) and apply the rules indicated above to their customers, their products and their services as well as their skills. Standards and other entrance barriers lead to competition not only of individual suppliers but also of complete supply chains. Each company must analyze the possible business networks and try to establish a position of maximum influence in the networks offering the greatest potential. If a bank succeeds in securing its presence as a credit solution amongst as many car owners as possible by means of a credit software and special services, it will also find access to a large number of car dealers and thus expand its position. Current experience shows that early entrance into a business network improves the chances of assuming a dominant role.

2.2.5 Focusing

Networking promotes specialization. If cooperation with a South American tire manufacturer runs just as smoothly as with a European manufacturer, if the credit rating is performed better externally than inside the bank and if external payroll accounting costs less than doing it inside the company, then the appropriate supplier will be selected. A process of deassembly and reassembly is initiated in which companies consider each of their processes and decide whether it is better to operate them themselves or to buy them in. If the suppliers to the car dealer can sell their products and services directly to the car owners they will bypass the car dealer (disintermediation); if the car dealer creates additional benefits for the customer by integrating services, the car dealer can act between customer and supplier (intermediation).

However, each one will focus on the processes which it can do best (worldwide): the bank on credit handling, the car journal on information relating to the car, the car dealer on the car owner process and the integration of services. All other processes will be outsourced to specialists.

New kinds of services which are purely electronic and in some cases cover very small tasks will intensify the focusing. One example would be automated information on the traffic flow in a highway tunnel. A traffic information service could easily integrate this information into a route specific information for one driver.

2.2.6   Process Efficiency

If no monopoly situations arise which cut out the market, the Internet will always promote the selection and combination of the most efficient processes. That means processes with high reliability, low price, short cycle times and high flexibility.

A high level of process competence and properly planned and executed processes will become the foundation for business in the information age. This will be based as far as possible on integrated application systems for the planning, execution and control of intraorganizational and interorganizational processes. Networking presupposes efficient processes, it does not replace them.

2.2.7   Networkability

Today, business relationships on the Internet are almost exclusively 1:n in the form of online shops or online purchasing. This means that a supplier has a relationship with several customers or a customer communicates with several suppliers. One (1) company sets the rules and the formats (standard), the customers or suppliers (n) have to accept it (or leave it). Even the marketplaces on the Net rarely go beyond this constellation. This can be compared to a rail network with different gauges and power supply systems. If you want to use it, you have to accept the standards.

The breakthrough for business-to-business networking will occur when the car owner works with bank A today and bank B tomorrow without any additional cost involved, e.g. for the installation of new software (multi-bank capability), and conversely when the bank can communicate with all car owners using the same standard. We call this the m:n capability.

On the one hand we still have a long way to go before we arrive at m:n capability, on the other it is not necessarily in the interests of dominant market participants. A company will try to see that its solution becomes embedded in the market as standard or latch onto the standard with the greatest chances of dominance.

Eventually, a set of standards will enable the m:n capability. Some standards will apply for specific business networks, others will be generally accepted.

Networkability as described in Chapter 1 is not merely a question of IT, but to a far greater extent one of business alliances. Networkability is of strategic importance for every business wishing to become part of a business network.

2.2.8   Change Management

The development towards the information society will take at least another 30 years. Until then, all building blocks of an enterprise will remain in a state of flux. Businesses must sharpen their skill in recognizing developments and above all in mastering change. An important consequence will be the need to install change management alongside operative management. Shareholder value is a catalyst of change. It not only forms the basis for evaluating the company and for acquiring capital but also helps in the systematic analysis of factors determining the success of change - with the aid of value drivers - and in controlling them by means of key performance indicators.

2.3   Seven Trends

Seen by a business point of view the numerous IT developments are responsible for seven fundamental trends in business transformation.

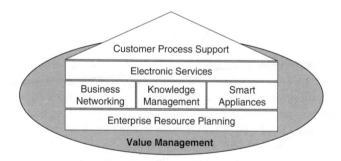

Figure 2-2: Seven Trends on the Road to the Enterprise of the Information Age

- *Enterprise resource planning,* i.e. the operational execution of business, runs almost imperceptibly in the background. Integrated applications for administration as well as for product development and technology make it possible to concentrate on business rather than on administration.

- *Knowledge management* supplies each task within a process with the necessary knowledge about customers, competitors, products, etc. and above all about the process itself.

- *Smart appliances* take information processing to the point of action. Traffic information is supplied via the satellite navigation system (GPS) to the motorist, point of sale information from the cash register to the product manufacturer and machine faults via sensors to the service engineer.

- *Business Networking* makes collaboration between two companies so simple that they appear to be one enterprise. Information on sales of the end product is immediately available to all the companies in the supply chain.

- Many subprocesses which companies still operate individually at the moment will be available from the Net as *electronic services.* One example could be customer profiling. In addition to the supplier, a third party online-database provider and the customer him or herself can take over the responsibility of his or her profile and offer it via an electronic service.

- Companies will not simply be selling products or services but will be supporting entire *customer processes.* Transport businesses will take on the logistics process, doctors will support the whole therapy process and insurance companies will handle the claim processing instead of the customer.

- Corporate management will no longer merely focus on financial results but also on factors contributing to these results. Financial management will become *value management* which keeps an eye on key performance indicators for the success of the business.

2.3.1   Enterprise Resource Planning

Over the past thirty years, companies have used IT primarily for improving internal processes. Between 60% and 90% of IT investments were aimed at internal supply chain processes, such as purchasing, production and distribution, at support processes, such as finance, human resources and IT as well as at the management process. Computer aided design and manufacturing round off this picture for development and production. This assessment applies to service companies (banks, travel agencies, etc.) along similar lines to those seen in manufacturing.

Operative strength is decisive for the competitiveness of many companies. This explains why a mid-sized textile mill, such as Getzner Textil AG, in a country

with high labor costs, such as Austria, has succeeded in attaining a leading position in the EU market for top-fashion fabrics. Consistent process development
based on the standard software R/3 enabled this company to reduce time expenditure in administration from 233 person years p.a. to 177 and order cycle time from
eight to six weeks, within the space of five years. This was achieved in spite of a
tripling in the number of orders and articles during this period. The customer focus, which is so critical for the competitiveness of the company, calls for a wide
spectrum of variants, small lot sizes and short time-to-market, from the customer-
specific design through to delivery. Getzner Textil AG acquired these capabilities
on the basis of a highly integrated software.

Transactional systems for materials management, sales, finance, etc. manage operating resources, such as orders, articles, and customers (see Figure 2-3). All
activities belonging to business processes (e.g. procurement, production, distribution and management) plan, execute and monitor the use of resources. The transactional systems give staff the tools for performing activities, e.g. the transactions
order entry and price change. A company can make transactions, such as stocking
or ordering directly, available to the customer or supplier for the processes of sales
or purchasing.

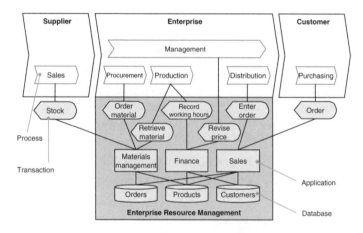

Figure 2-3: Transaction Processing and Business Process

Transactional systems are usually referred to as enterprise resource planning
(ERP) systems. More precisely we would talk about enterprise resource management, since these systems support all phases of the management cycle, namely
planning, execution, and control. SAP's 'solution maps' provide a good overview
of the modules which an ERP system typically comprises today.

In the context of banks and insurance companies, ERP systems are usually termed
back office or processing systems and include transactional systems for e.g. funds

transfer, securities settlement, the administration of insurance policies or customer profiling.

We say that an ERP system is integrated if all process activities have real-time access to the same state of the same data (see Figure 2-3) and if the required relationships between data exist. So controlling must be in a position to determine the effective costs of a customer order, customers must have access to the manufacturing progress of their orders (order status tracking) and it must be possible for sales to assess the consequences of squeezing in a rush delivery.

Processes are determined by business strategy. Ideally, the ERP system will support every organizational solution. In other words, it is business strategy and not the software manufacturer which should decide questions, such as whether a member of the sales staff registers customer orders or whether the customers place orders themselves by means of electronic commerce, whether the company manages its own raw materials store or the suppliers offer consignment stock (vendor-managed inventory) and whether staff pay is performance-related. The transactions stocking and ordering in Figure 2-3 point to the fact that these organizational variants merely require a little additional functionality but access the same databases.

Needless to say, the functionality of the modules, and in particular the database structure of the ERP systems limits the scope for organizational design. However, most companies utilize only a fraction of the possibilities available to them.

The business processes, the customizing of the ERP software and, last but not least, the packaged software represent corporate strategy as it is practiced. They determine how the business is actually run and how much strategic room to maneuver is possible. Many companies still have a long way to go before this fact is properly recognized [e.g. Rodin 1999, 156].

In future, ERP systems can be expected to take on a role similar to what we have seen up to now in the case of operating systems, database management systems, Internet browsers and office suites:

- Companies invest huge amounts in one particular product.

- One or few products survive in the market.

- Innovative add-on products are oriented towards the dominant product and its environment.

- Integration is more important than best-of-breed. Linking up two software products is expensive, involves a great deal of effort with each new release and precludes many solutions due to the incompatibility of concepts.

- Only a basic innovation is able to replace a dominant product. In the past, for example, such innovations were the personal computer and the Internet. In the case of ERP systems, message-based modular packages could replace data-integrated monolithic packages (see item on Business Networking). Nothing more than first pilots can be expected over the next five years. In the area of customer relationship management (e.g. Siebel) we are more likely to see such powerful systems arising outside the traditional field of ERP packages. CRM systems have the potential to take over parts of the dominant role from ERP systems.

Seamless processes based on integrated operative transactional systems form the foundation for the enterprise of the information age. They will continue to tie up a large proportion of resources as a result of:

- New software and hardware functionality (new releases),

- The improvement and adaptation of business processes (continuous process improvement),

- The opening up of the ERP system for business partners, customers and suppliers,

- The restructuring of businesses: globalization, acquisitions, mergers, deregulation, outsourcing.

Consequences

Networking presupposes operatively independent and efficient units. Intraorganizational integration is the prerequisite for interorganizational networking. The following tasks remain to be solved, depending on the status of a company's operative processes:

- *Coordination of strategy, process and transactional system.* The company must utilize the opportunities provided by integrated transactional systems in its strategy and set the objectives for the processes on the basis of that strategy.

- *Wall-to-wall support of processes and business units.* Business Networking and other innovative solutions are based on a productive, integrated ERP system. Missing pieces may limit these solutions drastically.

- *Process optimization.* Many companies have been quick to replace their old transactional systems with standard software with the objective of achieving Y2K compatibility. In many cases this has not included process redesign. Competition will force them to build up process competence, to bring processes into line with customer needs and to increase their efficiency. Key performance indicators from the ERP systems make the level of maturity of processes transparent.

- *Process standardization.* Globalization, supply chain management and restructuring demand proven processes with clear interfaces. Standardized subprocesses, which are critical to coordination, are the prerequisite.

- *Internal software standardization.* Each additional software platform (additional software supplier) generates additional complexity.

- *External standardization.* Irrespective of whether this is emotionally desirable, the operative basis of an enterprise must be aligned with the standards which are going to be the most workable in the long run. And in the case of software, these are molded by the market leaders and by market expectations.

The dawning of the next millennium, coupled with the introduction of the Euro in Europe, caused many companies to speed up their investments in ERP systems. This has produced an unprecedented boom in the software product and software consultancy market. While it may come as no surprise that growth rates in this market segment are not continuing at the pace of the past few years, it is all the more amazing to note that sales revenues have persisted at the same high level and have not slumped. The many observers who conclude from the present stagnation in sales that the ERP philosophy is in crisis may have overlooked the context mentioned above. Forecasts for this software market are in fact assuming an annual growth rate of between 10% and 20% over the next five years [Cole et al. 1999, 7]. "Smart companies view enterprise application purchases as an essential investment. [...] a strong IT infrastructure aligned with core business processes is the key to competitive advantage" [AMR 1998].

2.3.2 Knowledge Management

Knowledge is increasingly determining the value of a company. The value of a company, particularly on the stock exchange, is no longer based on its physical and financial assets but on its ability to operate a particular business profitably in the future [cf. Stewart 1997]. This ability depends on knowledge about technologies, products, services, processes, customers and other market participants (cf. Chap. 7, [Davenport/Prusak 1998], [Probst et al. 1999]). In a networked economy, every company will specialize in a limited number of products and processes but in view of globalization will have to attain world class in those products and processes.

Knowledge management is not fundamentally new. Organizational development, organizational learning, artificial intelligence and other approaches were all pointed in the same direction. So how can investments in knowledge management be justified? What barriers to classic knowledge management does IT remove? The answer is that multimedia technology eliminates integration breaks by substituting paper; every form of documented knowledge becomes available electronically. Networking removes transport times and thus makes knowledge globally and concurrently accessible.

ERP systems have taken on the job of structuring, processing and storing the formatted data (transaction processing); knowledge management systems perform structuring, processing, editing and storage of multimedia documents (referred to as weakly structured data). Multimedia documents include text files, spreadsheets, presentation graphics, images, video and audio files and links to other documents. Together with the formatted data of the transaction systems, the electronic documents represent what is termed explicit knowledge.

However, multimedia and networking do not just make existing knowledge available, they also allow new forms of presenting knowledge and above all new forms in respect of creating, searching for and utilizing knowledge. Examples are groupware systems, search engines, expert maps (for utilizing implicit knowledge) and discussion forums as well as multimedia and interactive explanations of products, to name but a few.

Companies are given the possibility of making any documented knowledge available to all employees for the tasks they perform in processes, a precondition for a world-class performance. Knowledge management, therefore, does not mean creating new, additional business processes but equipping existing business processes with knowledge. In addition to the transactions of the ERP system, employees also receive computer support for the utilization and processing of knowledge (functions like revise drawing, print brochure and view product in Figure 2-4).

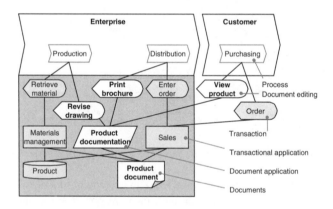

Figure 2-4: Document Processing and Business Process

In the simplest case, this can mean that employees and, where necessary, customers have access to the latest product information. Examples are a travel service, such as TIScover, which provides detailed information on travel destinations from hotels and sports activities to the latest weather report, or aircraft documentation which Boeing makes available to its staff and to customers via an Intranet.

The LGT Bank in Liechtenstein has built up systematic knowledge management for its customer advisory service, based on the model of business knowledge management [cf. Bach/Österle 1999] (see Figure 2-5). They first determined which external and internal knowledge (financial data, product information, etc.) was necessary and available for the advisory process, structured it (knowledge structure), then formulated and implemented the processes and responsibilities for setting up and maintaining this knowledge. Finally, they created the technical infrastructure in the form of an Intranet which integrates heterogeneous systems, such as Reuters or an object management system and documents (systems and documents). The system paid for itself within a year through the cost reductions in paper-based documentation and external information services alone. The main goal, i.e. improvement in the quality of advisory services, is being consistently tracked on the basis of key performance indicators, such as the hit rate for new accounts [cf. Kaiser et al. 1998]. A detailed description of LGT can be found in Chapter 7.2.

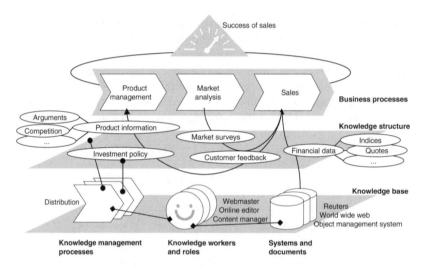

Figure 2-5: Knowledge Management in the Sales Process of the LGT Bank in Liechtenstein

A major component of the business knowledge management model is the systematic maintenance of the knowledge through clear responsibilities and processes (knowledge workers and roles as well as knowledge management processes). Just as master data maintenance is critical for a successful transaction processing, knowledge management is dependent on reliable maintenance of the electronic documents. Tasks include the authorization of a product description to be released to customers or removing documents which are no longer applicable.

A flood of information services from newspapers and magazines (e.g. Wallstreet Journal and AutoBild) through search engines and portals (e.g. Yahoo! and Point-Cast) to scientific information services, such as Brint, credit inquiry agencies (e.g. Experian), patent databases and stock exchange information services, such as Charles Schwab, are shifting the focus of information management away from internal sources and very strongly in the direction of external sources.

Knowledge management is not only beneficial in the process of customer advisory services and care. Other important fields of application are the processes of product development, organizational development and training. In the case of organizational development it is a matter of knowledge about business strategies, processes and systems, as systematically built up and maintained by consultancies nowadays. The corporate universities of large organizations cover conventional training activities on the one hand, but on the other have a much wider remit to collect and impart corporate knowledge.

Consequences

- *Knowledge utilization.* It is not the collection of knowledge but the utilization of knowledge which creates value for the enterprise. The business process determines what knowledge is required.

- *Knowledge value measurement.* Knowledge management must be based on the value for the process and must measure it by performance indicators.

- *Knowledge structuring.* Knowledge management starts with the recording and structuring of internal and external knowledge, based on its use in the business process.

- *Utilization of existing knowledge.* The most important task is to utilize the (explicit) knowledge which is already documented electronically in business processes. Only then will previously implicit knowledge become explicitized. A consultancy firm, for example, will first make use of the documentation from completed projects in new projects before urging project managers to document the most important findings from a project in addition.

- *Documentation of implicit knowledge.* The explicitization of knowledge is particularly successful if it leads to instructions (methods) and reusable documents or templates. A service technician needs an assembly instruction and not a database containing general experience with the functioning of components.

- *Knowledge management as part of business processes.* Knowledge management is the task of business managers and not the task of a new staff position. However, the organization/IS department must take on the same tasks for document processing as it has already done for transaction processing.

- *Strategic knowledge management.* It is the task of management to recognize the opportunities provided by knowledge management and to drive implementation forward.

2.3.3   Smart Appliances

Today, smart appliances, such as digital cameras, machine-tool control systems, electronic organizers, game computers, pace-makers or car engine management, are already taken for granted. The miniaturization and the fall in prices of processors and memories are contributing to the rapid growth of application areas, such as clearance monitoring in cars. However, there is a new feature of these appliances that will visibly change life at home and at work: the networking capability (cf. [Norman 1999, 62], [Davis/Meyer 1998], [Strauss 1998]).

The car navigation system (GPS), the mobile telephone (GSM), the pager, the TV set top-box, road-pricing systems, Internet-enabled maintenance computers on machines, the electronic book and the electronic tagging of prisoners are examples of networked appliances which are already in use. Video cameras, photographic cameras, audio and video systems are increasingly becoming digitalized and have also found their way to the Internet - in some cases via the PC. Smart cards are a special form of smart appliance used for a wide spectrum of applications, from authorization to electronic cash. All these appliances offer a specially adapted form of access to the Internet and/or to the networks of individual companies from the home or while on the road (see Figure 2-6).

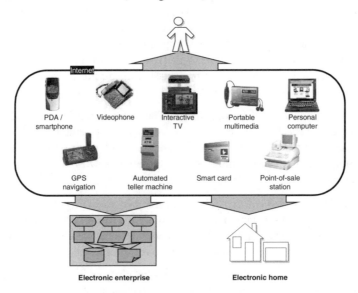

Figure 2-6: Multi-mode Access Through Smart Appliances

The business flight of the future might proceed as follows: the passenger books his flight via the Internet or through a call center. A few hours prior to departure, the electronic organizer of the passenger's mobile phone reminds him to confirm his flight and, once authorized, forwards confirmation to the airline. In the event of a delay, the airline sends the passenger an SMS message or a voicemail to his mobile phone. On approach to the airport, the GPS tells him where parking spaces are available in the airport's multi-story car park and guides him there. The road-pricing system automatically charges the parking fee. The automatic airport check-in registers the passenger's presence through the arrival of his mobile phone within the zone of the airport. An SMS message, tells him at which gate he can board and the number of his seat. When boarding the aircraft the passenger identifies himself with his customer card (smart card). Once on board his mobile phone and PC have Internet access which allows him to work just like in the office.

Airlines already have many of the features described in this scenario in the pipeline. Similar scenarios are to be found for patient home care, service engineers performing machine maintenance, entertainment with audio, video and games as well as in other areas.

The parcel service FedEx supports its order tracking system with PDAs (previously Apple Newton, now PalmPilot) [cf. FedEx 1999]. This allows customers to call up the status of their parcel deliveries at any time via the FedEx web site. As well as improving customer service, FedEx is also reducing costs through savings in staff who provide information on the telephone.

The Palm VII Connected Organizer via the proprietary network Palm.Net provides access to news channels like BBC News, financial information like Bloomberg, or a hotel guide like Fodor's, it locates the nearest three cash machines or gas stations, connects to a translation service, and allows access to existing travel itineraries.

The company Grenley-Stewart Resources (GSR) sells diesel fuel to over 1,200 gas stations in the USA. Customers are the owners of truck fleets who obtain fuel at a significantly reduced price than at normal gas stations through a contract with GSR. The high consumption and large distances covered by a truck mean that even relatively low differences in the fuel prices of various suppliers can add up to large sums.

Diesel prices fluctuate on a daily basis and vary from one place to another. In order to inform truck drivers on the current prices at GSR gas stations, GSR publishes its latest prices on its own web site which can be accessed by the fleet owners free of charge. As distributing the information by telephone is too involved, GSR offers its customers access via PalmPilot as an additional service. Drivers can investigate local diesel prices whenever they wish and can also request graphic route plans to take them to the required gas station [cf. Korzeniowski 1998].

A few technical developments have made all this possible (e.g. [Davis/Meyer 1998], [Bill 1998]):

* *Digitization.* Digitization makes it possible to communicate all information, be it music, measured values from sensors or images, by simple means.

- *Internet.* The Internet has provided an extremely low-priced method of globally available networking.

- *Low-priced processors.* The drop in processor prices has made it possible to equip appliances with additional functionality, a simple user interface and access to the Net.

Where appliances are concerned, a trend can be observed towards both the integration of functionality and specialization (cf. [Burrows/Reinhardt 1999], [Kuri 1999]). On the other hand, mobile phone manufacturers, for example, are packing more and more functions, such as planners, e-mail, SMS messages, address database, Internet browser, remote control for any appliances and video communication into their products with the aim of creating a universal PDA (Personal Digital Assistant). On the other hand, there is a tendency for game computers, TVs, refrigerators, heating systems and machine controls to be equipped with their own specialized processors, network connections and control units.

At the same time there is a fully fledged battle going on between operating system manufacturers for a standard application platform: Windows CE versus Java versus PalmOS versus EPOC. More decisive for the networking of smart appliances is the competition between middleware, such as UPnP, Jini or WAP and alternative networks. The most important versions here are peripheral access devices (cable connection, e.g. IEEE1394, USB), telephone line (Phone Line, e.g. HomePNA), power line (Power Line, e.g. CEBus, X-10), radio and/or infrared in the local area (e.g. HomeRF, Bluetooth, IrDA) and long-distance radio (e.g. GSM, CDMA). In the end, a combination of technologies, each with a dominant market standard will win through. In addition, we can expect to see whole series of new broadband standards gaining wide diffusion in the next few years, including UMTS (universal mobile telecommunication standard) for mobile communication or ADSL (asymmetric digital subscriber line) for linking households to the Internet. In view of its huge volumes, consumer electronics technology will also provide the standards for businesses, as was already the case for personal computers.

The following general scenario is possible within a few years:

- Every machine has access to all the information which any computer keeps on the Net. In other words, the navigation system has access to road maps, traffic reports, weather reports, hotels, restaurants, car repair garages, etc.

- Consumers and employees have real-time (with no delays) and global access to all private and business information. They use the most suitable appliance in each case (multi-mode access, see Figure 2-6).

- Data entry takes place at the point of action. The smart card and the point of sale cash register record the payment transaction, the purchased articles, the time and the location. The bank, department store and department store supplier have real-time access to these data.

- Use of these appliances ensures general computer literacy. Communication with computers and an understanding of computer functions become a matter of course.

According to IDC [cf. Hwang et al. 1998], 18 million consumer information appliances will be sold for home use in the year 2001, topping personal computers for the first time. Datamonitor [cf. Hofer 1999] states that in the year 2001 consumers will purchase 8 million games consoles alone (USA and Western Europe only). In addition, 34% of the population in the USA and 13% in Europe will then have a personal computer with access to the Internet according to a study by Forrester Research [cf. Sawyer 1998]. If we include additional categories of appliances (GPS etc.) we begin to get an idea of the potential which smart appliances represent.

Consequences

The consequences of smart appliances are still difficult to assess. Who would have thought three years ago that the MP3 format developed by the Fraunhofer Institute in Erlangen, which allows the compressed digital storage of music, in conjunction with the Internet would succeed in restructuring the complete music sector within a few years [cf. Gomes 1999].

- *Appliance and software manufacturers.* The greatest challenge of all is that facing the manufacturers of appliances and software. This ranges from the electronically monitored label printer and the escalator to the office coffee machine which sends information on coffee consumption to the service company for replenishment purposes. MP3 (more precisely: MPEG Audio Layer-3) and other multi media standards (e.g. SDMI) are leading to the creation of a new generation of appliances for audio/video storage and reproduction. They will revolutionize not just the appliances (players etc.), but the music industry and the music distribution channels as a whole.

- *Service providers.* Networked smart appliances are usually only meaningful in conjunction with a special service. In the air travel example, this would be check-in and boarding, in the case of FedEx order tracking, with MP3 the music distribution service and with Grenley-Stewart the diesel price information system.

- *Suppliers of conventional products and services.* Smart appliances are changing business in many areas. Entrepreneurs must ask themselves the following questions:

Which information and electronic services generate added value at the point of action for consumers, employees or machines (e.g. a personal telephone directory on the Net, a regional weather forecast via the mobile phone)?

Which information can smart appliances provide at the point of action (e.g. sales data from point of sale cash registers)?

Which market participants are in a position to offer our products and services by better or more economical means (e.g. business news from the point of view of a daily newspaper)?

Despite the fact that this technology - compared to ERP systems for instance - is still far from mature, it points the way to serious transformations in business processes and in the private sphere. In some countries at least this is giving rise to widespread fears of technology and big brother taking over.

2.3.4   Business Networking

Business in the information age is a network of processes. During the past ten to twenty years, business process redesign has created integrated processes within companies; database systems have made this integration possible. During the next ten to twenty years, Business Networking will link processes above and beyond company boundaries and serve consumers directly; networks, such as the Internet, will provide the means. Interorganizational coordination will change business far more fundamentally than intraorganizational integration has done.

The result will be a worldwide network of specialists, each of which will play its part in value creation with its core competence. The path will lead via the deassembly of existing enterprises into independent processes and via reassembly of enterprises and supply chains [cf. Wigand et al. 1997, 2]. Business is at the start of a dramatic transformation and Business Networking is a main driver.

Experiments in the automotive industry with new forms of supply chain networks should be mentioned as a reference for the many reorganizations in the financial sector, in the pharmaceutical industry, in tourism and in other areas. With Micro Compact Car (MCC) [cf. van Hoek/Weken 1997], DaimlerChrysler realized an enterprise which largely performs the coordination of processes which it has outsourced to specialists. Ford is currently in the process of handing over parts of its final assembly to specialists and transforming itself into an enterprise for consumer goods and services [cf. Burt 1999].

A few examples allow us to identify the types and principles of Business Networking (see Figure 2-7):

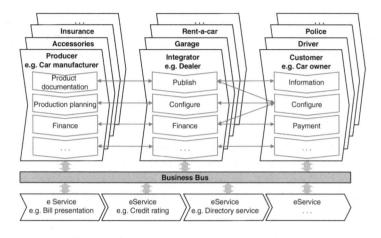

Figure 2-7: Model of Business Networking

- *Electronic commerce.* The most commonly known form of Business Networking is the Internet shop. In sell-side electronic commerce or eSales (cf.
Chap. 4.3.1), manufacturers, banks and many others use the Internet as a new
sales channel to corporate customers and consumers [cf. Barling/Stark 1998].
Customers, in the example shown in Figure 2-7 the car owner, perform their
subprocesses information, configure, payment etc. jointly with the subprocesses publish, configure, finance etc. of the intermediary, in this case the car
dealer. The car dealer retrieves the customer's address data from an electronic
directory service, the credit information from an electronic service for credit
rating and settles payment through a payment service.
The role of the intermediary (integrator) in the supply chain is to group products, services and information together to form a package, to allow the customer to compare the offerings of many manufacturers side by side (eBay,
Yahoo!, e-Steel, eTrade, Dell, etc.), and, if needs be, to match supply and demand (in an auction e.g. buy). The value added by the intermediary is the integration [cf. Klein 1999].
At the heart of the Internet shop is the electronic replacement of the conventional ordering process using paper-based catalogs and fax [cf. Kala-
kota/Whinston 1997, 3]. ETA, for example, a manufacturer of watch movements within 'The Swatch Group', has arranged for its customers (i.e.
watchmakers) to order movements and spare parts through an Internet shop
(cf. Chap. 6). This rapidly gives rise to an intermediary which expands its
range by including other non-related articles, additional services (e.g. maintenance) and information (e.g. sales forecasts), such as Dell or Cisco. Cisco
makes 40% of its turnover, i.e. USD 3 billion, via the Internet.

- *MRO procurement.* While the examples mentioned up to now have related to
the sell-side, MRO procurement focuses on buy-side electronic commerce (cf.

Chap. 4.3.1). The process of procuring indirect goods (MRO: maintenance, repair and operations) is built around the customer process. UBS, one of the world's leading banks with 30,000 staff, has set up an Intranet shop with 10,000 articles for the procurement of MRO products (office stationery, furniture, information technology, etc.) [cf. Dolmetsch 1999, 13]. External suppliers maintain a warehouse and supply to some 3,000 authorized purchasers in the organization. Now, six months after introducing the system, 2,500 different articles are processed on a daily basis. The benefit lies in a drastic simplification of the ordering process, plus volume discounts and reduced inventory. MRO procurement starts from the customer's procurement process, creates multi-vendor product catalogs with the intermediary, links the suppliers, utilizes electronic services for logistics, payment, product catalogs, etc. (cf. Chap. 10).

• *Supply chain management.* The goal of supply chain management is to optimize purchasing, production, inventory management, and transport across all the elements in the supply chain network [cf. Handfield/Nichols 1998, 2]. From the boutique (customer) via the garment manufacturer (integrator) and the textile manufacturer back through to fiber production (producer), supply chain management exchanges sales forecasts, effective sales, inventory levels, delivery dates, customs papers, payments, etc. For this purpose it uses electronic services for credit ratings, payment and transport organization (logistics). It creates an additional service 'available to promise' which takes on scheduling tasks for all the participants in the supply chain. Most members in the supply chain act as producer as well as integrator and customer (cf. Chaps. 4.3.2, 6.2 and 9).
Riverwood, a packaging material manufacturer, has closely linked its production and distribution planning with that of its customers (e.g. Miller Breweries). This has enabled Riverwood to drastically increase delivery speed and accuracy, and to achieve a quantum leap in customer relationships (cf. Chap. 5).

• *Shared services.* Large corporations group together subprocesses, which occur in a similar form in several business units, to form shared services. BP Amoco, for example, has turned its processes tax, auditing, legal services, human resources as well as purchasing and materials management into shared services which all business units in the group can access. In this case the shared services are producers of services, the group is the integrator and the business units are the customers. This type of organization is dependent on electronic services for master data coordination, transporting messages, charging services, etc. However, shared services can also be bought in from independent companies. ADP handles the payrolls for 425,000 customers, which means over 30 million wages and salaries [cf. ADP 1999].

• *Online service.* Companies, such as Intel and Cisco, offer their customers the choice of a broad spectrum of information and services for the use and operation of their products online. Nowadays, the customers of technology companies have come to expect Internet services of this kind, the quality of which is considered to be a major differentiating factor [cf. Association 1999]. 80,000 registered users take advantage of Cisco's online service [cf. Rodin 1999, 213].

The speed at which Business Networking will change the face of business will largely depend on the following technical and business factors:

- *Intermediary.* Customers will only place a large proportion of their purchases via the Net if an intermediary packages a large number of suppliers, products and services in such a way that they conveniently cover the customer's needs in a particular process. Any company can act as intermediary without having to invest much effort. However, the competition between intermediaries is going to be phenomenal. Only few intermediaries will survive worldwide in each business area (customer segment, customer process and range of articles). Standard software for intermediaries, which is currently developing under the heading of customer relationship management (e.g. Siebel), will further increase the dynamics in this area.

- *Electronic services.* Payment transactions, credit ratings, multi-vendor product catalogs, trust, etc. are services which are needed time and again in many forms of Business Networking. The more of this type of service that is available and accepted by a large number of market participants, the easier it will be to set up an electronic business relationship.

- *Business bus.* The Internet is a technical standard for data communication (TCP/IP) and presentation (HTML, SGML, XML) around which a rich infrastructure of products and services has formed. By analogy, the business bus is the term used to describe the totality of technical, applications and business standards on which software solutions, electronic services, etc. are based. These include EDIFACT, cXML (commercial XML), RosettaNet, OAGIS (open application group integration specification) and OAMAS (open application group middleware api), de facto standards for business objects, such as those in the SAP environment (incl. the BAPIs as methods) or those of Microsoft's BizTalk [cf. Microsoft 1999a], process standards like CPFR, and finally 'laws' for Business Networking, e.g. generally valid rules for dealing with delays in delivery as now agreed in some cases between the participants in a supply chain. An example of the business bus in a banking sector is the order transport management system from PricewaterhouseCoopers.
  The business bus produces the m:n capability of Business Networking. Today, virtually all business networks are either 1:n (e.g. Amazon) or 1:1 relationships (e.g. Riverwood). As a result, the effort involved in setting up and operating every additional business relationship is too high. The availability of standards which improve the m:n capability will more than anything else

determine the speed with which business becomes networked. Ideally, the business bus will supply a standardized socket and the plug to go with it.

- *Networked enterprise resource planning.* Today, ERP packages are structured liked classic enterprises. They only support new forms of networked businesses in part, if at all. The distribution of the human resource process between a shared service and the outsourcing company, the coordination of production planning in one company and the supply chain planning in another, the matching of an order with an MRO supplier with the purchaser's order, etc. must first be developed step by step. While it should be considerably easier to expand proven ERP solutions by network versions of the processes than developing complete ERP systems based on network solutions, there is still a great deal of development work to be done here.

On the basis of these considerations it is possible to sketch out the following scenario:

- *Technical infrastructure.* A broadband, low-cost communication infrastructure will shortly become available (UTMS, ADSLetc.).

- *Business bus.* "An infrastructure designed around information flow will be the 'killer application' for the twenty-first century." [Microsoft 1999b]. The large corporations in this market are fighting an intense battle for domination of the business bus. Major players are Microsoft with its development environment, in particular BizTalk, and with Microsoft Network, Oracle with Oracle Exchange, SAP with mySAP and above all with network-compatible ERP functions (BAPI, APO, etc.), Siebel with customer relationship management software, portal providers, such as AOL, Yahoo! and PointCast. Outsiders, such as Commerce One with an electronic service for multi-vendor catalogs (MarketSite.net), should also be watched (cf. Chap. 3.2.5).

- *Killer application.* MRO procurement could prove to be the killer application of Business Networking. A lot of large corporations take advantage of the possibilities for savings when purchasing secondary materials, at the moment frequently using solutions which they have developed themselves. If Ariba, for example, was able to dominate as a supplier of procurement solutions and catalog services, then its data structures and semantics would be able to establish themselves as a de facto standard. When a company masters the processes and applications for the procurement of part of its articles, the tendency is to extend this solution to cover other articles. As customers like Ariba introduce the corresponding sell-side solution onto the market in addition to the buy-side solution, the same applies for the sell-side. Once a company has established a Business Networking software platform for the purchasing process, it will want to use it to network other processes.

- *ERP and CRM.* Enterprise resource planning and customer relationship management (CRM) are variously described as possible, separate directions for the development of enterprise software. In a Forrester Report, [Cole et al. 1999] come to the conclusion that the wide range of isolated solutions for CRM are growing together and will form their own platform with an interface to ERP systems. As the CRM applications access the same data as the ERP applications, however, the systems will have to be integrated. The question is whether the CRM package will be extended to include the ERP functionality or vice versa. If we look back at similar developments in the past, there is a lot to be said for concluding that the core of networked units (e.g. the operating system Windows and travel booking system SABRE) will dominate and not the Net. However, this only applies if the ERP systems acquire Business Networking capability fast enough. Inadequate cooperation between companies which function well on their own is more probable than perfect cooperation between units with inadequate internal processing.

Consequences

In many cases the question is not whether investments in Business Networking will pay in the short term but whether the customer will be prepared to accept a supplier who does not offer its product catalog and associated services electronically. In accordance with the model of Business Networking shown in Figure 2-7, a company has a series of options:

- *Products and services.* Which new products, but above all which services will be feasible via the Net? A configurator for products, support for troubleshooting or a chat room for customers are examples. Which internal services can the company also offer in the marketplace? Does the company perform internal services which it could offer as an electronic service without too much effort? One example would be the soil database of an agrochemical manufacturer which documents the quality of the soil according to region and which the manufacturer has used up to now to sell its fertilizer but could possibly be sold more profitably as a service via the Net.

- *Customer segment.* Business Networking creates an additional channel to existing customers but also access to other customer segments. In particular, it extends the geographical scope to the whole globe.

- *Supply chain.* In which supply chain is the company involved? Which networks will establish themselves on the market? Which positions can the company hope to occupy in these networks? Which alliances should be forged? Can the company organize a supply chain or does it act as a supplier and customer?

- *Procurement.* Is the company familiar with the products and services which are offered via the Net and does it use them as a customer? Does it make use of the global access to suppliers? Which processes need to be redesigned? What about market research?

- *Outsourcing of processing.* When communication between companies no longer involves much more effort than communication between departments within a company, a company can gain striking power by concentrating on strategic processes and buying in all the others from outside. A financial institution, such as the German MLP, for example, specializes in providing a comprehensive financial service for a narrow customer segment and purchases all handling processes, such as credit scoring, collection, securities settlement, payment, etc. from specialized financial service providers. A pharmaceutical corporation may understand the management of its complex research and development process plus marketing and distribution as core processes and outsource all the others, such as the performance of research, the testing of substances and production, to specialists.

- *Critical mass.* Business Networking presupposes a critical mass. The customer will purchase from the online bookshop with the biggest selection of books. In the case of an exclusivity clause, the supplier will supply to the bookshop which has the largest number of customers. The investments for setting up (development and marketing) an electronic bookshop are very high, the marginal costs extremely low. Being able to allocate the investment costs to as many transactions as possible will decide profitability. What is true for the bookshop applies by analogy for the investment service of a bank, for training or for the marketing of construction materials.
  Many networking solutions, while useful in themselves, are not even begun if the path to reaching the critical mass is either too long or too uncertain. The best example is the introduction of new technologies, such as DVD (digital versatile disk), which do not establish themselves until long after they become technically available when all the participants in the network believe in the success of the technology.

- *Networkability.* Networkability is a core competence for every enterprise of the information age. In addition to concrete interorganizational processes, an enterprise must build up the capability to offer new services quickly via the Net and to integrate new customers and suppliers with minimum effort. This includes not only the standards of the business bus, but also the networkability of the enterprise's own applications and last but not least a functional, integrated enterprise resource planning.

Business Networking will change more in business than the ERP systems have done. The potential is so huge that many are talking of a new industrial revolution. Despite the initial euphoria, there are nevertheless many factors exerting a braking effect, first and foremost that of standardization. Interorganizational solutions do not come about unless all the necessary participants stand to benefit and the solution will achieve the critical mass within a foreseeable time span.

2.3.5 Electronic Services

Road traffic has paved the way for complete business sectors: police, road construction, maintenance, repair workshops, snow clearance, traffic information, navigation, etc. Business Networking will give rise to a new business sector for electronic services: Net access, directories, payment, portals, etc. Electronic services either perform coordination tasks (e.g. payment transactions) or they are subprocesses which many companies require in a similar form and therefore purchase in electronic form. A huge business sector is growing up around Business Networking. Figure 2-8 classifies electronic services and names examples:

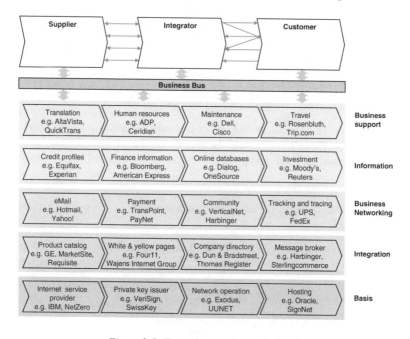

Figure 2-8: Examples of Electronic Services

- *Basic services* provide the technical infrastructure on which all other services are based.

- *Integration services* are services which support the coordination of processes across enterprises. They ensure the safe transfer and logging of messages to and from selected network participants (messaging, routing), help in the search for and identification of market participants (directory services, e.g. customer Meier from Buttwil), products, etc. (multi-vendor product catalogs), assist in the reconstruction of a failed web transaction involving several participants and link objects from different data pools (e.g. all producers of products containing genetically modified corn). In other words, integration services do the same as a database management system does within a company for the integration of applications and processes. At the moment, the form integration services will take is only identifiable in outline. While directory services, for example, have been introduced for telephone subscribers, multi-vendor product catalogs are still in their infancy (e.g. in the case of General Electric) and in terms of the infomediaries, as designed by [Hagel/Singer 1999, 21], only exist as a vision.

- *Business Networking services* are services which almost every company needs when working with other companies and which are therefore to be found on most of the more highly developed web sites [cf. Giaglis et al. 1999].

- The Net offers a vast maze of *information services*. The content might be news or research reports, stock exchange prices or credit ratings for business partners. The information may enter the company's own portal as a channel, be pushed internally as a clipping service or - for example in the case of financial data - be directly included in calculations (e.g. current price in a foreign currency). Classical media companies will be transformed in broad variety of specialized and integrated media services [cf. Hess/Schumann 1999].

- *Business support services* include processes which companies outsource and can largely purchase in electronic form. This can be an automatic translation service or payroll accounting.

Electronic services have the following in common:

- They permit collaboration between companies, and/or between companies and consumers.

- They are largely electronic, i.e. with no manual intervention.

- They are accessible via computers or smart appliances.

- They can be used individually or as a package.

- Their service components are highly standardized.

- In the majority of cases they are charged according to use.

Most of the services mentioned above do not exist in the pure form, i.e. service providers try to cover customer needs as comprehensively as possible by bundling services and thus keep the entry barrier for competitors as high as possible.

After a period in which many start-ups created innovative services, such as Hot-Mail, a free email service, which proved to be successful, only very large companies which can absorb high investments with long pay-back periods and have global access to a broad customer base can now keep pace with the packaging and establishment of services, despite the fact that large opportunities still remain in niche markets.

This can be explained by an example. Paper-based correspondence between consumers and insurance companies, banks, public administrations, schools, travel agencies, etc. involves a large time and effort on both sides. Files and records in private households are not only cumbersome but usually also inadequate. Strack-Zimmermann, the CEO of iXOS AG, has designed a document exchange and filing service, the value of which is immediately obvious to all concerned [cf. Strack-Zimmermann 1998]. Despite the fact that a service of this kind could operate highly profitably, the barriers confronting the establishment of the service are difficult to surmount: the companies will have to accept the standard stipulated by the service provider, a sufficiently large number of consumers must be online and able to operate the service and ultimately be prepared to dispense with the tangible medium of paper.

For every type of service only a limited number of suppliers can survive per customer segment as all participants have an interest in having only one supplier for each task or process, just as they only have one power or telephone connection. In addition, service customers want to have integrated services so that they will not have any interface problems. The reader should consider the question of how many private key issuers or payment services are possible worldwide. These considerations form the background to the exorbitant increases in 'Internet shares'.

Consequences

Companies can draw the following conclusions from these considerations:

- *Development of own services.* If a company has leading know how for a specific service and has opportunities for establishing that service globally - e.g. through alliances and branding - then, this is a highly attractive economic proposition.

- *Utilization of services.* Business Networking means taking advantage of a broad spectrum of electronic services. Each of these services represents part of the standard of the business bus. It is not the best service but the combination of services with the greatest market penetration which will establish itself. Investments based on the wrong standards are expensive and delay the development of the networked business.

2.3.6   Customer Process Support

Customer process support utilizes all the developments mentioned above to service the customer's problem-solving needs comprehensively and from a single source.

Customer centricity has long been a guiding principle for many businesses. However, this is usually limited to marketing existing products and services with as strong a customer focus as possible (cf. Chap. 7). Corporate strategy remains basically product-centered. The web sites of most companies provide the best evidence of this fact.

The enterprise of the information age focuses on the customer process. Networking, multimedia and high IT functionality at the customer's end make it possible to place the emphasis on the customer's problem rather than on the product [cf. Kühn/Grandke 1997]. Innovative companies have already gone over to supporting the complete customer process, i.e. the process which a customer goes through in order to satisfy a need. They offer customers every product, every service and every piece of information they need from a single source and guide them in this process. They become service integrator and specialist for this process.

With its help desk, the Zürich insurance company is pursuing its goal of supporting the customer throughout the complete process of handling a claim. Ideally, the insured party calls the help desk, e.g. following a car accident, which from that moment on assumes responsibility for the process. The help desk takes care of vehicle repair, the provision of a substitute vehicle and the settlement of claims, etc. Zürich is pursuing a dual aim here: firstly, its many years of experience in the field and its trained network of specialists enable it to handle the claim much more efficiently than the client can; this reduces the claim costs. Secondly, Zürich is relieving the client of tiresome tasks. This service becomes possible when Zürich can handle claims with a large number of partners so efficiently by means of information technology that it costs less than the conventional solution.

An example of a customer process which has already proved highly successful is logistics. Companies, such as Kühne & Nagel, Danzas or FedEx, offer their customers not just transport services but also a large number of additional services, such as e.g. order tracking or inventory management. In extreme cases they even assume responsibility for the customer's complete logistics process. Automatic communication between the logistics service provider and customer management, order entry and production as well as with the financial accounting at the customer's end make this solution fast and economical.

Another example with considerable effects on the whole branch of industry is the process 'car ownership'. Car manufacturers, car dealers (AutoByTel), car magazines (AutoBild) and Internet shops (CarPoint) are starting to offer not just car sales, but all products, services and information from the selection and running of a car through to its disposal, from a single source (as already indicated in Figure 2-7). In the past, customers had to take care of every partial task in the process 'car ownership'. They read the test reports in the car magazines, visited the dealer, studied brochures, obtained a loan, registered the car with the appropriate authority, kept an eye on service intervals, obtained road maps, planned travel itineraries, obtained traffic reports, navigated, placed an ad for their used cars, etc. In other words, the car owner had to act as an expert for the process without actually being able to become one, and was compelled to communicate with a large number of service providers, resulting in considerable time and effort both for customer and supplier.

The special feature of the development in the automobile trade is the fact that new providers are entering these markets by means of the Internet - portal providers and a car magazine. These are not tied to a particular brand of car, in fact their very strength lies in their independence. They begin with a topic portal which merely represents a loose collection of information and services, develop into a business community in which the participants of this network work closely together (e.g. exchange of quality problems) and finally try to offer not only all information, services and products for the process of car ownership but also to manage the process.

Avnet Marshall (cf. Chap. 3.2.3) is a leading US distributor of electronic components and appliances (with 2,300 employees). Avnet Marshall supports - as embedded in its strategy [cf. Rodin 1999] - the customer process procurement of electronic components. In 1998 their web site was voted world best business-to-business site for a second time by the online magazine 'Advertising Age' (ahead of Cisco Systems, Dell Computers and Compaq Computers). This corporation is a typical intermediary which sees its position in the supply chain network in the age of electronic commerce and supply chain management as being to enrich the pure trading in products and services to such an extent that the corporation becomes attractive to both suppliers and customers. With this in mind, Avnet Marshall set about shifting its activities to electronic platforms in a big way in 1993. Today, Avnet Marshall offers a product catalog covering a large number of suppliers, a news service, online seminars, a supply chain service and numerous other services around the product 'electronic components' on the Net (see Figure 2-9) in addition to electronic commerce. Avnet Marshall's customers outsource part of their procurement process to Avnet Marshall.

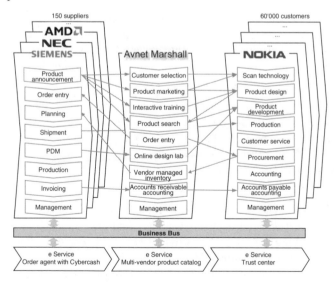

Figure 2-9: Service Integrator Avnet Marshall

An example of support for the complete customer process from the software sector is SAP. Over the past few years this software company has expanded its sale of software to include a large number of services and is pursuing the goal of supporting customers in all aspects relating to the optimization of their business processes. The focus, of course, is on introducing the software. SAP offers process management using the ASAP method, reference processes for reorganization (SAP Solution Map), templates for customizing, training for business engineers and users, remote consulting for specific questions, online information services regarding errors, plus newsgroups and list servers for communication between user companies. SAP provides remote maintenance (early watch) for system operation and even outsourcing of the operation [cf. Muther 1998]. Prior to and following introduction, SAP offers aids, such as e.g. key performance indicators and benchmarks [www.mysap.com], to assess potential and monitor achievements.

Further interesting examples of service integrators on the Net, which attempt to cover the customer process as widely as possible are Quicken, Charles Schwab, eTrade, Consors, Pointcast and SmartMoney for financial services or Travelocity and TIScover for tourism. These portals are also referred to as process portals. [Mertens et al. 1998, 18] analyze the products and services provided by 15 so-called virtual enterprises and end up with a similar picture of the networked enterprise [cf. Mertens et al. 1998, 64].

The following features can be identified from the examples given:

- *Specialist for customer process.* Service integrators master customer processes better than the customers themselves as, unlike the customers, the service integrators make these processes their strategic core processes.

- *Customer resource life cycle.* Customer centricity is based on the customer process. It attempts to resolve the process and thus the customer's problem in the sense of the customer resource life cycle [cf. Ives/Learmonth 1984] and to combine as many products, services and information as possible for this purpose.

- *Virtual community.* The extended form of the service integrator also comprises a virtual community which provides customers on the one hand with organized access to all the knowledge of relevance to them and their processes, and on the other hand makes direct communication possible between customers and also between customers and suppliers of the individual services [cf. Hagel/Amstrong 1997, 57].

- *Customer data.* The support for the complete customer process makes it possible to collect detailed data on customers and on their utilization and purchasing behavior [cf. Hagel/Amstrong 1997, 128]. For data protection reasons, but equally for reasons of integration, a large part of these data could be located at the customer's in the form of a personal or business profile which they could make available to business partners on a selective basis, depending on the application.

- *Service packages.* Service integrators typically offer multi-vendor product catalogs, product search, configurators, order registration and processing, payment, logistics, industry news, access to information services, seminars, discussion forums, help desks and product-related services, such as support for the assembly of electronic components.

- *Globalization.* Service integrators rapidly break free of conventional regional boundaries and become global providers.

- *Outsourcing of process elements.* Customer process centricity begins with the support for a few services and can go as far as complete outsourcing.

A service integrator offers the customer considerable added value (Figure 2-10):

- *Everything.* The customer obtains all products, services and information from a single source and only needs one business relationship.

- *One-stop.* The customer can complete his transaction in one stop. He never has to wait for the supplier - with the exception of the physical transportation of goods.

- *Anyhow.* The customer receives process support by the method she prefers.

- *One-to-one.* Communication with the supplier is tailored to the requirements of the customer (customer profile), from marketing to after-sales service.

- *Everywhere and non-stop.* The customer receives the services at any time and any place in the world.

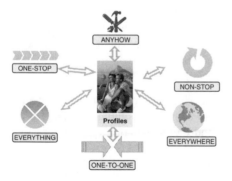

Figure 2-10: Characteristics of Customer Process Support

A service integrator, such as Avnet Marshall, uses the whole spectrum of IT applications outlined in connection with the five previous trends. The following should be emphasized however:

- The low-cost networking of all market participants via the Internet,

- The simple and cheap availability of multimedia solutions to communicate any form of knowledge,

- A broad spectrum of systems under the heading of 'Customer Relationship Management' (e.g. Siebel). A collection of customer care tools is to be found in the tool database of the Institute of Information Management of the University of St. Gallen [www.ecc.ch].

Consequences

Over the next three years, many companies will try to establish a strong market position as service integrator. Classic corporations will try to extend their offerings in this direction, new companies will want to establish themselves in this form. The most important tasks along the way will be:

- *Customer process.* The provider must not only understand the customer process but also build up superior know how relating to the customer process.

- *Role in the business network.* A business has to decide the customer services for which it can itself act as service integrator, the service integrators to which it is going to deliver and/or the customers to which it is going to sell directly.

- *Critical mass of customers.* The service integrator needs a high market share, on the one hand in order to allocate the high investments involved in setting up the business to a sufficiently high number of transactions, and on the other in order to convince the suppliers that it is offering the right network. Service integrators may well compel suppliers to enter exclusive agreements [cf. Hagel/Singer 1998, 169].

- *Critical mass of suppliers.* Providers must convince the suppliers of the required services to offer these to the market through them. Customers will work with the service integrator in which they have the greatest confidence on the basis of the name and who offers them access to the greatest number of suppliers [cf. Hagel/Singer 1998, 169].

- *Business community.* The greater the number of cooperating processes between the members of a business community, the greater the derivable benefit from the network and the greater the level of attractiveness for the participants.

Avnet Marshall consider the following factors to be critical for success in their sector: customer service, product range (extent to which customer needs are covered), degree of product availability, price, technical information (knowledge) and value-added services.

2.3.7 Value Management

Shareholder value is the catalyst in the transformation from the industrial to the information age. It drives entrepreneurs to look for new business solutions on the basis of IT, serves as a standard of valuation for investments, ensures the supply of capital for risky innovations and controls implementation. Shareholder value will dominate in turbulent times of change, but in a networked world it is dependent on other dimensions of stakeholder value (see Figure 2-11).

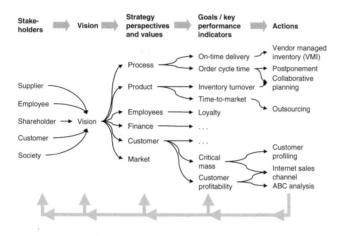

Figure 2-11: Dimensions of Stakeholder Value

The vision of the enterprise is gaining in significance. The resulting corporate strategy determines the areas which will be critical for success. In the information age there will be a new emphasis: on the customer base, employee values, know how, services, processes and networking.

Strategy defines goals and the key performance indicators. The information system supplies objectivized and updated actual values for all managers. It links the key performance indicators to the employee compensation scheme.

The classic enterprise is dominated by unidimensional, financial management. Sales revenues and, at most, contribution margins determine planning and controlling and performance-related remuneration. At Avnet Marshall, Robert Rodin realized one of the most radical changes in the management of a trading company: he dispensed with every form of commission for the complete management and subsequently for the entire sales force, and introduced fixed salaries. He then went on to develop a 'performance matrix' for assessing personnel according to their skills and performance in the areas which were critical for success (key performance indicators). In retrospect, Rodin describes this step as the most important prerequisite for mastering the transformation from a classic retailing business to an Internet intermediary of the information age [cf. Rodin 1999, 104, 238].

The characteristics of value management are (see Figure 2-11):

- Stakeholders have a common vision. This is the basis for the shareholders, for employee loyalty and for customer confidence. It determines values.

- Strategy concretizes the vision; it determines the areas critical for success (perspectives, critical success factors, value drivers) and formulates goals and measures.

- Management in the information age is therefore multidimensional. It sets objectives for financial performance, objectives for process quality [cf. Österle 1995, 105] and objectives for transformation of the enterprise.

- Management becomes future-oriented. Financial indicators document the past, while order cycle time considers customer satisfaction and thus the financial results in the future.

- Management becomes more direct. Sales revenues and costs represent aggregated information which tell the individual employee little about what she can do better. Customer returns, customer profitability, etc. are applicable to day-to-day business.

- Measures have to be adopted to implement strategy. The planning, execution and control of measures are at the heart of transformation.

What is new in all this? Strategic management, critical success factors, balanced score cards, key performance indicators and scoring systems have been around for some time and have triggered various management trends - and nevertheless only been partly successful. So what is different in the information age?

- *Process measurement.* The ERP and CRM systems track all business transactions in detail. For the first time in the history of business management theory it is possible to record the key performance indicators for all areas which are critical for success automatically and objectively - and not just the financial performance indicators from accounting and costing - and to distribute them to employees on a daily basis [www.img.com/pmb]. The Internet and smart appliances provide a flood of new data on customers, purchasing behavior, etc.

- *Knowledge management.* Knowledge management now makes not only transaction data, but also less formalized knowledge from sources within and outside the business readily accessible.

- *Data warehousing.* ERP, CRM, process measurement and external sources of information provide an unprecedented flood of data. Data warehousing provides the tools which make it easier to structure data, to store them separately from the operative systems and to generate evaluations to suit exact requirements.

- *Transformation management.* During the transformation - and this will take at least 30 years - change management will take on special significance. Management en route to the information age therefore means operative management of the business on the one hand and transformation management on the other.

Consequences

The information age, but above all the road which leads to it, demands new management skills and tools. Important steps in this direction include:

- *Vision and values.* The management team develops a common vision and common values which permit this vision to be realized.

- *Multidimensional management.* Management must be easy to communicate. It must focus on a limited number (less than ten) key performance indicators [cf. Brecht et al. 1998] and concretize these down to the goals of the individual employees.

- *Compensation scheme.* Performance indicators must be reflected in employee assessment and compensation.

- *Transformation management.* Transformation management requires its own system of performance indicators, from project portfolio management, via migration planning and project management through to continuous improvement.

- *Management process.* It is not the all-embracing data collection but the management process which determines what management will be based on and which data will be needed.

3 The Networked Enterprise

Elgar Fleisch, Hubert Österle

3.1 Introduction 56

3.2 Business Networking Case Examples 57
    3.2.1 Dell: Supply Chain Management and Customer
        Relationship Management..57
    3.2.2 Amazon.com: Supply Chain Management and Customer
        Relationship Management..59
    3.2.3 Avnet Marshall: Supply Chain Management and
        Customer Relationship Management 61
    3.2.4 SAP: Customer Relationship Management...............................62
    3.2.5 MarketSite.net: Procurement and Sales 63
    3.2.6 UBS: Procurement 65
    3.2.7 Migros Cooperative: Development..66
    3.2.8 Commtech: Procurement, Finance, Real Estate and Taxes........67

3.3 Networked Business Processes 69
    3.3.1 Networking Through Coordination..70
    3.3.2 Collaborative Processes 71

3.4 Model of a Networked Enterprise 75
    3.4.1 eServices 75
    3.4.2 Standards...76
    3.4.3 Model..76

3.5 Networkability as a Competitive Factor..77
    3.5.1 Concept and Design Objects of Networkability.......................78
    3.5.2 Approaches to Measuring Networkability 79

3.6 Consequences for Management: Design for Networkability...............81

3.7 Conclusions..84

3.1   Introduction

"The revolution under way will be driven not by changes in production but by changes in coordination." [Malone/Rockart 1991, 128] "The use of IT for coordination is more complex than much of the academic and practitioner literature suggests."[Kling et al. 1999]

In the early 90s enterprises started to improve internal efficiency and customer responsiveness with aligning their organization along business processes. They realized, that business processes do not end at the boundaries of a cubicle, subsidiary or division. With the help of ERP systems as the main instrument for process integration, they teard down internal organizational walls and achieved remarkable results.

At the end of the 90s the next level of rationalization appeared at the horizon. New information systems, such as supply chain management or customer relationship management systems, helped enterprises to integrate business processes even across companies boundaries. Terms like eBusiness or Business Networking were born. Now enterprises are looking for design models for the engineering, implementation and further development of IT-supported business relationships.

This Chapter develops an approach which links process orientation and networking. The result is a model of a networked enterprise, that is an enterprise which sees itself as a node of several business networks.

Linking up businesses to form networks has been the object of numerous investigations in the fields of economics, sociology and informatics (cf. [Alstyne 1997], [Klein 1996], [Sydow 1992]). These investigations describe network phenomena and as a rule offer very abstract approaches to network classification and structure (cf. [Williamson 1991], [Snow et al. 1992]). Neither transaction cost theory, network theory, network economics nor any other of the theories examined provide comprehensive help in answering practical questions.

Network theory, for example, describes business networks as an organizational form between market and hierarchy, provides a comprehensive description model of the design areas of a network and considers the business unit[1] or the networked enterprise as the primary unit of reference. However, a finer degree of granularity is required for describing and ultimately for designing networks. Practice shows that as a rule businesses participate in several networks simultaneously. They take part in development and procurement communities at the same time, for instance, enter into strategic marketing partnerships and are involved in different value chains with different products and/or services. Thus they can be part of several internal, stable and dynamic networks all at once, and at the same time these net-

---

[1]   Business units are economic units, such as e.g. corporations, divisions, national subsidiaries, profit centers or small and medium-sized enterprises.

works may mutually influence one another (cf. Figure 3-1). In the process, they use different information systems and information technologies, depending on the business processes to be coordinated.

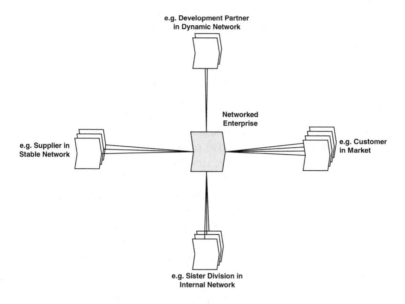

Figure 3-1: Networked Enterprise as Part of Various Networks

3.2   Business Networking Case Examples

Every interdependency between the business processes of different business units leads to networking. Based on this definition, there are a great many examples and variants of networking to the found in the real world. The case examples taken from business practice and described here help to illustrate the concrete organizational forms of inter-company coordination frequently encountered. The case examples represent part of the empirical basis for derivation of the model of a networked enterprise. They reflect a special view of the company presented and, as far as this Chapter is concerned, merely represent items of focus.

3.2.1   Dell: Supply Chain Management and Customer Relationship Management

Dell Computer Corporation, Round Rock (TX), USA, is a leading manufacturer of computer systems. With a workforce of 24,000 employees Dell achieves a sales volume of USD 18.2 billion. Dell sells computer systems to a value of USD 14 million via the Internet on a daily basis. The corporation serves consumers (1/3 of sales) and companies (2/3 of sales) [cf. Dell 1999].

Dell's success is based on the two concepts of direct selling and build to order [Preisig 1999] which have been consistently incorporated in the sales and supply chain management systems (see Figure 3-2).

Dell uses its sales system to collect experience with each individual customer. The emphasis is on the creation of a *1:1 relationship* which is specific to the person or company. This individuality refers both to the products offered and to the additional services, i.e. to the entire value creation system. Every computer system purchased from Dell is specially configured and assembled to suit the specific customer. Even in the case of collective orders for e.g. 100 computer systems of the same kind, each system actually passes through Dell's complete supply chain individually as an order in its own right. *Individual additional services*, such as product catalogs specially geared to corporate clients (which only contain products approved by the customer), automatic individual pricing, a single contact point (account management), a special service arrangement provided locally by the manufacturer direct, or an online or telephone service tailored to the customer's computer system, form the basis for a partnership-oriented business relationship between Dell and its customers.

The creation of this radical 1:1 relationship is largely dependent on the *design of the supply chain* and its information systems. Dell manufactures each system to order and delivers within 12 days. This means that Dell operates with virtually no warehouse of its own. Its suppliers' warehouses are located within 15 minutes' drive of the production site. This allows the corporation to provide the high degree of innovation in its products which is in particularly strong demand in the computer sector.

Each customer has the possibility of tracking their order status online. This service is used approximately 20,000 times a day [Preisig 1999]. Dell exchanges *supply chain information,* such as capacity, inventory levels, cost structures, quality information, current forecasts, demand, market prices, with its suppliers in *real time*.

Dell estimates that by the year 2002, 50% of all its customer transactions will operate through the Internet sales system (www.dell.com). With its 'Dell Talk Forum' the corporation offers its customers a *platform for the exchange of experience*. Today, there are already 50,000 registered users who provide each other with mutual assistance in the use of Dell Computers, thus taking some of the load off Dell's personnel.

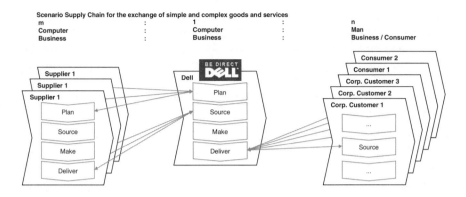

Figure 3-2: Networking at Dell

Dell coordinates with its corporate clients and consumers via the processes of sales and customer relationship management, with its suppliers via the process of the supply chain. The information system www.dell.com supports the processes of sales and customer relationship management[2] while a supply chain management system supports the processes of the supply chain. The example of Dell shows the relevance of the interaction between networking scenarios: here, the potential resulting from networking can only be realized with a combination of supply chain and customer relationship management.

3.2.2   Amazon.com: Supply Chain Management and Customer Relationship Management

Amazon.com, Seattle, WA, USA, is the leading online bookshop.[3] With a workforce of some 2,100 staff (status 1998, [cf. Hoovers 1999a]), Amazon.com serves around eight million customers, 64% of whom are regular customers, and sells approx. 4.7 million different books, CDs, videos, games and gifts [Amazon 1999]. In 1998, Amazon.com recorded a sales volume of USD 610 million [cf. Hoovers 1999a].

---

[2]   Manufacturers of such catalog systems include Netscape with Seller Xpert, Vision Factory with Cat@log, Microsoft with the MS Site Server and Intershop.

[3]   [Absatzwirtschaft 1995, 28] states that "trade in the institutional sense covers institutions whose economic activities can be assigned exclusively or primarily to trade in the functional sense. In official statistics, an enterprise is assigned to trade if the value creation resulting from its trading activities is higher than that obtained from a second or from several activities." Trading companies take many different forms. [Müller-Hagedorn 1998, 31] defines the three most important *organization types* for trade as being that of the wholesaler, retailer and trade intermediary (cf. [Falk/Wolf 1992, 18], [Lerchenmüller 1998, 17], [Barth 1993, 81], [Becker/Schütte 1996]). When applying these criteria to define the organization types, Amazon.com can be classified as a retailer.

From the consumers' point of view, Amazon.com is characterized by the *user friendliness* of its Web presence [Keen/Ballance 1997, 267] and a visible orientation towards customer requirements. This takes place largely on the basis of the information collected during the relationship with the customer. After a customer has searched for a given book title A, for example, Amazon.com will propose alternative titles based on previous purchases: the consumer is given a list of all the books which other consumers have purchased along with title A.

The orientation towards customer requirements is also reflected in new *completeness* of the service. In the case of Amazon.com, a large part of the complete customer problem 'reading' is supported: from recommendations, reviews, bestseller lists to simple and transparent purchasing, payment and order tracking, through to the contribution of own reviews.

By processing information, Amazon.com also changes the *supply chain* from the publishers via the bookshops through to the consumers. Up to now, publishers have had up to 50% of the books they deliver returned as not sellable. The publishers have to foot the bill for lost profit and disposal.

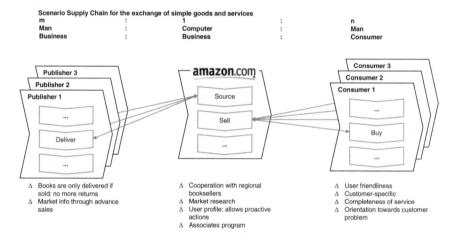

Figure 3-3: Networking at Amazon.com

Amazon.com only orders books from the publishers on the basis of confirmed orders received from consumers. The only books which Amazon.com stocks are the top 200 in the best seller list. This means that the publishers no longer have books returned. In addition, Amazon.com operates advance sales of books before they are published, thus passing on the obtained *market knowledge* to the publishers.[4] In order to reduce delivery times, Amazon.com includes regional booksellers in its logistics.

To promote rapid diffusion and thus receive more customer information, Amazon.com offers 5% to 15% commission on sales resulting from links established by associates in its *associates' program*. Associates currently include Yahoo!, Excite, AOL plus many small and medium-sized businesses.[5]

3.2.3   Avnet Marshall: Supply Chain Management and Customer Relationship Management

Avnet Marshall, El Monte (CA), USA ranks amongst the largest distributors of industrial electronic components and production supplies (cf. Chap. 2.3.6).[6] Avnet Marshall's 2,300 staff supply 170,000 different products and services to approx. 40,000 customers, generating a sales volume of USD 1.4 billion (cf. [Avnet Marshall 1999] and [Hartman 1997]).

Amongst others, Avnet Marshall offers design, materials management, logistics and information system services. Avnet Marshall adds value to the products from its 150 suppliers for example by applying static methods of *quality control*, by testing components, by *mass customizing* and programming.

Global connection is the name of the trading system which Avnet Marshall uses to match customer requirements with supplier offerings. It offers customers and suppliers alike a *24-hour service* from any location in the world. Customers can track their orders right up to the time that the goods reach their own production units, obtain information regarding stock levels and calibrate their material consumption with forecasts.

The global connection system provides suppliers with a real-time feedback regarding *movements in the market* with the granularity of article numbers, region, USD or units. On this basis suppliers can then draw up their production plans, pricing structures and forecasts. In addition, they profit from Avnet Marshall's *marketing efforts*.

For Avnet Marshall, the introduction of global connection has meant being able to replace hand-written sales reports, paper-based catalogs, endless telephone calls between customers, salespersons and warehouses by digital information and information system functions. Global connection handles some 700,000 transactions

---

[4]   An analysis of the Amazon.com's competitor situation and pricing structure is to be found in [Downes/Mui 1998].

[5]   In March 1998, there were over 35,000 Amazon.com associates [cf. Shaprio/Varian 1999, 129].

[6]   Using the criteria which define organization types for trade according to [Müller-Hagedorn 1998, 31], Avnet Marshall can be classified as a wholesaler.

a day, which are used to develop *customer profiles,* for example. Today, it is first and foremost information which Avnet Marshall processes and sells.

With E.N.E.N. (the education news & entertainment network), Avnet Marshall offers its customers and in fact the entire electronics industry a comprehensive Internet service which supports a large number of its customers' *'life events'* with e.g. interactive live training courses, product announcements and technical descriptions via video.

3.2.4   SAP: Customer Relationship Management

Dell and Avnet Marshall already show examples of the formation of *customer communities.* The aim of communities is to achieve a customer relationship by increasing the customer's product competence (cf. [Belz et al. 1997], [Hagel/Amstrong 1997] and [Muther 1998, 73]). Communities generate greater customer loyalty, further tighten the customer relationship and provide more detailed insight into *customer requirements* through observation of communication processes.

SAP, Walldorf, Germany offers an impressive example of community building (cf. Chap. 3.2.4 and [Muther 1998]). In addition to a large number of user groups (SAP user groups) organized according to regions and business areas, SAP offers the following electronic tools to provide its customers with comprehensive solutions to their problems:

- *Information* on new releases, technical developments, contacts, etc. can be accessed by customers through the SAP WWW site.

- Customers can download *software updates* via the SAP Net, a web site accessible to a restricted circle of users, conduct technical discussions with other customers and SAP specialists, order or download *brochures* and register for SAP courses.

- The online service system offers, amongst other things, the latest information on the status of product development, an error database and *various trouble-shooting services.*

- In an *electronic discussion list* run by the Massachusetts Institute of Technology, customers exchange information on problems, developments and new features of SAP products by e-mail. Customers only receive e-mails concerning the subjects which interest them. 3,500 users currently benefit from this service [cf. Muther 1998, 21].

- With video conferences and remote log-in into the customer's SAP system, SAP operates *remote consulting* and trouble-shooting. The savings (time savings, reduction in travelling costs) for customers amount to up to 15% of consulting costs [cf. Muther 1998, 21].

- The *documentation* for implementation, system management, database management, migration and operation of SAP products is supplied on CD-ROMs.

- With its international demonstration and education system (IDES), SAP offers a complete R/3 system for the purpose of *testing and demonstrating* R/3 functionality.

- 25 regional *helpdesks*, distributed across Europe, the USA and Asia, are available to all customers by telephone and fax 24 hours a day, 7 days a week.

- In Internet newsgroups customers discuss *any and all topics* related to SAP.

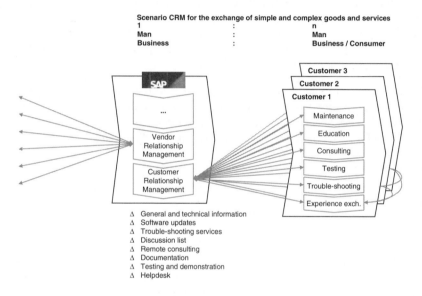

Figure 3-4: Networking at SAP

3.2.5   MarketSite.net: Procurement and Sales

Commerce One, Walnut Creek (CA), USA is in its own words the leading manufacturer of business-to-business purchasing systems and the founder of Market-Site.net, an electronic market for indirect products.[7] Commerce One puts the purchasers of indirect goods in touch with suppliers. Together with three leading telecommunications companies, Commerce One first set up three independent eMarkets for indirect products: in the USA, Europe and Asia. In 1999 these three

---

[7]   Using the criteria which define organization types for trade according to [Müller-Hagedorn 1998, 31] MarketSite.net can be classified as a trade intermediary.

eMarkets now represent a *joint purchasing power* of USD 160 billion and are only in the early stages of their development [Commerce One 1999b].

Each marketplace supports *a large number of process and information standards*. A customer possessing the right standards is in a position to contact all the suppliers participating in the marketplace via its own purchasing system, just as if the processes, systems and data were individually coordinated with one another. Networking with MarketSite.net automatically gives vendors access to new markets.

By eliminating individual technological links between customer and supplier, *centralizing content and functions for the management of transactions,* Market-Site.net is attempting to exploit the benefits of the law of *increasing returns*[8] through economies of scale. Over 5,000 suppliers now offer their products through MarketSite.net. As the number of customers who stand to gain high savings through the use of purchasing systems which are compatible with the standards of MarketSite.net, Ariba.com or MySap increases (cf. also [Aberdeen-Group 1999], [Dolmetsch et al. 1999] or [Ginsburg et al. 1999]), so too will the number of suppliers for whom MarketSite.net is of interest.

MarketSite.net offers purchasers *real-time access* to the most important information in respect of suppliers. Examples are prices, availability and order tracking. In addition, MarketSite.net incorporates support services, such as transport, payment, taxation and trust services plus basic services, such as directories.

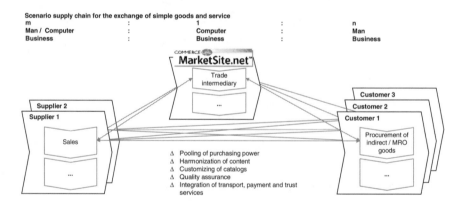

Figure 3-5: Networking at MarketSite.net

In the area of catalog content management, MarketSite.net depends on Commerce One transactive content management, for example. The most important tasks relating to catalog content management include quality and completeness checks on catalog data, standardization and addition by means of a metadata layer, mapping

---

[8] A scientifically founded analysis of increasing returns and increasing economies of scale can be found in [Arthur 1989].

of the different classification schemes and the customizing of product catalogs [cf. Commerce One 1999a]. Other well-known trade intermediaries are Harbinger and Ariba.com (cf. Chap. 10) as well as mySap.com from SAP.

3.2.6   UBS: Procurement

UBS, Zürich, Switzerland, is Europe's biggest bank. Measured in terms of its turnover, UBS ranks amongst the world's big five. In 1997, UBS generated USD 19 billion with 27,600 employees at 500 branches in 40 countries [Hoovers 1999b].

Prior to 1999, UBS procured all indirect/MRO products via its legacy and ERP systems, and was thus confronted with high process and fixed costs in procurement. In the past many industrial corporations, like UBS, paid scant attention to their relationship with the suppliers of indirect/MRO products, i.e. products which are not used directly in the end product or, in the case of trading companies, which are not resold directly (cf. [Grieco 1997, 1], [Killen&Associates 1997, 1]). On the procurement side, greater attention was always paid to the direct area which is frequently supported by supply chain management concepts and EDI links [Dolmetsch 1999, 1]. The average process costs of a procurement operation for an indirect/MRO product show potential for rationalization, however: for Switzerland, [Dolmetsch 1999, 4] gives process costs of between CHF 80 and 180, while [Grieco 1997, 15], [Killen&Associates 1997, 13], [Laaper 1998, 6], [Margherito 1998], [Marks 1996] state USD 80 to 120 for US companies.

Today, UBS classifies its indirect/MRO products according to the groups A (1,900 different items of merchandise), B (approx. 4,200 stocked items) and C (800 consumer goods and 4,000 durable consumers)[9].

3,800 authorized staff, referred to as 'purchase requisition creators', can order 100% of the standard products in the area of consumer goods in all three categories through a *shop system*. The shop system has been developed by UBS itself on the basis of the Internet transaction server, a new product in connection with SAP R/3. For category A products, UBS regularly receives an electronic catalog from a company called Gate, which is a joint venture between the suppliers Furer, Waser, Mühlebach and Serlog. The content of the catalog is defined by UBS in dialog with the Gate partners. UBS maintains the catalog for category B and C products and updates it after every procurement operation.

In the first months after going live in early 1999, some 2,400 items (55% category A, 42% B, and 3% C products) were handled daily via the shop system. In view of the high level of acceptance and the immediate cost savings of the shop system,

---

[9]   This case is described in detail by [Dolmetsch 1999].

UBS anticipates that the project will have paid for itself in far less than a year. The cost savings include:

- *Reduction in process costs.* UBS now pays invoices for category A products monthly on the basis of electronic bills which allow automatic allocation to the appropriate cost centers. The costly task of verifying invoices is replaced by plausibility checks on the part of the cost center manager once the cost center has been debited and/or by random checks by outsourcing management on the basis of the suppliers' records of electronic transactions.

- *Reduction in fixed costs.* For a large part of the indirect/MRO products, inventory was outsourced to the suppliers Mühlebach and Serlog. Today, orders and goods movement transactions are exchanged with all business partners by electronic means.

Major standard software suppliers in the area of desktop purchasing include Ariba Technologies with ORMS, Commerce One with BuySite / MarketSite, Netscape with the BuyerXpert, SAP with B2B Procurement [cf. Dolmetsch 1999, 141].

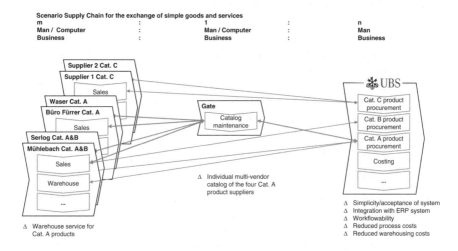

Figure 3-6: Networking at UBS

3.2.7   Migros Cooperative: Development

The Migros Cooperative (Migros) is Switzerland's largest retailing organization. With its 72,000 employees, Migros makes a turnover of USD 11.3 billion, almost 80% of that figure through its retail trading activities [Migros 1999]. Migros produces a large part of its own food products. These include bread and cakes, meat, preserved products and mineral water [cf. Benz 1999].

Migros is very much a decentralized organization. Ten largely independent cooperatives together own the Migros-Genossenschaftsbund (MGB - Migros Federation) which provides a whole series of services for the cooperatives, the production units and other Migros operations.

A large number of internal and external Migros business units are involved in the creation of food packaging. They include printers, packaging and multimedia companies, production units, design, translation and food analysis departments plus graphic designers. The MGB introduced a document flow application to coordinate the creation of food packaging. This is helping to limit the throughput time for design orders for individual articles to 30 days and for article groups to 60 days, thus radically reducing the time to market. The first priority was therefore to create regulated information flows and clear areas of responsibility. The system ensures joint order scheduling and deadline monitoring, and permits the joint processing of centrally stored order data and documents as well as notification of the next business unit in line when a task has been completed [cf. Benz 1999].

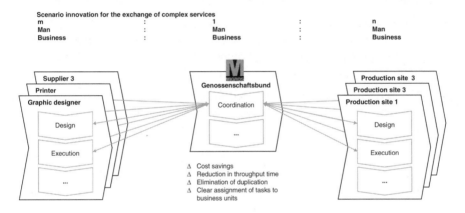

Figure 3-7: Networking at Migros

3.2.8   Commtech: Procurement, Finance, Real Estate and Taxes

Commtech[10] is a globally active corporation in the communications sector, headquartered in North America. With a workforce of 130,000 employees, Commtech generates revenues of USD 23 billion. The corporation is divided into four business units and is spread over 45 countries. Its principal products are enterprise communication solutions, microelectronics for manufacturers of communications equipment and consumer products.

---

[10]   Name changed for the purposes of this book.

As a relatively young spin-off enterprise, Commtech had to reorganize its internal business network. Its management was pursuing two goals. On the one hand, largely autonomous business units were to improve the effectiveness and flexibility of the business processes in the scenarios innovation and customer relationship management. On the other hand, shared service centers were to pool services which were similar throughout the company and to exploit synergetic effects. The business units were thus responsible for the business processes sales, distribution, logistics, controlling, material management, quality management, service management and production planning. The shared service centers assigned to corporate management were responsible for the processes used jointly by all business units, such as finance, real estate, taxes and global procurement.

The CIO's greatest challenge was to design a generally acceptable application architecture which would permit and implement the new organization. In order to secure the coordination of the business units involved, processes and master data were standardized and/or homogenized and integration scenarios were defined. The application architecture made it possible to exploit the following potential:

- The implementation of finance as a shared service center had the effect of reducing finance-related costs from 2% to 1% of Commtech's revenue. Additional savings were made through improved functionality in the areas of accounts receivable and internal hedging and netting.

- The reorganization of real estate led to better use of the buildings and to a reduction in real estate-related costs from 6% to 3.5% of revenue.

- Greater reliability, visibility and real-time 'drill-down-transactions'[11] helped to save taxes amounting to 0.6% of Commtech's revenue.

- Global procurement reduced the purchasing costs for one third of all purchased products and services by 7.5%. This corresponds to a saving amounting to 0.6% of Commtech's revenue.

---

[11] Real-time 'drill-down transactions ' allow a corporate management operative, for example, to break down a summary entry into its constituent parts, whereby the detailed entries are called up from the information systems of the business units in real time.

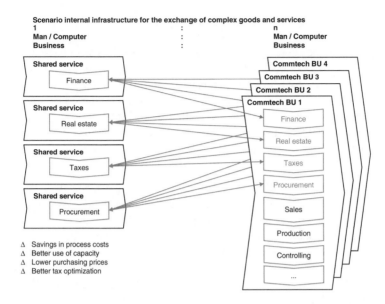

Figure 3-8: Networking at Commtech

Processes can be outsourced to external and internal business units or shared service centers [cf. Kris 1998]. Examples of external business units are companies, such as ADP [cf. ADP 1999], which now already perform payroll accounting for 10% of all US employees as an external service provider, or outsourcing partners, such as Andersen Consulting [cf. Barling/Stark 1998].

3.3   Networked Business Processes

In literature with an economics slant, design recommendations are usually linked to the *business unit* as reference object. For the description of networks on a greater level of detail required for the deduction of concrete procedural instructions for designing and implementing networks, the granularity of a business unit would appear to be too coarse.

In real-world projects, the business process has proved itself to be a suitable reference object for the purposes of networking in addition to the business unit. Here, the focus is on the coordination of the cooperating business processes of different business units. We now introduce the process view in the context of networking business units in order to permit the subtle differentiation of conclusions required for the implementation.

3.3.1 Networking Through Coordination

The processes of the coordinating business partners, together with the outputs they produce, form the operative side of the business relationship. Figure 3-9 shows two business units - two 'average' industrial enterprises - along with their most important business processes. These processes are based on the process models of [SCOR 1998], [Teufel et al. 1999], [Boutellier et al. 1999], [Porter 1992b], [SAP 1998a] and [GPS 1997]. The networking of processes describes the organization of dependencies between the processes and/or tasks of the various network partners.

[Malone/Crowston 1994] define coordination as the 'management of dependent activities'. We define networking as coordination in networks. Along with his coordination theory [Malone 1988] provides a 'set of principles' for describing and solving dependencies (an up-to-date taxonomy can be found in [Crowston 1994b]). Tasks are then interdependent if they access the same resources. Tasks are performed by resources (e.g. personnel) on the one hand and consume resources on the other. According to [Crowston 1994b] resources are all subjects and/or objects which come into contact with a task. Examples of resources are machines, tools, storage spaces and employees.

The resource information takes on a special role in this Chapter. This is due to the fact that while it obeys the laws of information processing and thus, unlike raw materials for example, is reusable and divisible, it can also depict all other resources for coordination purposes. In Figure 3-9 the processes on both sides of the value chain rely on the same information and are therefore interdependent.

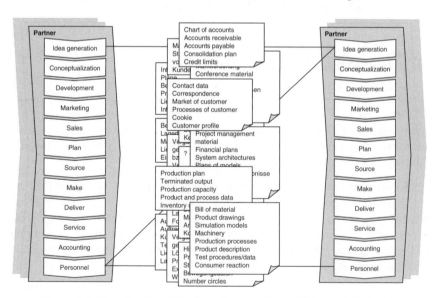

Figure 3-9: Coordination of Business Partners Through Shared Information

According to [Österle 1995] processes are coordinated exclusively by means of outputs. By virtue of this fact, coordination must therefore be an output or part of an output in the sense of the above definition. Consequently, the potential of inter-organizational networking lies in suitable design of the coordination capability (networkability) of outputs and all associated design areas such as process, IT, people, organization structure and culture [cf. Alt et al. 2000]. Business Process Redesign and integrated information systems have already shown how potentials arising from the organization of internal dependencies can be realized.

3.3.2 Collaborative Processes

Figure 3-9 illustrates the wide variety and great complexity of inter-organizational networking. However, network design requires a level of complexity which is manageable. In order to reduce complexity, areas are sought which show high dependencies. Based on the concept of integration areas [Österle et al. 1993], we refer to processes (of different business units) which are characterized by high dependency and therefore require a high degree of coordination as 'coordination areas". Areas are usefully delimited if the sum of all dependencies between the areas is low and the sum of all dependencies within the areas is high.

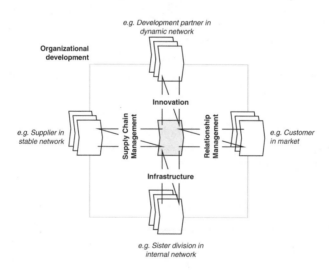

Figure 3-10: Coordination Areas

Integration areas and coordination areas both refer to processes and their tasks. The integration area pursues integration through integrated information process-ing, the coordination area pursues integration through the organization of depend-encies. In addition to integrated information processing this includes for instance the modularization of outputs and the design of new incentive systems for employees. The criteria used for delimiting coordination areas include goal, culture, partners, form of coordination, coordinated processes, resources and information systems. By applying these criteria to the case studies we arrive at the five coordination areas Supply Chain Management, Relationship Management, Innovation, Infrastructure and Organization Development (see Figure 3-10 and Table 3-1).

- The goal of *supply chain management* is to handle operative planning and execution processes as efficiently as possible. Unlike innovation, supply chain management does not redesign anything but multiplies clearly defined outputs and tries to utilize the effects of economies of scale in order to achieve profit. As a rule, supply chain management realizes its attempts to achieve efficiency through a large integration depth in the coordination of its well-structured processes. High repeat numbers and integration depths require stable structures. Supply chain management prefers the forms of coordination of an internal and/or stable network.

Coordination Area	Goal/Culture	Coordinated Processes	Main Form of Coordination[12]	Main Coordination Technology
Supply Chain Management	Efficiency through utilization of 'economies of scale', large integration depth	Planning, procurement, production distribution	Stable network	Supply chain planning systems; transaction-oriented electronic commerce systems
Customer Relationship Management	Effectiveness through utilization of 'economies of scope'	Marketing, sales, service	Market	Customer relationship management systems; document-oriented electronic commerce systems

---

[12] According to [Snow et al. 1992].

Innovation	Rapid development of successful products, dynamic	Idea creation, concepts, development	Dynamic network	Information systems for distributed innovation [Boutellier et al. 1999]
Infrastructure	Efficiency through service culture	Accounts, asset management, master data management,	Internal and stable network	Distributed enterprise resource planning systems
Organization Development	Network-capable employees and partners	-	All forms of coordination	-

Table 3-1: Coordination Areas

- The goal of the coordination area *innovation* is the rapid creation of new products. In accordance with the 'loose-tight' hypothesis [Gassmann, 1997], innovation requires a dynamic environment in the early phases. As a project advances in maturity so the streamlining of the organization increases. In the case of innovation, a business unit will thus coordinate with a large number of different partners and, depending on the task in question, follow the rules of different forms of coordination.

- The area *infrastructure* distinguishes itself from supply chain management in terms of content (e.g. payroll accounting). In addition, this content does not necessarily show a high degree of repetition (e.g. preparation of a corporate balance sheet), and its transactions may be complex in nature (e.g. outsourcing of IT). As a rule, there is a high level of dependency between the infrastructure partners which calls for the relationship to be stable.

- *Organization development* secures the willingness of own employees and those of partners to cooperate. It employs special procedures for assessing and honoring performance, developing partnerships and winning partners.

Every business unit is always linked to other business units across all the coordination areas described in Table 3-1. The sector and the position in the network determine the priority with which business units approach the task of consistent network design.

The (inter-organizational) dependencies within areas are contrasted by the (intra-organizational) dependencies across areas. Both play a decisive role in the networkability structure of businesses (cf. Figure 3-11).

(a) The goal of relationship management is to create a relationship with business partners such as customers or key suppliers which is as close, long-term and thus profitable as possible. The success of relationship management is dependent on the quality of supply chain management and vice versa. In the context of relationship management, businesses make information and capabilities available to their customers for example, which are generated in the area of supply chain management. This information includes things like availability checks or track & trace information in real time, capabilities include things like mass customizing.

On the other hand, supply chain management relies on relationship management information and capabilities. Examples here are correctly configured customer orders or current detailed information on payment terms and the customer's delivery address. A further indication of the interdependency of these two areas is provided by numerous case studies: as a rule, companies which consistently apply relationship management implement the complementary supply chain management at the same time.

(b) Relationship management provides the area of innovation first and foremost with market analyses, competitor strategies and products and concrete customer requirements. At the same time, relationship management relies on the area of innovation for information on new products, for instance, or ongoing research projects with image value.

(c) Innovation and supply chain management are connected via product design and the process required to produce it. Jointly used documents here include parts lists and production process descriptions.

(d) The infrastructure area supplies the 'operating resource' information to all other areas. Relationship management, supply chain management and innovation rely on information from external and internal accounting as well as from data management.

(e) Organization development forms the basis for all other coordination areas by ensuring suitable organization structures and/or cultural and political attitudes on the part of the organization units involved. The success of the operative coordination areas is dependent on organization development at both the intra-organizational and inter-organizational levels.

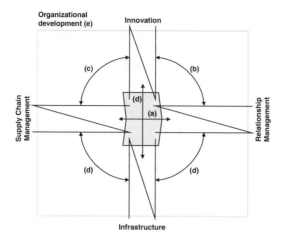

Figure 3-11: Inter-area Dependencies

3.4   Model of a Networked Enterprise

"Describing and categorizing organizational forms remains a central problem in organization theory" [Crowston 1994a, 2].

We know from the fifth phase of computerization (cf. Chap. 1.1.2) that cross-company business processes rely on a new infrastructure, also referred to as eServices (cf. Chap. 2.3.5), and new standards. Together with the coordination areas they form a basic model of the networked enterprise.

3.4.1   eServices

Decreasing coordination costs through the use of enterprise resource planning (ERP, supply chain planning (SCP), electronic commerce (EC) and enterprise application integration (EAI) systems are leading on the one hand to the *substitution* of IT-supported forms of integration for integration through employees. On the other, we see decreasing coordination costs through *demand elasticity* leading to an increasing number of economical transactions (e.g. small lot sizes, micropayments). Both effects favor the creation of coordination-intensive structures which include eServices [cf. Malone/Crowston 1994].

In this context, [Tapscott 1995, 55] expands by saying that: "Every economy needs a national information infrastructure. This is the utility of the twenty-first century - a broadband highway for a broadband, high-capacity economy. And every organization needs to plug into this utility with an enterprise information infrastructure. The new infrastructure will change economic activity as significantly as did electrification. Just as business and wealth creation would be unthinkable today without electrification, so the new economy would be impossible without the power of information." Frederick W. Smith, Chairman, President and CEO, FDX Corporation, quoted in [Jones 1998], summarizes that: "Mastery of logistics is as vital to success in the digital economy as it was to the extraordinary success of the Roman Empire".

New IT, such as e.g. the n:m trading systems are often the basis for new services. Every enterprise has the strategic option of offering a new service. Chapter 2.3.5 gives an overview of the new infrastructure and thus some of the strategic options.

3.4.2   Standards

Customers, suppliers and services which link customers with suppliers have to be able to 'understand' each other at many different levels of their relationship in order to be able to organize their interdependency. Standards make this 'understanding" possible. We define standards as objects which are accepted and shared within a community (cf. [Cargill 1989], [Buxmann 1996]). Objects are understood to mean hardware, software, processes, date, function, protocol, etc. Communities are e.g. business units, value chains, sectors or geographical regions. Bodies or enterprises within these communities commit themselves to disseminating the appropriate standards.

Standards are an integral part of the model of the networked enterprise. Just like the DIN standards in engineering (e.g. thread size M8, fit H7, steel grade ST37 or test procedure DIN 68858), they make it possible to realize economies of scale at the same time as individualization, and constitute a central coordination mechanism. Unlike the widely accepted standards in the engineering field, however, those for communication only apply to the technical and/or syntactical level. Standards for semantic and pragmatic integration remain a huge challenge for Business Networking.

3.4.3   Model

"For every problem there is a solution that is simple, neat ... and wrong", H.L. Mencken, quoted in [Rodin 1999, 60].

The model derives from a process-oriented and enterprise-centered view of the networking of business units. We do not consider the topology of a network but the networking of partners from the point of view of the individual, 'selfishly' acting business unit. In Figure 3-12 a company to be analyzed can equally well take on the role of supplier or that of the customer. It sees itself at the center of its networks and practices networking in order to strengthen its position and/or to improve its profit ratios.

Splitting networking into the four operative coordination areas of relationship management, supply chain management, innovation and infrastructure takes into account the complexity inherent in networking which is observable in practice. These four areas pursue different economic goals, implement different types of network, are characterized by widely divergent cultures, link different partners, have interdependencies based on different resources and use different information systems for coordination purposes. Each business unit must nevertheless be capable of developing all these relationships in the interests of their own business strategy, i.e. of adapting to the new demands of the information age.

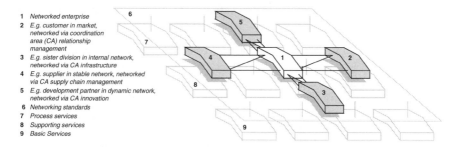

1 Networked enterprise
2 E.g. customer in market,
   networked via coordination
   area (CA) relationship
   management
3 E.g. sister division in internal network,
   networked via CA infrastructure
4 E.g. supplier in stable network, networked
   via CA supply chain management
5 E.g. development partner in dynamic network,
   networked via CA innovation
6 Networking standards
7 Process services
8 Supporting services
9 Basic Services

Figure 3-12: Networked Enterprise

Even if a business unit does not operate its own development or outsources every conceivable support process to suppliers, it must nevertheless be familiar with and actively maintain its relationships with partners, which according to [Hagel/Singer 1999] are customers, output integrators, innovators or infrastructure companies. The model of the networked business enterprise helps here by bringing together in a single architecture those design areas of a company which are most important from the networking point of view. On the one hand it provides an indication of how to usefully break down the networking problem, without neglecting the interdependencies of the delimited areas. On the other hand, the model serves as reference framework for deriving recommended action while taking into account the central role of IT, services and standards.

3.5   Networkability as a Competitive Factor

The objective of every networked enterprise is to increase competitiveness through higher networkability. This leads to increased process efficiency and opens up new business opportunities. The following subsections will provide you with a framework for the consistent and practice-oriented design and implementation of networkability.

3.5.1   Concept and Design Objects of Networkability

Business networking tries to increase process efficiency and to enter new business segments by forming innovative networks of value creation. According to [Wigand et al. 1997, 11], new innovative strategies are based on three models: (1) forms of organization for rapid and permanent orientation to the market, (2) forms of personnel leadership for developing and utilizing employee potential, and (3) forms of networking for creating an internal and external ability to cooperate. The concept of networkability is developed in the following to take into account all the dimensions of business engineering in addition to the organizational ability to cooperate.

Networkability is the *internal and external ability to cooperate as well as the ability to rapidly and efficiently establish, conduct and develop IT-supported business relationships.* Corresponding to the dimensions of business engineering, networkability has different aspects or design objects. In the case of all design objects, there are relationships of dependence between the network partners, whereby networkability expresses the attribute needed for management of these relationships of dependence. Networkability is thus a continuation of coordination theory which sees coordination as the management of relationships of dependence [Malone/Crowston 1994, 90]. In relation to the design objects of networkability (see Figure 3-13), this means:

- *Products and services.* Networkable products and services can be altered quickly and inexpensively for specific partners or be integrated in other products. This includes the personalization of services, such as mySAP.com, and configurability regarding the information needed (e.g. status information, use of partners' article numbers).

- *Process.* Networkable processes can quickly and inexpensively establish and conduct a relationship of coordination with corresponding processes. Automatic requests for various catalogs or automatic orders when stock levels fall below an agreed safety level are examples of this.

- *Information systems.* Networkable information systems can be linked up to other IS quickly and inexpensively and support communication on the system level. This especially applies to setting up an EDI link with a business partner.

- *Employees.* Networkable employees are the essence of personal networks. They are oriented to the customer, understand the relevance of win-win situations and are also assessed according to the way in which they maintain and look after relationships between partners.

- *Organizational structure.* Networkable organizations can be adapted quickly and inexpensively to new market requirements. Examples of this are the rapid creation of temporary inter-company teams, the relocation of business processes or the joint execution of processes (formation of so-called shared services).

- *Company culture.* Networkable company cultures promote cooperation by being open to change and by basing cooperation between business partners on a relationship of trust instead of mutual checks (on costs).

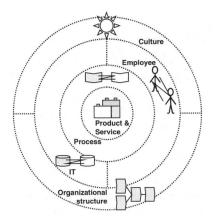

Figure 3-13: Design Objects of Networkability

3.5.2   Approaches to Measuring Networkability

A precondition for appropriately designing networkability, according to the management cycle of [Ulrich 1984, 54], is measurement and evaluation of the design objects. It is only when the existing nature of these objects and the required nature of these objects have been determined that concrete ideas to close a specific networkability gap can be obtained in relation to the design object. Above all, the requirements of the partners involved have to be carefully assessed since the goal is not to achieve maximum but appropriate modification of the design objects.[13] For example, it would be inappropriate to implement an EDI link when the coordinated processes only involve infrequent transactions.

The correct estimation of appropriateness has a direct effect on the cost-benefit ratio of networks because measures for increasing networkability are usually asso-

---

[13]   For a definition of quality as the relation of performance to expected performance see [Fleisch/Wintersteiger 1999].

ciated with higher costs. In some circumstances, a company which wants to intensify its business relationship with *n* customers will outsource some services and
products, adopt new products and services, adapt its information systems to new
process and communication standards, introduce new information systems, redesign processes and re-train its employees. The basic criteria for measuring networkability are *time, costs and the quality of the change*. Table 3-2 shows some
examples of criteria relating to the design objects. Networkability thus indicates
what changes in business relationships a company can cope with and in what time
and at what cost it can do so.

Design Object	Quantitative Change Criteria (Time/Cost)	Qualitative Change Criteria
Products and Services	Costs and duration of combining individualized products and services or integrating additional services, e.g. payment services.	Degree of modularization with regard to products and services Degree of specificity of the adaptations Degree of multiple use of products and services
Process	Costs and duration of adapting planning or handling processes to the processes of the partners (customers/suppliers) Costs of relocating a standardized process to a specialized service Expenditure for establishing cross-company controlling	Transparency of the process for the partners Openness of information exchange Existence of a conflict management system Interorganizational monitoring of processes Coordination scenarios employed
Information System	Costs and duration of automating an IT-supported business relationship, e.g. establishing of an link. Costs of data preparation or syntactical and semantical integration	Use of application and communication standards Form of IT integration (e.g. EDI, shared databases, remote log-in, ERP@Web) Security mechanisms, access rights
Employees	Costs and duration of employee replacement Time needed for building up personal basis for business relationships	Ability to look after and maintain personal networks Ability to organize oneself Degree of harmony of vision Ability to acquire information

Organiza-tional Structure	Costs and duration of a decision-making process Duration and costs of establishing new organizational structures, e.g. profit centers or a new regional company Duration and costs of establishing a new external symbiotic cooperative venture	Distribution of power Homogeneity of the organizational structures Granularity and flexibility of the organizational units Number of internal and external partners
Culture	Costs and duration of information acquisition Costs and duration of training	Distribution of benefits between the partners (reciprocity) Intensity of the exchange of knowledge and experience Lived openness Dealing with the question of trust

Table 3-2: Examples of Criteria for Networkability

3.6 Consequences for Management: Design for Networkability

Activities for designing a company's networkability have three basic effects: (1) Reduction of time and costs when new business relationships are established or when transactions are conducted, (2) reduction of the specificity of investments and increased flexibility of existing investments, and (3) improved opportunities for detecting and occupying new market segments at an early stage. These effects can be seen in various examples: the supply chain integration service of Riverwood International described above, the MarketSite.net procurement service of Commerce One (cf. Chap. 3.2.5), or the described services of GW.

Coordination theory is a useful tool which can be used to determine various possibilities of entrepreneurial action for increasing networkability (e.g. drawing up profiles of partners or designing application architectures) because coordination is a basic element for designing interorganizational relationships. Coordination theory regards coordination as the management of relationships of dependence and tries to identify generally applicable mechanisms for regulating these relationships [Malone/Crowston 1994]. When recommendations for action are formulated, *coordination mechanisms*, i.e. processes or rules which organize the relationships of dependence between tasks, are the starting point. In order to develop concrete ideas on the action to be taken, we interpret the coordination mechanisms more broadly as *rules for objects with the property of networkability.*

Different coordination mechanisms can be defined for each design object and these mechanisms form the basis for various alternatives of action. The following alternatives of action can be derived (see Table 3-3):

- *Design of products and services.* [Austin et al. 1997, 11] see the design of products as a very powerful but, up to now, rarely considered alternative of action for integrating value creation in networks. The most important coordination mechanisms include modularization, standardization and digitalization of products and services. For example, modularized, standardized and digitalized products and services enable rapid and efficient bundling to create comprehensive products and services which can be directed at solving specific customer problems (mass customization). Concerning physical products, the coordination mechanisms of standardization and modularization allow considerable postponement of the time when a product receives customer-specific modifications.

- *Design of processes.* Process coordination describes the consistent design of interorganizational processes of planning and implementation. The coordination mechanisms include process standards and the form of process integration. Standardized processes, such as those developed by OBI or CPFR, reduce the effort involved in coordination and, in the ideal case, lead to integration on a pragmatic level or electronic workflows between anonymous partners. Principle mechanisms of process integration are loose and close links of processes. The first, for example, is known in the area of indirect procurement (so-called MRO procurement [cf. Chaps. 10.1 and 14.2.2]) and allows an appropriate degree of flexibility by means of catalog solutions (e.g. rapid addition of suppliers). Close process links, for example, can be encountered in supply chain management and allow coordinated and completely automated processes in real time (e.g. strategies of automatic stock-keeping).

- *Design of information systems.* The networking of IS is the basis for designing new products/services and new business relationships. Products and services, processes and organizational structures thus depend on the networkability of the 'basis-forming' IS [Schmid 1997]. The most important mechanisms for increasing the networkability of IS are communication and data standards as well as the integration of internal information systems. Templates, for example, use the same type of configuration for distributed ERP systems to solve the problem of standardizing data and messages and thus achieve integration on the semantic level (cf. Chap. 11). At the same time, they are the starting point for linking partners according to the same pattern. Finally, system integration allows a high quality of data and real-time processing of this data.

- *Design of organizational structure.* The organizational structure in the sense of the network topology describes the individual business units in a network. The coordination mechanisms of virtualization, modularization [Wigand et al. 1997] and distributed responsibilities are used for designing different networking structures, e.g. dynamic, stable or internal networks [Snow et al. 1992]. For example, in dynamic networks, several small (modularization) companies cooperate to pursue shared business goals (virtualization) with each participating company being responsible for their own business (distributed responsibility).

- *Design of people's roles and company culture.* The role of the employees and managers in networks is distinguished from the roles found in classical hierarchies mainly by "an increase in the requirements for an ability to make decisions and assume responsibility for complete, customer-oriented processes as well as the capacity for teamwork, communication and innovation [...]." [Wigand et al. 1997, 459]. The important coordination mechanisms are openness, the identification and control of goal-conflicts as well as trust-creating measures [cf. Hilb 1997]. For example, openness and trust-creating measures enable to establish and maintain personal networks.

Design Object	Networkability of Design Object	Coordination Mechanisms	Objectives of Networkability
Products and Services	Rapid and inexpensive individualization of products or services	Modularization Standardization Digitalization	Mass customization [Klaus/Krieger 1998, 344] Postponement [Klaus/ Krieger 1998, 380]
Process	Rapid and flexible establishment and use of appropriately coordinated processes	Process standardization Process integration	Pragmatic integration Real-time coordination Appropriate flexibility
Information System	Rapid and inexpensive establishment of an individual communications link between information systems	Communication standards and data standards System integration	Semantic integration Making information externally available High data quality Real-time data processing

Organi-zational Structure	Flexible organizational structures which enable participation in several different networks	Virtualization Modularization Distributed responsibilities	Internal networks Stable networks Dynamic networks
Culture and Employees	Cooperation-promoting company culture and employees with the capacity for internal and external cooperation	Relative openness Identification and control of goal-conflicts Trust-creating measures	Autonomy Communicative competence Information acquisition Establishing and maintaining personal networks

Table 3-3: Approaches for Designing Networkability

The design areas are closely interlinked. Provision of a service or product for the customer, for instance, depends on numerous processes which, in turn, depend on the abilities of the people and IS involved. In addition, the modular design of products and services only leads to an increase in competitiveness if processes and IS support this modularization. The challenges encountered in the formulation of concrete alternatives of action for increasing networkability therefore are in the simultaneous coordination of several objects according to the method of concurrent engineering.

3.7   Conclusions

Business engineering enables the transformation of companies to adopt business networking strategies, business models and the 'underlying' information systems. The starting point is always a specific company which appropriately creates its customer and supplier network. This involves the exploitation of process efficiencies by means of electronic information exchange between partners (e.g. electronic order entry, exchange of planning data) and the development of new processes and roles (e.g. gateways, auctions, multi-vendor catalogs).

Model of a Networked Enterprise

The proposed model of a networked enterprise combines a company's position being part of several business networks with its needs to organize along cross-company business processes. It helps businesses to identify the importance of processes in the network and to split the networking problem into five clear areas, each of which is homogeneous in itself. At the same time, it shows the connection between the individual areas. Describing networking with the aid of coordination areas allows a networked enterprise to consistently orient itself towards the processes of its partners, in particular those of its customers. The model of a networked enterprise thus provides:

- *An orientation aid for potential analysis.* Networked enterprises can orient themselves towards the discussed potentials of the individual coordination areas when evaluating their coordination strategies. This Chapter distinguishes between potentials derived from (a) process efficiency through networking, (b) enhanced customer benefits and (c) new business opportunities.

- *An orientation aid for strategy evaluation.* Experience has shown that networked enterprises sometimes have a tendency not to devote enough attention to dependencies between coordination areas. They try to coordinate sales processes within an internal network, for example, and neglect the fact that the organization of master data is a prerequisite for a 'global' process network. The model lists the major dependencies between coordination areas and can thus serve as the basis for strategy evaluation.

- *An orientation aid to increase networking manageability.* By splitting up the networking problem into coordination areas, the model of a networked enterprise creates domains which differ in terms of culture, employees, processes and information systems and which consequently the management of networked enterprises can design and run as one unit. At the same time, the model identifies the most important dependencies between the coordination areas and thus creates the right conditions for inter-area management, e.g. for the required calibration of the coordination areas supply chain management, relationship management and infrastructure.

- *A means of deriving management tasks for inter-company coordination.* The model of a networked enterprise supports the derivation of management tasks in a networked enterprise. The most important tasks in connection with networking include (a) strategic positioning of the networked enterprise in the various networks, (b) organization of the coordination areas relationship management, innovation, supply chain management, infrastructure and organization development, (c) organization of internal integration of the coordination areas and (d) organization of IT, standards and services, on which the coordination is built.

- *Infrastructure positioning from the business point of view.* Supply chain management, relationship management and innovation are immediately dependent on the coordination area infrastructure. While most companies recognize this connection, the infrastructure area, in particular data management, is underdeveloped. Companies usually lack the business arguments to support the time and cost-intensive harmonization and networking projects. The model of a networked enterprise establishes the link between the supply chain, relationship management and innovation processes, which are considered to be strategic, and the supporting infrastructure processes, thus simplifying the business argumentation for infrastructure projects.

- *Positioning of standards and services.* The most powerful elementary goal of networking is the m:n capability. This permits the automation of new business functions and at the same time makes it possible to exploit the effects of economies of scope (n customers generate a demand for individual, comprehensive output systems which can be configured from standardized outputs) and economies of scale (m suppliers specialized in individual outputs). Standards and services are the central mechanisms which permit an m:n network. The model of a networked enterprise positions them accordingly and thus shows the increasing significance of and necessity for a well-founded evaluation process for the selection of standards and services.

Networkability Framework

To show and support the path towards a networked enterprise, the networkability concept has been formulated as a management variable in which several business engineering dimensions are combined as design objects. For increasing networkability, there are various alternatives of action, starting from the design objects. These alternatives depend on different coordination mechanisms. Two factors are especially relevant to management:

- The goal of networkability is to arrive at appropriate solutions so that the benefits of networking exceed the costs involved. Different criteria can be identified for assessing these solutions.

- Human resources are at the center of new networked products/services, processes, information systems and organizational structures. It is on the individual person that the quality and feasibility of the new solutions depend.

Whereas, today, only innovative companies possess a networkability which contributes to their competitiveness, the cost efficiency of Internet technologies as well as increasing standardization will lead to a general increase of networkability. Networkability will be incorporated in companies' strategies for achieving their objectives, in the development of project methods and in the operative controlling of projects and transactions. The criteria, objectives and coordination mechanisms will be developed further as business networking spreads. In the future, the challenges to be faced will not just be encountered in the management of networking between organizations and processes but in the networking of everyday goods (consumer goods, raw materials etc.) that are equipped with chips.

Part 2

Business Concepts

Part One: **Building the Foundation**
Chapter 2: Enterprise in the Information Age
Chapter 3: The Networked Enterprise

Part Two: **Business Concepts**
Chapter 4: Strategies for Business Networking
Chapter 5: Business Networking Lessons Learned: Supply Chain Management at Riverwood International
Chapter 6: Electronic Commerce and Supply Chain Management at 'The Swatch Group'
Chapter 7: Knowledge-enabled Customer Relationship Management

Part Three: **Information System Concepts**
Chapter 8: Future Application Architecture for the Pharmaceutical Industry
Chapter 9: Overview on Supply Chain Management Systems
Chapter 10: Electronic Commerce in the Procurement of Indirect Goods
Chapter 11: Templates: Standardization for Business Networking
Chapter 12: eServices for Integrating eMarkets

Part Four: **Key Success Factors**
Chapter 13: Key Success Factors for Business Networking Systems
Chapter 14: Towards a Method for Business Networking
Chapter 15: Application of the Business Networking Method at SAP
Chapter 16: Architecture Planning for Global Networked Enterprises

4 Strategies for Business Networking

Rainer Alt, Thomas Puschmann, Christian Reichmayr

4.1 Introduction 90
    4.1.1 Strategic Relevance of Business Networking 90
    4.1.2 Overview of Strategies..91

4.2 Organization Strategies 92
    4.2.1 Outsourcing – Externalizing Non-core Competencies..............93
    4.2.2 Insourcing – Strengthening Existing Competencies 94
    4.2.3 Virtual Organizing – New Segments with Cooperation
          Partners 95
    4.2.4 Developing New Business Segments...96
    4.2.5 Summary of Organization Strategies 98

4.3 Networking Strategies 99
    4.3.1 Electronic Commerce – Transaction Perspective....................101
    4.3.2 Supply Chain Management – Flow Perspective 104
    4.3.3 Customer Relationship Management – Relationship
          Perspective 107
    4.3.4 Summary of Networking Strategies 108

4.4 Interaction of Business Networking Strategies 109

4.5 Conclusions 110

4.1   Introduction

4.1.1   Strategic Relevance of Business Networking

As the networking scenarios in Chapter 3 revealed, Business Networking provides a strategic concept enabling new and/or more efficient processes to be introduced by extending the application of IT to relationships a company has with its partners. A broad variety of strategies are under discussion, such as outsourcing, virtual organizing, electronic commerce or supply chain management. Apart from clarifying the value added of each conceptual approach, differentiation of strategies helps in deciding how strategic goals, such as strengthening an existing market position, can be achieved.

This is shown by the example of Diamond Multimedia Systems, Inc., which was aquired by S3 Inc. in Sepember 1999. S3 is a USD 350 million manufacturer of multimedia devices for home and business computer systems located in Santa Clara (CA), USA. In 1998, Diamond introduced the 'RIO' music player, a portable device able to store and play back 60 minutes of music using the MP3-format which is typically downloaded from the Internet. At that time Diamond only possessed an Internet store which was managed by Diamond's customer service [cf. Diamond 1999]. The company knew that same-day shipments and near flawless execution would be critical for successful selling on the Internet.[1] Since Diamond recognized that it would be unable to provide the necessary response times it turned to Skyway, a well-established logistics provider who also serves Dell, Cisco Systems, Compaq, and Hewlett Packard. With their 'Concerto suite', Skyway offered electronic support for demand planning, warehousing, order management, and fulfillment [cf. Skyway 1999]. Concerto provided Diamond with a system to handle the high-volume, one-at-a-time orders which were expected for RIO without having to invest in modifying their existing internal system. The savings in manual labor estimated at between USD 250,000 to USD 500,000 are marginal compared to the advantages in terms of time and quality.

The Diamond example highlights the various strategic elements that have to be addressed within a Business Networking strategy: (1) What are the company's core competencies today and what are future business segments, (2) What are the partnering characteristics (number of partners, closeness of cooperation), and (3) which are the processes to be addressed with a Business Networking strategy?

---

[1]   Before introducing the RIO, Diamond distributed its products primarily through indirect channels via system integrators, value-added resellers, distributors and retailers.

4.1.2   Overview of Strategies

Generally speaking, strategies are to be designed to sustain the creation and rein-
forcement of a unique and valuable competitive position [cf. Porter 1996, 68].
According to [Hinterhuber 1992, 7], strategies encompass four main activities:

1. The analysis of the initial strategic situation.

2. The decision about the future position to be established in a competitive environment.

3. The selection of differentiation elements (technologies, etc.) that determine the
   competitive advantage and the appropriate allocation of resources.

4. The commitment to criteria and standards that can be communicated and that
   permit a strategy's success to be measured.

Many theoretical approaches have been proposed in recent literature to answer the
strategic questions in Business Networking. Firstly, there are general approaches
to be found in the strategic management literature (cf. e.g. [Porter 1996], [Pra-
halad/Hamel 1990]) which address the analysis of the existing situation and the
development of future competitive strategies. Secondly, there are specific approaches put forward in the organization literature which aim at shaping the cooperation with partners. Examples include the transaction cost framework, literature
on virtual organizations and (strategic) networking [cf. Sydow 1992]. Thirdly, we
have some more technology-oriented approaches that are geared to providing
electronic support for specific business processes, such as electronic commerce for
procurement or sales activities.

These three strategic approaches will be combined in two main strategy dimensions of Business Networking.[2] On the one hand, decisions are required on strategic positioning and the type of partner relationship to be adopted. For example,
Diamond decided to concentrate on producing the RIO while outsourcing necessary non-core competencies, such as the transaction infrastructure, to Skyway.
This dimension will be referred to as organization strategies. On the other hand,
Diamond supports sales and distribution via an electronic platform. Developing
decisions on which business processes should be supported and what technological concept should be applied (e.g. electronic commerce) is the object of the second strategy dimension, the networking strategies.

---

[2] A comparable distinction has been suggested by [Venkatraman 1991, 141] who distinguishes two
   strategies for business network redesign: (1) strategies for business governance, and (2) strategies
   for IT governance.

4.2   Organization Strategies

Business Networking strategies have to connect to the general business strategy as
seamlessly as possible. This means that the potentials of Business Networking are
part of the overall strategy and that strategic goals can be directly translated into
consequences for Business Networking. This is the purpose of organization strategies.

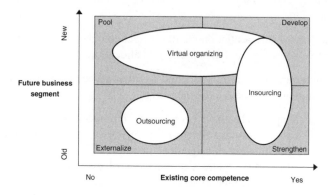

Figure 4-1: Alternative Organization Strategies

As Figure 4-1 illustrates, we need to identify whether a Business Networking
relationship supports business in an existing or a new business segment. To a large
extent, this decision depends on what the existing core competencies are[3]:

- Develop new resources with existing core competence in a new business
  segment

- Externalize resources if it is a non-core competence in an old business segment

- Pool resources with partners if a new business segment is to be entered
  without having all required core competencies to be competitive in this field

- Strengthen resources with an existing core competence in an old business
  segment

Table 4-1 also shows that several organization strategies are available in theory
and practice for designing the partner relationships in these four cases. From the
variety of existing approaches (see Table 4-1) three organization strategies will be
elaborated in more detail: insourcing, outsourcing and virtual organizing. The

---

[3]   According to [Prahalad/Hamel 1990], core competencies: (1) provide potential access to a wide
      variety of markets, (2) should make a significant contribution to the perceived customer value, and
      (3) should be difficult to imitate for competitors [see also Reve 1990].

special fourth quadrant shows an overlap of two strategies and will be described separately.

Approach	Options	Reference
Transaction cost economics/ organization theory	Hierarchy, market, hybrid	[Williamson 1985]
	Electronic markets, Electronic hierarchies	[Malone et al. 1987]
	Inhouse manufacture market supplier, partnership	[Clemons/Reddi 1993]
Telecooperation	Hierarchical organization Networked organization, Modular organization, Virtual organization	[Reichwald et al. 1998]
Strategic networks	Internal networks, stable networks, dynamic networks	[Snow et al. 1992]
	Quasi-externalization, quasi-internalization	[Sydow 1992]
Virtual organizations	Intraorganizational, interorganizational	[Davidow/Malone 1992], [Bleicher 1996], [Scholz 1997]
Resource-based approaches	Pooling, allying, linking	[Moss-Kanter 1989]

Table 4-1: Existing Approaches to Organization Strategies

4.2.1   Outsourcing – Externalizing Non-core Competencies

Traditional business resources which are not part of a company's existing and/or future core competencies are typical objects of an outsourcing strategy. For example, *Trust Bank* is a regional bank with over 50 locations in Australia. Trust Bank is structured around four strategic areas: the bank network, electronic banking, personal banking as well as commercial banking and manages over USD 1.8 billion in assets [cf. Hewlett Packard 1998]. In 1991, Trust Bank acquired Tasmanian Bank and was having problems to integrate the two different IT systems into one. Due to the critical nature of systems for the business, IT operations were outsourced to Hewlett Packard's operations services division. Trust Bank is now concentrating on developing custom applications and creating new IT based services within their core competencies (see Figure 4-2).

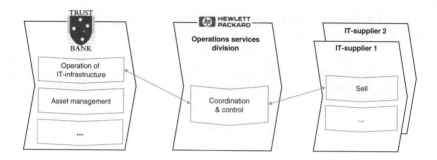

Figure 4-2: IT-Outsourcing at Trust Bank

Outsourcing is an organization strategy which allows major, non-core functions to be externalized to specialized service providers that established a core competence in this specific area [cf. Sägesser 1999, 25]. Outsourcing is different from classical subcontracting since it concerns non-core activities which are traditionally performed inside a company, e.g. an activity in Porter's value chain model (cf. [Koppelmann 1996], [Lacity/Hirschheim 1995]).

In 1997, the Dun & Bradstreet Corporation and The Outsourcing Institute released an outsourcing index designed to measure the changes in the level of outsourcing activity in the United States. According to a study [cf. Outsourcing Institute 1999] six main areas of outsourcing can be distinguished: finance (11%), human resource (15%), information technology (30%), marketing & sales (14%), administration (8%) plus some minor ones (22%). The study reveals that U.S. companies with over USD 80 million in revenue expect to increase expenditures for services they outsourced during 1997 by 26% to approximately USD 85 billion. Over the next three quarters, outsourcing activity is anticipated to rise by 16% to USD 146 billion [cf. Outsourcing Institute 1999].

4.2.2   Insourcing – Strengthening Existing Competencies

Compared to outsourcing, insourcing concentrates on the acquisition of competencies that are apt to strengthen already existing core competencies (cf. e.g. [Andrade/Chapman 1998], [Westkämper/Wildemann 1993]). For example, the German post office organization, *Deutsche Post*, acquired the Swiss Danzas Group which bought the European transport and distribution division of Dutch Royal Nedlloyd N.V. Plans are for Deutsche Post to take over Nedlloyd's parcel business and Danzas' logistics business to integrate them into their own organizations [cf. Schnitzler 1999]. Both acquisitions clearly strengthen the scale and scope of Deutsche Post in its existing market segment, the transportation of parcels [cf. Deutsche Post 1999]. Similar insourcing activities can be observed in other industries as well. Examples are telecommunications (e.g. AOL/Worldcom merger) or the automotive sector (e.g. DaimlerChrysler).

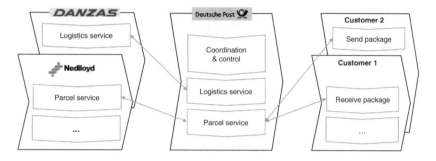

Figure 4-3: Insourcing at Deutsche Post

4.2.3   Virtual Organizing – New Segments with Cooperation Partners

Virtual organizing is a strategy that emphasizes the network as an entity. Although various legally independent partners cooperate within this network, an integrated product is offered on the marketplace. It is a central characteristic of a virtual organization that none of the participants could offer the same service individually and that virtual networks are temporary in nature (cf. [Davidow/Malone 1992], [Byrne 1993]). According to [Faucheux 1997], [Venkatraman/Henderson 1998] and [DeSanctis/Monge 1998], the term virtual organizing has been chosen instead of virtual organization in order to emphasize the process nature and to denote all possible organizational arrangements between market and hierarchical coordination forms.

An example of virtual organizing is *Enba*, a start-up venture which offers Internet based financial services from Dublin, Ireland. Although Enba does not possess the necessary resources, it sees its competitive advantage in a virtual business model that pools different, legally independent companies under one brand, but appears as one company to external parties. In contrast to vertically integrated competitors, Enba works with a selected group of internationally renowned partners, each chosen for its individual expertise in providing a specialist contribution to the overall service offering. For instance, The Royal Bank of Scotland is responsible for clearing and settlement, the Merchants Group takes responsibility for all call center operations, whereas stock orders are forwarded to Dresdner Kleinwort Benson who take on the execution. All processes are automatically run on the Internet, controlled by accompanying information systems. These systems enable customers to easily set up or delete accounts or calculate stock values and price risks. At the same time, they provide the platform for the integration of all participating partner companies and Enba is able to offer stock orders 50 % cheaper than its competitors.

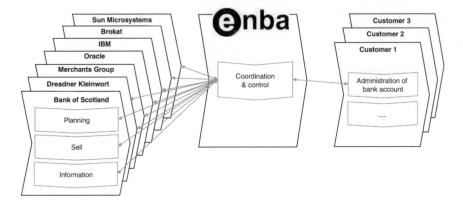

Figure 4-4: Virtual Organizing: Enba's Business Network

Enba constitutes the center of a business network in which the company concentrates on its core competence: the coordination of a pooled business network consisting of legally independent companies (see Figure 4-4). A virtual organizing strategy can therefore be defined as an *organization strategy in which a collection of legally independent companies, institutions, or individuals come together quickly to cooperate for a particular mission*. Its characteristics may be summarized as follows (cf. [Mertens et al. 1998, 3], [Arnold et al. 1995, 10]):

- *Common business objective.* All partners strive at providing a common service or product. Each member brings to the cooperation his core competencies and all act as an entity vis-a-vis the customer.

- *IT-platform.* Compared to internal coordination, virtual organizing involves more coordination, e.g. exchanging order, invoice or status information. These requirements are compensated by process standards and IT platforms.

- *Trust.* Because of the need for speedy action, not all aspects of the relationships can be backed up by formal agreements. Therefore, it is crucial that a large amount of trust should exist among members.

4.2.4   Developing New Business Segments

Both insourcing and virtual organizing may also be applied by companies aiming at entering new business segments that are in line with their existing core competencies. Developing existing core competencies to enter new business segments can basically be achieved by teaming up with partners or by making strategic acquisitions.

For example, *Ariba* offers an operating resource management system (ORMS) to manage the procurement of MRO goods within an enterprise. By implementing the Ariba.com Network, the company aims at developing its core competencies in ORMS to build up a new service that connects buyers and suppliers over the Internet (cf. Chap. 10.2.1). To meet these challenges, the Ariba.com network incorporates a number of Internet services including catalog and content management, order transaction routing, and multi-protocol support for numerous standard ways of exchanging content and transaction information. Ariba developed its existing core competence (ORMS) for the new (Internet) business segment.

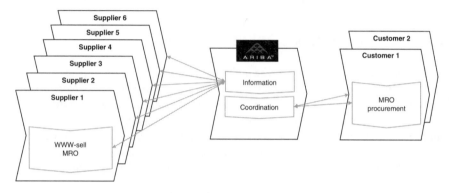

Figure 4-5: Ariba's WWW-Site

Ariba is also an example for the next development in Business Networking: electronic services (eServices). Increasingly, existing business-to-business relationships will be enhanced to offer individual services that generate new revenue. These eServices are available over the Internet and a high degree of standardization and modularity allows them to be integrated into internal application landscapes (cf. Chap. 2.3.5). eServices are a consistent continuation of outsourcing and concern areas, such as payroll processing, Web-site development and hosting, and credit card processing. Increasingly, eServices are evolving for more business oriented areas as well: bill presentment and reconciliation, credit checking, freight forwarding, customs clearance, field service, inventory management, and supply replenishment.

The strategy framework clearly shows that the development of new business segments (e.g. eServices) can either be done by pursuing an insourcing strategy (e.g. Ariba) or a virtual organizing strategy. The latter has been done by *AFB Software* in Munich who initiated a cooperation with *AutoBild,* a German automobile magazine. In March 1999 they launched 'Autokatalog', an Internet catalog for prospective buyers to configure a car to suit their preferences. It includes more than 3,000 models and more than 250,000 available after-market items. From Autokatalog, a customer may also obtain such information as actual market surveys, interior and external views of the car and a calculation of individual leasing, financing and insurance facilities [cf. AFB 1999]. AFB is linked to various finance and insurance companies, permitting real-time calculations and cooperation with existing dealers. Inquiries are routed to the nearest dealer who will fix an appointment for a test drive.

All companies involved in this eService cooperate to serve a new market with their existing core competencies. AutoBild, for example, uses its brand recognition to enter a new market segment – the sale of cars. Insurance, finance, and leasing companies are enabled to extend their business segment and develop their core competencies by offering the new services.

4.2.5   Summary of Organization Strategies

All examples discussed above have emphasized the role of core competencies and the future positioning in the market. They have shown that Business Networking can support various strategic goals that have to be decided in close coordination with the general business strategy. Business Networking consequently extends a company's core competence strategy. For example, by allowing a company to focus on core competencies, Business Networking can strengthen its position in an existing business as well as enable it to exploit new business opportunities (e.g. eServices).

Each of the organization strategies has a specific profile characterizing the cooperation (see Table 4-2). The strategies vary according to the number of partners involved as well as the depth and the duration of the partnership. For example, insourcing relationships are more of a long-term nature than virtual organizing relationships. Virtual organizing is the strategy that yields the highest flexibility (e.g. to respond to changing market demands), whereas insourcing is not really very flexible in changing existing internal partnerships.

Strategy / Criteria	Outsourcing	Insourcing	Virtual Organizing
Number of Partners	1	1	n
Depth of Cooperation	deep	deep	medium
Duration of Cooperation	long	long	medium
Flexible Response	medium	slow	fast

Table 4-2: Profiles for Organization Strategies

4.3   Networking Strategies

As explained above, networking strategies put their focus on the processes between business partners and the applications supporting these processes. In Chapter 3, the relationship between Business Networking scenarios and Business Networking strategies has already been indicated. Three main networking strategies
have been mentioned [cf. Kalakota/Robinson 1999]: electronic commerce, customer relationship management, and supply chain management. The networking
strategies are designed to address different types of processes (see Figure 4-6)
with the emphasis on different aspects:

- *Customer relationship management* (CRM) aims at supporting the whole
  relationship a company has with individual customers. To characterize CRM
  functionality the customer buying cycle is used which includes marketing,
  evaluation, buy, and after-sales activities.

- *Supply chain management* (SCM) focuses on supporting four main business
  processes: source, plan, make, and deliver. These processes from the SCOR-
  model aim at designing a smooth flow of goods, information and funds.

- *Electronic commerce* (EC) focuses on transaction processes and can be applied at the links of various business processes. For example, EC can support
  the outsourcing of payroll activities, the auctioning of surplus capacities in
  sales, the procurement of indirect goods and the like.

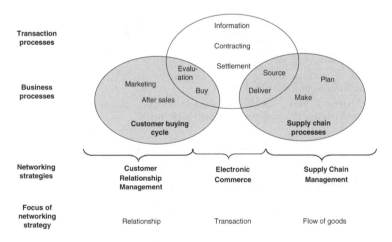

Figure 4-6: Processes in Different Networking Strategies

Business Networking integrates the three networking strategies that have emerged
as separate fields from a holistic perspective. The isolated evolution of each strategy explains the heterogeneity of the process models. For example, the processes

of information, contracting, evaluation, buy, and source are inherently similar. The same is true for settlement and deliver processes. From this, two insights can be derived:

- Business Networking strategies involve overlaps which indicate that links between the strategies have to be taken in consideration. Consequently, EC or supply chain strategies need to be enhanced by elements of other strategies.

- Business Networking strategies have individual emphasis which justifies the distinction of three different networking strategies. EC concentrates on shaping transactions, especially information and contracting processes, CRM concentrates on relationship processes, i.e. processes that go beyond individual transactions, and SCM concentrates on planning and production processes.

Therefore, Business Networking involves conceptualizing and managing multiple networking strategies at the same time (see Table 4-3).

Electronic Commerce	
Entire collection of actions that support commercial activities on a network	[Adam/Yesha 1996, 5]
Any form of economic activity conducted via electronic connections	[Wigand 1997, 2]
Use of digital processes to improve efficiencies of commercial transactions and processes as well as a means to offer new, digital product	[Choi et al. 1997, 12]
Supply Chain Management	
Integration of all activities associated with the flow and transformation of goods from the raw materials stage to the end user	[Handfield/ Nichols 1998, 2]
Management of upstream and downstream relationships to deliver superior customer value at less overall cost	[Christopher 1998, 18]
Process of examining buying and use of purchased materials and services and linking the resources of suppliers to the strategic goals of the company	[Riggs/Robbins 1998, 4]
Customer Relationship Management	
Use of IT in supplier-customer relationships concerning all points of contact (awareness, evaluation, settlement, and after-sales) between a company and their customers	[Österle/Muther 1998, 109]
Three computer-enhanced capabilities – information management, interactive communication and customized products - are integrated to create a 'customer feedback loop' with each individual customer	[Peppers/Rogers 1997, 13]
The management of customer relationship in business media comprises the design, development, and application of holistic concepts in order to manage relationships to economically valuable current or future customers	[Körner/Zimmermann 1999, 461]

Table 4-3: Overview of Approaches to Networking Strategies

4.3.1   Electronic Commerce – Transaction Perspective

Electronic commerce is a buzzword that is frequently applied without reference to the processes that are specifically included. In order to implement an EC strategy, 'doing business electronically' is not sufficient. The main processes which are used to characterize EC are developed from a transaction perspective. Transaction cost theory (cf. e.g. [Williamson 1985], [Wigand et al. 1997]) has been applied early by [Malone et al. 1987] to discuss electronic markets and hierarchies. The established phase model distinguishes three phases [cf. Schmid/Lindemann 1998]:

- In the *information phase*, relevant partners and products/services are identified. For example, electronic product catalogs are used to compare products and relevant conditions (prices, delivery deadlines, etc.). This phase is supported by a large number of services, e.g. search engines, such as Altavista, Yahoo! or Lycos, content providers (e.g. Ariba), or community pages (e.g. [http://bec.iwi.unisg.ch]). The main thrust is towards establishing multi-vendor platforms permitting thorough comparisons of competing offers.

- The *contracting phase* continues the transaction and establishes a formal, mutually binding relationship between the partners. Contracting includes agreeing on terms and conditions, such as terms of payment, delivery date, delivery conditions, warranty, service levels, etc. Clearly, electronic contracting presupposes the redesign of existing legal rules and appropriate technologies. In both areas, a variety of promising initiatives are under way which will foster the volume of commercial transactions [cf. Schmid et al. 1998].

- The *settlement phase* finalizes a transaction. Physical or virtual goods are delivered and funds are transferred. Currently, many actors are aiming at offering integrated services for settlement processes which have been described as computer-integrated logistics (CIL) [Alt/Schmid 2000]. Examples are electronic commerce services by Deutsche Post or virtual order by Federal Express. The big challenge is to overcome the traditional physical/financial dichotomy and to integrate financial solutions. Modular financial services, such as bill presentment services (e.g. PayNet [www.paynet.ch]) and eCash systems, are being developed.

These transaction processes are used to characterize EC more precisely. *EC denotes the electronic support of information, contracting and/or settlement processes. EC requires that at least information and order entry processes should be supported electronically.* Within EC, various fields have been distinguished. The established differentiations are:

- Depending on the application context, EC can be conducted within an enterprise (intra-business), with business partners, such as suppliers and corporate customers (business-to-business), and with end-customers (business-to-consumer) (cf. e.g. [Kalakota/Whinston 1997], [Schwede 1999]). The focus of Business Networking is on the intra-business and business-to-business areas.

• Depending on the underlying business processes, EC has evolved for procurement and sales processes. This has led to buy-side and sell-side EC applications (see Table 4-4).

	Sell-side (eSales)	Buy-side (eProcurement)
Potentials	• Additional revenue generation • Improved after-sales service • Set-up of virtual communities	• Higher cost efficiency • Higher process efficiency • Improved supplier management
Technology	• Web-sites/catalogs • Trading platforms • Hosting services	• Workflow/catalogs • Procurement services • Hosting services

Table 4-4: EC-Potentials and Technologies

An example for a buy-Side EC-application is provided by *W.W. Grainger's* procurement system. W.W. Grainger, Vernon Hills, USA, brought together six different suppliers of MRO goods and created a one-stop online buying center.[4] Via OrderZone.com, customers place their order and receive one invoice across multiple suppliers [cf. Order Zone 1999]. OrderZone.com routes the orders to each supplier for fulfillment (see Figure 4-7). When customers are finished, a completed order form containing all necessary information (such as shipping, billing information, multiple quantity and total calculations, etc.) is generated and various schemes are offered for payment (such as credit cards, and open-account billing). OrderZone enabled Grainger to create a new service and to enter new market segments. It streamlines the procurement process and standardizes trading procedures which has led to a 10% reduction in buying costs for Grainger. Delays and errors in procurement are reduced and all interaction with customers is performed via one channel.

---

[4] Participating companies include: Cintas Corp. (uniforms), Corporate Express (office supplies), Lab Safety Supply (safety supplies), Avnet Marshall (electronic components), VWR Scientific Products (lab supplies), and Grainger Industrial Supply (MRO supplies).

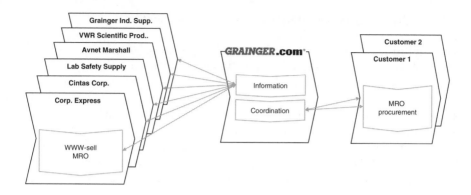

Figure 4-7: Buy-side EC at W.W. Grainger

Blaupunkt Extr@Net is an example of an eSales application. A subsidiary of Robert Bosch GmbH in Hildesheim, Germany, Blaupunkt is a manufacturer of car communication technologies, e.g. car audio, traffic telematics, and radiophones. With about 7,000 employees (2,600 in Germany) and a volume of five million car radios per year, Blaupunkt is a European market leader in car radios [cf. Blaupunkt 1999]. In July 1998, Blaupunkt introduced an Internet-based electronic catalog which enables specialized traders and after-market customers to order products and to obtain information about products, prices, delivery status and backlogs (see Figure 4-8). The catalog is divided into 13 sub-product groups (from antennas to accessories) and may also be downloaded. Customers can place articles into a simple shopping basket specifying desired delivery dates. Further benefits are: no order and express forwarding expenses, information about delivery times, available products and campaigns. For Blaupunkt the largest benefit came from the savings in manual order entry which took up about one third of the time the sales people spent on this operation before the solution was implemented.

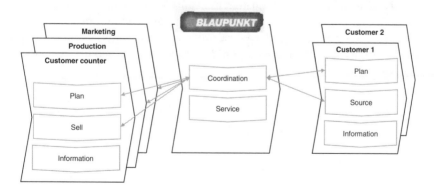

Figure 4-8: Sell-side EC at Blaupunkt

4.3.2 Supply Chain Management – Flow Perspective

Another Business Networking strategy that mainly evolved from the logistics discipline is supply chain management. SCM aims at optimizing the flow of goods between multiple processes [cf. Handfield/Nichols 1999, 2]. First logistics approaches were geared to overcoming the functional orientation within an individual company which involved the coordination of materials management along procurement, production, warehousing, and distribution activities in order to reduce inventories and increase flexibility to react to changing market demand. With the advent of ERP systems many companies have achieved considerable levels of internal supply chain optimization. The current developments are focused on enhancing these solutions in two respects:

- Improve coordination of physical and financial flows in order to reduce cash cycles, and

- Extend supply chain optimization efforts to external partners, such as suppliers, distributors, retailer, and, ultimately, customers.

Clearly, extended supply chain solutions are made possible by the use of potentials of information technology which reduces the specificity of technological investments and increases interoperability among IT systems [cf. Dubois/Carmel 1994]. An example of this networking strategy is the *Taiwan Semiconductor Manufacturing Company* (TSMC) in Hsin-chu, Taiwan. TSMC is the world's largest contract manufacturer of integrated circuits, with revenues exceeding USD 1.5 billion. TSMC's competitive advantage has traditionally come from technology, capacities, and pricing. With increasing competition, TSMC realized the need to focus on superior customer service aiming at better differentiation. It was mainly in respect of two criteria that performance was to be improved: visibility into the off-site manufacturing process and order lead time [cf. Orths 1995, 29]. The solution was to remove the internal/external barrier and to give partners access to the same amount of information as available to internal production units. TSMC's first business partner was Adaptec, the USD 1 billion manufacturer of networking and I/O equipment. To reduce order lead times, information links were established for Research & Development (R&D), forecasting and the execution of supply chain processes (see Figure 4-9).

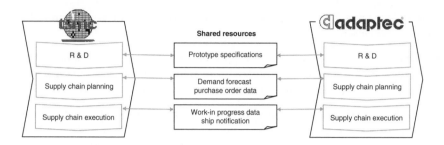

Figure 4-9: Supply Chain Scenario at TSMC and Adaptec

To take advantage of scale effects and to increase supply chain efficiency with other partners, TSMC wants to roll out the scenario to other customers as well. Although the solution will be customized for each customer, TSMC estimates that 80 % of its customer base are eligible for this solution. The benefits resulting from the solution are significant (see Table 4-5) and illustrate the potentials of Business Networking to create win-win situations with partners. But above all, TSMC has been able to achieve its goal to stay competitive and to become an industry leader.

TSMC's Benefits	Adaptec's Benefits
• Increased customer satisfaction through customer's increased real-time visibility into their supply chains, the reduction in lead time and inventory levels, and improved on-time deliveries • Customer's product lead time reduced by as much as 25 % • Reduction in work-in-progress inventory carrying costs due to cycle time reduction • Improved capacity planning with demand forecasts	• Increased customer satisfaction through reduction in lead times and improved on-time delivery • Cycle times cut by as much as 50 % • Inventory levels reduced by 25 % • Integrated processes for invoicing, sharing of quality data

Table 4-5: Benefits of SCM at TSMC and Adaptec

The advantages at TSMC are mainly based on exchanging information on forecasts, stock levels, orders, work-in-progress data and the like (see Table 4-5). This is also reflected in supply chain models, such as SCOR[5], which builds supply chains using four core logistic processes (plan, source, make, deliver) and three core management processes (planning, execution, infrastructure). A combination of both dimensions (Table 4-6) serves to develop a detailed functional view of

---

[5]   SCOR is a process reference model and was first published as version 1.0 in November 1996 by the Supply Chain Council (SCC) as a cross-sector standard from 73 Fortune 500 companies. The prime goal is to provide a language standard for intra and inter-company communication with SC partners [cf. Supply Chain Council 1998]. For the SCOR model, see also Chapters 6 and 9.

supply chain processes that are contained in the more general type of supply chain strategies, such as:

- *Integrated logistics solutions.* Supply chain processes are bundled into an integrated logistics solution. Often, these solutions focus on planning and delivery processes. Prominent providers are such integrators as FedEx.

- *Global supply chain visibility.* Information about supply chain performance (status of resources and flows) is pooled in centralized databases. Euro-Log, for example, performs the tracking & tracing between multiple business partners.

- *Global sourcing.* Sourcing activities are consolidated across organizational boundaries which involves designing vendor contracts, demand planning and the like (Table 4-6).

- *Vendor-managed inventory (VMI).* Inventory at the customer is managed by the vendor. This strategy involves elements of all four processes and will be described in more detail in Chapter 5.

- *Quick response (QR).* An order system permitting fast reaction, based on EDI over the whole supply chain, to customer individual demands [cf. Walker 1994].

- *Continuous replenishment (CRP).* A continuous, standardized and automated system of supplying materials based on scanner data direct from point of sale (POS), e.g. Wal-Mart [cf. Klaus/Krieger 1998].

	Planning	Execution	Infrastructure
Plan	• Supply network planning • Life cycle planning	• Supply chain configuration • Make-or-Buy decision	• Long-term capacity planning • Product line planning • Transport vehicle planning
Source	• Vendor contracts • Demand planning	• Purchase • Payment	• Vendor certification • Warehouse mgmt. • Sourcing quality mgmt.
Make	• Production planning	• Manufacture: - Make-to-stock - Make-to-order - Engineer-to-order	• Product quality mgmt. • Facility/equipment maintenance • Short-term capacity planning
Deliver	• Order mgmt.	• Pack • Load • Deliver	• Warehouse mgmt. • Packing mgmt. • Crossdocking mgmt. • Car pool mgmt.

Table 4-6: Examples of Supply Chain Processes

Conventional ERP systems were unable to cope with the variety of supply chain strategies and the complexity of process configurations. This has led to the evolution of specific supply chain applications which focus on calculating demand patterns, simulating production capacities, etc. An overview of these advanced planning systems (APS) is provided in Chapter 9.

4.3.3   Customer Relationship Management – Relationship Perspective

Compared to EC which has its focus on transactions and SCM which focuses on flows, the third Business Networking strategy presents a distinct relationship perspective. While EC assumes an atomistic transaction perspective, SCM is production-centred with marketing or sales activities being secondary considerations. Customer relationship management recognizes that customer relations stretch across atomistic transactions and that pre-sales and after-sales activities are an inherent part of customer-orientation in Business Networking.

LGT Bank, Liechtenstein, for example, as described in Chapter 7.2, increased its focus on the needs of clients in order to remain competitive. As a result, the bank decided to integrate front- and backoffice processes via a common information system to create a customer-centric organizational structure. Another compelling example of customer orientation is *SAP AG* (cf. Chap. 3.2.4) which aims at achieving and maintaining customer relationship by offering a large number of electronic services and setting up a virtual community. Avnet Marshall (cf. Chap. 3.2.3), a company which succeeded by structuring the entire organization around the customer, created the junction box, a series of IT systems that support relationships between Avnet Marshall's cutomers and suppliers. Transaction functionality (EDI, Web order entry) has been enhanced with Avnet Marshall's Intranet (Avnet MarshallNet), an electronic catalog, a 24 h ordering facility, customized customer Web pages (PartnerNet), the creation and monitoring of customer profiles, a scheduling and replenishment system, as well as training and consulting services [El Sawy et al. 1999].

Customer relationship management means increasing revenues and profitability by coordinating, consolidating and integrating all points of contact that enterprises have with their customers, employees, partners and suppliers which is what in effect integrates sales, marketing, customer service, enterprise resource planning and virtual sales office [cf. Österle/Muther 1998, 108]. CRM primary focuses on the marketing, sales and after-sales processes.

- *Marketing process.* CRM supports the customer and the business itself with information on products, campaigns, customer profiling, etc.
- *Sales process.* CRM supports the customer with call center activities, product configuration information, etc.

- *After-sales process*. CRM supports the customer with problem analysis, guarantees handling, etc.

Between the after-sales and sales processes, we have order processing activities taking place that are not part of the CRM processes themselves. The tasks of these processes are supported by enterprise resource planning (ERP) systems (cf. Chap. 2.3.1). The three CRM processes and the process of order processing can be assigned to the four stages of the customer buying cycle [cf. Muther 1998, 17]. From the identification of customer needs, and the compiling of product and price information, purchase handling right through to the service phase of the customer buying cycle reflects all possible interfaces between providers and customers.

4.3.4   Summary of Networking Strategies

Networking strategies are the second strategic element in Business Networking. Since each strategy emphasizes different processes, the networking strategies complement each other. In general, the profiles of the strategies are (see Table 4-7):

- *Cooperation intensity*. EC deals with a vast number of partners but depth of cooperation, i.e. electronic ordering, is low and duration short. In the case of SCM and CRM, depth of cooperation is great and duration long, in other words, each partner has to be an individual part of the value chain and each customer wants individual attention even when he is not ordering at the moment.

- *Flexibility*. EC and CRM are flexible in responding to changing requirements, i.e. the creation of new catalogs, specific information, etc., whereas SCM is relatively inflexible due to the long period of time required for installation.

- *Specificity*. As elaborated by [Malone et al. 1987], asset specificity largely determines the number of partners and the ease of switching partners. Typically, EC solutions are conceived for a large number of partners and involve a limited depth of cooperation. Low specificity results from using standardized technology and low levels of integration with business processes. SCM requires high levels of process integration and often involves proprietary solutions. Standards in EC and SCM will result in a high degree of process integration at low specificity.

Strategy / Criteria	EC	SCM	CRM
Number of Partners	n	1:n	n
Depth of Cooperation	low	deep	medium - deep
Duration of Cooperation	short	long	medium - long
Flexibility	high	low - medium	high
Specificity of Investments	low	high	low - medium

Table 4-7: Profiles of Networking Strategies

4.4 Interaction of Business Networking Strategies

The concept of Business Networking strategies boils down to the idea that every Business Networking solution has two dimensions and requires decisions in terms of organization and (networking) processes. Therefore, each example can be positioned regarding these two dimensions (see Figure 4-10). For example, Blaupunkt intended to strengthen their market power in the field of car communication technologies and decided to insource with a combination of EC, SCM and CRM: a business-to-business eSales solution, a guaranteed delivery channel (SCM), and after-sales activities (CRM), such as order status tracking, complaint management, training facilities, information databases, etc. A similar case is W.W. Grainger which combines the multi-vendor catalog with a direct delivery channel and after-sales functionalities.

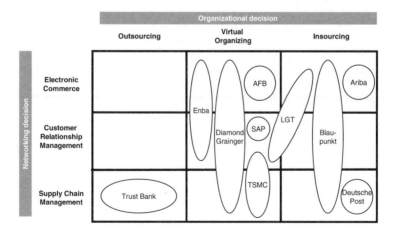

Figure 4-10: Interaction of Organization and Networking Strategies

The examples cited and feedback from interviews show that organization strategies are inherently of a long-term nature being that the cost of switching strategies are high. Networking strategies often have for their object the development of process solutions. An electronic catalog, for example, might be supplemented with a direct delivery channel (see the ETA case in Chap. 6) and, as a later stage, relationship management elements, such as virtual communities and FAQs, could be added.

4.5   Conclusions

Conceiving and implementing a Business Networking strategy requires top-management attention and decisions. It has been attempted in this Chapter to show that organization strategies link up with a company's competitive strategy and determine how competencies in a certain field should be organized. The processes behind each strategic decision are addressed by networking strategies that have different, but complementary, emphasis. Adopting a Business Networking perspective overcomes the problem of conceiving and implementing isolated solutions, a fallacy often observed in literature and practice.

Although the approaches proposed to formulate specific strategies are many and various and involve a certain amount of complexity, there are distinct benefits to be derived from a clear understanding of the interaction of strategies. First, it allows a distinct separation of organization and process issues. Second, it is helpful for planning the set-up and the evolution of a Business Networking solution. It would be possible, for instance, to start by implementing an electronic catalog and by enhancing it step by step with other networking features, such as shipment tracking, a discussion forum, auction functionalities and the like.

Due to the focus of this book being on processes, the following chapters will present a more detailed view of networking strategies. Chapter 5 concentrates on SCM, Chapter 6 on (sell-side) EC and SCM and Chapter 7 on CRM. Finally, both organization and networking strategies are also reflected in the method proposed for Business Networking which will provide concrete guidance as to when and how to adopt any of these strategies (cf. Chap. 14).

5 Business Networking Lessons Learned: Supply Chain Management at Riverwood International

Elgar Fleisch, Hubert Österle, Robert Betts

5.1 Business Networking Is Customer and Supplier Integration...............112

5.2 Establishing the Business Networking Vision 113

5.3 Implementing the Business Networking Vision....................................114

5.4 As the Tide Comes In all Boats Go Up..115

5.5 Shaping Competitive Advantage..116

5.6 Creating the Coordination Backbone 117

5.7 Becoming Part of the Business Networking Infrastructure 118

5.1   Business Networking Is Customer and Supplier Integration

In 1996 the management of Riverwood International, an integrated paperboard and packaging supplier with head quarters in Atlanta, GA, USA, set out to create a new level of customer service within the industry. Riverwood wanted to enhance its competitive position by improving the flow of information to and from the customer. This information flow will be determined by the uniqueness of the commercial relationships between each customer, and in some cases each 'ship to' location of each customer. Riverwood has developed capabilities that enable small customers to process orders, inquire into order status, and monitor global inventory position with direct access to Riverwood's information system via an Internet based solution. In the case of large customers, Riverwood is implementing new global materials management strategies, negotiated delivery and production schedules and shared sales and purchasing forecasts. Implementing these strategies, Riverwood and their customers will realize the benefits in the areas of inventory reductions, lower process costs, and greater flexibility for retail market response.[1]

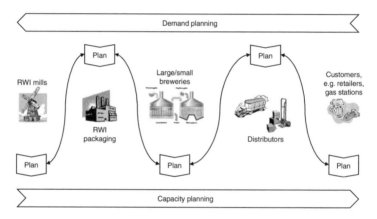

Figure 5-1: Supply Chain of Riverwood

Riverwood found itself primarily confronted with the following questions: How to approach the customers and how to arrive at a true win-win situation? What cooperative strategies should be considered? How to calculate the return on investment (ROI) for this inter-business project? What are the critical success factors for this project? What activities will have to be included in the project timetable? Which business processes implement the strategies? What organizational changes will be

---

[1]   For further discussion of the Riverwood International case see Chap. 14.3.

necessary? Which information systems and standards should be used? Which services could be used and/or provided?

Potential benefit of cooperation strategy	Stock turn Stock days of supply Returns Age of existing inventory Obsolete inventory	Labor hours to plan Degree of rework Number of "emergencies" Scheduling errors System availability	Capacity utilization Inventory accuracy Packaging machine-units per day per style	Promotion reaction time Volume reaction time
Consigment inventory	0	0	0	0
Vendor managed inventory	0	++	+	+
Automated vendor replenishment	0	++	+	0
Global inventory visibility	++	++	++	++
Backflushing from distributor plan	0	0	0	0
Collaborative production planning	+	++	0	0

++ High   + Middle   0 Low

Table 5-1: Supply Chain Potentials at Riverwood

Today, executives can pick up any management magazine and read about the latest business and information technology trends in the area of inter-business integration, supply chain management, electronic commerce, outsourcing, etc. and about the overwhelming benefits for the modern business. They read the advertisements of consulting firms who are building core competencies in the area of Business Networking, and full-page spreads from new and well-known names in software industry who are bringing innovative software components for business partner integration onto the market. Exactly how this potential can be harnessed remains largely unclear, however, Business Networking aims to provide the answers.

Business Networking encompasses the professional design and maintenance of the link between business partners and constitutes the sine qua non for the implementation of a large number of effective strategies for the future. The same principles of Business Networking apply when it comes to translating strategies into functional processes and information systems, irrespective of whether we are dealing with supply chain integration, outsourcing, globalization, electronic commerce in sales or purchasing.

5.2   Establishing the Business Networking Vision

The first question, which Riverwood asked itself, was: who are my business partners today and who will they be tomorrow? From the huge number of business partners comprising customers, suppliers, authorities and the general public, the management selected those who were the most important: in the case of River-wood *all* customers. The next question was: what are the forecasting, planning, purchasing, replenishment and payment processes of these customers going to look like tomorrow? Riverwood's sales personnel sat down with the customer's staff or managers and drew up profiles for each and every customer. Customer profiles record the current status and target developments in the customer's business and information management. Examples are organization structure, cooperation strategies, classifications, information on business processes and exceptions as well as the architecture of the relevant information systems.

Customer profiles provide on the one hand a systematic and largely objective overview of the current partner situation and thus the basis for wide-area integration; on the other, they represent for sales staff a welcome means of enhancing customer loyalty and strengthening the relationship with the customer. Business Networking visions can be derived from the general business trends and the specific statements of the customer profiles. In Riverwood's case the vision was: every customer is important. Every customer, whether they are an international beverage producer or a micro-brewery with three employees, should be given a specially customized link. The example of Riverwood follows the generally observable business trend towards mass customization: it is not only the products which are individualized but also the services associated with the product, the customer relationship. "Riverwood has always provided high quality products and services. Traditionally, these services focused on transportation and warehousing. In the future, these services will provide integration between end buyers, manufacturers, and suppliers. The boundaries that have traditionally restricted cooperation have been eliminated, now all that remains is the ability of management to properly utilize these capabilities."

5.3   Implementing the Business Networking Vision

A large number of strategies with differing design focus were open to Riverwood (cf. [Fine 1998], [Austin et al. 1997]):

- Strategies leading to more efficient and more effective Business Network structures: How do I reduce the number of suppliers through one additional intermediary? How do I outsource the entire transport logistics including finishing to an external service provider?

- Strategies which aim to improve the quality of a large number of major entrepreneurial decisions by integrating inter-business information: How do I convince my customers to forward their production schedules, delivery schedules or point of sales data to me? How can I initiate an inter-business forecasting system and thus minimize the number of demand signals? How can I make relevant information available to my partners online?

- Strategies which make it possible to create individual products and services: How must product components be designed in order to ensure that they can be assembled to form a product specifically geared to the requirements of an individual customer at a later date? What information technology support do I need in order to be able to offer every customer individual after-sales service?

- Strategies that reduce the time and effort necessary for coordinating business partners Who will manage my raw materials warehouse? At what point in time does ownership and thus product risk pass to my customer? When can I dispense with order acknowledgements, when can I use a clearing method to settle accounts?

On the basis of the Business Networking vision and the partner profiles, management then decides to implement the most effective strategies in the catalog. The effectiveness of a cooperation strategy largely depends on its acceptance among the business partners involved.

5.4   As the Tide Comes In All Boats Go Up

How do I create this acceptance? How does Business Networking benefit the businesses involved? Business Networking is put in place in order to improve the return on investment of new and existing resources. The costs and benefits of Business Networking are described in terms of the effectiveness and efficiency of the new form of inter-business cooperation. With Business Networking, *efficiency* applies more to the company internal effects and can typically be measured quantitatively. Frequently used metrics here are internal costs (production costs, warranty costs, costs generated by returned products), the costs of administrative processes (e.g. costs of procurement) and the development of inventories (cash-to-cash cycle time, inventory days of supply, asset turns). *Effectiveness* describes effects directed outward towards partners. In some cases, these can only be determined qualitatively. The effectiveness of a solution is described in terms of delivery quality metrics (delivery performance, order fulfillment performance, perfect order fulfillment) and flexibility (supply chain response time, production flexibility).

For Riverwood, one of the greatest challenges lays in the lack of information on customer processes and customer feedback on Riverwood's products and services. Riverwood's service processes were largely manual and reactive and thus costly and slow. Information on production processes was very scant. Riverwood's service personnel received no support in achieving sustainable customer loyalty and consequently morale sank. By linking Riverwood's goals, strategies, processes and information systems to those of their customers, Riverwood plans to (a) reduce the order to cash cycle by 60 days, (b) go from 8 weeks of finished goods to 2.5 weeks, (c) reduce cost to serve by 50%, (d) cut order fulfillment process cycle times from 14 days to 2 hours, (e) increase the accuracy of invoices sent out, (f) achieve a minimum customer service rate of 95% and (g) raise the morale of the workforce.

How does Riverwood convince its business partners of its Business Networking vision? Business Networking questions always deal with n:m relationships, in other words, relationships between n suppliers and m customers. Thus Riverwood sells its products and services, for example, to some 2000 customers and each of these customers purchases from between 5 and 20 packaging manufacturers. In order to simplify handling, it is frequently only the individual 1:1 relationships which are analyzed and managed in today's inter-business projects. As a result, the interdependence between these 1:1 relationships is lost and solutions that need a critical mass (cf. Chap. 2.2.3) of business partners are not considered. In order to convince the critical mass of partners in favor of a new Business Networking solution, a *Win-Win situation* must be created and communicated. Win-Win situations are those in which the ROI of each partner is improved by the new networking solution (cf. Chap. 13.3.3)

5.5   Shaping Competitive Advantage

From its customer profiles and the selected mix of cooperation strategies in the area of warehouse management and the inter-business integration of information, Riverwood evolved standard services which it would like to offer its customers in future. Such standard services are management and IT based. Envisaged management services for customers include, e.g., advanced shipping notices, order acknowledgements, 7*24-hour ordering facility, 7*24-hour current status information from production and logistics; envisaged IT services range from simple Web solutions developed and provided by Riverwood, including hardware and maintenance and allowing direct access to Riverwood's order management system, to the integration of the customer's ERP systems with Riverwood's ERP systems. For each customer, Riverwood composes an individual package from these standard services for customer integration. It is only through the individual combination of a few standard services that the costs and complexity of individual partner integration can be mastered. Individually programmed links at the information system level lead to a blind alley.

The new services help coordinate Riverwood's business processes with those of its customers. As a result, new planning data from key account customers in some cases automatically initiate Riverwood's planning processes, inventory movements in the warehouses run by Riverwood on customer premises automatically affect Riverwood's production and logistics. The business processed involved must be designed so that they coordinate themselves under normal circumstances. The managers of coordinating processes have to agree threshold values, such as minimum inventory levels in the warehouses, at the outset. In addition, they have to arrive at joint decisions in respect of the applicable microprocesses, such as the correct way to process inventory or the storage method to be applied. Management attention should only be required in exceptional cases. There are two major questions to be considered here:

- Who is responsible for coordination in exceptional cases? In the case of Riverwood and its customers it is the process managers of the self-coordinating processes, i.e. Riverwood's vice president sales and the vice president of purchasing for the customer concerned. They and their staff meet not only to deal with exceptional cases but also get together twice a year to further develop their processes and coordination mechanisms as well as to nurture their cooperation culture.

- What procedure is to be followed in exceptional circumstances? An intensive integration of customers and suppliers may well mean heavy dependence on the part of both partners. What happens if one side fails to provide an agreed coordination service? If, for example, a supplier receives an incorrect production schedule from its customer or is not informed that the vendor managed inventory has already dropped below the minimum level this may lead to short deliveries and consequently to lost production. Exceptional arrangements clarify the question of who bears the costs in such cases and whether penalties are to be applied. Together with its partners, Riverwood developed a comprehensive set of rules governing obligatory microprocesses, threshold values and exceptions.

5.6   Creating the Coordination Backbone

The architecture of information systems follows the architecture of the business. This also applies in the case of Business Networking. During the eighties and nineties, software manufacturers followed the call of business for data integration to be as comprehensive as possible, first and foremost SAP with its products R/2 and R/3. With the transformation of the business model towards greater specialization and decentralized structures, the once highly integrated packages are increasingly being distributed or supplemented by special software components. This distribution or development of new components is occurring where the market demands it: in the process areas assigned to Business Networking. Highly regarded manufacturers of these new components for integrating business partners are i2, Manugistics and SAP in the area of advanced planning systems (cf. Chap. 9) and Ariba, Commerce One, Netscape and SAP in the area of electronic commerce purchasing systems (cf. Chap. 10).

These new software components support the coordination of inter-business processes and permit the inter-business integration of data, which are accessed by the cooperating business partners. They represent connecting elements with special functionality between the business partners' ERP systems. To support its inter-business processes to the customer, Riverwood installed the APO planning system from SAP and integrated it firstly with its own R/3 system, secondly with the relevant systems of its customers and thirdly with the Web solution. The *integration* with the internal and external information systems is the greatest challenge for the architecture and implementation of Business Networking systems. The *information system standards* used play a decisive role here: the wrong standards will lead to a blind alley. Active management of these information system standards ensures the flexibility and integrity of a Business Networking solution (cf. Chap. 8).

Amongst others, Riverwood would like to give its customers the possibility of calling up the current order status at any point in time. That means that Riverwood must first be in possession of this information. This simple example clearly demonstrates that a properly functioning internal organization and the internal integration of information systems are prerequisites for Business Networking.

5.7 Becoming Part of the Business Networking Infrastructure

In order to be able to implement its cooperation strategy Riverwood must depend on the services of trust centers, e-cash providers, security providers, network providers, master data providers, etc. These services are standardized and are increasingly becoming an inherent part of the infrastructure of the business world in the information age (cf. [Tapscott 1995], [Barling/Stark 1998]). Riverwood's goal is to outsource all services that do not belong to its core business. The smooth integration of the providers of these infrastructure services is dependent on well-known interfaces and service levels. The sum of all providers with whom Riverwood could integrate is referred to as the 'business bus' (cf. Chap. 2.3.4). Riverwood regularly follows developments in the Business Bus and thus ensures that innovations in the relevant service market are used to the corporation's advantage. The spectrum of services offered by the Business Bus is continually increasing. At the same time the services are increasingly taking on more business functionality (payroll services, etc.).

The management of Riverwood found that "in the future Business Networking will be a primary product of Riverwood. We are creating customer supply chain integration centers to ensure that each participant in the supply chain derives benefit from the relationship."

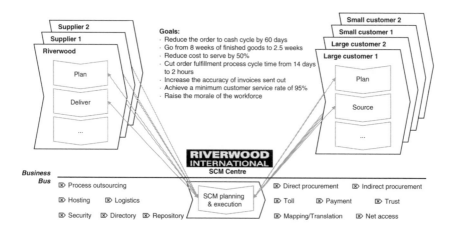

Figure 5-2: Riverwood-Business Networking Model

Business Networking describes the far-reaching capabilities of a corporation to position itself and hold its ground in a network of other corporations and to design the strategies, processes and information systems so vital to any corporation in order to communicate with the outside world.

The St. Gallen business model (cf. [Bleicher 1995], [Ulrich 1984]) is based on the conception of a business as a living social system, and over the years it has drawn on many ideas from the fields of biology, cognitive science, ecology and evolutionary theory. If we view a business as a living social system which strives to survive within its environment, i.e. its business network, then the significance of 'networkability' can be clearly illustrated: the ability to survive, to learn and to think will always depend on the business's communication capability.

With applying the core lessons of Business Networking Riverwood is achieving networkability. Those core lessons are:

- Customer and supplier integration is an entrepreneurial challenge.

- Partner profiles and processes help defining the Business Networking vision.

- A mix of cooperation strategies implements the Business Networking vision.

- Create and communicate a win-win situation.

- Business Networking creates USP characteristics and changes business strategies.

- New information systems and standards support the integration of business partners.

- New Business Networking services emerge and transform the business world.

6 Electronic Commerce and Supply Chain Management at 'The Swatch Group'

Rainer Alt, Karl-Maria Grünauer, Christian Reichmayr, Rudolf Zurmühlen

6.1 Introduction 122

6.2 Comparison of Concepts 122

6.3 Case Study: EC and SCM at ETA SA...124
    6.3.1 Goals of EC and SCM at ETA SA 124
    6.3.2 Initial Problems at ETA SA 124
    6.3.3 Phase I: Re-engineering the Supply Chain...............................125
    6.3.4 Phase II: Introduction of a EC Solution 126
    6.3.5 Complementarity of Concepts and Implementation..................128

6.4 Critical Success Factors at ETA SA...129
    6.4.1 Master Data Management as 'Hidden Success Factor' 129
    6.4.2 Strategic Alignment with Marketing Strategy 130
    6.4.3 Reciprocity of Benefits 130
    6.4.4 Common Basis for Communication...131
    6.4.5 Method for Structured Procedure...132

6.5 Conclusions and Next Steps...133

6.1   Introduction

Electronic commerce (EC) and supply chain management (SCM) are two Business Networking strategies that are enjoying widespread popularity. As mentioned in Chapter 4 both are concepts designed to sustain networking among businesses and as such are attracting considerable management attention these days. This is explained by the substantial growth in electronic sales that is expected to take place in the coming years. According to [Forrester 1998] five percent of all global sales will be through electronic media by 2003. While EC is often put on a level with such sales solutions as electronic catalogs, malls and auctions, all sales involve supply chain activities as well. The latter cover the entire production process from procurement to distribution and for some products at least have reached a remarkable degree of sophistication. Examples are immaterial products (e.g. news, and software) as well as some physical products such as CDs, books or computers. Compared to the potential of physical products, electronic sales are still negligible. Prominent exceptions such as Dell or Cisco have had a measure of success due to their efficient link to EC and supply chain solutions. But for many companies this still remains an intricate task. Reasons for that are:

- Solutions for EC and SCM have evolved from different backgrounds: The former from sales and marketing and the latter from physical logistics, production and materials management.

- Companies are faced with the trade-off problem to quick develop an EC solution to be present on the market and to integrate transaction data in the back-end systems which is a time-consuming and expensive task (cf. Chap. 17).

In the following, we will outline how industrial companies can reap benefits by jointly managing EC and SCM. We believe that the pursuance of integrated strategies which include both areas is vital for expectations in electronic sales to materialize. We will present a case study to show how ETA SA implemented an EC and SCM strategy. This will include a description of the solution and an evaluation of the major benefits for the participants. Important lessons learned and critical success factors deduced from this project will be dealt with in Chapter 6.4. Finally, in Chapter 6.5 we will discuss the conclusions to be drawn for the management of the inter-relationship between the two concepts.

6.2   Comparison of Concepts

The theoretical analysis of EC and SCM reveals that both concepts have two aspects in common (cf. Chap. 4.3). First, buy-side and sell-side overlap with the source and deliver activities that are core elements in supply chains. Second, information on supply chain planning processes is required within the contracting phase when the availability of goods or the scheduled delivery time for a specific configuration is to be determined. This functionality, called 'available to promise' (ATP), clearly requires information from the supply chain. ATP checks have become an important feature of SCM systems from i2 Technologies, Manugistics or SAP (cf. Chap. 9). It is equally important that these systems should make use of the information on EC transactions in determining demand forecasts.

Figure 6-1 illustrates the relationship in a sourcing scenario: The source activity is initiated when demand emerges from an ERP module or is determined manually. Such demand triggers off the EC transaction and goods are selected, negotiated and delivered via close interaction of customer and supplier systems. On the supplier side, a supply chain link exists between the information phase and the plan process which enable the ATP check to be performed. All other links focus on the settlement phase for the production and delivery of the goods ordered.

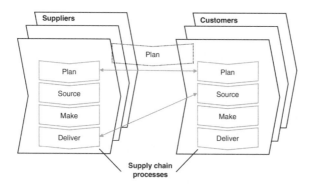

Figure 6-1: Complementary Relationship Between EC and SCM

While there is considerable overlap of the central functions in the two concepts, marked inherent differences exist in the scope of design and quality of the underlying relationships. In EC, the main emphasis is on shaping information and contracting processes within transactions. SCM is designed to provide control of the underlying flow of goods, an element reflected in supply chain planning, delivery and payment processes. From the transaction perspective, the latter mainly take place within the settlement phase and, except for a slight overlap resulting from the exchange of availability information noted above, orders emerging in the contracting phase may trigger off SCM activities. As regards the quality of the relationship, it can be observed that SCM arrangements tend to occur in long-term relationships with a substantial intensity or depth of cooperation. Often, EC tends to produce opposite effects seeing that the costs of switching catalog providers are marginal.

Thus, an analysis of the two concepts – EC and SCM – reveals a complementary relationship with some overlapping. EC concentrates on shaping information and contracting activities (e.g. designing electronic catalogs and matching functions) whereas SCM is primarily concerned with planning processes and the organization of various flows of goods. Specifically, SCM has developed techniques and methods for streamlining the designing, implementing and operation of settlement processes. Indeed, both concepts are bound to have an important impact on day-to-day business [Kalakota/Whinston 1997, 285]: "The integration of electronic commerce and supply chain management is changing the way businesses work internally and work with each other."

6.3   Case Study: EC and SCM at ETA SA

6.3.1   Goals of EC and SCM at ETA SA

'The Swatch Group' is a globally operating producer of watches for brands such as Blancpain, Omega, Rado, Longines, Tissot, Certina and Swatch. The Group consists of a number of individual companies which, inter alia, mainly engage in the production of watch movements and components as well as in research and development. The production of watches for the individual brands is undertaken by various member companies of the Group. ETA SA Fabriques d'Ebauches of Grenchen, Switzerland, employs about 10.000 people worldwide and supplies the movements for watches to all brands of 'The Swatch Group' which, in turn, organize the production and distribution of the finished products. As the world's third largest manufacturer of movements, ETA has over 15 production sites in Switzerland, Germany, France, Thailand, Malaysia and China. Revenues in 1998 exceeded one billion Swiss francs.

In the case of ETA SA, Business Networking makes for increased customer-orientation, improved cost-efficiency, reliability and global presence. Together with the Institute of Information Management at the University of St. Gallen (IWI-HSG), ETA has conceived and already introduced new procedures for the distribution of spare parts which incorporate SCM and EC elements. The ETA case highlights the potential of both strategies for cutting costs and for streamlining customer service processes in a typical business-to-business setting.

6.3.2   Initial Problems at ETA SA

When ETA started its 'business network redesign' project in 1996, there were three main problems that were considered to be of strategic importance: (1) the redesign of the introduction process for new movements, (2) a new distribution strategy for spare parts as well as (3) the installation of a new distribution channel for spare parts. A two-phase project was set up to tackle these challenges: Phase I addressed the reengineering of the supply chain and phase II the introduction of the EC solution.

To start with, a number of customer workshops and a customer relationship analysis were conducted in order to explore networking potentials and problems [cf. Benz et al. 1999]. The main problems reported were:

- Customers, i.e. mainly the different brands within the Swatch Group, were lacking information about the interchangeability of parts (one part may be used in several movements) and comprehensive up-to-date technical information on the movement, assembly information for the production of watches, manuals and specific information on special questions such as necessary stocking etc.

- Specimen movements, spare parts and movement-specific tools were not available as new movements were coming on the market.

- Low level of customer service (ETA-CS) performance due to long cycle times for the repair of movements and the distribution of spare parts and frequent misunderstandings resulting in the delivery of wrong parts.

- Rudimentary information on ETA customers, their sales history concerning spare parts as well as their preferences.

6.3.3   Phase I: Re-engineering the Supply Chain

As shown in Figure 6-2, the distribution of spare parts involves a complex distribution network of warehouses, both inhouse and outside. Each brand orders spare parts from ETA-CS and delivers them to their customers, e.g. 'The Swatch Group'-country organizations (CO) and independent agents. Brands receive the parts from the ETA-CS and store them in their own warehouses. After analyzing the existing supply chain, it was found that there are three major advantages to be gained from direct deliveries to the brand's customers:

1. *Concentration of inventory holding locations at ETA.* Today, ETA had about 12 different levels of inhouse warehouses which were scattered all through the distribution process. A new high-bay warehouse has been installed to eliminate the need for small warehouses. Concentration of inventories has not only reduced overall inventories at ETA but also ensured more efficient stock-keeping, i.e. quick retrieval of necessary parts.

2. *Elimination of warehouses at the brands.* With spare parts delivered directly to the brand's customers, warehouses at the individual brands will become redundant obsolete in some cases and outphasing them will result in reduced inventory costs and improved capacity utilization.

3. *Delivery guarantees for customers*. Eliminating warehouses also entails reduced bufferage within the distribution network. Brands that were reducing
their warehousing capacities insisted that ETA should guarantee specific times
for delivery. So ETA-CS established two distribution channels, Distributions A
only for EC orders, with cycle times of 24 within Switzerland and 120 hours for
the rest of the world, and Distribution B for non-EC orders, with same cycle
times as before, respectively.

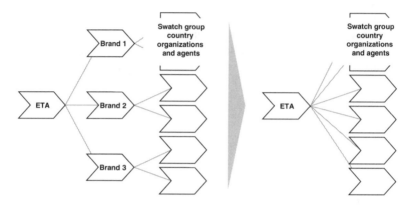

Figure 6-2: Redesign of the Distribution Network at ETA

6.3.4   Phase II: Introduction of a EC Solution

As explained in Chapter 6.2, the main activities of EC are associated with the
design of information and contracting processes. At ETA, orders were traditionally sent via fax or mail to the ETA-CS. Their main problem was that consistent
information on available products was lacking and orders often were for just '40
gears with 14 teeth'. Translating this order into processing terms, i.e. finding out
the relevant article number, was very time consuming for the ETA-CS and it
might take hours to identify the relevant article. After this matching process the
order was finalized and entered into ETA's ERP system.[1] Obviously, incorrect
matches would result in wrong parts being delivered.

The project team identified inconsistent product master data as the main problem
and went about to elaborate a homogeneous master data structure. The master data
homogenization of the collection 1999 (117 movements with about 5'000 artticles)
was finished in November 1999. All articles of the actual collection and all other

---

[1] ERP stands for Enterprise Resource Planning (ERP) and characterizes a company's integrated
transaction and administration system. Prominent examples are systems from Baan, SAP, People-
Soft etc. (cf. Chap. 2.3.1).

movements ETA-CS is responsible for - articles out of production – will be homogenized until beginning of 2001.

Information on products was initially conceived for distribution via CD-ROMs which contained article numbers, part descriptions, and pictures. However, updating in this solution involved some additional effort and order entry was still relying on conventional media, i.e. mail or fax. Therefore, an EC solution was conceived which enabled the integrated support of information and contracting activities via the World Wide Web (see Figure 6-3).

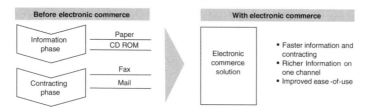

Figure 6-3: Convergence of Information Flow

The ETA Online Shop started in April 1999 with Swiss pilot customers and is available to all customers since December 1999. In the initial phase only selected pilot customers were able to order spare parts this mainly concerned those individual Swatch brands which account for the largest share of ETA's revenues. Once registered in the EC solution, customers can browse through the electronic catalog and obtain specific information about (new) products, prices, discounts, etc. Selected components are added to a shopping basket. The total order amount will be calculated and after choosing a specific payment method (e.g. credit card payment) the order process is completed. An (electronic) order acknowledgement is sent and order tracking will be possible throughout the entire order cycle. The main benefits to be gained from implementing the EC solution are as follows:

1. *Efficiency of information processes for the customer.* The convergence of information in the EC solution (see Figure 6-3) enables customers to obtain all relevant information on existing and new products (prices, technical descriptions, sales conditions, and interchangeability) via one channel. Since the site is maintained centrally, the ETA-CS can easily assure that information is up-to-date and benefit from cost savings in producing and distributing catalogs, price lists and technical documents.

2. *Improved level of customer service.* Additional, previously unavailable, features have been introduced with the EC solution and will yield significantly higher service levels. Such features include the shopping basket, electronic order payment options (credit card payments were unavailable before), technical document downloads and electronic order tracking. Additional functionalities are currently being conceived and will include enhanced customer profiling, indi-

vidual customer shopping baskets, customer communities, frequently-asked-questions databases (FAQ), online complaint management as well as auctions to sell refurbished or old parts.

3. *Efficiency of order processing for ETA SA.* With the EC solution, order processing efficiency has increased remarkably. This has been mainly due to the homogenization of master data which reduces matching efforts and, consequently, eliminates misunderstandings as well. Increased efficiency allows ETA-CS to cope with an increased order volume and enables the personnel to concentrate on intensifying customer relationships (e.g. acquisition of new customers, answering individual questions).

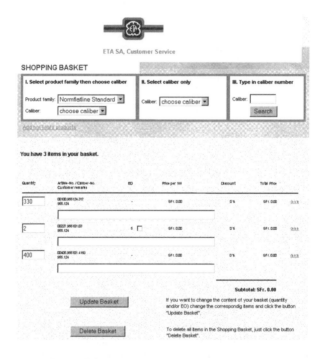

Figure 6-4: Sample Screen of ETA's EC Solution

6.3.5   Complementarity of Concepts and Implementation

The case of ETA SA underlines the complementarity of EC and SCM which was elaborated in Chapter 6.2. Supply chain activities were started by optimizing the flow of physical goods from ETA to the customer. A central aspect was establishing a direct delivery channel as well as enhanced capabilities for monitoring and controlling the distribution processes which has made it possible to offer guaranteed delivery times. The fact that no specific supply chain planning system was implemented goes to show that supply chain performance may be improved even without setting-up complex planning systems.

Direct customer contact has also been accomplished with the EC solution with customers being able to directly browse through ETA's catalog and use the same platform for order entry. Clearly, the main areas of the EC effort were the design of the catalog and the order entry channel. EC implementation was accomplished via a proprietary, tailor-made solution. Linking the ERP and the EC system is first done manually with the integration of both systems being the object of the next step.

The overlapping of the two concepts was manifest from several aspects. First, the attractiveness of the EC solution increased as direct order entry *and* direct delivery became practical possibilities. This was mainly due to the fact that both cycle times and uncertainty of delivery were significantly reduced as a result. Before, the complex warehouse structure and incoherent master data had impeded quick and reliable deliveries. ETA's long tradition in business notwithstanding, the new electronic channel made it possible to obtain distribution structures comparable to Dell's (cf. Chap. 3.2.1) and Cisco's (cf. Chap. 8.1). Second, an analysis of the financial flow resulted in an additional payment method being introduced, i.e. payment by credit card. Third, there are plans now to integrate logistic function-alities from third-party-distributors to track orders through the entire order cycle and to calculate prices including the accurate shipping costs.

6.4   Critical Success Factors at ETA SA

The study of the ETA case revealed a number of critical success factors which were responsible for the success of the company in introducing its Business Net-working solution.

6.4.1   Master Data Management as 'Hidden Success Factor'

Both solutions, SCM and EC, were dependent on the standardization of processes and master data. In the ETA case, this involved identifying the applicable stan-dards for handling orders via the 'customer counter' of the ETA-CS and possible modifications of the existing master data scheme. This led to a far-reaching stan-dardization and maintenance initiative in the area of product and customer master data. As explained earlier, the most time-consuming part of order processing was translating an order into ETA's article numbering system. This concerned mainly the processing of interchangeability information, consolidation of pricing infor-mation (for special packaged quantities) as well as the integrity of article and technical descriptions. Neither of the two concepts directly includes this activity in its scope, but without master data management the benefits described would not have been possible. Therefore, master data management has been recognized as a 'hidden' success factor.

6.4.2   Strategic Alignment with Marketing Strategy

EC and SCM tend to mark a turning point in a company's established marketing strategy in as much as these strategies introduce a new distribution channel with novel functionalities (direct order entry and direct deliver). Interestingly enough, EC initiatives often originate in a company's IT department and SCM on the production side. For this reason, the first step to be undertaken should be to make sure that the marketing department is convinced of the initiative's benefits and strongly believes in the necessity to act.

In the case of ETA SA, the benefits and possibilities of implementing the new distribution channel were clarified with the company's top management when best practice EC solutions from Dell, Cisco and others were demonstrated. An intensive discussion process ensued and the positive effects of the planned solution on the company's marketing as well as on customer's sourcing strategy were identified. As a result, a clearer understanding was obtained of the benefits to be expected, costs and project timescale. As a side effect, it was possible at an early stage of the project to clarify such upcoming questions as security issues and legal aspects of EC.

6.4.3   Reciprocity of Benefits

The first activity on starting the project was to communicate the current status of development work to the partners on the basis of the isolated EC solution (no ERP integration). This provided a pretty clear picture of the scope the solution at this early stage and enabled the partners to assess their specific win-win situation. For this purpose, the project team conducted workshops where win-win situations were elaborated in terms of improved effectiveness (guaranteed delivery times, higher information level, transparent order tracking information, interchangeability information for customers of the EC solution) and higher efficiency (lower order fulfillment costs for ETA SA and cost-saving potentials for the brands' local warehouses). It was decided that the 'selling proposition' for the EC solution should consist in superior supply chain performance, mainly guaranteed delivery times, rather than price incentives.

6.4.4   Common Basis for Communication

As strategies for business networking, EC and SCM are inherently interorganizational in nature. In determining the scope of a joint solution and the degree of synchronization of processes among independent business units, it was important to establish a common basis for communication. At ETA, the previously mentioned SCOR model proved helpful in as much as it aims at improving communication between supply chain partners.[2] SCOR distinguishes multiple analytical levels of which the upper three were used at ETA.

- At level 1, management and relevant supply chain partners jointly elaborated a *business network* that enabled an overview to be provided of the internal and external organizational units for the product groups affected by the solution. Included was an overview of production and distribution locations on ETA's procurement side as well as intermediate storage facilities, distribution centers, wholesalers, retailers and end customer groups on the distribution side. With the aid of this chart, ETA defined which of the distribution levels should have access to the EC solution in the future.

- At level 2, relevant business processes and exchanged outputs were defined using the generic SCOR distribution processes such as 'make-to-stock', 'make-to-order', 'deliver stocked products' and 'deliver made-to-order products' (cf. Chap. 4.3.2). At ETA, this *execution process network* mainly consisted of execution and planning processes. For example, 'plan make' was used to coordinate the order-based production process with the order-based delivery process.

- At level 3, the *process elements* relevant to EC were analyzed and refined. For example, outputs exchanged such as product description, customer inquiries, order acknowledgements, etc. were specified. An important step was the application of the metrics provided in the SCOR model (e.g. lead times, number of perfect orders, etc.) since this forms the basis for measuring the performance of the SCM/EC solution in the future.

SCOR clearly helped in rapidly mapping out processes and in compiling an unambiguous documentation of the future supply chain configuration. However, it turned out that SCOR was conceived for supply chains and, when applied to the modeling of an EC solution, it permitted only delivery processes in the settlement phase to be modeled with the pre-defined elements. Despite its shortcomings in the area of information and contracting activities, SCOR was chosen for the introduction of the EC solution since the 'selling proposition' consisted to a high degree of supply chain performance.

---

[2]   SCOR comprises a standard description for management processes, a framework for relationships among the standard processes, standard metrics to measure process performance, management practices that produce best-in-class performance, and standard alignment to software features and functionality [cf. Supply Chain Council 1998].

6.4.5   Method for Structured Procedure

The ETA project clearly brought out the specifics of Business Networking which are non-technical to a great extent. Business Networking needs strategic management attention and requires organizational standards and rules. Important examples are homogenized master data and clear responsibilities between marketing and IT for the design and operation of the EC solution. Both SCM and EC involved business relations to other members of 'The Swatch Group' that are largely independent. Therefore, hierarchical pressure to participate in the SCM and EC solutions was no viable option to ensure the acceptance for the solutions. Once the internal organizational measures had been initiated, a possible scenario was developed and benefits for potential partners were estimated. Based on these expected benefits pilot partners were convinced to participate in the further development of the EC solution. This mainly involved completing a change request and also offered the possibility of shaping the final solution according to their requirements. After a series of change requests from internal and also from pilot partners the EC-solution was ready to be rolled out to all customers.

Phase 1: SCM	Phase 2: EC
• Homogenization of product master data • Redesign of distribution network: Concentration of existing inventory holding locations • Redesign of warehouse management, e.g. high-bay warehouse • Redesign of supply chain process networks based on common basis for communication	• Strategic alignment with marketing strategy • Homogenization of customer master data, including customer specific discounts in a rebate matrix • Calculation of customer benefits • Communication of customer benefits and selection of pilot partners • Set-up of EC steering committee • Selection of pilot products • Design, plan and implement EC pilot • Collection of change requests • Roll-out EC solution • Enhancement of EC solution (ERP integration)

Table 6-1: Steps Undertaken in Business Networking at ETA

The major steps in the ETA-project are shown in Table 6-1 and were used in the development of a method for Business Networking (cf. Chap. 14). The structured approach is also apt to improve efficiency where further Business Networking processes are to be implemented.

6.5   Conclusions and Next Steps

This Chapter discussed the steps and procedures used in implementing a business-to-business EC solution based on a redesign of the supply chain for industrial products at ETA SA. In executing the EC solution, the supply chain proved a critical element and direct delivery and direct order entry facilitated a direct link to the customer. The performance of the supply chain was, in fact, used as a selling incentive with a view to fostering the diffusion of the EC solution. At the same time, the EC-system was instrumental in improving such supply chain activities as order entry and payment. There are many other aspects, too, that underline the complementarity of EC and SCM, i.e. the flow perspective of SCM versus the transaction perspective of EC.

More importantly, the project also reflects the intricacies of inter-business projects that involve multiple Business Networking strategies. It was crucial for the success of the project that it had the management's support and that not only IT and customer service were involved, but the marketing department, too. As far as external partners are concerned – the individual brands at ETA – here is a case that bears witness to the importance of reciprocity. Creating mutual win-win situations is clearly a sine qua non for the successful diffusion of an inter-business solution. Addressing these challenges and the hidden success factors that became apparent in the course of the project, is a complex task. The method adopted provided a structured procedure model and systematic guidance in identifying roles, problems, success factors, milestones, budgets, and other key elements.

It should be pointed out, however, that work on both the method and the EC/SCM solution is ongoing. Important steps to be undertaken next are to develop an extended cost-benefit analysis and to define metrics to assess the performance of the EC/SCM solution as well as to establish links with customer relationship management functionalities, e.g. complaint management, customer communities or self-information services.

7 Knowledge Enabled Customer Relationship Management

Jens Schulze, Frédéric Thiesse, Volker Bach, Hubert Österle

7.1 Introduction 136
    7.1.1 Business Trend: Customer Centricity 136
    7.1.2 Technology Trend: Tools for Marketing, Sales and
           Service Automation 137

7.2 Case Study: LGT Bank 139

7.3 Managing Customer Knowledge..141
    7.3.1 Knowledge Management 141
    7.3.2 Relationship Marketing...142
    7.3.3 Knowledge Enabled Customer Relationship Management......143

7.4 Towards a CRM Reference Model..144
    7.4.1 Business Processes...145
    7.4.2 Knowledge Structure 148
    7.4.3 Knowledge Infrastructure 150
    7.4.4 Knowledge Measurements...151

7.5 Knowledge in Business Networks..152

7.1   Introduction

The redesign of business processes and the implementation of standard software for enterprise resource planning (ERP) in recent years has led to significant improvements in both process performance and service quality (cf. Chap. 2.3.1). Now that the classic reengineering trend is slowing down, companies have come to realize that efficiency in itself is no longer sufficient if they are to compete for customers in the 21st century. In many markets we are currently witnessing a major move away from market and product centricity towards a complete realignment of business processes in order to integrate with customer processes, which creates additional customer values and finally leads to lasting customer relations. The efforts directed at building and maintaining long-term relationships with customers are usually summarized as 'customer relationship management (CRM)'. CRM represents one of the networking strategies in Business Networking (cf. Chap. 4.3.3) and is driven by both business and technology:

7.1.1   Business Trend: Customer Centricity

Although many companies claim to be customer-oriented, even new services are mostly product-centric, i.e. customers have to adapt to the way a company works but not vice versa. In essence, customer centricity is a business strategy which aims for the complete redesign of a firm's processes to meet customer needs. The main goal of any customer-centric strategy is to solve a customer's problem in its entirety through the creation of a complete solution package containing all the necessary services and products, and to offer it as part of a one-to-one relationship (cf. Chap. 2.3.6).

An example is *Travelocity*, an Internet-based travel agency which integrates a broad range of vacation planning activities in one platform. Instead of booking a flight with airline X, making a room reservation with hotel Y and looking for a car at rental car agency Z, customers are guided through their entire planning process by an Internet application that seamlessly combines all these services (see Figure 7-1).

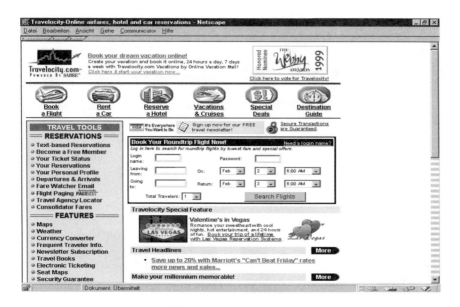

Figure 7-1: Travelocity [www.travelocity.com]

7.1.2 Technology Trend: Tools for Marketing, Sales and Service Automation

Emerging technologies, such as mobile computing and document processing, allow novel applications in the front-office. Sales force representatives have access to transactions and functionalities of the ERP system in their company's headquarter as well as to document repositories and dynamically generated reports. All sales information is available on the road and at the customer's office. Other technologies enable highly sophisticated marketing and service applications, e.g. customer profiling and computer- telephony integration.

For example, the *Siebel Enterprise* software package integrates with existing SAP installations and allows for transaction and document-oriented information processing. Data and documents on accounts, leads, market campaigns etc. can be downloaded to any mobile PC and thus distributed to a company's sales force. The system offers a variety of analysis features and reports on sales activities and customer profiles (see Figure 7-2). Order data can be entered and automatically transferred to an SAP system, where corresponding production processes are triggered.

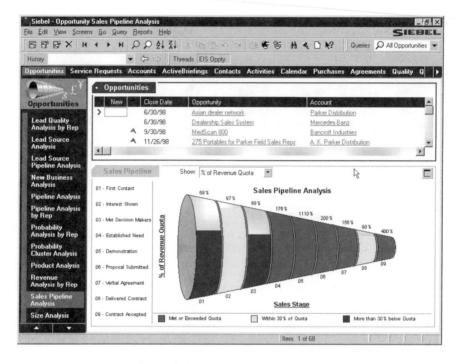

Figure 7-2: Siebel Sales Enterprise [www.siebel.com]

The first step towards CRM in a firm is a complete understanding of customers, their processes, needs and preferences. Processes in the front office are highly unstructured, mostly non-transactional, and are virtually impossible to standardize. Their performance is predominantly influenced by the underlying supply with up-to-date knowledge about products, markets and customers. Therefore the foundation for any customer relationship management initiative is the implementation of a an effective knowledge management infrastructure.

In this paper we outline the relevance of knowledge management techniques to the management of customer knowledge and the redesign of the corresponding business processes. Starting with an analysis of the core processes of CRM, we illustrate the underlying knowledge structures and support processes. We also give an overview of the opportunities for IT support in this context. We regard this framework as a first step towards a reference model for customer relationship management.

The CRM framework described in this paper is based on the results of the research project 'Competence Center for Business Knowledge Management (CC BKM)'. CC BKM is part of the research program 'Business Engineering (BE HSG)' at the Institute of Information Management at the University of St. Gallen (cf. Chap. 1.3).

7.2   Case Study: LGT Bank

The LGT Bank in Liechtenstein is an internationally active private bank. In view of the increasing importance of customer orientation in the banking sector, the bank revised its corporate strategy in 1996 with the aim of changing from a product-driven to a customer-centric organization and thus improving client benefits. Banks must increase their focus on the needs of clients if they are to remain competitive in an environment characterized by the globalization of markets, tighter margins due to increasing competitive pressure and the trend towards concentration in order to utilize synergies. As a result, changes became necessary in the bank's structures and processes and new demands were made on its information systems.

The project team started with an analysis of the sales process and other related processes, i.e. product management and market analysis. The information needs of these processes led to a novel knowledge structure, which could then be mapped with existing information systems and other information sources. New roles and support processes had to be designed, e.g. for the publication of market reports. Finally, a set of additional measurements was defined for process controlling purposes (see Figure 7-3).

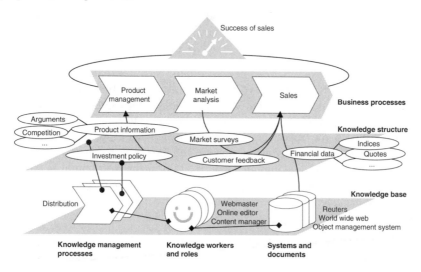

Figure 7-3: Knowledge-oriented Redesign of the Sales Process at the LGT Bank

The bank decided to implement the new concept with an Intranet application and to integrate front and back-office processes via a common information system named the KUNO front system [cf. Kaiser et al. 1998]. The functionality of the applications enables the administration of clients, accounts, custody accounts, portfolios, loans and funds, the processing of orders in the name of the bank or others and the analysis of market positions and trends. Employees no longer have to be specialists for individual products. Instead they have to serve as generalists and must be able to provide clients with sound, comprehensive advice about the bank's complete range of products and services. The KUNO front system is composed of logical modules as depicted in Figure 7-4.

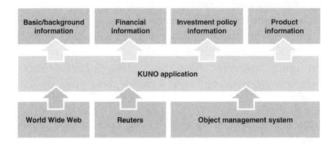

Figure 7-4: Modules of the KUNO Front System

KUNO represents the interface between the bank's sales process and its product management and market analysis processes. Information created by these processes is provided directly via the KUNO front system and called up when required by the client advisor. Conversely, the advisor has the possibility of providing feedback to the product manager and the analyst via the system. The KUNO front system therefore integrates the sales, product management and market analysis processes.

The front system offers quantitative benefits in the field of financial information. So far the bank has maintained approx. 120 Reuters terminals resulting in monthly costs of approx. CHF 500 per connection. Thanks to the integration of information in the front system, the bank expects to reduce the number of Reuters terminals by 50, which would generate savings of about CHF 300,000 per year. The bank also expects to make annual savings of CHF 165,000 in the distribution of printed information material for individual products. In the provision of support for client advisors, the bank hopes to attain substantial capacity savings of up to 30% in the administrative sector.

From the qualitative viewpoint, the client advisor is able to prepare himself far more efficiently for an advisory discussion due to the fact that all the relevant information is integrated under one interface. Moreover, the information is available in electronic form, which substantially simplifies advisory meetings with clients at a location away from the bank because the advisor no longer needs to take large quantities of printed information material with him. For the first time, binding product information is available. Above all, this facilitates the training and familiarization of new employees but also enables clients to be given comprehensive advice in accordance with their actual needs. Placing the responsibility for the information objects within the scope of the staff's work procedures also ensures that they are kept up to date. The client advisor therefore has a 'virtual' expert on call.

7.3   Managing Customer Knowledge

7.3.1   Knowledge Management

Corporate transformation processes take place at the levels of strategy, business processes and information systems [cf. Österle 1995]. From this point of view, instruments for the improved management of knowledge can be categorized as depicted in Figure 7-5:

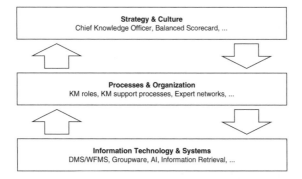

Figure 7-5: Instruments of Corporate Knowledge Management

Strategy

In the area of strategy development, knowledge management belongs to the so-called resource-oriented approaches that began to appear at the beginning of the 1990s as an answer to traditional market-oriented approaches. Instead of a detailed analysis of markets and competitors, the goal of this 'resource-based view of the firm' [cf. Collis/Montgomery 1995] is the development of a unique combination of core competencies [cf. Prahalad/Hamel 1990]. At the same time, corporate knowledge was identified as an important or even crucial strategic resource [cf. Nonaka/Takeuchi 1995]. At the strategic level, therefore, the activities of knowledge management aim for the creation of a corporate culture which will promote and enable the acquisition, maintenance and use of knowledge in all departments of an organization. As a result senior management is supported through the definition of knowledge goals and a set of suitable measurements, analogous to conventional financial indicators.

Business Processes

Nearly all established approaches to corporate knowledge management focus on the introduction of new processes or the improvement of existing ones. Their structure is usually based on a generic phase model (e.g. 'building blocks of knowledge management' [Probst et al. 1999], 'knowledge cycle' [Steier et al. 1997], 'operations on knowledge' [van der Spek/Spijkervet 1997]). This view tends to ignore the fact that the primary objective of knowledge management is not the pointless accumulation of knowledge but its use in the context of specific business processes [cf. van Heijst et al. 1996]. Therefore the central starting point needs to be a business process and consideration of the respective information processing activities. For this purpose, methods for analyzing knowledge needs and flows within business processes are required. Other aspects include the design of support processes for knowledge creation, maintenance, distribution, and also the embedding of the corresponding responsibilities within an organization.

Information Systems

The effects of knowledge management initiatives on the IS infrastructure of an organization are manifold due to the lack of integrated systems for knowledge processing. On the other hand, many software producers use the term 'knowledge management' in order to market DMS, WFMS, groupware and other technologies as suitable IT solutions. A clear distinction between knowledge management-oriented tools and conventional systems is barely discernible and usually depends on the respective application domain [cf. Ware/Degoey 1998].

7.3.2   Relationship Marketing

In several markets, products have become indistinguishable due to their technical and qualitative homogeneity. This development has led to weaker relations between customers and vendors. In many industries the creation of long-term relationships therefore requires integrated problem solutions which include value-added services [cf. Meffert 1998].

Whilst it has long been acknowledged that the fundamental purpose of marketing is the 'getting and keeping' of customers, the truth is that more attention has typically been paid to attracting customers than to keeping them. More recently a recognition has emerged that marketing needs to place, but also to develop processes that will enhance long-term customer loyalty. This viewpoint is the foundation for the development of the concept of relationship marketing, at the heart of which lies the proposition that the fundamental purpose of marketing is the creation and development of long-term, profitable relationships [cf. Christopher/McDonald 1995].

It would be incorrect to think that relationship marketing is a replacement for marketing as it has been practiced to date. It is more a case of broadening and refocusing the marketing concept with the emphasis placed upon strategies to enhance customer retention and loyalty. Some of the major differences in emphasis between the traditional approach, which we label 'transactional', and the 'relationship' focus are shown in Table 7-1.

Transactional Focus	Relationship Focus
• Orientation to single sales	• Orientation to customer retention
• Discontinuous customer contact	• Continuous customer contact
• Focus on product features	• Focus on customer value
• Short time scale	• Long time scale
• Little emphasis on customer service	• High customer service emphasis
• Limited commitment to meeting customer expectations	• High commitment to meeting customer expectations
• Quality is the concern of production staff	• Quality is the concern of all staff

Table 7-1: Shift to Relationship Marketing[1]

7.3.3   Knowledge Enabled Customer Relationship Management

The characteristics of knowledge work have already been discussed intensively in the pertinent literature [cf. Shum 1997] and there is a common understanding of knowledge-oriented processes as a set of activities that depend significantly on past experiences, expert knowledge, information from heterogeneous sources etc. At a high level of abstraction, these can be summarized by the following two attributes [cf. Eppler et al. 1999]:

- *Knowledge intensity.* Since we regard knowledge management as an extension of BPR and KM applications and a complement to ERP software, we use a pragmatic definition of knowledge as the totality of information outside existing ERP information systems. From this point of view knowledge intensity is therefore based on the need for knowledge from heterogeneous, not necessarily computational information sources.

- *Process complexity.* Process complexity implies that extensive knowledge is necessary for the execution of the respective process. This can either be caused by the process's complicated structure or by the absence of clear

---

[1]   [cf. Christopher/McDonald 1995].

structures. Research and development activities are an example of the second category.

Note that there is a strong correlation between these attributes, i.e. processes that combine high complexity with low knowledge intensity or vice versa cannot be found in reality. Thus, we can identify two – usually overlapping – classes of business processes (see Figure 7-6).

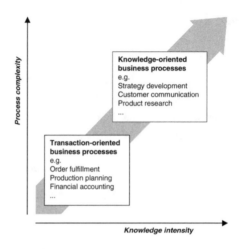

Figure 7-6: Knowledge-oriented Business Processes

As we have demonstrated in the previous chapters, CRM processes can be considered as an example of knowledge-oriented processes as described above. Furthermore, several surveys indicate that the management of customer knowledge is of great concern for most industries (cf. [Delphi 1997], [KPMG 1998], [Murray/Myers 1997], [Skyrme/Abidon 1997]) and also an important factor for the success of knowledge management projects. We can therefore expect further research to be relevant for both science and practice, and it should result in a CRM-specific reference model.

7.4   Towards a CRM Reference Model

Reference models contain consolidated problem solutions which have been derived from empirical knowledge [cf. Reiter 1999]. Typical examples of reference models are process models, IT architecture models, project models and so on. A process-oriented reference model for knowledge management (KM) comprises the following elements [Bach et al. 1999]:

- Descriptions of knowledge-intensive *business processes*.

- *Knowledge structures* and *knowledge flows* on which these processes are based.

- A knowledge infrastructure which consists of *systems and documents, knowledge roles* and *support processes*.

- *Knowledge measurements* for knowledge-oriented controlling and leadership.

Advantages of such reference models include

- *Quality.* A reference model can be used as a base for precise project drafts. Since the model can be regarded as a description of an optimal KM solution, it also ensures that all relevant aspects of a KM implementation are taken into account.

- *Cost efficiency.* The reference model enables more efficient project planning and project control activities. It prevents the project team from doing the same work twice or wasting time with unnecessary tasks.

- *Best practices.* Reference models allow standardized documentation and the reuse of experiences from former projects. They can also be used as a tool for the creation of process or architecture reference models.

- *Common language.* The corresponding method manuals guarantee that all project members have the same technical and methodical background and are able to communicate from the very start.

7.4.1 Business Processes

The entire CRM macro process consists of three distinct subprocesses, the marketing process, the sales process and the service process (see Figure 7-7). These subprocesses can be distinguished by the target group at which their activities are directed [cf. Stender/Schulz-Klein 1998]:

- *Marketing process.* The target group consists of an anonymous market, identifiable prospective customers and existing customers of an enterprise. In the case of an initial personal contact between a representative of the market and the enterprise, the anonymous representative becomes a prospective customer. This contact event connects the marketing process to the sales process.

- *Sales process.* Activities of the sales process are directed at prospective customers and existing customers only.

- *Service process.* Once delivery has been completed, the activities of the service process are triggered and are then directed exclusively at existing customers.

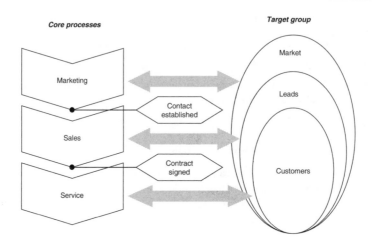

Figure 7-7: Core Processes of CRM

Each process consists of a set of various tasks which can be assigned to one of the following management layers (see Table 7-2):

- *Output management* includes all planning and monitoring tasks that refer to a company's marketing, sales and service activities as a whole, e.g. market segmentation and sales planning.

- *Process coordination* tasks are required for the management of specific process instances, e.g. call planning and field service coordination.

- *Transaction/information handling* summarizes all activities that refer to CRM knowledge bases and transaction-oriented information systems, e.g. information retrieval, contract management etc.

	Marketing	Sales	Service

Output Management	• Product management
	  - Product analysis
	  - Life cycle analysis
	  - Portfolio management
	• Market segmentation
	• Market analysis
	• Campaign planning &
	  analysis
		• Sales planning
		• Sales analysis
		  - Pipeline analysis
		  - Regional analysis
		• Call center management
		  - Call list assembly
		  - Call statistics
		• Sales force management
		  - Territory assignment
		  - Activity analysis
			• Service planning
			• Problem analysis
			• Customer analysis

Process Coordination	• Campaign coordination
	  - Event planning
	• Market research
	• Coordination
	  - Call planning
		• Call process management
		  - Call planning scripting
		• Time management
		  - Group scheduling
		  - To-do lists
		  - Activity reporting
			• Incident assignment
			• Escalation
			• Field service coordination
			• Time management
			• Group scheduling
			  - To-do lists
			  - Activity reporting

Transaction / Information Handling	• Customer profiling
	• Product configuration
	• Information retrieval
	  - Markets
	  - Branches
	  - Competitors
	  - Products
		• Contact handling
		• Account management
		  - Proposal
		• Generation
		• Contract
		• Generation
		  - Order entry
		  - Account history retrieval
		• Information retrieval
		  - Markets
		  - Branches
		  - Competitors
		  - Products
			• Guarantee / service
			• Contract handling
			• Solution development
			• Spare part handling

Table 7-2: Tasks of the CRM Processes

The three CRM processes can be assigned to the four stages of the customer buying cycle. From the recognition of customers needs, via product configuration and price information, purchase handling through to service and support, the customer buying cycle reflects all possible contact points between a company and its customers (see Figure 7-8).

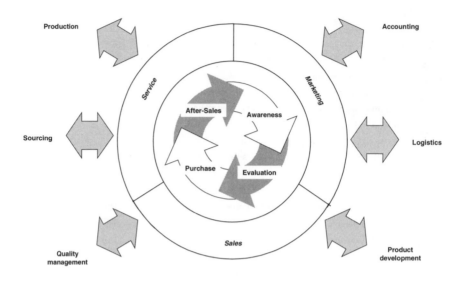

Figure 7-8: Customer Buying Cycle and CRM Reference Model

7.4.2   Knowledge Structure

The design of a KM solution for the CRM processes presented requires in-depth analysis of the underlying knowledge structures. This includes both static and dynamic aspects, i.e. relations between knowledge repositories and a process must be considered as well as knowledge flows between a set of processes. The knowledge needs of the three CRM processes can be distinguished using the following categories:

- *Markets & competitors.* Market news, strategies and products of competitors, market analysis reports etc.

- *Customers.* Contact data, the customer's markets and processes, correspondence etc.

- *Orders & contracts.* Past and current orders and contracts, sales managers responsible, production and delivery status etc.

- *Products.* Data sheets, product configurations, current product research projects etc.

- *Problems & solutions.* Past and current complaints, best practices for solutions, expert maps etc.

Linking these knowledge categories with activities from the CRM processes results in a conceptual knowledge architecture. In a next step, this view must be extended by a physical layer which contains the actual sources that feed the described knowledge sets. The list of information systems that are relevant for CRM includes a variety of sources, ranging from classic ERP software, additional CRM applications (e.g. sales force automation systems), external sources (e.g. WWW, Reuters) to document management systems and data warehouses (see Figure 7-9).

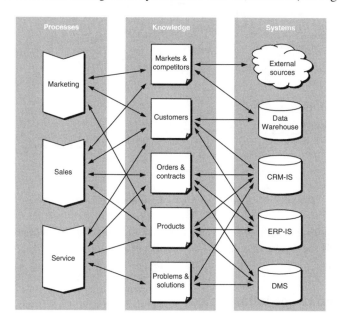

Figure 7-9: CRM Knowledge Repositories

Besides these knowledge repositories, we also need to identify and model knowledge flows between processes in order to optimize knowledge creation and reuse. This analysis is not limited to CRM processes but rather illustrates the relationships with other processes within an organization (see Figure 7-10). It also helps us find 'missing links' between certain activities, e.g. the flow of knowledge about typical complaints from customer service to quality management and back to product development might prove extremely useful for the continuous improvement of a company's products. Another example is the flow of knowledge from customer service to the sales process, where a company can reuse information about customer-specific needs in order to sell additional services or products.

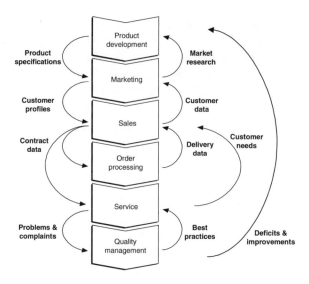

Figure 7-10: Knowledge Flows Between Business Processes

The two resulting diagrams serve as a basis for the creation of a suitable IS infrastructure and the design of a set of KM support processes.

7.4.3   Knowledge Infrastructure

IT Support

IT support for CRM processes includes a broad range of KM technologies and systems, such as:

- *Data warehouse/data mining.* One of the most important reasons for implementing a data warehouse (DW) is the possibility of analyzing the customer information hidden in vast amounts of operational data. Market segmentation and customer profiling are two typical tasks of the marketing process that can be supported by DW tools.s

- *Sales force automation.* Systems for sales force automation (SFA) are designed to increase the effectiveness of sales representatives by integrating opportunity management systems, marketing encyclopedias, product configurators and team selling functions across multiple distribution channels. Their purpose is to support the expanded role of the salesperson as sales project coordinator, linking various departments of an enterprise and its information systems in order to satisfy the needs of the customer [cf. Siebel 1996].

- *Document management/optical archives.* During personal customer contact, it is necessary to access many different documents, such as product descriptions, electronic forms, correspondence and so on. All documents should be up to date and must be available as quickly as possible. In addition, modification and distribution of documents must be possible, e.g. if an existing contract should be adapted and the printed document must immediately be handed out to the customer.

- *Workflow management.* Standardized and repetitive activities within the CRM processes can be automated using workflow management systems (WFMS). Typical examples are complaint handling and technical field service tasks.

- *Information retrieval.* As we have illustrated, CRM processes are based on a variety of heterogeneous knowledge repositories. Information retrieval techniques can be used in order to find and reuse the knowledge from past experiences stored in these repositories, e.g. knowledge bases for customer sales and support that contain processed requests and associated activities.

Other examples include artificial intelligence techniques (e.g. case-based reasoning), Internet technology for the integration of external information sources and skill databases. As already mentioned in Chapter 4.3, there is a strong interrelationship between CRM and electronic commerce. CRM not only supports traditional CRM processes but also allows novel applications, such as Web self-service, customer surveys by e-mail and product configuration, on the Internet which are closely related to electronic commerce solutions.

Knowledge Roles and Support Processes

Besides IT, building a functional knowledge structure also requires the implementation of support processes for knowledge acquisition, filtering, distribution and maintenance. These processes must be designed in order to provide business processes with information and keep knowledge bases up to date. Support processes are associated with knowledge roles, e.g. knowledge editors for the design and maintenance of product data sheets, knowledge scouts for the filtering of information from external sources etc.

7.4.4 Knowledge Measurements

As with other business processes, CRM processes require a set of measurements in order to monitor their performance and efficiency. These measurements include conventional indices (number of fulfilled orders, revenues per sales representative etc.) as well as knowledge-specific indices (number of contributions to the service knowledge base, time reduction for information retrieval etc.).

7.5   Knowledge in Business Networks

Against a background of virtually indistinguishable products and services, the value of long-term customer relationships is destined to become a critical factor for many businesses in the 21st century. Placing the customer at the center of all corporate activities requires innovative concepts for customer relationship management. Newly designed marketing, sales and service processes require a mixture of process innovations, including instruments, such as multi-channel management, Internet self-service, customer profiling methods etc.

As we have demonstrated, knowledge can be regarded as the foundation for the creation of relations between a firm and its customers covering the whole buying process (see Figure 7-11). CRM processes are highly knowledge-oriented business processes, which makes them suitable for the application of knowledge management techniques. Knowledge management should therefore be considered as a crucial aspect of a Business Networking strategy.

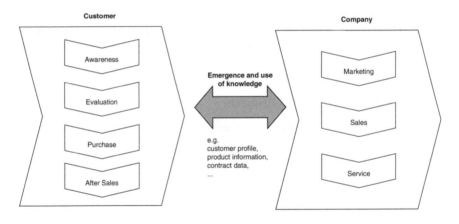

Figure 7-11: Knowledge in Business Networks

Part 3

Information System Concepts

Part One: **Building the Foundation**
Chapter 2: Enterprise in the Information Age
Chapter 3: The Networked Enterprise

Part Two: **Business Concepts**
Chapter 4: Strategies for Business Networking
Chapter 5: Business Networking Lessons Learned:
            Supply Chain Management at Riverwood
            International
Chapter 6: Electronic Commerce and Supply Chain
            Management at 'The Swatch Group'
Chapter 7: Knowledge-enabled Customer Relationship
            Management

Part Three: **Information System Concepts**
Chapter 8: Future Application Architecture for the
            Pharmaceutical Industry
Chapter 9: Overview on Supply Chain Management
            Systems
Chapter 10: Electronic Commerce in the Procurement of
            Indirect Goods
Chapter 11: Templates: Standardization for Business
            Networking
Chapter 12: eServices for Integrating eMarkets

Part Four: **Key Success Factors**
Chapter 13: Key Success Factors for Business Networking Systems
Chapter 14: Towards a Method for Business Networking
Chapter 15: Application of the Business Networking Method at SAP
Chapter 16: Architecture Planning for Global Networked Enterprises

8 Future Application Architecture for the Pharmaceutical Industry

Thomas Huber, Rainer Alt, Vladimir Barak, Hubert Österle

8.1 Introduction – New Business Models Are Emerging..........................156

8.2 From Business Model to Application Architecture............................157

8.3 Future Business in the Pharmaceutical Industry 159
    8.3.1 Elements of the Business Model..160
    8.3.2 Relevance of the Seven Trends for the Pharmaceutical
    Industry 162

8.4 Application Architecture of the Information Age 164
    8.4.1 Flexibility..165
    8.4.2 Networking - Capability of Integration....................................165
    8.4.3 Standardization 166

8.5 Components of the Application Architecture.....................................166
    8.5.1 Future Application Architecture Areas 166
    8.5.2 'Extended' Make-or-Buy Decision 168
    8.5.3 Application Architecture Components.......................................170

8.6 Summary and Outlook 173

8.1   Introduction – New Business Models Are Emerging

As described in Chapter 2 profound changes are taking place in the way business is being done in the information age. An excellent example is provided by Cisco, the leading supplier of Internet-equipment, such as routers, switches and the like. Sales amounting to some USD 8 billion. highlight that only few companies have better understood the far-reaching management consequences of new technologies than Cisco. The company has been in the front line whenever it came to transforming management practices through the use of the new technologies. Cisco is thoroughly organized as a network. Existing and prospective customers, suppliers, other business partners and employees are tightly interlinked. This year, Cisco expects to sell products for more than USD 5 billion (more than half of its total sales) via the Internet. Cisco's Business Networking solution links the systems of suppliers, contract manufacturers and assemblers to Cisco's production processes. To the outside world, i.e. to customers, Cisco appears as a single enterprise. Through the Cisco Intranet, the contract partners directly process the orders placed by Cisco's customers and deliver the selection of items ordered directly to the buyer, frequently without Cisco seeing the items at all. Outsourcing of 70% of production has enabled Cisco to boost its sales four times without the need for additional facilities and, on top of this, Cisco has succeeded in shortening the time to market for new products by two thirds. At the same time, seven out of ten customer requests for technical assistance are dealt with electronically; and this at high degrees of customer satisfaction. The consistent utilization of the network for its after-sales service has made it possible for Cisco to save more money than its biggest competitor spends on research and development [cf. Byrne 1998].

The Cisco example clearly shows that the economy is in the process of radical change (e.g. [Naisbitt 1994], [Laszlo 1997], [Byrne 1998], Chap. 2.3). Today, the environment of international companies is marked by globalization and individualization of products and services, specializing and networking of companies, more complex technologies, shorter product life cycles and increased competition in many industries (cf. Chap. 2.2). In face of these developments it is no longer sufficient for companies to pursue a policy of small steps to improve their performance in the areas of critical success factors, such as quality, costs and speed. Instead achieving repeated quantum leaps is the challenge. Furthermore, the ongoing reduction in vertical integration and concentration on core competencies have led to a higher degree of international division of labor.[1] Cooperations and strategic alliances are being formed which call for enhanced inter-enterprise coordination of processes (cf. Chap. 3).

On the one hand, these general economic developments dictate the requirements to be addressed by the technological infrastructure of enterprises while, on the other

---

[1] An explanation provides the theory of comparative cost advantages [cf. Porter 1992a] or for greater detail [cf. Caves et al. 1990].

hand, it takes the developments in the technology landscape to make them possible. It is primarily the developments in the fields of information and communication technologies that are not only changing the way business is being done but are also causing paradigm shifts in the organization. They are ultimately transforming the industrial society into the information society [cf. Österle 1995] (see Figure 8-1).

Figure 8-1: Eras of Change

8.2 From Business Model to Application Architecture

"The bridge to the 21ˢᵗ century is under construction, and the only way we're going to be able to build it quickly and correctly is if we understand the technological challenges ahead of us" [Millett 1997].

The development of a future application architecture presupposes an understanding of the future business model, the *business model of the information age* (cf. Chap. 2). A certain vision of future strategies and processes is critical to identify the systems which support those processes. Conversely, it takes an analysis of current trends in the areas of management and technology for a vision of future business models to be obtained (see Figure 8-2).

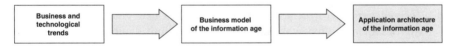

Figure 8-2:Trends Leading to the Application Architecture

Since some of the central business and management trends (e.g. globalization, specialization, virtualization) have already been mentioned earlier, this Chapter focuses on developing an application architecture for the information age. This architecture represents an implementation of the business model of the information age (cf. Chap. 3.5.1) at the IS/IT level. In the following the architecture will be elaborated and illustrated with the technological trends and examples which are especially relevant to the pharmaceutical industry.

An investigation carried out by the Battelle Institute [cf. Battelle 1998] highlights the general development of technologies. The ten technology-driven development are:[2]

1. *Affordable home-based health care.* Market forces are shifting health care from hospitals and HMO's to private homes.

2. *Personalized consumer products.* Many mass-produced products for mass markets will not be competitive in the 21st century.

3. *Convergence of technology in the home.* In the next ten years, the home will be the place of convergence for private and public lives.

4. *Protecting the environment and natural resources.* Easily accessible resources are now largely tapped out, so further growth will come from the smart management of remaining resources and our ability to use alternatives.

5. *Human interfaces.* As more complicated technology floods the home and the workplace, consumers will demand interfaces that go the next step beyond 'user-friendly'.

6. *Nutritional health.* Technologies are being developed now to engineer natural foods that will be packed with more vitamins, protein, other nutrients.

7. *Mobile energy.* The automotive industry's needs for alternative mobile power sources are obvious. In 10 years, many more cars, though not a majority, will operate on alternative-fuel systems.

8. *Micro-security.* Technology's security challenge will shift from national security – protecting nations from invading armies or missiles - to personal and community security.

9. *The renewed infrastructure.* New materials and new construction methods will be required to renew the infrastructure with limited public funding.

10. *Global business competition.* To achieve business growth in this environment, companies will have to improve and expand their efforts at finding technology, acquiring it and putting it to work around the world.

---

[2] The developments referred to here and in the following chapter should be looked upon as examples which are intended to demonstrate trends rather than attempt precise forecasts and dating. Predictions like those of Battelle are also available from other institutions (e.g. Gartner Group or IDC, International Data Corporation, http://idcresearch.com).

8.3   Future Business in the Pharmaceutical Industry

There is little doubt that the trends described above will fundamentally change business processes, rules and players. Specific, high-impact factors for the pharmaceutical industry are:

- Globalization and regionalization of certain business processes[3],

- Cost pressure from government authorities (health care authorities),

- Time and cost-intensive development processes with shorter product life cycles,

- Shifting of selling and marketing activities from bulk buyers and hospitals to the medical practitioners and even the individual patients, and

- Concentration and optimization of manufacturing and administration processes.

On their way to the information age, companies will have to radically review their value proposition, strategic positioning, and organization. An industry-specific business model facilitates these activities. On each of the seven developments (cf. Chap. 2.3) we can distinguish two perspectives (Figure 8-3):

- *Business view.* The business view of future developments analyzes the opportunities and risks as well as the changes caused by developments described to the structures of a company's organization and operations. The pharma-specific business view of the business model of the information age will be discussed in Chapter 8.3.2.

- *IS/IT-view.* The IS/IT view focuses on the technical implementation of the developments. The emphasis here is on the analysis of techniques, tools and applications that help to transform the seven foreseeable developments into profitable business solutions. For a discussion of the IS/IT view of the business model of the information age (cf. Chap. 8.4).

---

[3]   Globalization, e.g. in the areas of finance, controlling, planning and R&D processes, and, partly, the production processes; regionalization, e.g. in the areas of selling and distribution processes and some certain production processes.

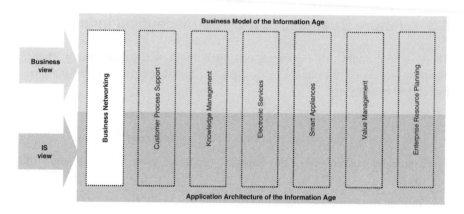

Figure 8-3: Views on the Business Model of the Information Age

8.3.1   Elements of the Business Model

In the business model of the information age, information, services and products are systematically sourced from external partners. Existing and, above all, emerging communication media (e.g. e-mail, phone, message, video, EDI, receipt, net operation, chat room services) and market services (e.g. information, news, payment, directory, master data, public key, broker services; cf. 4.3.2) will support both the internal and external processes. The entirety of these services may be reduced to the mental construct of a 'business bus' (see Figure 8-4 and Chap. 2.3.4).

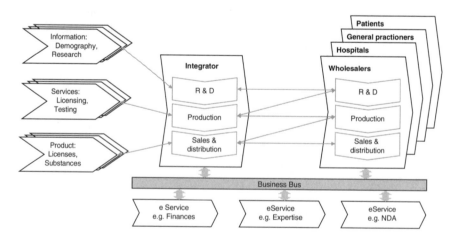

Figure 8-4: New Business Model for the Pharmaceutical Industry

Figure 8-4 shows the business model of the information age as applied to the pharmaceutical industry. Despite a great variety of information, services and products are obtained from outside partners, the pharmaceutical companies are still relying on a (horizontally) very wide basis. From R&D through procurement, warehouse management and production to marketing and sales, many activities are still sited inhouse. Table 8-1 depicts areas where pharmaceutical companies are already linked-up with outside partners.

Area	Relations to/for
Research	• In-licensing: licenses/patents on substances from outside research partners • Information services • Cooperations with research partners • Inter-divisional networks for new products
Development	• In-licensing: licenses for products from outside research partners • Clinical tests • 'Virtual Company' in development • Regulatory authorities (NDA) • Expertise network
Marketing	• Purchase of information (competitors/demography) • Onward development of products • Customer network (for various types: hospitals, whole-salers, general practitioners) • Electronic commerce (Internet presence)
Production & Distribution	• Outsourcing of certain process steps • Suppliers network (for production components)
Finance	• Regional shared services • Relations with finance service providers

Table 8-1: Business Networking Relations in the Pharmaceutical Industry

One of the questions arising relates, for instance, to what role the companies will be playing within a future health-care network. The companies may perfectly well operate in central role within such a network. They may act as the vendor of the health care process (i.e. operate as a clearing center in the health-care process as shown in). Such strategic decisions will directly influence the application architecture of the enterprises, since the information systems act as the central enablers for such networks.

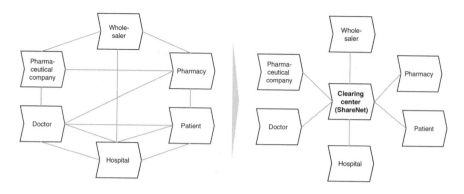

Figure 8-5: Clearing Centers in the Pharmaceutical Landscape

8.3.2   Relevance of the Seven Trends for the Pharmaceutical Industry

The six out of the seven trends of the business model will have direct effects on the future application architecture:

1. *Business Networking.* *"Inter-corporate networks and inter-corporate computing are fundamentally changing worldwide patterns of commerce"* [Martin et al. 1995]. As discussed earlier in the introductory chapter, many of the current developments in the economy and in management are pointing towards a higher degree of networking between enterprises. Since these developments are IT enabled, Business Networking forms the first and decisive pillar in the business model of the information age on which the other six aspects are more or less directly built on. Added to this is the fact that pharmaceutical companies are devoting more attention to identifying their role in a networked economy (e.g. in the areas of R&D, production or distribution) and that the information systems or rather the application architecture of these enterprises will be implemented by such components as APS/SCM and electronic commerce (cf. Chap. 8.4).

2. *Customer Process Support.* The alignment of internal to customer processes has various consequences for a pharmaceutical company. Its ultimate customer, for instance, may not just want to buy some medicine but may look to it for full coverage of his or her health process. This would include diagnosis, treatment, advice, alternatives, insurance etc. If possible, he or she would prefer to have all these services from a single source. Obviously, we are at present still far from being able to offer such a service. But as far as the comparability and the ordering of medicines are concerned, there are indeed a first few online pharmacies engaged in this business sector. A typical example is PlanetRx [www.planetrx.com]. Aside from providing the possibility of com-

paring and ordering medicines online (including medicines obtainable on pre-scription), vitamins, health food or medicinal appliances, the company's of-fering also includes advice and the latest health information. The customer centricity concept will in the future application architecture be represented by the component CRM or SFA (cf. Chap. 8.4).

3. *Knowledge Management.* Knowledge management is one of the most impor-tant factors in the R&D area of pharmaceutical companies. Pfizer Inc. (Viagra), for instance, has had all its R&D documents digitalized and, inci-dentally, is sending these also electronically to the food & drug administration (FDA) which in the USA has to approve all medicines. In the past, this in-volved the submittal of large amounts of paper and whenever questions were raised on the part of the FDA, it was necessary to sift through piles of paper-work by hand. Today, Pfizer uses Internet technologies in this area and has been able to cut the time for the approval process by half [cf. Hamm/Stepanek 1999]. A separate component is envisaged in the future application architec-ture to support knowledge management (cf. Chap. 8.4).

4. *Electronic Services.* Companies will have to decide which Business Net-working processes they intend to handle internally and which will be procured on the market (cf. Chap. 4.3.2). According to Chapter 2.3.5, we will refer to the latter as electronic services (eServices). An example of an already existing eService in the health sector is ShareNet [www.sharenet.org] which operates an EDI platform for the processing of electronic transactions (exchange of patient data, billings, etc.). The clearing center service lets participating com-panies exchange information without having to implement individual EDI links between themselves. Since eServices are sourced from the market, they are not included in the future application architecture. Nevertheless, they are an important element of the future business model (cf. Chap. 8.3.2).

5. *Smart Appliances.* In the area of the intelligent appliances, mobile phones, electronic agenda, Internet, TV, etc. are rapidly merging. These technologies inherit multiple potentials, for example, a patient to could be told electroni-cally to take his or her medicine, and infrared interfaces could be used to transmit pulse beat, blood pressure, etc. Diagnosis instruments could be con-nected via the Internet with provider systems and a patient could have the necessary medicines delivered as required. The intelligent home concept re-fers to the developments in the private homes and would not be found directly in the future application architecture of the enterprises. However, enterprises would have to be prepared to communicate with their customers through dif-ferent channels.

6. *Enterprise Resource Planning.* Contrary to previous business process redes-ign approaches, reengineering in the business model of the information age differs as the challenge is to (re)design complete networks rather than internal processes. Online, realtime, integration of customers, suppliers and external

service providers are the key words which are relevant in this context. Tough competition continues to force companies in many industries to optimize their internal business processes. To this end, ERP systems will continue to be used in the future. Therefore, they form an important component in the future application architecture, too. Apart from the classical ERP systems, there are two other components which will be increasingly resorted to in order to improve processes: data warehouses and Master Data Management applications. The former concentrate on consolidating data from the different – mostly heterogeneous – ERP systems. The latter contain the key data of all parts of the enterprise will be and contribute to vital standardization in business processes. An important consequence will be the streamlining of communications among internal ERP systems.

8.4   Application Architecture of the Information Age

Webster's Dictionary defines architecture as the art or science of building. Indeed, developing an application architecture is some form of art since trends in the extremely fast-moving IT industry are extremely hard to anticipate. However, this is definition is of little use in our context. Therefore, the following definition of application architecture [cf. Tibbetts 1995] has been adopted: Application architecture describes the individual technical components (application types) of a corporate information system as well as the relations (interfaces) between these components. In the first place, an application architecture for the information age has to meet the challenges emerging from the business model of the information age. For example, companies, such as Wal-Mart or Amazon.com, have succeeded in strengthening their competitiveness significantly by managing the flow of goods and information through all stages of the value-added process. The management of these relations forms the core of *Business Networking* which comprises the optimization of planning, implementation and monitoring of the value-added processes beyond corporate boundaries as well as the increasing customer-orientation. Both efficiency and effectiveness of Business Networking are determined by the degree to which information (e.g. on required planning data, orders, controlling information, etc.) is accessible in the whole network of partners. The Business Networking capabilities of existing systems still have to be enhanced and a number of standard software applications are available which better meet these requirements than classical ERP systems. Examples are advanced planning and scheduling systems (APS), customer relationship management systems and electronic commerce applications. Some of these have been brought on the market by the established ERP vendors (e.g. SAP's Advanced Planning and Optimization - APO - module), others by newcomers that have not been present on the ERP market (e.g. i2, Manugistics, Siebel or Harbinger). The main questions which emerge for designing the new application architecture are:

- Which requirements have future application architectures to meet?

- What applications support internal and interorganizational processes?

- How can new applications be integrated into existing architectures?

Two factors that future application architectures have to meet follow from the discussions in the preceding chapters. These are: flexibility, networking, and standardization.

8.4.1   Flexibility

A necessary feature of an application architecture of the information age is its flexibility to adapt itself to constantly and rapidly changing environmental conditions. Relevant environmental conditions are:

- *Changes in the processes.* Globalization and specialization of enterprises are ongoing processes. News about mergers and acquisitions, joint ventures or outsourcing continue to make the headlines in the business press. There are no signs of consolidation in the foreseeable future. Therefore, it is crucial that application architectures should define corporate information systems in a way to render them capable of supporting constantly changing processes.

- *Changes in the IS/IT domain.* The rapid technological developments in the field of the information and communication technologies are only very difficult to predict. On the one hand, the definition of the architecture should be sufficiently precise to serve as a blueprint for an enterprise but, on the other hand, it should be open enough to permit any future IT developments to be taken advantage of.

A major benefit of flexible application architectures is the improved coordination of disparate current and upcoming IT projects. In this process, the architecture blueprint establishes a set of principles for the IT projects [cf. Metagroup 1998]. In addition, such a set of principles permits an evaluation of the individual projects for their importance in realizing the planned architecture.

8.4.2   Networking - Capability of Integration

Both the specialization and the globalization of enterprises call for a higher degree of networking between the companies and their customers and suppliers. This is why high levels of networkability are necessary in the information age (cf. Chaps. 3 and 5). For instance, Heineken (USA) stated that its new SCM system has halved delivery times. Instead of having a Heineken salesman call, big distributors now log on Heineken's system to update their planning data online [cf. Stein 1997]. The key to realizing modern forms of cooperation is in the integration of information flows along a supply chain. An efficient cooperation calls for processes that are automated to a maximum extent. However, automated coordination of processes is possible only if the systems supporting these processes are highly integrated with internal integration forming the basis for external integration. A requirement of highly integrated (internal) systems is for standardization of business objects (cf. Chap. 11.2). At a technical level, message-based solutions have been variously recommended (cf. [Jonsson 1998], [Metagroup 1997]) to connect information systems. Clearly, a change is occuring from the classical EDI messaging types, such as EDIFACT or STEP and proprietary networks (WAN, LAN), towards the more flexible Internet-standards (e.g. XML).

8.4.3 Standardization

As described in Chapter 2, standards significantly reduce the coordination needs between trading partners and, at the same time, provide the basis for integrated information flows. Internet standards, such as HTML, SMTP or TCP/IP, have been important enablers for the development of electronic commerce. Only the availability of these general accepted, formal specifications for communication between heterogeneous information systems has permitted the efficient integration of the information flows between suppliers, producers, customers and supporting service providers. Standardization facilitates the transfer of information between the individual system elements of corporate information systems. From an economic perspective, standardization leads to reduced information costs and enhanced information value. However, full standardization of the system elements would restrict heterogeneity and, consequently, might result in a less than optimum support for the user. In other words, pervasive standardization would entail opportunity costs resulting from sub-optimal support of the users (or processes) [cf. Buxmann 1996].

8.5   Components of the Application Architecture

8.5.1   Future Application Architecture Areas

Based on a number of workshops the following 22 basic areas have been identified which reflect the activities which have to be supported in multi-national companies. These activities are always important, even though individual applications and the distribution of these applications among business partners and systems are subject to change. The areas are:

- *Development.* Applications and services supporting the development process, e.g. CAD, product data management applications and graphic design tools.

- *Research.* Applications and services supporting the research process, e.g. CAD, graphic design tools and statistical applications.

- *Demand planning.* Applications and services permitting an as accurate as possible planning of customer demand, e.g. SAP's i2 or APO.

- *Requirements planning.* Applications and services permitting supply planning, e.g. SAP's APO.

- *Production planning.* Applications and services supporting production planning, e.g. ERP systems.

- *Procurement management.* Applications and services to manage the procurement of materials for production processes, e.g. ERP systems.

- *Inventory management.* Applications and services supporting materials management, e.g. SAP's R/3 module for materials management (MM).

- *Production.* Applications and services supporting the production processes, e.g. SAP's R/3 production planning module (PP).

- *Distribution / transport.* Applications and services to handle distribution and transport, e.g. parts of SAP's R/3 sales and distribution module (SD).

- *After-sales service.* Applications and services for after-sales processes.

- *Human resources.* Applications and services supporting the management of personnel data.

- *Payroll accounting.* Applications and services to process payroll accounts, e.g. payroll services provided by ADP.

- *Accounts payable administration.* Applications and services for the administration of accounts payable.

- *Accounts receivable administration.* Applications and services for the administration of accounts receivable.

- *Internal/external financial accounting.* Applications and services to handle the internal and external financial accounting, e.g. SAP's R/3 FI module.

- *Desktop purchasing.* Applications and services permitting individual employees to order indirect articles on their own initiative.

- *Sales.* Applications and services to handle sales processes, e.g. SD modules.

- *Executive information.* Executive information systems (EIS) concentrate on the graphical processing and manipulation of data, e.g. Seagate's HOLOS.

- *Groupware*. Applications and services, such as Lotus Notes or Microsoft's Outlook.

- *Document management*. Applications and services for the management of documents in different formats and distributed environments

- *Data standardization*. Applications and services for the standardization of master data for customers, products, materials or accounts.

- *Data collections*. Data warehouse applications and services, e.g. SAP's Business Warehouse.

The consistent use of the terminology, applications or services is intended to suggest that, in the future, many of these areas need not necessarily be covered by a company's own applications and that the functionality required can be bought from a service provider instead.

8.5.2   'Extended' Make-or-Buy Decision

For each of the application areas identified above, a company will have to make two decisions. First of all, it will have to decide whether it wants to build the necessary applications inhouse (make) or rather employ a vendor to supply the required functionality as a service (buy). The second decision is on whether it wants to have the functionality standardized on a corporate level or allow decentralized decisions from the individual divisions. Standardization in this context relates both to the processes and the data (especially the master data) that are to be adopted (see Figure 8-6). There are no hard and fast rules and a company's decision will essentially depend on its strategic concepts in designing its own processes and positioning them in a network.

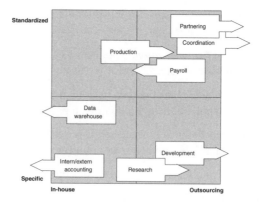

Figure 8-6: Example for 'Extended' Make-or-Buy Decision

Nowadays it is already possible for enterprises to buy quite a number of services from external providers. Table 8-2 shows a list of such services with individual services being enumerated in the rows of the table. Listed in the columns of the table are the 22 application architecture areas. This permits the services to be related to the individual application architecture areas (gray fields). These relations provide guidance in identifying the possible uses of the services. The ultimate combination can only be decided individually for each situation.

	Development	Research	Demand Planning	Requirements Planning	Production Planning	Procurement Management	Inventory Management	Production	Distribution/Transport	Service	HR	Payroll	Accounts Payable	Accounts Receivable	Financial Accounting	Desktop Purchasing	Sales	EIS	GroupWare	Document Management	Data Standardization	Data Gathering
I-Netprovider																						
Directory Services																						
eMail, Whitepages, Yellowpages									■	■	■						■			■		
Reference Server (Masterdata)			■																		■	
Passport Services																						
Customer Profiling									■								■					
Certification (Certification Authority)						■																
Public Keys					■																	
Financial Services																						
Credit Information									■								■					
Payment Service (e.g.micro)						■							■	■	■	■	■					
Funds Transfer													■	■	■	■						
eMarket																						
Tradepoint						■											■					
Request for Proposal						■																
Intermediary	■	■	■	■	■	■	■	■	■	■							■					
Broker	■	■	■	■	■	■	■	■	■	■							■					
Community Builder																						
Content Broker	■					■			■	■							■					
Chatroom	■																					
Newsgroup	■																		■			
Listservers	■																					
Lean Communication																						
eMail, Phone, Video	■	■	■	■	■	■	■	■	■	■	■	■	■	■	■	■	■		■		■	
Content Provider																						
Information Services	■	■	■	■	■	■	■	■	■	■							■					■
Content Broker																						
Market Intelligence (Infomediaries)	■	■				■			■	■							■					
Search Engines	■	■															■					
News Services (PointCast, NewsPage)	■	■																				
Process Services (Shared Services)																						
Personnel Administration										■	■	■										
Marketing																	■					
Database Marketing																	■					
Customer Profiling																	■					
Web Presence																	■					
Virtual Enterprise																						
Coordination Service	■	■	■	■	■	■	■	■	■	■							■					
Transaction Services																						
EDI		■	■	■	■	■	■	■	■	■			■	■	■	■	■		■			
Receipt						■	■	■	■													
Data Processing Center																						
Net Operation																					■	
Software Distribution	■				■												■					
Archiving, Online					■				■												■	
Call Center																						

Table 8-2: Services for Application Architecture Areas

8.5.3   Application Architecture Components

From the workshop discussions eight application components were defined which build on the 22 application areas. These application architecture components will have to be included in the planning of future architectures (see Figure 8-7).[4] The components include applications for master data management, classical ERP systems, data warehouse applications, advanced planning and scheduling applications (APS) for an integrated supply chain management (these may also be described as DSS - decision support systems), electronic commerce applications, customer relationship management (CRM), applications for knowledge management and finally EIS - executive information systems. All these applications are based on data and process standards which the individual companies will have to define.

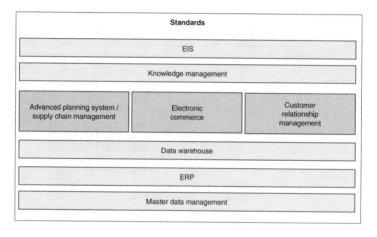

Figure 8-7: Application Architecture Components

The following table (Table 8-3) shows how the architecture areas and components can be related. It helps in determining and clarifying what functionality application components include and to identify overlaps.

---

[4]   Generally speaking, specialized applications might be used for all 22 application areas. However, with a view to minimizing the interfacing effort and a consistent integration of the applications, it would not make sense to use different applications for all areas.

Application Areas \ Applications	Master Data Management	ERP-Systems	Data Warehouse-Systems	Planning-/Scheduling Applications	E-Commerce-Applications	Customer Relationship Management	Knowledge Management	EIS – Executive Information Systems
Development							■	
Research							■	
Demand Planning				■				
Requirements Planning				■				
Production Planning				■				
Procurement Management		■						
Inventory Management		■						
Production		■						
Distribution/Transport		■						
Service						■		
HR		■						
Payroll		■						
Accounts Payable		■						
Accounts Receivable		■						
Financial Accounting		■						
Desktop Purchasing		■						
Sales					■	■		
Management Information								■
GroupWare							■	
Document Management							■	
Daten Standardization	■							
Data Gathering			■					

Table 8-3: Combination of Architecture Areas and Components

The application architecture components will be described in greater detail in the following paragraphs.

- *Master data management.* The standardization of processes and data is a prerequisite for the integration of heterogeneous applications (cf. Chap. 3.4.2). Whereas the standardization of processes is effected mainly by guidelines (also called business rules) in the form of written documentations, an automated approach would be required for master data. In future, enterprises will be using an increasing number of specialized applications that are designed only to create and distribute master data.

- *ERP systems.* ERP systems will continue to form the core of corporate application architectures. These ERPs are required to be closely integrated with the APS, electronic commerce and SFA applications in order to fulfil the requirements of Business Networking (cf. Chap. 3). Especially in the fields of payroll accounting, inventory management, transport and accounts payable administration, there are service offerings on the market. ADP, for instance, is a leading provider in the field of payroll accounting and handles payroll accounts for approx. 20 million employees in the US.

- *Data warehouse applications*. Data warehouse applications provide decision makers with a consistent data base. The relevant data from the various (heterogeneous) productive systems are collected and processed for analysis. While the employees in production, sales, bookkeeping, etc. use the operative systems, those individuals who deal with the analysis of the data (e.g. controllers) can draw on the data accumulated in the data warehouse. This approach ensures that these analyses which place an enormous load on computer capacity will not impair the operative work.

- *Advanced planning and scheduling applications*. In the last decade, process optimizations in production have brought about mass customization, efficient customer response programs (ECR) and vendor-managed inventories (VMI). Each of these challenges boils down to more goods to be planned with reduced lot sizes. This has moved the supply chains of the enterprises into the focus of attention [cf. Bermudez/Girard 97]. Shorter supply chain cycle times and a shrinkage of inventories have become the main targets. These targets can be achieved only if all enterprises along a supply chain cooperate and, for instance, agree to release their planning data to their upstream suppliers. Standard applications have come on the market during the last two or three years to support integrated planning (e.g. SAP's APO, i2 or Manugistics).

- *Electronic commerce applications*. Electronic commerce applications provide catalogues and ordering facilities for customers (cf. Chap. 4.3.1). Being mostly Internet-based, electronic commerce applications have provided new interaction channels with existing customers and have been successfully used to reach new customers. This is combined with significant cost reductions and time advantages in the area of the sales processes.

- *Customer relationship management applications*. Customer relationship management applications have emerged in various industries. These applications provide functions for after-sales service, marketing and sales, help desk, call centers, market research and for the interaction with the customers through the Internet. Among leading vendors of such systems are Siebel and Vantive.

- *Applications for knowledge management*. Included in this category are a number of applications, such as data bases, archiving and imaging systems (from the SAP environment, mention may be made of the products from the house of IXOS), groupware, document management and workflow systems.

- *Executive information systems*. Executive information systems (EIS) are designed to support the management activities. Typically, EIS support planning and financial processes. These systems are designed to collect and to analyze both internal and external data. In most cases, EIS are built up on data warehouse applications. The functionality of EIS includes, for instance, drill down analyses, trend analyses, graphical processing of data and the special presentation of information.

8.6 Summary and Outlook

Starting from the business model of the information age, it has been the aim of this Chapter to outline a business application architecture which has been derived from the business model of the information age. The example of the pharmaceutical branch has been used to illustrate these efforts. Two main elements of the application architecture are (1) the application areas where a total of 22 areas have been identified, and (2) the application components (see Figure 8-7) which are influenced by existing applications, such as master data management, ERP, DW, APS, EC, SFA, KM, and EIS systems.

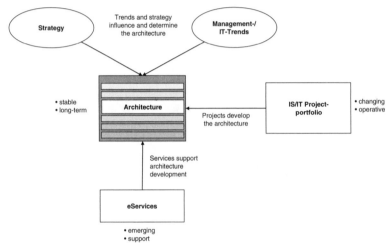

Figure 8-8: Application Architecture and IS/IT Project-Portfolio

In continuing this work it will be necessary to focus on the relations of the individual components of the architecture to each other. It will be necessary to analyze precisely which data are required to be exchanged between these components and what the requirements are that integration has to fulfil.

The real benefit of an application architecture for the enterprises of the information age is that it allows for a better coordination of different IT projects. In this process, the architecture blueprint will serve to establish a set of principles [cf. Metagroup 1998] for the IS/IT projects. Such a set of principles permits an evaluation of the specific projects to assess their relative importance in accomplishing the planned architecture. Another starting point for the continuation of the work is in the necessity to match the application architecture with the IT project portfolio of an enterprise. From the practical side of business, too, authors have stressed the need to analyze this aspect in greater depth and to match the application architecture with a company's project portfolio and the available eServices (see Figure 8-8).

9 Overview on Supply Chain Management Systems

Karl Maria Grünauer, Elgar Fleisch, Hubert Österle[1]

9.1 Introduction 176
    9.1.1 Objectives 176
    9.1.2 Supply Chain Pyramid 177

9.2 Planning Processes and Planning Horizons 179

9.3 Software Concepts for Supply Chain Management 180
    9.3.1 Transaction and Planning Systems 180
    9.3.2 Material Requirements Planning (MRP I) 181
    9.3.3 Manufacturing Resource Planning (MRP II) 181
    9.3.4 Advanced Planning Systems 183

9.4 Brief Overview on Advanced Planning Systems 185
    9.4.1 Functionality and Modules 185
    9.4.2 Rhythm Solutions of i2 Technologies 188
    9.4.3 Manugistics6 of Manugistics 189
    9.4.4 APO of SAP 189
    9.4.5 Numetrix of J.D. Edwards 190

9.5 Conclusions 190

---

[1] The authors would like to thank Alexander Blount, The Information Management Group (IMG), for his valueable input.

9.1   Introduction

For decades industry has been trying to match supply with demand. Supply chain management (SCM) is process-oriented management of the complete logistics network through the planning and control of material, information and funds flows on the basis of new information and communication technology. This gives rise to the question of 'old logistics wine in new IT bottles'. At the end of the eighties, the CIM concept (computer integrated manufacturing [cf. Scheer 1990a]) was already based on the idea of an integrated, holistic view of logistics from order receipt to shipment, thus "building a bridge from work flows based on the division of labor to integrated processes" [cf. Bothe 1998, 33].

According to [Scheer 1998, 3] the CIM concept failed for two basic reasons:

1. At the time the necessary tools in the form of software and open hardware were not available.

2. The end users were insufficiently involved and ultimately overwhelmed.

In this Chapter we investigate whether a similar fate to that of CIM is likely to befall the SCM concept due to a lack of suitable IS systems. It then goes on to look at the advanced systems currently available on the market for depicting interorganizational planning processes.

In summary, suitable IS systems are available for managing the supply chain. The real challenge lies in managing the cooperation between the business units involved in the supply chain (cf. Chap. 14). Cooperative behavior on the part of the project initiator plus the involvement of all the relevant partners in the supply chain is the only way to ensure that the required transactional data will be available so that the functionality provided by advanced planning systems can be utilized in line with business objectives.

After looking at business objectives (cf. Chap. 9.1.1) we start off by visualizing the planning process and planning horizons for supply chain management (cf. Chap. 9.2) and examine the existing software concepts MRP I, MRP II and APS for planning tasks (cf. Chap. 9.3). The assignment of typical modules of an APS solution to generic SCOR planning processes shows that functional requirements are depicted; a brief overview of four selected APS systems provides an indication of the focus and trends amongst various software vendors (cf. Chap. 9.4).

9.1.1   Objectives

The partners in a supply chain can be suppliers, manufacturers, wholesalers or retailers. Individually, these partners need to balance the supply chain objectives of customer service levels (maximization), supply chain assets (minimization), and supply chain costs (minimization) to achieve the greatest ROA (return on assets). Supply chain management takes this one step further and seeks to allocate these costs and benefits equitably across supply chain partners.

Service Levels

One of the major requirements is to provide the end customer with a suitable *service level*. This refers to the capability of a supply chain to deliver to the customer the right product in the right quantity and the right quality at the right time and at the right place. Building on from here, it is possible to develop objectives, such as improvement in quality or reduction in cycle and response time, which, for example, lead to an increase in customer satisfaction and secure sales revenues for all the business units in a supply chain for the long term.

Supply Chain Assets

The service level can, however, only be maintained if the partners in a supply chain build up *assets*. This can be done by means of current assets in the form of inventory, or fixed assets, such as production plant or information systems. Examples of objectives for supply chain asset management are quantitative targets for reducing the inventory days of supply and cash-to-cash cycle time, or for increasing the asset turn.

Supply Chain Costs

Providing the required service level and building up assets lead to *costs* for all the business units in the supply chain. Costs include order fulfillment costs, material acquisition costs, inventory carrying costs, logistics costs as well as manufacturing labor and overhead costs. This gives us objectives, such as the reduction of total supply costs or value-added productivity.

9.1.2   Supply Chain Pyramid

Selecting the right level of service for the customer means ensuring that the customer can be served in accordance with his needs. This leads to sales revenues at all value creation stages in the supply chain.

The customer may, for example, demand a high level of product availability. In the case of make-to-stock production, this can be achieved by stock levels, for example, in the case of make-to-order through short lead times. At each stage of the supply chain, provision of the required service level is paid for with assets and costs.

Intraorganizational objectives, such as the ROA, give partners in a supply chain an indication of the ratio of benefits (achieved sales or profit) to expenditure (assets and costs). The challenge lies in managing these objectives which are interwoven and mutually influence one another. This is shown for one business unit as a gray triangle in Figure 9-1, intraorganizational planning processes in procurement, production and distribution ensure the internal optimization of ROA.

However, it is not sufficient for each partner to try and optimize its ROA on an individual basis. A household appliance manufacturer, for example, may set up a cost-efficient manufacturing process. This will ensure an optimal ROA for the short term through efficient internal material requirements and production planning.

Unfortunately, failure to invest in projects aimed at improving communication between the manufacturer and downstream trading stages means that the retailer passes on information regarding changes in market demands to the manufacturer too late in the process. A lack of flexibility in the cost-efficient manufacturing process leads to delays in making the required changes to the efficient but no longer effective production operations.

Stock shortfalls occuring at the manufacturer and downstream trading stages are unable to provide the level of service required by the market. Delivery problems occur. Shortfalls in sales lead to a decrease in ROA for all concerned. Viewed over the long term, the complete supply chain is destined to fail.

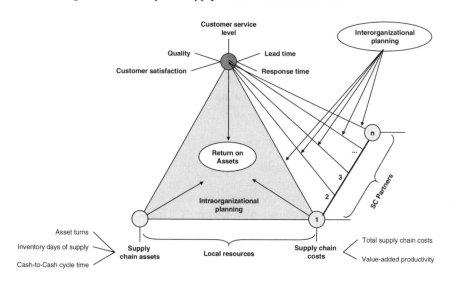

Figure 9-1: Supply Chain Pyramid[2]

Interorganizational planning between SC partners (see ellipse in Figure 9-1) ensures that in a first step customer requirements are identified, prioritized and aggregated throughout the whole supply chain. In a second step interorganizational

---

[2]   Compiled from ([Schary/Skjott-Larsen 1995, 20], [Christopher 1998, 286], [Bowersox/Closs 1996, 679], and [Becker/Geimer 1999, 32]).

planning balances these requirements with partner-internal procurement, production and distribution resources in good time.

The interorganizational and synchronized exchange of information between partners in a supply chain permits an optimal customer-oriented balance between service level, local supply chain assets and local supply chain costs at every stage in the chain. Viewed overall, synchronization means that a higher ROA is achieved for all concerned.

9.2   Planning Processes and Planning Horizons

Recently, the top down approach SCOR for capturing and designing supply chain configurations has been made publicly available[3]. On its top level, the SCOR model differentiates the supply chain processes plan, source, make and deliver (cf. Chaps. 4.3.2 and 6.2.1). On the next level, which is called the configuration level, SCOR defines four interorganizational planning processes P0: plan infrastructure, P1: plan supply chain, P2: plan source, P3: plan make and P4: plan deliver. These processes have planning horizons, which range between minutes, hours, days, weeks, months and years and can be classed as strategic, tactical and operative planning tasks (see Figure 9-2).

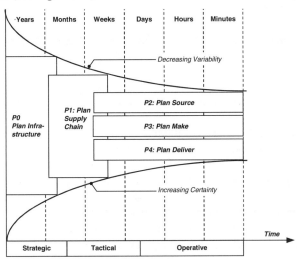

Figure 9-2: Types of Supply Chain Planning Processes

---

[3]   SCOR stands for Supply Chain Operations Reference-model (e.g. [Hankason 1999, 205], [SCOR 1998]).

P0: plan infrastructure is the SCOR process where the supply chain is reconfigured, make/buy decisions are made and long-term planning of capacities, resources and business plans are performed (e.g. [SCOR 1998, 56], [SCOR 1998 26]).

P1 starts with the identification, prioritization, and aggregation of supply chain requirements (P1.1) and of supply chain resources (P1.2). In the next two steps supply chain requirements are balanced with supply resources under consideration of product/process data and business rules (P1.3) and supply chain plans are established (P1.4). Outputs of P1 are courses of action over specified time periods that represent a projected appropriation of total supply chain resources to meet total supply chain demand requirements and executable sourcing/production/ delivery plans for customers and suppliers in the entire business network.

P2 balances materials resources with material requirements and establishes detailed sourcing plans. P3 balances production resources with production requirements and establishes detailed production plans. P4 balances delivery resources with delivery requirements and establishes detailed delivery plans.

Decreasing variability and increasing planning certainty in the transition from strategic via tactical through to operative planning tasks are shown in Figure 9-3 over various planning horizons (years, months, weeks, etc.) as a function of time.

9.3   Software Concepts for Supply Chain Management

9.3.1   Transaction and Planning Systems

BPR (cf. Chap. 3.3.1) projects and the introduction of ERP (cf. Chap. 2.3.1) systems have laid the foundation for the efficient execution of intraorganizational processes. ERP systems, such as R/3 from SAP AG, are primarily oriented towards depicting the as-is situation and managing transactional data. A trading company, for example, is provided with support for transactions in the areas of (a) stock management and procurement and (b) quotation, price and order management, invoicing etc. by the modules material management (MM), and sales and distribution (SD). As a rule, each business unit operates one or more ERP systems.

ERP systems provide up-to-date information e.g. on stock levels or the current value of orders. Non-order-based master data depict the structure of an object in the supply chain, for example, the bill of material for a product. The benefits of these systems for planning the supply chain as a whole consist mainly in the provision of a consistent database.

Planning systems on the other hand manage planning data, such as order forecasts or production plans. Viewed historically, three software concepts have developed for planning systems. In order of creation, these are material requirements planning (MRP I), manufacturing resource planning (MRP II) and advanced planning systems (APS). Each concept represents a further development of its predecessor.

In practice, the two traditional concepts MRP I and MRP II are often found to be integrated with the transaction systems in the form of the above mentioned ERP systems. APS represents independent applications that sit on top of ERP. Common to all planning systems is the use of master and transaction data embedded in the various transaction systems of a supply chain.

9.3.2   Material Requirements Planning (MRP I)

Material requirements planning is a batch-oriented determination of net requirements on the basis of gross requirements, such as current customer orders, rough-cut distribution and production plans, inventory levels and pending purchase orders. The breakdown of bills of material using fixed lead times gives planned production orders or ordering dates for bought-out parts.

With the MRP I concept the only planning principle taken into consideration is material availability. The availability of resources, for example through checking warehouse, transport or production capacity, is not taken into account. As a result it is not possible to guarantee that calculated plans are actually feasible, because there might not be sufficient capacity available.

9.3.3   Manufacturing Resource Planning (MRP II)

The disadvantages of MRP are toned down in the successor concept MRP II through the inclusion of additional planning modules. This results in a comprehensive planning and control system, which helps to achieve the following objectives simultaneously [cf. Pfohl 1994, 254]:

1. Ensure the availability of materials, components, and products for planned production and for customer delivery,

2. Maintain the lowest possible level of inventory, and

3. Plan manufacturing activities, delivery schedules, and purchasing activities.

The MRP II concept typically includes the following modules (cf. [Schary/Skjott-Larsen 1995, 144], [Winter 1991, 183]):

- Modules for financial planning and business forecasting,

- Modules for demand management for final products, such as production planning and master production scheduling (MPS),

- Modules for forecasting, such as demand management, production and sales planning and distribution requirements planning (DRP),

- Modules which take capacity considerations into account, such as resource requirements planning, rough cut capacity planning (RCRP) and capacity requirements planning (CRP),

- Modules for materials requirements planning (MRP I) and for controlling operations, such as purchase planning and control, final assembly scheduling (FAS) and production activity control (PAC).

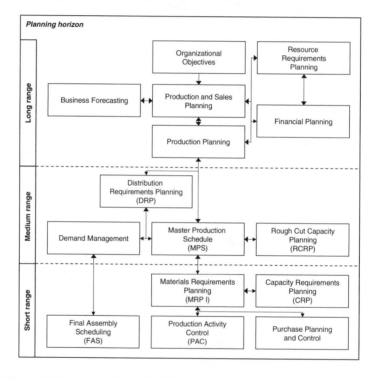

Figure 9-3: Structure of an MRP II System [cf. Schary/Skjott-Larsen 1995, 144]

The structure is based on steps, i.e. the results of long-range planning (e.g. production and sales planning) and medium-range planning (such as master production scheduling) are passed on to the next level (see Figure 9-3). If it is not possible to implement a plan (e.g. due to capacity restrictions in the case of master schedule items), successive solution approaches are pursued by feedback with the higher planning levels [cf. Gronau 1997, 66].

MRP II's most evident improvement over its predecessor concept is the expansion of planning to include capacity calculation [cf. Kilger 1998, 53]. On the other hand, there are a whole series of disadvantages to be considered. Uncertainties with respect to demand, lead times, etc. are not taken into account. In the case of lead times, waiting times due to capacity overload situations (waiting for capacity or waiting for material) are not recorded in the system. MRP II systems are also batch-oriented: capacity requirements planning (CRP), for example, is performed independently of material requirements planning (MRP I). If boundary conditions are encountered (e.g. insufficient capacity) the material requirements planning has to be executed again. Long throughput times for calculation makes producing plans an arduous task and also means that they cannot be readily adapted to new situations [cf. Kilger 1998, 54]. Orders are processed in the order in which they are received (first come–first served principle). The user has no means of including objectives in real time, reserving material or correcting existing plans. MRP II systems are site-oriented. This prevents the integrated planning of the interorganizational supply chain from material procurement via the various stages of the production process through to the delivery of products to customers. While MRP II systems optimize individual elements of a supply chain locally, the lack of an overview of dependencies along the supply chain makes it impossible to arrive at an optimal solution for the supply chain as a whole.

9.3.4   Advanced Planning Systems

The existing deficits of MRP II systems have provided the motivation for developing Advanced Planning Systems (APS)[4]. The main object of APS is the total optimization of an objective, such as ROA. This presupposes that the topology of a supply chain with its various resources and the consideration of boundary conditions, such as capacity constraints, are visible. For this reason, APS systems are based on an interorganizational model of a supply chain[5].

In the case of the household appliance manufacturer, an interorganizational planning model supports not only the production and material requirements planning but also the downstream distribution and sales planning in coordination with the business units further along the supply chain, such as retailers. Integrating the transaction systems of the retailers with the manufacturer's APS system ensures that data, such as forecast quantities or actual customer order quantities, are com-

---

[4]   According to [Prockl 1998, 443] the abbreviation APS stands for advanced planning systems, however this abbreviation is not always used to mean the same thing in the available literature. Authors such as (e.g. [Lapide 1998, 3], [Pirron et al. 1999, 69]) understand APS to mean 'advanced planning and scheduling'.

[5]   The model of an interorganizational supply chain includes e.g. suppliers, plants, various stages of distribution centers and points of sale.

municated in time. This enables the manufacturer to react quickly to fluctuations in demand and to plan more flexible production capacities.

The main advantages of APS relate to the following points (e.g. [cf. Prockl 1998, 443], [i2 1997], [Fritsche 1999, 50], [AMR 1999], [Simchi-Levi et al. 2000, 223]):

- *Depiction of complex, interorganizational supply chains.* Modeling of realistic restrictions ('constrained based systems') is made possible through the use of object-oriented technologies. Analyze. plan activities and make trade-offs based on information from the entrie supply chain.

- *Simultaneous planning philosophy.* In the case of APS, contrary to the sequential planning philosophy of MRP II, all planning processes are considered simultaneously; interaction and restriction infringements are checked (concurrent planning).

- *Incremental planning capability.* While MRP II systems create plans from scratch, APS can update requirements, inventory and capacity data and show the effects of the respective changes.

- *Bi-directional communication of changes.* Changes to plans are immediately transmitted upstream and downstream.

- *Positioning as DSS.* The departure from rigid planning processes, as was the case with MRP II, positions APS as decision support systems (DSS). Target groups, such as e.g. product managers, procurement planners or stock planners, can simulate the effects of changes by means of 'what-if' analyses.

- *Integration with transaction systems.* Middleware allows APS to be linked with transaction systems[6] in order to load operative data and conversely to be able to make planning results available to the transaction systems.

- *Main memory-resident data storage.* Leads to high processing speeds which allow good response times; enhanced information capability through available-to-promise in real time).

- *Single-point-of-contact:* Access any data in the system from a single-point-of-contact

---

[6]   On the transaction system side there are standardized interfaces, one example being the production optimization interface (POI) from SAP.

9.4   Brief Overview on Advanced Planning Systems

9.4.1   Functionality and Modules

With APS, planning processes in the areas of source, make and deliver are depicted against the background of various planning horizons in integrated modules with mutually complementary functionality. Figure 9-4 represents individual APS modules in three main areas: (1) supply chain design, (2) supply chain planning and (3) tactical/operative planning.

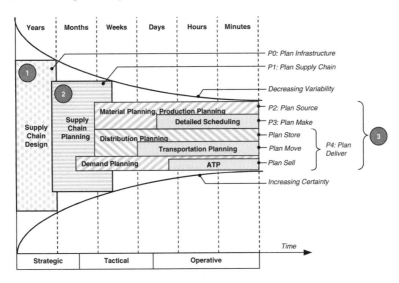

Figure 9-4: Modules of APS Solutions (cf. [Pirron et al. 1998, 62], Pirron et al. 1999, 70], Hiemenz 1998, 57])

(1) Supply chain design modules cover strategic planning with a time horizon, which can span months or years. It ensures that an optimal structure is found for a supply chain in the long term. This is done, for example, by simulating and evaluating investment alternatives. This might mean answering the question of whether existing warehouse capacity should be expanded, whether it would make sense to set up new distribution stages or whether it would be advisable to aim for consolidation. Supply chain design corresponds with the SCOR-process P0.

(2) Supply chain planning modules correspond with the SCOR-process P1. They operate within the supply chain design model with all its constraints. This enables the modules to plan the flow of materials, components and products along the entire supply chain by the synchronized exchange of sourcing, production and

distribution plans between entities, such as suppliers, plants, distribution centers and transportation lanes.

(3) The different tactical planning APS-modules correspond with the SCOR-processes P2: plan source, P3: plan make and P4: plan deliver. Functionality for enabling P2 and P3 processes are typically provided by material planning and production planning/detailed scheduling modules:

- Material planning ensures that sufficient quantities of critical material are available before beginning production. Time-phased material availability, dynamic part/ingredient substitution and synchronized material allocation to reduce work-in-process inventories enable business units to position the right materials effectively.

- Based on customer service, profitability, and cost, *production planning* and *detailed scheduling* allocates constrained production capacities to the appropriate parts. It optimizes the use of machines, labor, and material within each production facility by providing multi-site planning, detailed scheduling, and real-time communication with the plant floor.

Typically, software vendors distinguish between the sub-processes plan store, plan move and plan sell when depicting SCOR's P4 process. The corresponding APS functionality can be found in distribution planning, transportation planning, demand planning and available-to-promise (ATP):

- Distribution planning helps to optimize the flow of goods throughout the network of distribution centers and local warehouses.

- Transportation planning helps to optimize mode and carrier selection and consolidate freights to create shipments in the most cost-effective manner.

- Demand planning provides demand signal visibility (cf. Chap. 13) which helps to understand the current market dynamics and to accurately predict future customer demand (forecasting).

- ATP increases customer service via reliable confirmation dates by performing high-speed availability checks against stocks, allocation plans, forecasts etc. at the time of order entry.

Different APS manufacturers depict the modules with different emphasis. Solutions have been developed by an evolutionary process centered around the planning modules for tactical/operative tasks.

Additional functionality required has been added successively by the APS manufacturers through buying or collaborating with specialized software houses; this applies in particular to supply chain design and supply chain planning. As a result, the module landscapes within the APS systems tend to be heterogeneous.

This brief overview of APS systems covers the following four manufacturers[7],

- Market leader i2 Technologies with the *Rhythm Supply Chain Management (SCM) solution*,

- Their strongest competitor Manugistics with the product *NETWorks solution set* based on the predecessor *Manugistics6*,

- The newly developed APS solution from SAP which goes under the name of *Advanced Planner and Optimizer (APO)*,

- J.D. Edwards with their SCM products offerings based on *Numetrix/3* and *Numetrix/xtr@*.

Both i2 Technologies and Manugistics are independent software manufacturers who specialize in APS solutions. Together they accounted for over 50% of worldwide sales in the APS market segment in 1998.

As market leader in the field of ERP systems, SAP is in a position to offer customers a complete solution from a single source thanks to the new development of APO, which started in 1997. ERP manufacturer J.D. Edwards pursues the same objective. However, this company avoided self-development by acquiring Numetrix in the summer of 1999. This acquisition is part of a continuing trend. In the past we have seen e.g. Peoplesoft consolidate its position as a provider of SCM solutions (transaction system and APS solution) by taking over Red Pepper, or Baan, acquiring CAPS Logistics and the Berclain Group.

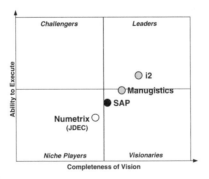

Figure 9-5: Leading APS Vendors

Figure 9-5 shows the positioning of the four manufacturers in the four cells of the Gartner Group matrix [cf. Enslow 1999]. Software vendors are classified according to their ability to meet current market demands 'ability-to-execute', and ac-

---

[7] For a detailed explanations of the functionality of APS tools (cf. [Benchmarking Partners 1997], [Bermudez/Girard 1997], [Pirron et al. 1998], and [Pirron et al. 1999]).

cording to their ability to meet new market challenges 'completeness of vision'. Niche players like Numetrix/J.D. Edwards focus on a small market segment, whereas visionaries (Manugistics and SAP) are already performing well but show weaknesses in meeting future market challenges. Gartner Group sees i2 Technologies as the only vendor in the leaders quadrant. New APS market studies like [IML-FHG 1999, 150] and [FIR-RWTH 1999, 322] will show, whether Manugistics and SAP can move into the leaders quadrant.

[AMR 1999] estimated that sales revenues from the worldwide APS market reached approx. USD 800 million in 1997 and around USD 1,300 million in 1998.

Table 9-1 shows the latest annual revenue, the 1-year revenue growth trend and the current market capitalization per manufacturer. For SAP[8] and JD Edwards we estimate, that the anual revenue from APS sales amounts to 15%-20%.

Company	Latest Annual Revenue in Millions of USD, 1-yr Revenue Growth in %	Market Capitalization in Millions of USD (08/24/00)
JD Edwards	USD 944.2 (10/1999), -4.9%	USD 2,424.21
Manugistics	USD 152.4 (02/2000), -6.8%	USD 1,632.66
i2 Technologies	USD 571.1 (12/1999), +64.8%	USD 30,826.09
SAP	USD 5,146.0 (12/1999), +0.2%	USD 44,103.00

Table 9-1: Latest Annual Revenues and Market Capitalization of Leading APS Vendors[9]

9.4.2   Rhythm Solutions of i2 Technologies

Originally founded in 1988, this company's sales are over 50% higher than those of manufacturer No. 2 (Manugistics): in 1998, i2 Technologies recorded total sales revenues of over USD 362 million with a workforce of over 2,300 employees. The company's background lies in realizing software based on the 'Optimized Production Technology' concept (OPT) of Goldratt/Cox (e.g. [Bermudez/Girard 1997, 11], [Goldratt/Cox 1995]) in the area of production planning.

A major factor contributing to the success of i2 in sectors, such as high-tech (electronics and semiconductor industry) or the steel industry, is the value-added sales approach. Introduction projects are billed according to the benefits achieved

---

[8]   [Bermudez/Richardson 1999, 19] estimate that SAP will achieve sales revenues for APO of around USD 810 million in the year 2001, which equates to roughly 16% of SAP's total sales for 1998.

[9]   [cf. MGFS 2000].

for the customer. The potential customer benefits of a solution are reduced costs, delayed or avoided expenses, increased responsiveness to customer demand and increased revenue growth. According to [Miller-Williams 1998], i2 generated customer benefits to the tune of USD 3,537 million during the period 1996-98.

The company's intention is to expand its market leadership e.g. through electronic Business Process Optimization (eBPO). With this initiative i2 Technologies is attempting to tap new market segments, such as product life cycle management or customer relationship management (CRM), alongside its traditional area of supply chain management (SCM). i2's acquisition of the CRM system manufacturer 'Smart Technologies' highlights the growing significance of CRM for supply chain management.

9.4.3   Manugistics6 of Manugistics

This APS vendor was set up in 1986 and focuses on short projects delivering rapid results, primarily in the consumer goods, process and automotive industries. Its background is forecasting and distribution requirements planning (DRP). After a restructuring in the beginning of 1999, the company has been trying to establish a foothold in the business-to-business (B2B) and business-to-consumer (B2C) area with its e-Chain™ concept and thus expand its APS product-suite called Manugistics6. This is aimed at giving the customer the possibility of linking its business processes with those of its partners and integrating end users via the Internet. One module in the suite is an implementation[10] of the CPFR standard (collaborative planning, forecasting and replenishment [cf. VICS 1998]).

With the middleware product, OAI/Net Manugistics is also endeavoring to improve the integration of transaction systems of various business units with APS solutions through the use of Internet technologies.

9.4.4   APO of SAP

SAP entered the APS market segment at the end of 1998 with its newly developed Advanced Planner and Optimizer (APO) against the background of anticipated saturation in its traditional segment of ERP systems (R/3). The high level of market penetration in the area of ERP will help SAP to achieve a leading position with APS systems as well: according to [Bermudez/Richardson 1999] 60%-70% of R/3 customers prefer to purchase their APS solution from the ERP supplier.

With the latest Release 1.1 and 130 installations worldwide to date [cf. SAP 1999a], SAP has developed a comprehensive solution within a short period of

---

[10]   This relates to the Manugistics product NetWORKS ™.

time. The 'grace of late arrival' [cf. Pirron et al. 1998, 67] meant that SAP was able to learn from the deficiencies of solutions already on the market. Beta tests were completed in the first quarter of 1999, and the first solutions are expected to go live as of mid-1999.

The APO concept includes all the APS modules shown in Figure 9-4. The strengths of the solution lie in the modules for strategic design and planning, and demand management [cf. Bermudez/Richardson 1999, 4]. In addition to the improvement in stability, the emphasis for Release 2.0 will be on the area of collaborative planning [cf. Kühn 1999] and enhanced user-friendliness (Enjoy SAP) among others.

9.4.5   Numetrix of J.D. Edwards

Numetrix was established in 1977 and a year later brought the first commercial application software for finite capacity planning (FCP) onto the market [cf. Benchmarking Partners 1997, 50]. The acquisition of the Numetrix/3 and Numerix/xtr@ solutions by J.D. Edwards expanded the supply chain planning competence of this ERP manufacturer. J.D. Edwards will integrate these products into its own SCOREx[11] supply chain solution. For Numetrix this could enable them to move beyond their previous niche position (see Figure 9-5).

In addition to sophisticated planning functionality, the special feature of the Numetrix products lay in the Internet-enabled supply chain planning strategy. Numetrix/xtr@ builds on the distributed object messaging system architecture (DOMA) and makes it possible to plan and optimize the complete supply chain via the Internet. A push procedure [cf. Pirron et al. 1998, 68] is used to forward planning data via a communication channel to internal and external business units. Numetrix/xtr@ permits the definition of business rules for running the channel and the conditions which initiate the exchange of information, notification or warning.

9.5   Conclusions

Information systems for managing the interorganizational supply chain take the form of ERP systems and planning systems (in particular APS). These allow business units to manage the necessary basic data consistently and to handle both intra and interorganizational planning tasks. APS system suppliers cover planning tasks with different functional emphasis, identifiable trends include (a) the use of the Internet for message-based system link-up, (b) the depiction of collaborative plan-

---

[11] SCOREx stands for supply chain optimization and real-time extended execution.

ning scenarios, such as CPFR, and (c) the expansion of APS focus and stronger customer focus through customer management.

While the systems are available, the challenge nevertheless remains to utilize the system functionality offered and to realize business potential. According to [Gartner Group 1998a] the majority of large corporations will not succeed in using APS systems in all three time horizons of supply chain planning tasks by the year 2003.[12]

Organizational measures, such as creating the necessary acceptance on the part of users both during operation and during the implementation of SCM systems, will thus become the most important task. An inability to gain this acceptance will doom SCM to failure, like CIM before it.

The implementation of SCM systems requires both technical and organizational skills. Since SCM systems involve data and processes of several different business units, the technical and organizational challenges required for its implementation top those of ERP systems. However, the future development in IT will make SCM systems more agile, easy to implement and easy to use. The complexity of cooperation among people and organizations will stay if not increase.

---

[12] "Through 2003, the majority of large enterprises will fail to achieve great supply chain management (SCM) because they will not master the application of advanced technologies in all three SCM time horizons: strategic planning, tactical planning and operational execution (0.8 probability)" [Gartner Group 1998a].

10 Electronic Commerce in the Procurement of Indirect Goods

Ralph Dolmetsch, Elgar Fleisch, Hubert Österle

10.1 Challenge in Indirect / MRO Procurement..194
    10.1.1 Introduction...194
    10.1.2 Current Procurement Scenarios 195
    10.1.3 Relevance of Indirect / MRO Procurement...............................197

10.2 Vendors of Desktop Purchasing Systems...198
    10.2.1 Ariba Operating Resources Management System of Ariba
           Technologies...198
    10.2.2 Commerce One BuySite / MarketSite of Commerce One 199
    10.2.3 iPlanet BuyerXpert / ECXpert of iPlanet 199

10.3 Overview of System Components and Functionality 200

10.4 Process and Workflow Functionality 201
    10.4.1 Catalog and Sourcing Services 201
    10.4.2 Purchase Requisition and Order Placement 202
    10.4.3 Delivery and Receipt..203
    10.4.4 Payment and Booking...204
    10.4.5 Process Management 204

10.5 Content Management 204
    10.5.1 Content Classification..205
    10.5.2 Content Aggregation..205
    10.5.3 Content Personalization 206

10.6 System Administration..207

10.7 Integration with Legacy / ERP Systems..207

10.8 Potential Savings of Desktop Purchasing Systems 208

10.1 Challenge in Indirect / MRO Procurement

10.1.1 Introduction

This article looks at a rather new and innovative class of Business Networking applications, referred to as desktop purchasing systems (DPSs). In recent years the face of many businesses has been changed radically by business process redesign and/or through the introduction of integrated standard software, referred to as ERP systems (cf. Chap. 2.3.1), e.g. SAP R/3, Oracle Applications or Baan IV. BPR projects essentially deal with the interface to external customers and rarely encompass the organization's procurement function.

Organizational design efforts in the area of procurement traditionally place a stronger emphasis on technology. In conjunction with the introduction of ERP or MRP II systems, many companies are in the process of redesigning the relationship with business partners on the supply side - in part driven by the need to modernize their systems in time for the next millennium. In this context they have largely concentrated on the area of direct procurement, i.e. on purchasing material for production. The result has been close partnerships with these suppliers, where the company's production planning and/or materials management systems frequently initiate procurement orders automatically with direct transmission to suppliers via EDI links.

The situation is quite different when it comes to the procurement of indirect/MRO products and services (maintenance, repair and operations), i.e. services which are not incorporated in the end product or are directly resold. In recent years, businesses have left the relationship with the suppliers of indirect/MRO services and the associated procurement processes within their organizations virtually unchanged [cf. Killen & Associates 1997]. It is precisely this area which harbors great potential for improvement through the use of modern information technology and, in particular, Internet technologies.

Nowadays, businesses frequently use their ERP systems to deal with the procurement of indirect/MRO services. These systems offer such a wealth of functionality that it is virtually impossible for staff who are not constantly using the system to handle it. For this reason, many companies are setting up the role of requisitioners in the indirect sector. A purchase requisition is an as yet unapproved purchasing order initiated by an employee. The requisitioner is responsible for a given number of employees and enters the purchase requisitions into the appropriate legacy or ERP system for his or her colleagues. In most companies typically secretaries, clerks, young technicians and laboratory assistants are requesting on behalf of their colleagues.

The advantages of this process are (a) that the requisitioner is practiced in using the system and (b) that the company needs a correspondingly lower number of user licenses for the ERP system. However, the disadvantages are (a) that the process is time-, work- and coordination-intensive and (b) that a detailed evaluation of procurement expenditure per employee is not possible or only possible if additional data are entered.

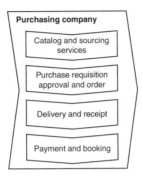

Figure 10-1: Core Process for Procurement

From the analysis of the procurement processes for indirect/MRO services in several corporations operating in different sectors we derived a generic core process [cf. Dolmetsch et al. 1999]. The core process for procurement was shown to consist of five process elements. Figure 10-1 represents the core process.

10.1.2 Current Procurement Scenarios

The problems involved in the procurement of indirect/MRO services can be illustrated with the aid of three typical scenarios.

Scenario 1: Decentralized Procurement Without Coordination

An employee in a large corporation needs a mobile phone in order to be able call customers when he is on a business trip. He inquires with the central procurement department and is told that the corporation does not have a preferred supplier for mobile phones. At the weekend he then sets off on his own initiative and collects offers from various suppliers. On Monday he asks his supervisor which one he should purchase. The supervisor, who bought a mobile phone himself only two months before, tells the employee to buy the same one. The employee buys the phone, fills out an expense form and presents the invoice to the accounting department. The data contained in the expense form has to be entered into the corporation's ERP system manually. At the moment, the expense forms for mobile phones, digital organizers, pagers and similar devices are piling up on the clerks' desks. This process doesn't help the purchasing department in collecting information about the actual needs and spending of the organization.

Scenario 2: Centralized Bureaucratic Procurement

In many companies, procurement activities are completely centralized so that volume contracts can be concluded with suppliers. If an employee needs a new notebook he will have to find out about the company's IT standards. The next step will be to ask the responsible procurement department which suppliers they have contracts with. As the relevant product catalog in the procurement department is already three months old, the employee requests new product catalogs from the contract partners. With the aid of these catalogs he decides on a particular model of the notebook, but is not sure whether the required configuration is technically possible. He sends the supplier a short query and asks them to send him a quotation direct. After receiving the quotation by fax, he checks it briefly and then sends it to the IT department by internal post along with the completed purchase requisition form as they are responsible for the technical approval of the purchase requisition. Once the employee's supervisor has granted his approval, the procurement department receives the requisition. They then check whether the price shown is in line with the agreed conditions. If everything is correct, the procurement clerk will then enter the requisition into the ERP system, post the order onto the existing frame contract, print out the order and send it to the supplier. Figure 10-2 shows the a drastically simplified as-is procurement process of a large industrial corporation.

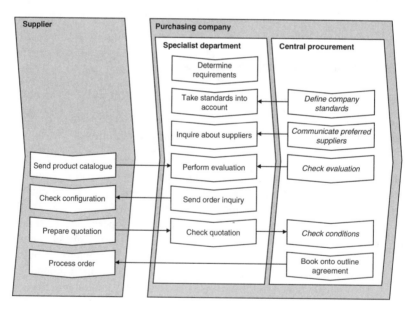

Figure 10-2: Excerpt of a Centralized Procurement Scenario

Scenario 3: Mixed Model

An employee needs a new paper punch, only to find that there is none left in the departments central stationery store. In addition to the possibility of borrowing a colleague's punch, the employee is faced with two options in this situation: one would be to go the stationer's round the corner, buy a punch and then submit a completed expense form to the accounting department in order to be reimbursed for the cost. The alternative would be to complete a purchase requisition form and pass it on to the procurement department. In this case, however, the employee will normally have to wait at least two weeks for the requisition to be processed and the item to be delivered. Table 10-1 summarizes the strength and weaknesses of the three scenarios.

	Scenario 1	Scenario 2	Scenario 3
Strengths	• High flexibility • Low cycle time • Low bureaucracy	• Potential for standardization • Potential for applying economies of scale	• High flexibility
Weaknesses	• Lack of standardization • Lack of applying economies of scale	• High cycle time • High bureaucracy • Low flexibility	• Lack of standardization • Lack of applying economies of scale

Table 10-1: Strengths and Weaknesses of Procurement Scenarios

10.1.3 Relevance of Indirect / MRO Procurement

Industrial corporations state that some 80% of all purchasing transactions relate to the procurement of indirect/MRO products and services (cf. [Intersearch 1998], [Netscape 1998]). Over 50% of savings related to the procurement of indirect/MRO products and services directly affect the bottom line (cf. [Killen & Associates 1997, 9], [AMR 1997, 4], [SAP 1998b, 3]). In view of this situation and the fact that, according to the results of a study, a purchasing transaction can often cost over USD 100, depending on actual order value [Intel 1998, 4], businesses have recognized Internet-based procurement to be an attractive area of inter-Business Networking [cf. Gebauer et al. 1998].

On the supply side, the range of available procurement solutions for the indirect sector is becoming increasingly confusing. DPSs are a category of application which have recently attracted a lot of attention. To date there have been very few productive implementations. In view of the high ROI for such projects, interest is growing rapidly amongst businesses and public authorities.

10.2   Vendors of Desktop Purchasing Systems

Many of the problems described above are attributable to a failure to provide employees with simple access to the latest information from suppliers and existing contracts. The DPS described below consolidate product and supplier information in multi-supplier product catalogs (referred to below as MSC) and at the same time incorporate access to the relevant data in the legacy and ERP systems. If a business is to support procurement processes with the DPS functionality efficiently, it will require suitable content and catalog management on the one hand, and integration with the relevant internal and supplier applications on the other.

In addition to a whole series of start-up companies, such as Ariba, Commerce One, Rightworks, Trade Ex or Netscape, ERP software manufacturers, such as SAP and Oracle, have launched their own solutions for desktop purchasing.

The DPSs now available on the market all have similar functionalities. The vendors develop additional features to meet pilot customers needs. Suite to the early stage of the market new releases are launched every couple of months. For this reason, it is not very meaningful to compare the systems on the basis of their functions. The principal differences between systems can be noted in (a) the strategy in respect of content and catalog management and (b) in system architecture with regard to integration with a company's internal information systems, the suppliers' systems and other Business Networking applications.

Based on the number of implementation projects, the market is at present largely dominated by three vendors. These three suppliers are looked at in greater detail below.

10.2.1   Ariba Operating Resources Management System

Founded in 1996, Ariba Technologies from Sunnyvale in California offers a system with a very user-friendly front end. The Ariba Buyer includes a high-performance search engine and an easy-to-use, graphical workflow component. For the integration with legacy and ERP systems, Ariba offers so-called adapters which are created as reusable interface solutions. Suppliers are expected to produce their product catalogs in Ariba's CIF-format (catalog interchange format). CIF is a simple comma separated value file suppliers convert their product catalog to (cf. [Ariba 1998a], [Ariba 1998b]). Ariba underlines the capability to depict services as well as physical goods in the product catalog.

In March 1999 Ariba announced the Ariba Marketplace. The Ariba Marketplace complements the ORMS software as a commerce network linking buyers and suppliers over the Internet.

10.2.2 Commerce One BuySite / MarketSite

Commerce One, headquarted in Walnut Creek, California, was founded in 1994. The company started off as a supplier of CD-ROM product catalogs before turning its attention to the buyer side in 1996. Before the cooperation with SAPMarkets, the DPS of Commerce One was called BuySite, and the new joint solution will be called Enterprise Buyer. BuySite is based on Microsoft commerce servers. Commerce One claims to have a component architecture, which permits the realization of individual solutions. Some companies, for example, prefer to use the already configured workflow component of their ERP system, rather than the BuySite workflow. Some employees then will continue to work directly with the ERP system, others will use the browser-based front end of BuySite.

The company has recently corrected its own product strategy again by increasingly placing the emphasis on what it has to offer in the area of catalog and content services as well as document mapping and routing using MarketSite.net. This eMarket will soon be renamed to MarketSet, a new solution provided by Commerce One and SAPMarkets. MarketSite.net is the core of the Commerce One strategy, which distinguishes this vendor from the growing number of competitors in the DPS software market. Like the Ariba Marketplace, the Commerce One MarketSite.net is a commerce portal, offering content management and routing services. In addition, MarketSite.net offers competitive buying. In order to compare products and services from different suppliers Commerce One rationalizes the product descriptions in the supplier catalogs. Besides that Commerce One recently introduced The Global Trading Web. This platform acts as a meta network which connects regionally or industry specific Commerce One eMarkets with each other.

10.2.3 iPlanet BuyerXpert / ECXpert

iPlanet eCommerce Solutions is a Sun-Netscape Alliance and was established in March 1999 by America Online, Inc. and Sun Microsystems, Inc. The company is headquarted in Mountain View, California. The procurement solution BuyerXpert was developed by Netscape and is now part of the CommerceXpert solution which also includes the components ECXpert, SellerXpert, PublishingXpert and MerchantXpert [cf. iPlanet 2000]. BuyerXpert builds on the ECXpert component which provides the basic functionality as well as the transaction management and security. Netscape products use open standards, such as CORBA for the application architecture and EDIINT as communication protocol. Netscape is also involved in the development of the OBI standard [cf. OBI 1998]. The company was one of the first vendors implementing the OBI standard into its products.

At this point we should mention the solutions of Aspect Development, Harbinger and TPN Register from GEIS and Thomas Register which also offer comparable functionality. Similar to Commerce One, these companies also act as content providers and maintain a comprehensive MSC containing the products of a multitude of catalogs from different suppliers. These content services are complementary to the functionality of the DPS and relieve businesses of many manual tasks related to content management.

10.3   Overview of System Components and Functionality

DPSs represent first and foremost a solution for the procurement of indirect/MRO products and services. These systems provide the user with access to a MSC containing previously negotiated products. The user interfaces of legacy or ERP systems contain deeply structured menu trees which are usually designed for power users. DPS support irregular use of infrequently requisitioning employees by the easy-to-use browser-based user interfaces.

All systems described above are based on a private MSC stored on the Intranet of the purchasing company. The user interfaces of these systems are in HTML and Java, and offer roughly comparable functionality.

The functionality of these systems supports the creation of purchasing requisitions and the approval workflow, as well as the tracking of authorization, order generating process, electronic ordering at the supplier's end and the financial booking of the purchased products and services.

Companies typically employ DPS for low-cost operating goods and services, such as spare parts or stationery, which are frequently ordered by a multitude of employees. At the moment, the field of application for such systems is thus limited to previously negotiated products and services which cannot by dynamically configured. All systems concentrate on catalog-based procurement. In the future, a XML based common business language could help to cover a wider range of different purchasing processes with DPS, such as auctioning and tendering.

The level of integration between DPS and ERP is different in every company and sometimes within one corporation between commodity groups. Purchasing card orders, direct orders and purchasing orders can be distinguished. The first two types of orders are directly send out to the supplier without generating a purchasing order in the company's ERP systems.

From the point of view of the existing ERP/legacy systems we distinguish between two different implementation strategies: the outside-in strategy, where the

DPS has its own transaction functionality - Ariba in particular pursues this strategy - and the inside-out strategy, where transactions continue to be handled in the ERP/legacy system [cf. Hantusch et al. 1997, 91-92] while the DPS is primarily responsible for the browser based user interface and the product catalog. The inside-out strategy requires real-time integration of the DPS via the appropriate APIs.

Figure 10-3 shows the functional and system components of a DPS in the form of a conceptional overview. In a concrete project the components depicted can be distributed amongst organization units of the customer, the suppliers or an intermediate catalog provider.

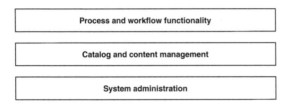

Figure 10-3: Components of Desktop Purchasing Systems

A critical success factor for the acceptance of a DPS is the immediacy and completeness of the product information in the company's private MSC. Ideally, complete, up-to-date data records for negotiated or relevant products of all suppliers will be stored in the private MSC. The user in the company does not have to request and scan the catalogs of various suppliers but can simply look through the company-specific (private) MSC. For this purpose, the data from the various suppliers will have to be consolidated in one catalog, suitably organized and stored in a metastructure. The metastructure is a hierarchy of product categories and groups which is derived from the requirements of the various purchaser groups within the company.

The system components shown in Figure 10-3 are dealt with in detail below. The main components are process and workflow functionality, content and catalog management, system administration, and integration with ERP/legacy systems.

10.4   Process and Workflow Functionality

10.4.1   Catalog and Sourcing Services

We structure the functionality according the core processes for procurement (see Figure 10-1). Among the functions of catalog and sourcing services are product configuration, product search, sourcing, availability check, and tenders and auctions.

Product configuration. At present, none of the systems investigated offers the rule-based configuration of complex products and dynamic price allocation. For this reason the pilot customers define a series of pre-configured products which they store in the MSC in accordance with the non-configurable products. In the area of computer hardware products this procedure accommodates companies' standardization efforts. This predefined, restricted selection means that employees can only select and purchase products which comply with the standard. Some vendors are planning to offer interfaces to optional configuration components of third party manufacturers.

Product search. All manufacturers offer convenient search engines for browsing in the MSC. The systems support (a) searching according to key words, (b) searching according to attributes and (c) browsing through the classification hierarchy.

Sourcing. If a product is offered by various suppliers, the order of the items found will show the prioritization in accordance with the company's procurement principles. The order can equally well be defined by the lowest price or by a preference for particular suppliers. If a company maintains its own warehouse, this can be assigned the role of an external supplier in the MSC and given a high priority.

Availability check. For availability checks real time integration with companies logistics systems is required. The DPS accesses the data via API from the database by calling up the relevant transactions in the productive ERP/legacy system.

Tenders and auctions. DPSs primarily address the purchasers of office and industrial equipment. Complex negotiation mechanisms acting on several attributes (such as product functionality, price and terms of sale), as used in particular by professional buyers in the direct sector, are not covered by the function scope of today's DPSs.

At the moment, none of the DPSs supports the posting of RFQs (request for quotations).

10.4.2 Purchase Requisition and Order Placement

Purchase requisition. The purchaser selects products and/or services from the MSC and makes up an electronic shopping basket from which an electronic purchase requisition can be generated. Frequently ordered items can be bookmarked and shopping baskets can be saved. This allows companies to store a shopping basket for a complete workplace for a new employee, for example. With most of the systems, a purchase requisition for this purpose can contain items from various suppliers.

Authorization workflow. Depending on the purchaser's user profile and the respective item ordered, the purchase requisition goes through an authorization workflow before the company sends it to the supplier as an order. The system informs the respective authorizing bodies by e-mail. In the case of DPSs, we identify different types of authorization workflows: (a) one authorization workflow per order, (b) one authorization workflow per purchase requisition and (c) one authorization workflow per item ordered. The systems investigated have varying levels of user friendliness in their workflow components.

Creating and sending orders. Once the purchase requisition has been authorized, the DPS automatically generates the order for each supplier and books these in the ERP/legacy system. The company sends the orders from the ERP/legacy system or from the DPS itself by e-mail, fax or EDI. In the case of a purchasing card or direct order the DPS sends the order out to the supplier directly. The whole process is closed later on by booking the back coming invoices directly onto the corresponding general ledger accounts.

Today it is not possible to hold back orders and bundle them in order to achieve a greater order volume per transaction.

10.4.3 Delivery and Receipt

Delivery of 'soft goods'. Unlike the delivery of s*oft goods*, such as software or electronic documents, it is not possible to handle the delivery of physical products and in some cases services entirely in the DPS. *Soft goods* do not need to be physically delivered, in fact the supplier can transfer these directly to the customer's DPS. Many software manufacturers already offer downloads via the WWW.

Receipt of goods and services. The receipt of an ordered good or service must be recorded in the DPS. There are two alternatives for goods receipt: delivery to the purchaser's/user's desktop or a central delivery (possibly with intermediate storage). DPSs support both alternatives. Companies have to investigate for each commodity group whether goods receipt makes sense at all regarding the absolute product price. Sometimes the caused process costs are higher than the product value.

The DPS does not show an ordering transaction as delivered until receipt has been confirmed. Tracking and reporting functionality allow the individual user or the central procurement department to check the current status of an order and the progress of a business transaction at any time.

10.4.4 Payment and Booking

Payment. In most cases, DPSs support the use of procurement cards. Pilot users investigated continue to use existing payment mechanisms with their suppliers after the introduction of a DPS. System manufacturers consider other electronic methods of payment, such as electronic cash, checks or smart cards, as belonging more to the business-to-consumer sector and therefore do not support them.

Financial booking. When initiating a purchase requisition for goods or services, the purchaser has to book the item onto cost centers and possibly activate it as asset. All the systems investigated allow the user to state a cost center for each individual item. Some manufacturers also provide the possibility of distributing the costs for an individual item amongst various cost centers.

10.4.5 Process Management

Tracking. The tracking functionality of DPSs gives the users an overview of both the authorization status of a purchase requisition or an order. Some manufacturers are planning to integrate the tracking of information in forthcoming releases, which is commonly offered by transport intermediaries. The tracking functionality also increases the transparency of procurement processes for the users. In comparison with paper form-based ordering processes, this additional transparency increases the purchaser's trust in the procurement processes.

Reporting. DPSs offer detailed reporting functionality. Companies can define procurement performance indicators per employee, per product or per product group and/or per supplier. In the past, the introduction of the role of dedicated requesters and processes frequently based on paper forms meant that companies had little management information and therefore little possibility of gauging procurement patterns or volumes or of assessing individual suppliers.

10.5 Content Management

In the case of content management, a company agrees on uniform data formats and records, as well as rules and mechanisms for replication within the framework of catalog updates with its suppliers. Here we focus on the classification, aggregation and personalization aspects of content management.

10.5.1 Content Classification

The aim of a classification scheme is to provide a system of categorizing product groups and products for MSCs which is independent of the supplier. Classification schemes are important for the maintenance and updating of MSCs and facilitate structured searching within an MSC. Unlike the DPSs investigated, ERP systems nowadays usually only allow flat classification hierarchies. SAP R/3, for example, only allows two categorization levels. The most important and frequently used classification schemes are as follows:

- The *standard product and services code* (SPSC) from Dun & Bradstreet [cf. Dun & Bradstreet 1998]. SPSC merged in 1998 with UN's CCS (common coding system), and is now called UN/SPSC.

- The *Thomas Register* scheme[1].

- The *NIGM* (National Institute of Government Purchase) which is a very detailed classification scheme especially used in public organizations.

At the present time, all the system suppliers investigated use the UN/SPSC standard. In addition to classifying the products, it is equally important for a business to determine the classification of each product category plus the attributes of a product data record. Here, we distinguish between character data and multimedia data, such as product photographs or PDF files for detailed function description. All the systems investigated allow the definition of specific data records for each product category.

10.5.2 Content Aggregation

A corporate customer needs the catalog data of different suppliers in order to be able to consolidate them in its private MSC. At the same time, the supplier will normally have various customers requiring different product data records in different data formats. This results in an n:m relationship. The effort involved can be reduced by the use of a content provider and the resulting n:1:m relationship. A content provider is an intermediary who has specialized in the aggregation and management of MSCs.

---

[1]   [cf. http://www.thomasregister.com].

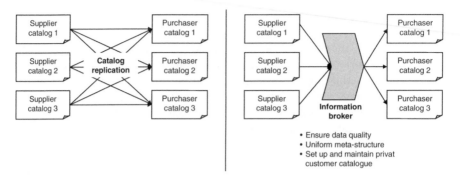

Figure 10-4: Role of Information Broker in Content Aggregation and Replication
[Aberdeen Group 1998, 4]

Up to now, no generally valid standards have emerged for the exchange of catalog data. For this purpose Ariba has developed and disclosed the CIF standard which is based on UN/SPSC [cf. Ariba 1998b]. The suppliers of Ariba customers use the CIF standard to code their catalog data. However, CIF is not a generally valid standard at the present time.

For this reason, all manufacturers offer their customers additional assistance with the adoption and integration of suppliers. Chevron, one of Ariba's first customers, also uses Harbinger as content provider. Harbinger is responsible for correcting, standardizing and formatting the catalog data of important Chevron's suppliers. Similar services are offered by Commerce One's MarketSite.net and TPN Register, a joint venture of Thomas Register and GEIS.

Commerce One is the only content provider which claims to offer its customers the possibility of calling up current prices and inventory levels in the appropriate supplier's system direct and in real time via the ECN.

10.5.3 Content Personalization

We distinguish between personalized corporate catalogs and user views of a personalized company catalog. Both Commerce One and Harbinger offer buy-side content management for *personalized corporate catalogs* MSCs. For the purposes of replication they take into account the metastructure of the catalog on the buy-side, the data fields of the product data records plus the prices for the specific company. The content provider stores different individual customer prices for each individual product.

MarketSite.net from Commerce One also performs automatic price degression. As soon as the market price drops below the individually negotiated customer price,

MarketSite.net updates the customer's MSC. This is an advantage in particular with high-tech products which are prone to pronounced price degression.

All the systems investigated allow companies to define special views of the MSC at employee or user group level. Depending on the individual user profile, the employee only has access to special products or product groups up to a defined maximum price after logging into the system. The company can define additional rules at will.

10.6   System Administration

Nowadays, all DPSs offer an administration component which accesses data on user profiles, supplier profiles and procurement rules. Depending on these data (a) a purchase requisition passes through an authorization workflow until it becomes an order, (b) the DPS gives the user access to a particular view of the MSC, (c) the user can only order products and services up to a defined maximum budget limit per time unit and (d) the system prioritizes suppliers.

In many companies, the relevant profile data are already stored in other systems. The DPS can either access the data of a given ERP/legacy system in real time or store the data in the DPS. In view of the fact that user profiles in particular are frequently used in various other systems, it is also appropriate to use directory services. At present, directory services are based on the technical standards X.500 or LDAP. Most DPS manufacturers are planning LDAP APIs for their systems.

10.7   Integration with Legacy / ERP Systems

In order to avoid the multiple input of data, the DPS has to be linked up with the internal information system of the purchasing company as well as with the information systems of the supplier. We distinguish between (a) asynchronous exchange of electronic documents, e.g. via industry-specific EDI formats and/or ALE-IDOCs in the case of SAP R/3 and (b) synchronous (real-time) exchange of and access to data via APIs (via the *application layer*).

Integration With the Internal Information System

A real-time access to data in the ERP/legacy system requires disclosed APIs. A lot of legacy systems, in particular the older ones, do not support access to system functionality via APIs. If this is the case, a company is forced to implement a message-based asynchronous integration. All DPS manufacturers claim to be able to realize a real-time link-up of the principal ERP systems from SAP, Oracle and Baan via APIs.

As the leading manufacturer of business management standard software, SAP AG has for some time now been pursuing the concept of BAPIs. BAPIs are APIs which facilitate the access to important data which have been semantically defined on the basis of the reference model and remain unchanged throughout several releases of the software [cf. Hantusch et al 1997, 113]. DPS manufacturers use BAPIs to extract the relevant data from the SAP R/3 system and write them back.

Integration With the Supplier's Information System

Real-time integration with supplier's system is mostly unnecessary for MRO goods. Today's Internet infrastructure does not offer the reliability of real-time integration. For this reason, the exchange of data with the supplier is usually asynchronous and message-based. Companies currently use EDI, e-mail and fax for sending documents.

10.8   Potential Savings of Desktop Purchasing Systems

However, savings potential is always present in the following three areas:

- *Procurement process.* The process is automated, faster and ties up fewer human resources for coordination. In some cases there is no need any more to maintain material masters for indirect goods in company's ERP systems.

- *More favorable prices.* DPSs make it possible on the one hand to bundle order volume by canalizing requisitions through the DPS as the company's intranet based purchasing portal and thus negotiate more favorable prices with the suppliers. On the other hand, these systems allow employees to compare products and prices and to purchase from the best supplier.

- *Inventory levels.* The complete procurement process is shorter and more transparent by status checks. Overall inventory levels can be reduced as a result. In some cases logistics can be outsourced to the supplier completely.

Unlike the introduction of ERP systems, there is frequently no room on the company's agenda of strategic IT projects for the realization of Business Networking applications and thus the implementation of DPSs. This aspect is taken into account in the project procedure in that a company is not expected to change over its processes from one day to the next with a 'big bang' introduction. It is much more customary to start off with a limited pilot which is then extended once a suitable level of acceptance is achieved.

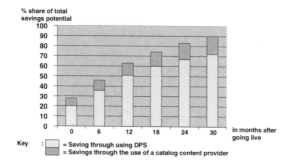

Figure 10-5: Savings Potential Realized[2]

What applies here for the changeover of processes is equally valid for the adoption of suppliers. When introducing the DPS, a company will normally start off with a product catalog covering its 3 to 10 preferred suppliers and later incorporate other suppliers and product categories. Figure 10-5 shows the typical progression of savings realized by companies.

Depending on the level of acceptance for the system and thus the progression of the curve shown in Figure 10-5, vendors speak of achieving a break-even between incurred project costs and realized savings after approximately 1 to 2.5 years.

"By Ariba's own estimates, its software can save between 5% and 15% in procurement costs-depending on the suppliers used and the items purchased." [Malik 1999]. Companies who already went productive with DPSs in 1998 inlcude VISA, Mastercard, Chevron, Pacific Gas & Electric, Country Los Angeles and Cisco.

Typically large, global corporations are implementing DPS. As described before DPS are integrated with buyer's back end systems, thus the benefit of integration also is with the buyer. We experienced that suppliers have a large interest to participate in DPS projects. They see the opportunity to have their products on virtually every employee's desktop. Frequently updates of the product range and prices are possible without the prohibitive high costs for distributing paper catalogues every couple of weeks.

"Ariba is on target to becoming a de facto industry standard.", writes [Malik 1999]. The vendors of DPS set widely accepted process and document standards for the procurement of indirect material. Once the companies know how to save money on their indirect purchase, they will leverage the standards to sell and purchase more complex goods and services. DPS thus have the potential to become a 'killer-application' of the new economy (cf. Chap. 2.3.4).

---

[2] Assumption: adoption rate of around 20% p.a. for suppliers and users within the company.

11 Templates: Standardization for Business Networking

Thomas Huber, Rainer Alt, Günter Lehmann

11.1 Introduction 212

11.2 Definition and Approaches to Standardization 213
    11.2.1 Definition and Dimensions of Standardization 213
    11.2.2 Requirements of Inter-process Integration 214
    11.2.3 Approaches to Close the 'Organization Gap' 215

11.3 Template Handbook 216
    11.3.1 Idea of a Template Handbook 217
    11.3.2 Components of a Template Handbook 217
    11.3.3 Activities in Template Design and Roll-out 218
    11.3.4 Who Should Design and Use a Template Handbook? 219

11.4 Template Handbook at the Robert Bosch Group 220
    11.4.1 Development of the Template Handbook 220
    11.4.2 Overview and Experiences 221
    11.4.3 Example Documents 223

11.5 Benefits of Templates in a Pharmaceutical Company 225

11.6 Conclusions 227

11.1   Introduction

Business in the information age depends to a large extend on the availability of accepted standards [cf. e.g. OECD 1996]. They significantly reduce the coordination requirements between business partners and are the basis for establishing integrated information flows. The availability of Internet standards, such as HTML or TCP/IP, has been a main enabler in the evolution of electronic commerce (EC) since the early 1990s. In providing specifications for the interconnectivity of information systems, which stretch across system platforms and user communities, they allowed the integration of heterogeneous sectors within an economy. Generally, we can distinguish two main thrusts towards standardization: business requirements and technological integration [cf. Venkatraman 1991].

Business requirements have changed fundamentally in the information age: large, established conglomerates are breaking up, innovative companies are emerging rapidly, and customer and process-orientation is becoming increasingly critical. Companies such as Walmart or Amazon.com derive competitive excellence from a thorough management of information and goods across all instances in their value chains. The management of these relationships is at the heart of Business Networking (cf. Chap. 1). From a technical perspective, this requires integrated information flows across all partners. This means that planning, order and control information need to be visible in real time within the entire business network.

Although the last decades have brought about significant technological improvements, today's information systems are still a far cry from this network-wide real-time visibility of information. The diffusion of enterprise resource planning (ERP) systems, such as SAP's R/3, Baan's ERP or Peoplesoft's BPCS has led to a higher level of internal integration (cf. Chap. 2.3.1). These systems are now being extended to include external partners. However, taking a closer look at the status quo of internal integration, we find that ERP systems are fragmented and distributed especially within large, multinational companies. The reason is in the high complexity of every ERP implementation project and the investments required in terms of time, capital, and manpower. Consequently, various individual ERP systems have evolved for different production sites, sales offices etc. Although, the distributed systems may use the same software products (e.g. R/3), they usually are configured individually with processes and master data being set-up differently. Consequently, the exchange of information between systems is difficult and specific interfaces are needed for establishing an integrated flow of information.

Standards for the configuration of the individual systems provide significant benefits in two dimensions. Firstly, the standardization of data, functions and processes leads to integrated information flows and permits improved processes, e.g. global credit limit checks, supply chain management and improved drill-down possibilities in financial reporting. Secondly, scale effects in the implementation allow reductions in the cost and time required to configure an ERP system.

11.2   Definition and Approaches to Standardization

11.2.1   Definition and Dimensions of Standardization

A broad variety of standards have developed in the field of information technology. Standards are available at various levels and originate from different standardization bodies. Although it would be desirable from a technological standpoint to have a single standard accepted worldwide, the variety also reflects the heterogeneity of the individual industrial sectors and the different power constellations within industries [cf. Brousseau 1994]. In the following, we will define standards as *objects that are shared and accepted within a specific community.*[1] Therefore, standards have three important dimensions (see Figure 11-1):

- The *objects* of standardization are hardware or software components with the latter comprising standards for data, functions, and processes.

- *Communities* are organizational and geographical in nature. Standards can be accepted within a single organization or between multiple organizations. From a geographical perspective, national, international, and global standards are distinguished [cf. Cannon 1993].

- *Standardization bodies* are closely related to the community and include private companies (e.g. Microsoft, IBM), industrial organizations (e.g. X/Open), national (DIN, BSI), international (ETSI, EWOS) and global (JTC1, ITU, IETF) bodies.

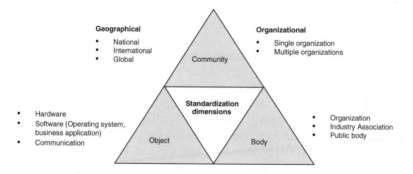

Figure 11-1: Dimensions of Standardization

The standardization dimensions are useful in analyzing standards that are on the marketplace. Standards which have had an impact in the marketplace concern

---

[1]   This definition uses elements of ([Cargill 1989] and [Buxmann 1996]).

proprietary or 'de facto' approaches to system platforms, such as the PC or DEC VAX, to operating systems such as DOS or Windows, to communication such as IBM SNA or DECNet, and to business software, such as SAP or Baan. Open standards are not owned by any single business or vendor and include such approaches as X/Open, the OSI model, and the Internet standards [cf. Chesher/Kaura 1998]. Starting from the late 1980s, the focus of businesses towards standardization has changed with the growing diffusion of open standards towards the upper layers (i.e. layers 4 to 7) within the ISO/OSI model (see). Moving to the higher levels mainly implied that interconnections among systems were taken for granted and that applications and the contents exchanged were becoming critical issues.

ISO/OSI-Layer	Examples
7. Application Layer	X.400, SMTP, DCA/DIA
6. Presentation Layer	X.400, ASN.1, FTP
5. Session Layer	X.225, X.224, ISO 8326/27
4. Transport Layer	X.225, X.224, TCP, ISO 8072/73
3. Network Layer	X.25, IP
2. Data Link Layer	X.25, ISO 8802, Arpanet, Ethernet, Token Ring
1. Physical Layer	X.25, ISO 8802, Arpanet, Ethernet, Token Ring

Table 11-1: Standards in the ISO/OSI Model

11.2.2 Requirements of Inter-process Integration

Integrating information systems means establishing communication between these systems. From the perspective of the well-known communication model, a common language is required which has four levels (see Figure 11-2). As long as communication involves human participants, there is a high degree of flexibility in interpreting the intended meaning. However, this form of integration is hardly efficient in the context of ERP where productive and high-volume data has to be re-entered manually in the system. Therefore, the following discussion will focus on inter-process integration, i.e. the direct coupling of applications. An outstanding example of for inter-process communication is EDI. Information is not only transmitted electronically, but also processed automatically in the receiving IS. Other forms of communication, such as human-computer interaction, are not within the scope of this Chapter.

Inter-process integration requires that all aspects of the communication should be identical in both systems. As [Kubicek 1992] showed, the ISO/OSI model has to be extended to include all necessary aspects. In addition to the communication services that are still covered by ISO/OSI, another three layers are required which, in essence, are derived from communication theory [cf. Zbornik 1996, 96]. In the first place, a common syntax is required which defines the order, length and the type of data being exchanged. Semantics add meaning to the individual data fields, e.g. EAN codes not only specify the 13-character syntax but also make sure that each article has a unique identification number. By referring to this unique number, meaning is added since it always leads to the same article name. The pragmatic element is optional and a feature of sophisticated workflow systems. It makes sure that transmitted data has not only been understood but that subsequent actions are triggered. For instance, the ERP would automatically issue an invoice once a product has been delivered.

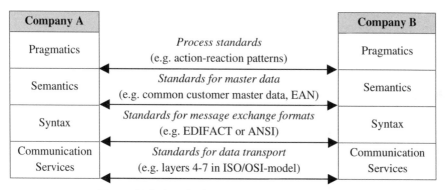

Figure 11-2: Standards in the Communication Model

11.2.3 Approaches to Close the 'Organization Gap'

Standards are the key to inter-process integration. In their early study, [Benjamin et al. 1990] reported that insufficient availability of standards has been the most important barrier to interorganizational integration. Up to date standards are mostly available for communication services and on the syntactical level (see Figure 11-2). Standardization on the semantical level has been set-up in some industries by industrial associations, e.g. the EAN codes in the food industry or the ISBN numbers for publications, or by independent providers, e.g. the Dun & Bradstreet (D&B) company numbers.[2] Standards on the pragmatical level are only available within companies and solutions which span across multiple organiza-

---

[2] Information on the D&B numbers (DUNS) is available at http://www.dnb.com.

tions still remain to be established. The neglect of semantical and pragmatical issues in such standards as EDIFACT has been referred to as 'organizational gap' [cf. Kubicek 1992].

Attempts to close the 'organizational gap' in inter-process communications have to address two aspects in general (see Table 11-2). First, the number and the type of systems involved are relevant. Normally, common semantics and pragmatics are no problem within a single ERP system. Additional systems may be other internal ERP systems or external systems, e.g. the ERP system of a supplier. The second dimension distinguishes two possibilities of standardizing semantics [cf. Scheckenbach 1997]: either the same codes and master data are used or matching tables are established ex ante which interrelate the individual codes. Clearly, using identical objects is a more efficient and pervasive way of integration, but requires the restructuring or re-customization of existing systems as well. A solution for the tight integration of ERP systems will be described in the following (shaded area in Table 11-2). Other possibilities are proposed and are being developed in the EDI community (e.g. basic semantic repository, automated negotiation), but these will not be dealt with in this book [cf. Lehmann 1996].

	Matching Tables	Same Objects
Single ERP System	—	Joint master data
Multiple ERP Systems	Converters	Network code
External Systems	Matching service (e.g. the translation engine from GEIS)	Industry code (e.g. D&B numbers)

Table 11-2: Options to Close the 'Organization Gap' in Inter-process Communication

11.3 Template Handbook

A solution for achieving standardized objects among multiple ERP systems is presented in the following. This template handbook is intended to provide a method for the semantical integration of individual ERP systems which is apt to be of substantial benefit in facilitating implementation and improving business process performance. The template handbook was developed in regular workshops and represents a pilot project with Robert Bosch GmbH in Germany. As part of this project, numerous interviews and workshops were undertaken with representatives from both the IS and the application side.

11.3.1 Idea of a Template Handbook

The implementation of ERP systems is a major challenge for companies. For different technical and organizational reasons, multinational companies need many different ERP systems, e.g. different R/3 systems for plants and for sales offices. In view of the complexities of each implementation project, different ERP systems have evolved with incompatible processes and/or master data. Consequently, each business process is limited to a specific area.

Insights gained from different practical partner company projects shows that semantical standardization is one of the most important issues when implementing ERP systems in multinational companies. Semantical standards enable an automated information exchange between the many different ERP systems – Bosch, for instance, has more than 30 productive SAP systems – supporting its business processes. The problem is in that there are different methods which support the implementation of ERP systems (e.g. SAP's ASAP method), but not the *standardization,* of such systems. An organizational gap needs to be closed in this area as well.

System templates are a solution for defining semantical standards for various applications. Such templates make sure that all applications are provided with a common customizing and a common set of master data. This is achieved, if templates are developed centrally and then rolled out to the different systems.

11.3.2 Components of a Template Handbook

Templates are well known from office packages such as Excel or Word, and denote predesigned documents that contain formats, styles or formulas. Apart from office applications, there are templates used in two other areas. First, programming languages, e.g. C++, make use of libraries that offer frequently used functions, e.g. pull-down menus. Second, there are systems built with the aid of CASE-tools that are called application templates [cf. Hofman/Rockart 1994]. However, the latter only target the development of new systems and, as a consequence, do not address the organizational gap. Therefore, the standardization of data, especially of customizing data and master data in ERP systems, still remains a topic for research.

For this purpose, the project group has defined ERP templates as *concepts or models for the standardization of processes, functions, and data that could be implemented in a physical (ERP) system.* Templates may as well be a 'piece of software' which can be distributed automatically on different systems, or some paper documents, e.g. manuals, which have to be implemented manually. The major components of ERP templates are:

- Preconditions for the set-up of the ERP configuration settings (e.g. the settings in the SAP R/3 implementation guide),

- Preconditions and recommendations for the common definition of master data,

- Test procedures, demonstrations, training documentation,

- Maintenance procedures, and

- External validation from authorities, customers, ISO 9000 etc. (if required).

With a view to enabling and ensuring multiple re-use of templates from different organizational units, establishing a *documentation* is highly relevant. Such documentation should cover the following aspects:

- 'Marketing' documentation (What can the template do?)

- Functional description for the implementation team (documentation of the template components; how does the template work?)

- Implementation guide (For roll-out and localization; how to install the template?)

- Users guide (How to use the template?)

11.3.3 Activities in Template Design and Roll-out

The template handbook embodies a method for the development and the roll-out of templates. The main activities of the method are shown in Table 11-3. For each activity, a result document is produced which can be used in projects, and there are also techniques that help to fill out a result document. Examples of the main result documents and techniques are presented in Chapter 11.4.3.

Template Development	Template Roll-out
1. Organize template development	1. Initial template selection
2. Document conditions for template deployment	2. Implement template locally
	3. Set up localization concept
3. Document template process	4. Conduct local template tests
4. Analyze the output exchange of the template process	5. Local approval of the template
5. Define customizing settings (overview)	
6. Define authorization concept	
7. Define customizing settings (detail)	
8. Document templates add-ons	
9. Define data storage guides	
10. Test template	
11. Prepare functional description	
12. Set up maintenance procedures	
13. Write user documentation	
14. Prepare implementation guide	

Table 11-3: Major Activities in Template Method

11.3.4 Who Should Design and Use a Template Handbook?

Templates can be used in large multinational companies as well as in smaller companies. However, the development process is very different. In larger companies, templates are designed to ensure minimal standards for the configuration settings in their ERP systems. Meanwhile, the development of a template method (or handbook) is mainly an IT driven project, whereas the development of a specific template (e.g. for the 'make-to-stock' processes in plants) calls for a profound understanding of the company's business processes and the ERP system that supports these processes. Therefore, people from the different business units (for which a template is to be designed) and from the IT department of a company have to work closely together in order to define the contents of a template.

In smaller companies, templates are used in a very different way. Such companies need templates for faster – and therefore cheaper - implementation of the complex ERP software products. In such cases, the term 'industrial sector templates' is preferred. Such templates are pre-configured ERP systems that may be implemented in different companies of a specific industrial sector. The development of a template is not normally done in these cases by the company that will use a template, but by a firm of consultants or by the manufacturer of the ERP software.

11.4   Template Handbook at the Robert Bosch Group

11.4.1 Development of the Template Handbook

The Robert Bosch Group is headquartered in Stuttgart, Germany, and has operations in over 130 countries worldwide. In its four business sectors, viz. automotive equipment, communication technology, consumer goods, and capital goods, Bosch generates approx. DEM 50 billion in sales and employees approx. 189,000 people (1998 figures). At Bosch, many different ERP systems support the business processes. Most of them, more than 30, are using SAP's R/3. ERP systems are in place for different organizational units, such as manufacturing facilities, sales offices, financial departments as well as for different geographical regions (e.g. Germany, USA, and Asia). With a view to enabling new business processes and reducing the costs for ERP implementation projects, Bosch decided to use templates for the:

- initial implementation of new ERP systems, and

- the deployment of new processes on existing ERP systems.

Regarding the dimensions of standardization (Table 11-1) the Bosch templates were defined to support the global operation within Bosch (standardization community). The standardizing body was QI (Querschnittsbereich Informatik) which is Bosch's central IT department and serves all its divisions. The objects to be standardized were configurations of the ERP systems as well as data structures and codes.

Because of all the experiences that Bosch had gathered in respect of its ERP systems, they were aware of the complexities besetting templates. Therefore, there was no doubt that an effective method would have to support the template development process. The development of the 'template handbook' (which in fact is the name given the method) was the subject of a joint project which involved people from CC iBN and up to seven people from Bosch. The people from Bosch came from its information management department and had a good knowledge either of the ERP systems or the business processes within different departments at Bosch. The template handbook was developed using the method engineering concept (cf. Chap. 14.1.3). The basic components of method engineering are:

- *Activities* which describe what has to be performed. The goal of an activity is to deliver one or several defined results. The procedural model of the method determines a sequence of activities.

- *Results* are produced or changed by activities. Various types of documents can be distinguished, such as tables, graphs or diagrams.

- *Techniques* which describe how to obtain a result. Every task has at least one corresponding technique. Techniques are guidelines for the production of results and can include best practices and lessons learned from prior projects.

- *Roles* which describe the responsibilities for a specific task. Within a method, people and organizational units assume certain roles which are a summary of activities from an actor's point of view.

11.4.2 Overview and Experiences

For Bosch, the two primary objectives in developing the template handbook reflect the motivations described above (cf. Chap 11.1). On the one hand, ERP systems should be capable of supporting Bosch's Business Networking requirements. An integrated flow of information between the individual ERP systems was the key to addressing this business need. On the other hand, the time needed for R/3 implementations was to be reduced through re-use of know how.

Table 11-4 gives a detailed view of the contents of the template handbook. Section A lists all the activities, techniques and result documents that were needed to develop a template. Section B comprises all activities, techniques and result documents needed to roll out a specific template to different ERP systems.

Activity	Technique	Result Document
A. Template Development		
1. Organize template development	Organization template development	Overview organization template development
2. Document conditions for the template deployment	Conditions for template deployment	List of conditions for template deployment
3. Document template process	Activity chain(s) template processes)	Activity chain diagram
4. Analyze the output exchange of the template process	Context diagram template process	Context diagram of the template process
5. Define customizing settings	Settings for customizing (overview) and authorization	Preconditions for customizing (overview)
6. Define authorization concept		Authorization concept

7. Complete customizing settings	Settings for customizing (detail)	Preconditions for customizing (detail)
8. Document templates add-ons		Overview template add-ons
9. Define data storage guidelines		Documentation of storage guidelines
10. Test template	Test of configuration settings	Test report
11. Prepare functional description	Functional description	Documentation of template functionality
12. Set up maintenance procedures	Maintenance procedures	Documentation of maintenance procedures
13. Write user documentation	User documentation	Documentation for end user
14. Prepare implementation guide	Implementation guide	Check list conditions for template deployment
		List of template add ons
		List of settings to be localized
		Change list for original objects
B. Template Roll-out		
1. Select templates for local use	Local selection of templates	List of selected templates
2. Implement template locally	Local template implementation	Experience report
3. Adjust template locally	Localization	Documentation of localization
4. Conduct local tests	Local tests	Local test report
5. Accept and release template	Acceptance and release	Configuration settings

Table 11-4: Template Handbook Overview

The whole development process for the template handbook took about 7 months and is now (Spring 99) in the phase of practical testing with processes – that should run on different ERP systems within Bosch – being defined and documented using the template handbook. The main challenge was to define all the aspects of a template that must be documented in some kind of result document. The goal was to document the entire template life cycle, thus covering development, roll-out and distribution, maintenance, release management, and re-use. The second challenge was to align all the activities that were necessary to produce the result documents. It took about ten group meetings to define the content of the result documents and the activities needed to build these documents.

11.4.3 Example Documents

As mentioned above, the template handbook specifies a result document and a technique for each activity. Both will be illustrated using the first activity of the method ('organize template development' Table 11-4). The document 'overview organization template development' is shown Table 11-6. The guidelines required to complete the result document fields are specified in the technique which is termed in analogy to the activity 'organization template development' (see Table 11-5). The following paragraphs show the constituents of this technique. All other activities, result documents and techniques of the method are documented as in the example discussed in this Chapter. Altogether, the template handbook now consists of approx. 70 pages.

Technique: 'Organization template development'

The first step of the method deals with the identification of the organizational framework needed for the development of a template. The following information is important:

- *Template Name*: Definition of a unique name for the template. The name should reflect the future function and the scope[1] of the template.

- *Kernel System*: Definition of the operating environment for the template. Here the decision is made on what types of systems the template will run (e.g. plant or distribution systems).

- *Application Type*: Detailed specification of the type (manufacturer and application name) of the application for which the template is to be developed (e.g. SAP R/3).

- *Release*: It is important also to specify the exact release number of the application type (e.g. 3.1.h).

- *Process-/Function Number*: Use, if available, the identification numbers for functions provided by the manufacturer (e.g. the SAP function numbers).

- *Development Board*: In this row are defined the persons (and organizational units they belong to) responsible for the development of the template.

- *Review Board*: Here the review board is defined (employees and organizational units). The review board has to crosscheck the contents of the template against the overall conventions that exist in a company (e.g. naming or programming conventions).

- *Authorization Board*: This row defines responsibilities for official authorization (final acceptance) of the template. Accordingly, the names of the persons appointed to the board and their organizational units are indicated in this row.

- *Pilot Customer(s)*: Definition of the pilot customer(s) of the template. Again, the names of the persons appointed must be indicated and the organizational units they belong to.

- *Template Roll-out*: Definition of the organizational units that must or could use the template. For each of these units, a decision is needed on whether the template must be implemented locally (enter 'M' for must) or whether the template could be implemented in a local system (enter 'C' for could) - if the unit wants to do so.

- *Localization*: A decision is needed for each organizational unit that must/could implement the template on whether a localization of the template (e.g. changes in the customizing definitions in the template) is allowed (enter 'Y' for yes) or not (enter 'N' for no).

- *Copying Model*: In a next step, a decision is made for each organizational unit on whether the template can be used as a copying model (enter 'Y' for yes) or not (enter 'N' for no). Copying model in these context refers to templates for an initial system set-up (this field is rather Bosch-specific).

- *Authorization Date*: At the end of the development process, the template needs to be formally authorized (accepted). If accepted, the place and the date of the authorization are entered in this document, the authorization board signs the document and the template is ready for roll-out.

Table 11-5: Technique 'Organization Template Development'

Document: Overview - Organization Template Development **Date:** 12.12.99
Status: Completed   **Author:** THU
Activity: Organize Template Development   **Page:** 1

Template Name: Purchase Demand Release		
Kernel System	• Plant systems (all plants within Europe) • Sales systems (multi-divisional sale systems)	
Application Type	SAP R/3	
Release	3.1. h (and higher)	
Process/Function Number	BANF	
Template Boards	Organizational Unit	Name
Development Board	• IS department • Plant representatives • Sales representatives	• A. Miller, F. Smith, C. Barns • H. Wilson, W. Walters • S. May, K. Muller, B. Gerber
Review Board	• IS department • Plant representatives • Sales representatives	• H. Hansen • K. William • P. Klein
Authorization Board	• CIO • Vice-president, plant management	• U. Lee • P. Guinness
Pilot Customer(s)	Strasbourg Plant, France	J. Bartoli
	Philadelphia Plant, USA	W. Clark
	Munich Sales Office, Germany	B. Gross
	Hong Kong Sales Office	E. Wu

Template Roll-out (M = must, C = can)	Org. Unit 1	Org. Unit 2	Org. Unit 3	Org. Unit 3							
	M	C	M	M							
Localization (yes/no)	Y	Y	N	N							
Copying Model (yes/no)	N	N	N	N							
Authorization Date	Frankfurt, January 24, 2000										

Table 11-6: Example of a Result Document

11.5 Benefits of Templates in a Pharmaceutical Company

Another example of the deployment of templates in multinational companies is taken from the pharmaceutical industry. In the case of this company, the pressure to develop templates was a direct function of the growing globalization of its business. The company is organized in multiple divisions which are located in various parts of the world. In order to better manage the divisional businesses, the company decided to move from existing, historically grown, local systems to global systems. Contrary to the former, which are cross-divisional, the latter provide global information flows within a specific division. The main objectives of this strategy were to:

- Establish consistency and integrity of group reporting,

- Ensure consistency with divisional business strategies (process view, integration, globalization),

- Enhance project flexibility (improvement in terms of time, costs and risks), and to

- Foster opportunities for sharing and re-use of knowledge.

In order to achieve these results, establishing standards for processes, data and systems configuration's settings were a prerequisite. The necessary templates were developed by divisional competence centers for two areas. First, the company developed a company core that defines the common elements for all SAP R/3 implementations across geographical sites and divisions, e.g. group master data, chart of accounts, organizational elements, etc. This core guarantees the support of the group reporting rules, definitions and accounting principles and ensures consistent and efficient reporting. The uniqueness of data is ensured by assigning different number ranges to the divisions.

Based on this core, the company developed further templates for each division which were called 'divisional kernels' (see Figure 11-3). These templates are pre-configured ERP systems (mainly SAP's R/3) and reflect common processes in a division based on best practices. They are used for implementing systems within the different regional and local businesses of a division. The objectives of the divisional templates are to:

- ensure globally/regionally homogenous systems which facilitate different global/regional processes,

- support local process improvements, and to

- reduce implementation time and costs.

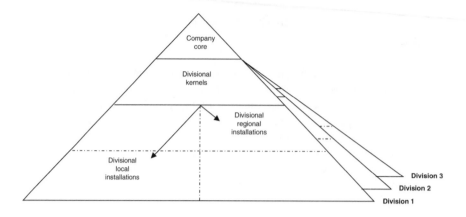

Figure 11-3: Distribution of Company Core and Divisional Kernels

As Figure 11-4 shows, between 40% and 80% of a local system's configuration is defined by templates (FI: financials, SD: sales and distribution, MM: material management, PP: production planning; FI, SD, MM and PP are modules of the R/3 system). Thus, templates were the important instrument to achieve global standardization among the different ERP systems. Having common, standardized systems in place tends to increase the efficiency of business processes and sustain strategic control and process improvements. Common systems and standardized implementations also tend to make for faster implementation and consequently, lower implementation costs.

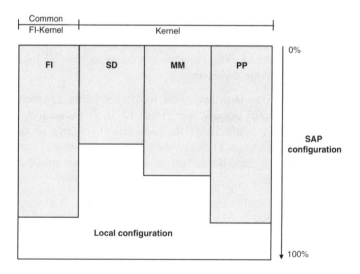

Figure 11-4: Pre-configuration Rates for Different Templates (in % of the Whole System)

11.6 Conclusions

In the present chapter, we emphasized the role of standardization in Business Networking and presented templates as instruments to achieve standardization of distributed ERP systems. As our project activities have shown, templates are apt to generate major benefits in two areas. First, templates sustain integrated information flows and foster new process perspectives such as one face to the customer as well as enhanced controlling and reporting possibilities. Second, templates are instruments to reduce the costs of implementing and coordinating distributed ERP systems inside large multinational companies. However, introducing, assessing and rolling out templates are complex processes which call for a systematic approach. This method we have termed 'template handbook'.

Besides the complexity of template development, other factors were found to have an impact on realization. First, templates presuppose the existence of application architecture planning. For example, a corporate decision would be needed as to whether local cross-divisional or global divisional systems are to be implemented. This degree of (de)centralization governs the design of templates. Templates with strong cross-divisional components, for instance, may differ from divisional templates. This may be due to the probability of different production strategies (make-to-order, make-to-stock etc.) being used greater in cross-divisional than in divisional production set-ups.

Second, templates are associated with significant scale economics since the costs of standardization are higher for pilot users. Every instance of the template being implemented will decrease its development cost and, due to learning curve effects, the cost of implementation. Consequently, organizations should strive for an as large a number of implementations as possible, making sure at the same time that pilot users are not penalized for participating in the development of templates. It is quite important, for the promoters of templates to consider creating incentives schemes which reward the pilot users.

Third, as all standards, templates have a strong political component. As [Brousseau 1994] pointed out, standards tend to be confronted with the dilemma as to whether universality or individuality should prevail. On the one hand, single, universal standards tend to yield the higher returns in terms of efficiency, whereas on the other hand, the different businesses within a company require individualized systems for maximal flexibility. For example, financial managers and forecasting departments would prioritize standardized and centralized systems. People in sales and production usually have a strong bias towards decentralized and individualized processes. In point of fact, the amount of individual fields and codes to be added to a template depends to a large extend on the political power of the individual business units.

Given the political power to implement standards and a strategy for the development and re-use of templates, the templates designed and the systematic method applied have shown a practicable way of how to close the organization gap. At the same time, they will enable the course of further research to be charted out. First, continued research will have to focus on how future (ERP) application architectures that are geared to Business Networking will look like. A specially interesting aspect will be to determine which parts of these architectures will lend themselves to the use of templates. Second, the method is proposed to be amplified to assist in answering the question as to what the optimal degree of standardization will be that a specific template should provide. Finally, in view of the growing autonomy and interdependence of business units, it should be borne in mind that the possibilities of a hierarchical roll-out of templates are likely to diminish. Instead, it will be necessary to convince users to develop and use templates, and this will involve not only an appraisal of the costs but also a transparent demonstration of the benefits to be gained from investing in templates.

12 eServices for Integrating eMarkets

Norbert Kaltenmorgen, Roland Klüber, Florian Leser, Rainer Alt

12.1 Business Networking and ERP Integration 230

12.2 eMarkets and eServices in Business Networking................................231
    12.2.1 Evolution and Market Potential 231
    12.2.2 Benefits of eMarkets...231
    12.2.3 Benefits of Process Integration 232
    12.2.4 Integration Requirements...232

12.3 eServices for Integration - Case of Triaton 234
    12.3.1 newtron and Triaton – eMarket and System Supplier..............234
    12.3.2 Considerations on eMarket Integration Potential.....................235
    12.3.3 Triaton eService 'A2A e-Link for eMarkets'...........................236
    12.3.4 Cooperation newtron and Triaton 237
    12.3.5 Business Process Support and Benefits....................................239

12.4 Implementation and Architecture of A2A e-Link for
    eMarkets...240

12.5 Digression: Solution Enhancement Potentials with IBM
    tpaML..243

12.6 Conclusions and Outlook 246

12.1   Business Networking and ERP Integration

Integration is a key element for Business Networking applications. First, many companies have introduced initiatives to restructure internal processes and integrate information systems by merging individual subprocesses into integrated information systems, such as desktop purchasing systems (cf. Chaps. 10 and 14.2). Second, the rapid evolution of new eMarkets, such Covisint in the automotive sector or ChemConnect in the chemical industry, as well as external eServices providers, such as inet-logistics in logistics or Deutsche Merchant in factoring. As partners of the businesses are concerned, these new business models take over subprocesses or replace business processes with new high-quality IT-supported processes which ideally should represent a seamless extension of company processes. This means integrating the ERP systems of companies and the infrastructures of eMarkets and eServices.

As a result of the speed at which the Business Networking (or eBusiness) sector has developed, ERP system suppliers have not yet succeeded in fully integrating outwardly reaching eBusiness activities, such as electronic markets or eProcurement with internal processes, even if they have already launched their own initiatives and developed new infrastructures within an extremely short space of time (e.g. mySAP.com from SAP). Integration with these new partners via electronic media has only just begun and is being boosted by initiatives such as eServices and e-speak from Hewlett-Packard or tpaML from IBM. eServices are therefore seen as the next revolution [Plummer/Smith 2000]. The integration of eServices into an existing organization brings new challenges as process, data, protocol and interface standards for dynamic eService access are still at the development or introduction stage. This is partly because in eBusiness the vast majority of IT infrastructures are proprietary developments. The Gartner Group forecasts that the market for these integration services will hit USD 100 billion by 2004, with an annual growth rate of more than 50% [GartnerGroup 2000].

Since the knowledge and competencies required to solve this problem are currently rare, the attractiveness of outsourcing these activities to third parties is growing. This trend is being accentuated by a desire to avoid past experience where the relationship-specific interfaces and applications used for EDI or CAD systems led to technically limited and expensive one-to-one solutions between business partners. The case of Triaton shows how an eService business model of an outsourcing provider offering the integration of eMarkets into ERP systems is developed and technically realized.

12.2   eMarkets and eServices in Business Networking

12.2.1 Evolution and Market Potential

Electronic markets have become a vital part of Business Networking strategies in all industries. Well known examples are Covisint, a joint venture of General Motors, Ford, DaimlerChrysler, Nissan, Renault and others, or ChemConnect, a joint venture of Bayer, BASF, BP Amoco, Eastman Chemicals, Celanese, Dow, ICI, and others. Many analysts expect the volume of electronic transactions to expand from just under USD 400 billion (today) to almost USD 2,500 billion in the year 2004. Optimistic estimates from AMR even go as far as putting the value at USD 5,700 billion. Merill Lynch und Forrester Research predict that the proportion of transactions handled by eMarkets will account for 10% – 20% of the total. [Blodget/McCabe 2000]. AMR, on the other hand, base their forecasts on over 50%, and consider a trade volume of almost USD 3,000 billion to be realistic. In addition, the number of eMarkets is expected to grow from the current level of around 600 (6/2000) to over 4,000 in the year 2004, with the number of users jumping from 400,000 at present to 12.2 million.

"It is questionable whether companies which do not participate in electronic markets will survive" is a popular argument put forward to persuade decision-makers to participate in eMarkets. Whether such assertions prove correct remains to be seen. What can be observed at the moment is the demise of certain electronic markets [cf. Hof 2000]. This trend towards consolidation will certainly increase until the critical mass (cf. Chap. 2.2.3) is reached. What is important is that businesses can derive benefits from participating in electronic markets.

12.2.2 Benefits of eMarkets

Compared to conventional procurement and sales channels, Internet-based eMarkets offer the advantage of lower transaction costs. Search costs (e.g. in catalogs or physical exhibitions) are reduced and it is easier to reach more customers. The catalogs for eMarkets combine the offerings of various suppliers in one sector (vertical integration) or across sectors (horizontal integration). The catalog for the Chemplorer marketplace, for instance, contains over 180,000 different products for the chemical industry.

Various mechanisms are available for coordination in eMarkets. In the first place auctions, exchanges and electronic requests for bids (RFB) help to achieve market transparency and higher market efficiency. The risk of not being able to find an alternative supplier in the event of procurement bottlenecks or having no buyers for remaining stocks is also reduced [cf. Kuper/Billington 2000, 33]. Companies succeed in achieving significant procurement savings through price reductions when using eMarkets in procurement (cf. Chap. 10.8). For example, Bayer AG was able to cut the price for packaging materials by 15% compared to the previous level through an auction [cf. Hübner 2000]. Contract costs were also reduced by using standard contract templates [cf. Merz 1996, 12].

12.2.3 Benefits of Process Integration

Further increases in efficiency can be achieved if internal processes are integrated with the processes of the eMarkets and other suppliers. Where indirect goods (eProcurement) are concerned, it has been shown that 80% of procurement costs can be saved in this way.

eMarkets try to differentiate themselves from their competitors by offering additional services, thus surviving the consolidation phase and winning new customers. Such measures allow them to increase liquidity on the one hand and tap new sources of income on the other. Services, such as news and monitoring, are easily provided on the basis of the existing eMarket IT infrastructure and the associated know-how. This means that additional know-how relating to ERP systems and integration tools is necessary for integration with the processes of eMarket customers.

According to a survey carried out by Forrester Research, only 6% of eMarkets currently have backend integration. In 2002, 42% of eMarkets are planning to offer their customers this service. The high requirements in terms of ERP integration, eMarket infrastructure know-how, and the growing demand for solutions represent a market opportunity for specialized service providers. Many eMarkets have already concluded cooperation agreements with IT partners to avoid being exposed to the risks of inadequate IT. More complex outsourcing scenarios will evolve for handling logistics, financing and process integration.

12.2.4 Integration Requirements

The prerequisite for integration is a suitable model which shows how an integration solution can technically be realized. This model has been derived from the Business Networking model (cf. Chap. 2.3.4) and focuses on integration aspects between intermediaries, eMarkets and eServices. At the heart of integration is standardization (cf. [Hartman et al. 2000], [Berners-Lee 1999]) at all levels in the communication model (cf. Chap. 11.2.2): pragmatics (standardized processes), semantics (standardized content), and syntax (standardized data fields). Current standards in general focus on the syntax level (e.g. EDIFACT) and significant activities are underway to provide semantical standardization (e.g. EAN, eClass).

From an implementation point of view three elements are relevant in the business model:

- *Business Bus.* A set of standards that supports the exchange of information, products and services among business partners. It is a logical space where (complex) services and products are flexibly and efficiently exchanged on the basis of previously agreed standards. Its purpose is to define a set of standards that enable 'plug&play' connections. Examples are standards for catalogs (e.g., BMEcat, eClass, cXML) or processes (e.g. CPFR, RosettaNet).[1] The standardized infrastructure of the Internet is extended to exchanging business information, services and knowledge on a semantic level. The concept builds upon the increasing availability of modular eServices and standards for processes, data and interfaces.

- *Business Port.* Information systems or services which enable a company to interface with a large number of partners. The first generation of business ports are already on the market (e.g. SAP Business Connector or systems for Enterprise Application Integration [cf. Linthicum 2000]) and are expected to develop with the diffusion of XML-related standards. These systems or external services form the layer that manages different syntax and semantics based on the standards defined by the business bus. It can be regarded as a customized layer to connect internal and external IT world, featuring high requirements on security, performance and service levels.

- *Standard Applications.* Increasingly standard software is becoming available for the individual Business Networking strategies. Standardized components (e.g. for CRM and EC) support the diffusion of processes and interfaces, i.e. the processes and interfaces being hardwired in the application. Another implication of standardized applications is that they can be outsourced to eServices more easily.

Figure 12-1 depicts an example of an intermediary who has networked systems with an eService and his partners via the business bus. All participants use the same set of standards and have to implement business ports in order to map their internal processes and data standards.

---

[1] CXML stands for Commerce Extended Markup Language and CPFR for Collaboration, Planning, Forecasting and Replenishment (www.cpfr.org).

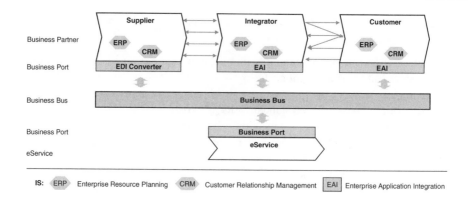

Figure 12-1: Integration Elements in Business Networking Model

12.3   eServices for Integration - Case of Triaton

In the following we will describe one of the first integration solutions which are offered as an eService. We believe that the Triaton – newtron case highlights an important solution for achieving critical backend-integration in Business Net-working.

A cooperation agreement was concluded with newtron in order to offer solutions for the ERP integration to newtron eMarket customers. This cooperation gives Triaton access to new business fields by bringing together and utilizing many years of integration experience and eBusiness strategies. The partners involved and the basic eService idea are presented briefly below.

12.3.1   newtron and Triaton – eMarket and System Supplier

newtron AG is a typical company of the 'New Economy'. Its core business areas include the development of eMarket software and the operation of eMarkets with own operating units (www.newtron.net). In autumn 2000, the company employed around 60 people at four sites. The eMarket software developed by newtron represents a trading platform to support business processes in sales and purchasing. The main task is to provide eMarket participants with the processes RFB and various forms of auction through the trading platform (see Figure 12-2). The platform is capable of flexible operation on various product supplier directories.

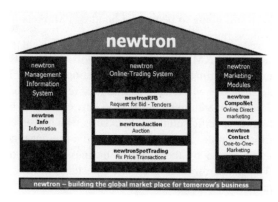

Figure 12-2: Processes Supported by newtron (Source: newtron AG)

Triaton GmbH (www.triaton.com) is a new system supplier of ThyssenKrupp Information Services Group which was founded in autumn 2000. The company was created through a merger between ThyssenKrupp Information Systems and HiServ, the former Aventis IT system supplier. The ThyssenKrupp Information Services Group employs a total of over 3,000 people, with a forecasted sales volume of almost DEM 1 billion for 2001. Triaton is positioned as a globally active, comprehensive system supplier. The areas on which it focuses include the automotive sector, agribusiness, chemicals, engineering, industrial trade, logistics, plant construction, the metal industry, pharmaceuticals, steel and other processing industries.

12.3.2 Considerations on eMarket Integration Potential

The competencies of Triaton include providing solutions for integrating application systems between companies with middleware and enterprise application integration systems. The idea of developing services and solutions for integrating eMarkets with the ERP systems of marketplace participants goes back to 1999. It was shaped by the following considerations and integration needs:

- eMarkets must offer their participants ERP integration by 2001 at the latest. Without the seamless integration of internal business processes (determination of requirements, ordering, etc.) with the processes of trading platforms (RFBs, auctions, etc.) it will not be possible to achieve the necessary growth rates for marketplace transactions.

- In view of the large number of existing vertical eMarkets, many businesses will have to confront the task of 'multi-eMarket integration'. Even if the anticipated eMarket consolidation goes ahead at a faster pace than generally expected, there are still going to be several hundred eMarkets in existence with significant business relevance in the year 2003.

- Although Internet and XML-based solutions will establish themselves, they will not do much to facilitate the task of integration initially. The vertical orientation of the eMarkets will tend to lead to a large number of different interfaces and protocols. In addition, competition between platform providers will encourage eMarket-specific solutions. Standards which even consider the role of eMarkets, for example, are not available at the present time. This is made more difficult of course by the different business models of the eMarkets themselves. The standardization of eMarket business processes would, however, be the prerequisite for interface standardization.

- Even if coordinated solutions were available from standard software vendors and eMarket operators, it would still take 1 to 2 years before these software versions were used by a reasonably large number of companies.

12.3.3 Triaton eService 'A2A e-Link for eMarkets'

Based on the considerations described above, Triaton developed the eService 'A2A e-Link for eMarkets'. This eService had to meet the following requirements:

- *Customers.* Concerning the target group, the eService was to focus on two groups: (1) eMarket operators who do not have their own integration infrastructure or who would like to outsource it to a partner for strategic reasons. This group also includes companies wishing to build up their own eMarkets exclusively for their own purposes. (2) Small and medium-sized enterprises as eMarket participants.

- *Flexibility.* Depending on the strategy of the eService customer, the eService must therefore allow flexible configuration, from a 'core business port' on the customer side and a suitably powerful business port on the e-Link side to the other distribution extreme: a powerful customer business port which only communicates with 'core business ports' of eMarkets.

- *Micro-expansions.* In principle, Although frameworks and tools are available, a classic software solution does not promise the desired success. What is lacking are the protocols implemented with these tools and 'micro-expansions' of the application systems (add-ons). Here, the emphasis is on a coordinated combination of education/knowledge services, consultancy and implementation services, operation and maintenance of customer and eMarket operator business ports including a fully integrated helpdesk, and the development of eMarket and ERP-specific adapters with the aid of middleware and EAI systems.

Finally, the eService must meet some additional criteria concerning timeframe, technological and economic constraints:

- It must be made rapidly available in an initial version for first customer projects

- It must be possible to implement it within one week (5 man-days per customer)

- The eService must have 'multi-protocol' capability

- Prices and services must be geared to target groups

Basde on the above requirements, an initial development phase would be dedicated to supporting the ERP system SAP R/3 MM/SD[2] on the customer side plus an eMarket platform. Development of the basic services and the market launch itself will take place during this phase. In spring 2000 a cooperation was reached with newtron to support newtron's trading platform within three months.

12.3.4 Cooperation newtron and Triaton

The newtron platform is now used in various eMarkets and newtron currently runs three eMarkets: (1) technical components (including mechanical and electronic engineering, electronics and plant engineering, measurement and control technology (www.newtronComponNET.com), (2) Maintenance, Repair and Operations (www.newtronMRO.com), and (3) telecommunications and multimedia (www.telbiz.com). The platform is also used Europe-wide in the plastics industry in an eMarket for raw materials belonging to ClickPlastics AG (www. clickplastics.com).

The supported business processes are requests for bids (RFB), auctions and multi-vendor catalog sales. newtron started its web presence 1999, based on the ComponNET catalog, which was extended to an eMarket. It offers buyers and sellers a platform providing information on products, producers, status; the exchange of product specifications and CAD files is included.

---

[2] MM and SD are the names of SAP R/3 modules for Materials Management and Sales & Distribution.

Figure 12-3: Example of a newtron eMarket CompoNET

In the cooperation newtron used its IT competencies combined with the content of other partners (Catalogic, Konradin, etc.) to set up a working eMarket. This eMarket offering has now been enhanced with the aid of Triaton to offer ERP integration to newtron's customers. This helps to increase customer retention and to improve the offering in order to realize efficiency gains on the buyer side. newtron is profiting from the early availability of this eService for its marketplace participants and, as a development partner arriving early on the scene, can influence how the eService is designed. In choosing newtron as a partner, Triaton was able to develop the eService within a short period of time and benefits from the dynamics and flexibility of being a start-up. The fair behavior of the partners towards each other and the recognition of the win-win situation laid the basis for the rapid transition from business idea to practical realization. The overview below shows how this cooperation works on the basis of the business networking model (see Figure 12-4).

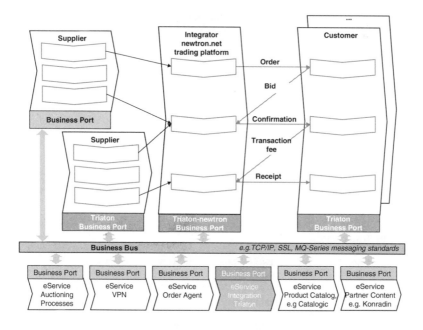

Figure 12-4: Business Networking Model of newtron and Triaton Partnership

12.3.5 Business Process Support and Benefits

Based on the business ports, newtron will be able to offer its customers a more complete solution including a seamless electronic integration of the request for bidding process (RFB) or auctioning processes as well as contracting. Process support by an intermediary (eMarket) is not yet included in the standard SAP R/3 software. The electronic integration will then include all transaction phases (cf. Chap. 4.3.1). The information and contracting phase will be implemented within newtron's electronic commerce solutions. The settlement phase will be implemented within the SAP R/3 system, based on data from the electronic commerce transactions made available by Triaton's eService. Using several eMarkets in his ERP system gives the customer an overview of all business processes operating in the marketplaces in which he participates, whether in a buying or selling role.

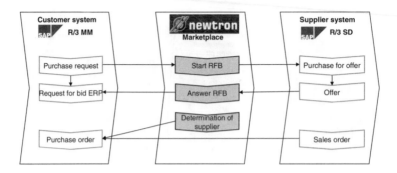

Figure 12-5: Process Flow via Individual Systems and Triaton Business Ports

Possible benefits for businesses using the eService 'A2A e-Link for eMarkets' include the following:

- Streamlined work processes and less duplication of data storage,

- Unread mailboxes and the misdirection of (mail-based) RFBs, invitations to auctions in the organization are avoided,

- eService enables quick and economic availability of eBusiness infrastructure,

- Increased acceptance and critical mass of connected eMarkets.

12.4   Implementation and Architecture of A2A e-Link for eMarkets

Figure 12-6 shows the architecture of the A2A e-Link for eMarkets. The process expansions required for the ERP system SAP R/3 SD/MM are grouped together in the applications components Sellers Port and Buyers Port. This is not a new applications package but minor extensions in the MM request for quotation/purchase order processing and the SD inquiry/incoming orders. The central component of the technical infrastructure is the e-Link Engine. This is responsible for communication between the ERP adapters on the customer side as well as the eMarket adapters. The important feature here is that the e-Link Engine is fully integrated with a service and helpdesk. Administrators can check the status of their own business processes, initiate and call up maintenance services at any time via the appropriate service portal. The flexibility with which components can be linked into this service and operating infrastructure on the customer side (e.g. SAP Business Connector) or marketplace side is decisive. A special prototype, known as the e-Link Configurator, has already been developed to manage the variety of configurations possible.

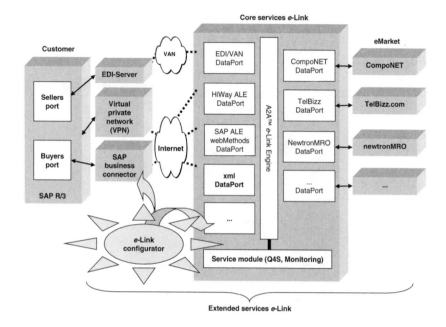

Figure 12-6: A2A e-Link System Architecture

The A2A e-Link Configurator is a graphical user interface-based tool which Triaton developed to implement seamless integration between multiple business systems and IT platforms. It manages and controls all interface requirements and allows the transformation and translation of data. Figure 12-7 shows the linking of the SAP R/3 MM (source) with the newtron eMarket (destination), as indicated by the line in the graphic.

The complete technical configuration can be generated with the Configurator, from selection of the application-specific dataports (ERP adapter, eMarket adapter), the communication middleware (messaging, etc.), the required data transformations and encoding through to distribution of the components to the servers involved.

The first step is to define the dataports. This is done by selecting one of the ports given in the pop-up window. The dataport contains the communication protocol with the appropriate application, eMarket or ERP system. The Configurator needs a transport and filter adapter in order to be able to generate runtime coding for that connection. While the transport adapter configures the physical data exchange between the servers, additional transformation and encoding rules required are included by means of the filter adapter.

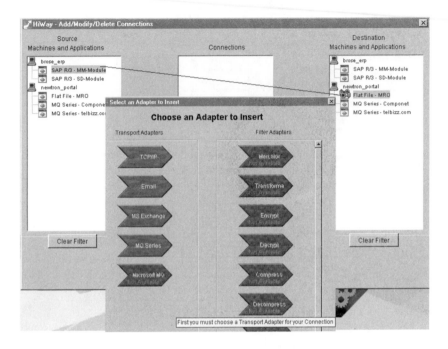

Figure 12-7: Screen Shot of the A2A e-Link Configurator

In this step the network protocols to be used, security requirements and messaging middleware are determined in order to set up the connection to the newtronCompoNET marketplace. The next stage represented in Figure 12-8 is to generate the code that implements the specified business port.

Further eMarket dataports and increasingly XML-based standards such as cXML, Common Business Library (CBL) or RosettaNet[3] standards will be implemented in the forthcoming expansion phase. Synchronous links will also be used more frequently. A major supplier for this type of dataport is webMethods (www.webmethods.com) and the SAP Business Connector. A specific expansion might be as described below.

---

[3] See www.ariba.com for cXML, http://www.commerceone.com/xml/cbl/index.html for Common Business Library (CBL) and www.rosettanet.org.

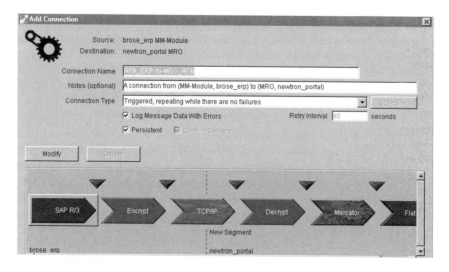

Figure 12-8: Business Port Elements to be Implemented by Configurator

12.5 Digression: Solution Enhancement Potentials with IBM tpaML

The business networking model recommends that a set of standards is used in order to obtain the required flexibility for business networking. To facilitate electronic contract definition and its implementation, IBM has developed the Trading Partner Agreement Markup Language (tpaML)[4].

tpaML aims to facilitate collaboration by standardizing the interaction of trading partners, ranging from the basic communication via data and document exchange to the business protocol layer. The XML-based tpaML documents capture the relevant information to enable the communication of applications and processes. Since it covers a high level layer many standards below have to be agreed upon and defined. The language and its standards are based on the following assumptions:

- Usually there is no common shared underlying middleware for inter-business processes. Setting up such a middleware would require a tight coupling of partners' software platforms with implications for security, naming and component registration.

---

[4] This is an open standard available on the Internet and submitted for standardization with OASIS xml.org initiative. TpaML is complementary to the Electronic Business XML initiative (ebXML) of the UN/CEFACT and OASIS.

- ACID principles (Atomicy, Consistency, Isolation, Durability [Gray/Reuter 1993] and one sphere of control are not desirable since hold locks would lead to a loss of autonomy.

- Current inter-business practices do not support rollback or compensation transactions, but rely on forward moving actions like explicit recourse actions (e.g. cancellation of a purchase). These can also be implemented in computer supported media.

tpaML relies on a conversation model of interaction that is based on a conversation history with mutually agreed permissible operations. Based on these, the external interactions consist of requests, responses, modifications or cancellations. As in the inter-Business Networking method [Klueber et al. 1999, 272] the developers of tpaML stress the importance of control and monitoring as well as trust [Sachs et al. 2000, 3].

Trading Partner Agreements (TPA) expresses the IT terms and conditions which participating parties must agree upon. This also entails configuration information and the interaction rules that must be executable. To achieve this, tools for authoring and code-generation are required.

The standardization of the business bus could be supported by tpaML on several levels (see Table 12-1). The hierarchy of categories defines a layer model of eService categories. It describes how different tasks are solved by tpaML standards or standards which tpaML uses itself. The values result from the description of tpaML [Sachs et al. 2000] in the subcategories language, content, protocol. However, not every layer is fully specified as yet.

tpaML goes much further than typical communication standards like TCP/IP or transaction standards. It aims to automate services previously not considered to be 'automatable'. It is moving towards covering semantic elements like the roles and business processes applied. tpaML is a prototypical effort of a set of standards to achieve a higher level of standardization on the semantic level which forms the focus of the business networking model.

These standards can be implemented via eServices. Thanks to tpaML the computability rises to levels where computer-supported task fulfillment was previously too complex in heterogeneous environments. However, further research is needed on the maturity and applicability of tpaML. It remains to be proven, for example, whether it meets the time and functionality requirements (e.g. degree of detail and adaptations for the bidding and auctioning processes) of the setting described above. Implementation questions such as integration into IBM's MQSeries as the first product implementing the standard must also be resolved before this option can be explored any further.

Furthermore, the authors of the tpaML themselves state limitations [Sachs et al. 2000]. Thus far, for example, only two party scenarios have been implemented on the basis of static negotiations. At the moment, no hierarchical TPAs are possible and monitoring and control procedures are yet to be included. In addition, it is not yet clear how trusted third parties can be integrated and who can perform this. If tpaML could be integrated as a meta language for describing the agreement process and enforcing this agreement, opportunities might be plentiful. One example would be to directly instantiate the monitoring process of agreed service levels, delivery times etc., which were part of the contract after the bidding process or auction. This could be done by importing that information into the SAP system or by means of an additional service offered by newtron or Triaton.

Content	Category	Criteria	Value
Prag-matics	Coordination Standards	Language	tpaML
		Content	Trading partner roles, sequencing rules
	Process Standards	Protocol	OBI, Rosettanet's Partner Interface Processes (PIP)
		Language	tpaML
		Content	Invoking actions at the partners' site
Semantics	Information Standards	Language	tpaML (contract), cXML (products) etc.
		Content	Bids, availability, contract information like conditions and service levels, etc.
	Transaction Standards	Protocol	Document interchange, message brokering
		Content	Workflow, audit logging, non-repudiation (MD5, RSA, DSA), authentication (X509.V3), message security, recovery procedures
Syntax	Data Standards	Content	Message formats (e.g. BASE64), exchanges, address parameters
	Basic Standards	Protocol	TCP/IP, SMTP (HTTP), SSL
		Content	Maximum allowed network delay

Table 12-1: tpaML Standardization Areas

12.6   Conclusions and Outlook

The integration of processes with new cooperation partners such as eMarkets and eServices presents a great challenge for eMarket operators, market participants and integration service providers. A model is required for the communication within and between participating partners. The requirements of this model are that it should highlight preconditions for the integration of eServices, such as the use of standards (business bus), standardized interfaces, software components and services (business port) and how these interact. These preconditions must be met if a complete offering in eBusiness is to be developed and delivered. The general model was applied to the case of a specific eService offering from Triaton, and the usability of the model investigated as well as its refinement in a real-life environment.

Triaton offers an eService to provide business ports for integrating ERP systems with the eBusiness solution of eMarkets. Long-term potentials lie in expanding the scenario described by using standards like tpaML on the semantic and pragmatic level. For businesses, these continuous changes in standards always mean one-off, high-risk investments in know-how and new interfaces. By working with outsourcing partners it is possible to utilize synergy potentials when dealing with integration problems.

Part 4

Key Success Factors

Part One: Building the Foundation
Chapter 2:   Enterprise in the Information Age
Chapter 3:   The Networked Enterprise

Part Two: Business Concepts
Chapter 4:   Strategies for Business Networking
Chapter 5:   Business Networking Lessons Learned:
              Supply Chain Management at Riverwood
              International
Chapter 6:   Electronic Commerce and Supply Chain
              Management at 'The Swatch Group'
Chapter 7:   Knowledge-enabled Customer Relationship
              Management

Part Three: Information System Concepts
Chapter 8:   Future Application Architecture for the
              Pharmaceutical Industry
Chapter 9:   Overview on Supply Chain Management
              Systems
Chapter 10:   Electronic Commerce in the Procurement of
              Indirect Goods
Chapter 11:   Templates: Standardization for Business
              Networking
Chapter 12:   eServices for Integrating eMarkets

Part Four: Key Success Factors
Chapter 13:   Key Success Factors for Business Networking Systems
Chapter 14:   Towards a Method for Business Networking
Chapter 15:   Application of the Business Networking Method at SAP
Chapter 16:   Architecture Planning for Global Networked Enterprises

13 Key Success Factors for Business Networking Systems

Rainer Alt, Elgar Fleisch

13.1 Challenges in Designing Business Networking Systems 250
    13.1.1 Adoption-lag of Interorganizational Systems 250
    13.1.2 Gap Between Business and IT Issues.....................................251

13.2 Characterization of Business Networking Systems............................252
    13.2.1 Types of Transaction-oriented Business Networking
    Systems 252
    13.2.2 Specifics of Business Networking Systems 253

13.3 Key Success Factors in Designing Business Networking
    Systems 255
    13.3.1 Cases for Business Networking Systems 255
    13.3.2 Setting-up Partner Profiles 257
    13.3.3 Reciprocity: Creating Win-Win Situations 260
    13.3.4 Networking Projects are Business Projects.............................261
    13.3.5 Nucleus and Rapid Diffusion: 'Grow by Chunking' 261
    13.3.6 Standards and System Integration as a 'Conditio Sine Qua
    Non'...262

13.4 Conclusions 263

13.1   Challenges in Designing Business Networking Systems

Relationships among business units have recently been gaining momentum in a broad variety of industries. Previous chapters have shown that Business Networking leads to process efficiency, such as reduced cycle times, reduced process costs, increased customer service, and new distribution channels (cf. Chaps. 5 and 6). The current figures for business-to-business EC, which forecast a growth from USD 43 billion in 1998 to USD 1,300 billion in 2003 [cf. Forrester 1998] witness to these strategic developments. In view of the major relevant management trends (cf. Chaps. 2 and 8) establishing networkability (cf. Chap. 1) is one of the most important determinants of a company's future competitiveness.

However, many businesses have concentrated on implementing and integrating internal information systems. In fact, they, possess only limited networking capabilities and modules for supply chain planning, electronic commerce (EC) and the like have only recently been added. Analyzing the current situation concerning the application of Business Networking systems (BNS), two main challenges can be observed: an adoption lag and the gap between business and IT issues. With a view to meeting both challenges, this Chapter proposes major success factors and techniques governing the implementation of BNS.

13.1.1   Adoption-lag of Interorganizational Systems

Information technology (IT) can only live up to its enabling role for Business Networking (cf. Chap. 1) if information systems are in place that provide the necessary functionality and will ultimately be used by the various parties involved. There is ample evidence that BNS did encounter adoption problems in the past. Relevant interorganizational systems, such as electronic data interchange (EDI) or EC applications have been available since the 80s, but only now are they finding wider acceptance in the business community [cf. DeCovny 1998]. In the first place, this was due to the fact that most companies were preoccupied with establishing integrated internal systems and considered extended supply chain and EC modules as consistent extensions. In parallel with the spread of EDI or EC, interorganizational systems have been evolving as more advanced technologies became available. As Figure 13-1 shows, both developments are in the process of converging and will, through a fundamental redesign of business, lead to what we have termed a 'networked economy' (cf. Chap. 1).

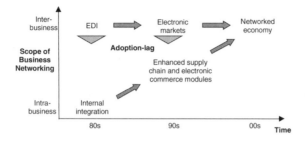

Figure 13-1: Evolution of Business Networking Systems

The evolution path depicted in the graph also reflects the degree of reluctance on the part of the business community to adopt either EDI or interorganizational systems. They were considered to be afflicted with high costs and a lack or insufficiency of functionality and participants/users. [Jimenez-Martinez/Polo-Redondo 1998] analyzed the diffusion and adoption lag of EDI in the European sector and identified several variables to be explained. According to [Kalakota/Whinston 1997, 379], there are five factors which determine the adoption lag of EDI: high costs, limited accessibility, rigid requirements, partial and closed solutions. Others (e.g. [Christiaanse et al. 1996], [Alt/Klein 1999]) found that electronic markets, such as air cargo community systems and electronic transportation exchanges, failed to catch on due to high costs, insufficient functionality and lacking network externalities on the infrastructure and application levels. Thus, attracting a critical mass (cf. Chap. 2.2.3) of partners continues to be one of the main challenges in the field of BNS.

13.1.2 Gap Between Business and IT Issues

In their empirical study, [Jimenez-Martinez/Polo-Redondo 1998] confirmed that strong hub companies and senior management support were critical factors in successful EDI implementations. The history of electronic market systems also indicates that cost structures, functionality and connectivity to other partners failed to match the requirements of businesses. We therefore deduced that the alignment of business and technological requirements is the key success factor for a wider acceptance of BNS.[1] In a horizontal study, senior executives and chief information officers (CIO) of 700 large enterprises throughout Europe and the US were asked what in their opinion were the main challenges CIOs are facing. 95% of all interviewees stated their IT organization was about to change dramatically. Only 2% (of the European companies) claimed to have a clear picture of their future IT and

---

[1]   This is also borne out by an empirical research study undertaken by the Gartner Group (cf. [Gartner Group 1998b], [Gartner Group 1998c]).

business vision. The research study is divided into two sections: IT management and technology. The two categories were also used by [Schnedl/Schweizer 1999] to structure the main challenges from a historical (1995-1997) and a future (1998-2002) perspective. As far as IT management is concerned, the alignment of IT and business strategy has always been the researchers' foremost concern which, indeed overshadowed others, e.g. strategic IT planning, the Y2K/Euro-problem or the management of distributed computing. From the technological side, client-server architectures, Inter-/Intranet-techologies and eBusiness were considered the main challenges from 1995 to 2002, followed by data warehousing, network management and the integration of applications.

13.2   Characterization of Business Networking Systems

13.2.1   Types of Transaction-oriented Business Networking Systems

Systems that support the coordination among business units are referred to as Business Networking systems (BNS). In general, transaction- and knowledge-oriented BNS can be distinguished. The former concern operative business trans-actions and stretch from information to settlement activities (cf. Chap. 6). The latter focus on less structured and more subjective information and knowledge.

This notion allows us to specifically address inter-company relations and to include relevant existing concepts, such as EDI, EC and supply chain management (SCM). They invariably involve more than one organizational unit and often integrate business partners (customers, suppliers, etc.) with a company's information infrastructure. Prominent examples are systems for EC and SCM. Although Business Networking is now receiving growing management attention, various types of systems have evolved since the emergence of EDI in the 70s. As Figure 13-1 shows, we can distinguish two evolutions paths, an interorganizational one which encompasses EDI, electronic markets and interorganizational systems (IOS), and an intraorganizational one which describes internal systems that are enhanced with Business Networking capabilities. In general, BNS are designed to link up the internal systems of individual business units that have been integrated mainly in the 80s with standard packages from vendors, such as SAP, Baan or Oracle. Enterprise resource planning (ERP) systems aim at providing efficient transaction processing by using integrated applications and data (cf. Chap. 2.3.1). However, implementing connections to other businesses in the same system offers only little flexibility and is bound to quickly reach capacity limitations. This is the starting point for the three different types of BN systems that we propose based on the previously mentioned evolution paths (see Figure 13-2):

- *Master data sharing* systems support the consistency of data by linking individual applications. This is the function of EDI-systems and proprietary systems, such as SAP's application link enabling (ALE), and intermediate documents (IDOCs) [cf. Hofmann/Killer 1995].

- *Supply chain management* systems or advanced planning systems (APS) offer functionalities for supply network planning, demand planning and the like (cf. Chap. 9). Usually, they are linked to an existing ERP system and are operated by one of the two parties involved. Examples are SAP's APO and the products from Manugistics or i2 Technologies.

- *Electronic commerce* systems are applications which concentrate on information and contracting activities and complement supply chain systems focusing on planning, managing and controlling of material and financial flows (cf. Chap. 6). Although ERP systems are now extended with EC-functionalities, specific applications (e.g. Open Market, Intershop) as well as specific services (e.g. electronic malls, auction systems) have emerged which have to be integrated with internal systems.

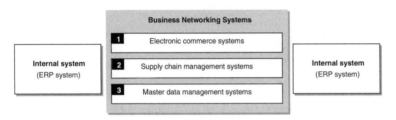

Figure 13-2: Types of Business Networking Systems

13.2.2 Specifics of Business Networking Systems

To describe the specifics of BNS we will use the three dimensions of Business Engineering that represents an approach geared to the business-oriented conceptualization of information systems. It combines various theoretical disciplines and "structures the organization, data and function dimensions at the business strategy, process and information systems levels" [cf. Österle 1995, 29].

As to the organizational dimension, BNS by definition support relationships between multiple organizational units. From a juridical standpoint, these may be internal, e.g. within a large conglomerate, or external, e.g. related to customers and suppliers. However, the blurring of organizational boundaries makes it difficult to clearly distinguish between the qualities of internal and external business networks. We therefore concentrate on the major organizational difference of BNS and (traditional) internal information systems (see Table 13-1). As interorganiza-

tional theory posits [e.g. Evan 1976], governance structures with authority, autonomy and dependency patterns are different in that interorganizational relationships
permit less direct influence and inherit higher conflict potentials than traditional
hierarchical relationships. In addition, there is usually only a lower level of
knowledge about the business partner's processes which is also a result of the
more frequent change in partners (lower stability).

	Internal Business Systems (e.g. Traditional ERP)	Business Networking Systems
Stability	High	Medium - low
Authority and Control	High	Medium - low
Autonomy of Partners	Low	Medium - high
Dependence	High	Medium
Conflict Potential	Low - medium	Medium - high
Process Knowledge	High	Medium - low

Table 13-1: General Specifics of Business Networking Systems

In the data and function dimension, BNS – just like any other business information
system – transform business data (or objects) using some business functions (or
methods). However, there are some specific requirements in both dimensions that
are summarized in Figure 13-3. In the first place, Business Networking processes,
such as collaborative forecasting, require single and homogeneous signals since
multiple parties base their actions on them. This is well known from the financial
sector where time lags in updating stock prices heavily influence investment decisions. An effect from the production field is the bullwhip effect described by [Lee
et al. 1997].[2] Since business partners make their decisions upon the data they receive, e.g. an automotive supplier schedules his production depending on the
planning data he receives from the manufacturer, accountability is a second requirement. Finally, information systems not only have to make sure that single,
accountable data are available but also that they are visible to all relevant actors,
i.e. they must be accessible to partners without any major additional effort.

In the functional dimension, we observe that BNS are built for real-time execution
since business partners require immediate responses to keep their processes running without interruption and to maintain consistent data (see also [Bradley/Nolan

---

[2]   First described by [Lee et al. 1997]and [Fine 1998] explains the bullwhip effect as a ‚law of supply
      chain dynamics‘. It describes a phenomenon whereby the volatility of demand and inventories in
      the supply chain tend to be amplified as one looks further upstream.

1998] or [Kelly 1998]). Real-time execution requires the integration of BNS and ERP systems among internal (e.g. APS or master data servers) as well as among external (e.g. electronic markets) systems. This n:m connectivity requires data and method standards that are accepted throughout a business network.[3] They also represent an important basis for the coordination processes and techniques [cf. Riehm 1997] that clearly have to be more sophisticated than in internal environments. Research on intelligent optimization algorithms, which, for example, support the simultaneous coordination of multiple actors and given the computational capacity, will continue to be an important issue for BNS (e.g. [SAP 1998c]). The degree of fulfillment of these requirements of BNS, in terms of logic and capacity, is referred to as the performance.

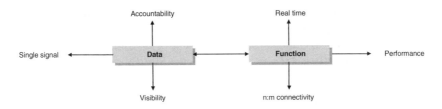

Figure 13-3: Business Networking Requirements for Data and Functions

Designing and implementing systems, to fulfill these requirements, are key challenges for the information management profession. Therefore, organizational, functional and data requirements have to be reflected in BNS concepts.

13.3 Key Success Factors in Designing Business Networking Systems

13.3.1 Cases for Business Networking Systems

To develop perspectives for closing the business IT gap and shortening the adoption lag, three different BNS-cases will be discussed. As Table 13-2 shows, each case has a different focus as it aims to highlight each BN type in a specific context, i.e. in interaction with internal and/or external business partners. Since all cases have been described in other chapters already, they will only be explained briefly:

---

[3]   For a detailed study of n:m issues of desktop purchasing systems see Chap. 10.

- *Commtech* (cf. Chap. 3.2.8) is a worldwide communication company that introduced shared service centers for some common areas in order to leverage economies of scale. Homogenized master data, process standards and integration scenarios were defined to ensure coordination among the participating units.

- *Riverwood International* (cf. Chaps. 5 and 14.3) is an integrated cardboard and packaging supplier located in Atlanta, USA. The company aimed at improving customer service by optimizing the flow of information to the customers. Small customers should be able to process orders and inquire order status whereas larger customers were offered global logistics strategies, such as vendor-managed-inventories (cf. Chaps. 4.3.2 and 14.3).

- *ETA SA* (cf. Chap. 6.3) is member of 'The Swatch Group' and manufactures watch movements. The main goal of the project (see [Alt et al. 1999], [Benz et al. 1999]) was to improve the management of information exchanged between ETA and its customers, i.e. mainly the Swatch group brands. Therefore, ETA redesigned their supply chain and introduced an EC solution.

Partners Type of System	Internal	Mixed	External
EC		ETA SA	
Extended Supply Chain			Riverwood International
Data Sharing	Commtech		

Table 13-2: Positioning of the Cases

In all three projects, similar steps were undertaken (see Table 13-3). The starting point was the identification of the main problem and the formulation of the project's goal in customer workshops. This input helped to derive the type of BNS that appeared to be a most likely solution to start with. As the next step, this initial system design was verified and elaborated in more detail with partner profiling. This technique systematically supported the design of the coordination technique and yielded the main input for creating win-win situations. Since project situation and BNS have already been described, we will now concentrate on partner profiling and coordination techniques (cf. Chap. 13.3.2) and the creation of win-win situations (cf. Chap. 13.3.3).

	Commtech	**ETA SA**	**Riverwood Int.**
Goal: Improvement of	Availability of internal process information	Information management in customer process	Organization of customer relationship
Type of BNS	Data sharing	Electronic commerce	Extended supply chain
Partner Profiling			
Partner Setting	Internal / few partners (5)	Mixed / few partners (15 represent majority of revenues); many small partners (approx. 1000)	External / many partners (approx. 2000)
Type of Partner Profile	Not used	Used in the form of customer workshops	Used for all small customers, for large customers in the form of customer workshops
Coordination Technique			
Scope of Standardized Data	Broad (multiple master data)	Low (material data only)	Medium (material, forecasting and planning data)
Standardization Tool	Harmonization	Mapping	Mixed (harmonization of material and mapping of forecasting and planning data)
Degree of Data Standardization	High (same syntax, same semantics)	Low (different syntax, same semantics)	Medium (high for material, low for forecasts and plans)
Standardization of Processes	High (global processes)	Low (ordering processes only)	Medium (supply chain processes only)
Win-win Creation	Transfer payments: New project due dates, new project budgets	Transfer payments: Shorter and guaranteed delivery times	Transfer payments: Price reductions, free hardware and software

Table 13-3: Main Steps and Topics in the Cases Reviewed

13.3.2 Setting-up Partner Profiles

Once a type of BNS had been identified as a starting solution, the partner setting was analyzed. To ensure networkability among a large number of partners and to limit the complexities of establishing and managing relationships, detailed partner profiles were designed at ETA and Riverwood for partner classification. However, for a small number of partners (as in the Commtech case) a qualitative description proved more efficient. Since business processes only communicate via business process outputs [cf. Österle 1995, 135], partner profiles aim at defining standardized outputs for coordination processes. These standard patterns are then tailored to specific partner requirements. Each individual profile contains the expected requirements in the organizational, functional and data dimensions. They can be represented as tables (see Figure 13-4) containing four components:

1. *Business relationship drivers* are generic factors influencing the design of business relationships. In terms of business engineering, a distinction is made between strategic, business process and information system drivers [cf. Österle 1995]. Figure 13-4 shows a customer profile as used in the Riverwood case. Detailed drivers were formulated which customers or sales reps were asked to simply mark them 'applicable' or 'not applicable'.

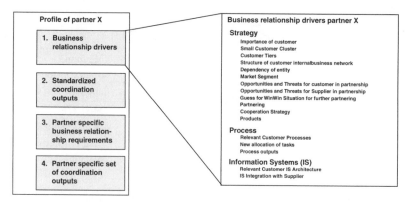

Figure 13-4: Components of Partner Profile

2. A catalog of *standardized coordination outputs* shows the possible components of a business relationship on the strategy, business process and information system level. Examples of coordination outputs are 'advance shipment notice' or 'order acknowledgement'. As shown in Table 13-4 for the three cases, outputs vary in scope and content. In addition, the catalog may also list some technical integration forms [cf. Riehm 1997], such as a partner accessing internal ERP data via the Internet.

	Commtech	ETA SA	Riverwood Int.
Data			
Accountability	Material, vendor, customer, …	Material	Material, forecasts, plans
Visibility	Credit limits, head counts, costs, taxes,…	Inventory, order status	Production plans, sales forecasts, inventories
Single Signal	Master data	Inventory	Demand signals
Functions			
Real Time	Credit limit check, One bill to customer, Global contracts, drill-down in taxes	Delivery dates, order status	ATP, vendor managed inventories
N:m Connectivity	Master data management	Delivery dates	ATP
Performance	Performance of distributed transactions	Interfaces to ERP systems	Performance of ATP server

Table 13-4: Requirements on IS-level

3. *Partner-specific business relationship requirements* are the outcome, if partner profiles are used as structured questionnaires. They reflect the specific needs of specific partners in respect of their relationship, support active partner management, and serve as the basis for individualized coordination. In the ETA and Riverwood cases, modular and standardized types of customer relationships were defined for different customer segments.

4. Once business relationship drivers and standardized coordination outputs have been defined, the partner-specific requirements can be translated into a *partner-specific set of coordination outputs*. Both partners would implement the processes and systems needed to obtain the partner-specific set of coordination outputs. The processes and systems implemented by Riverwood and ETA were designed to produce such outputs as advance shipment notice, vendor replenishment, vendor managed inventory, ordering and order tracking via the Internet.

In structuring business relationship requirements on various levels, partner profiles provide the basis for conceiving a specific coordination technique. While we cannot elaborate on alternative coordination techniques here, we may point out two aspects that have emerged from the cases reviewed:

- Standardization of master data and processes were the main coordination techniques used in different scopes in the cases (see Table 13-3).

- Standardization of master data was achieved by data harmonization and by implementing mapping procedures. Obviously, the former reflects closer coupling among partners.

13.3.3 Reciprocity: Creating Win-Win Situations

Stringent standardization requirements, to be sure, are not readily reconciled with the need for organizational autonomy inherent in business networks (see Table 13-1). In all three projects discussed, it took a great deal of persuading to have partners participate. Where an unbalance of costs and/or benefits exists among the partners, the chances of successful implementation dwindle rapidly. Therefore, creating win-win situations was an important change management effort in these cases.

As a first step, the impact on setup and running costs and the benefits was explored for the networking partners. Following the concept of life cycle costs [cf. Schelle 1989], we distinguish between setup and ongoing costs and benefits. A partner's setup costs encompass his total project costs and the costs due to integration effects with other projects:

- Project costs fall into costs for designing new processes, change management, indoctrination of employees, data standardization and costs for implementing IT based relationships.

- Costs incurred by integration effects reflect the networking character of networking projects. Interdependencies between networking projects and other internal projects have to be closely watched since they tend to be a source of delays.

- Costs of the new process, especially costs for designing and implementing the new coordination tasks, are part of the running costs (for detailed process cost drivers, [cf. Braun 1996]).

Thanks to the impact of the networking project, win-win situations can be designed for any individual partner or any type of partner. The partner profile provides the basis of a win-win situation by specifying the partner-specific requirements and includes further specifics, such as feasible coordination techniques or investment power. A crucial element in creating win-win situations is to establish reciprocity and trust which are known to be essential enablers in implementing business networks [cf. Klein 1996]. In the cases under review, success was owed to two facts:

- Partner-specific profiles kept transaction and investment costs low and generated networking benefits which it was possible to quantify.

- Compensation for investment costs, costs due to interdependencies with other projects and protection against opportunism was achieved in the cases under review by providing transfer payments. Examples include price reductions for the new services or hardware and software offered for free. In networks with hierarchical elements, such as Commtech, extra budgets and schedule concessions granted for other projects proved effective in maintaining the priority of networking projects.

Win-win situations are easy to communicate when real-life examples can be cited to illustrate them. For each networking project, the case study companies defined a project nucleus permitting the benefits of the networking project to be assessed by the project partners within a limited time and cost effort. The fact that it was possible to quickly reach a critical number of partners proved vital for the success of the BNS.

13.3.4 Networking Projects are Business Projects

Networking applications and technologies enable new business processes and business strategies and support them. In order to use them correctly, the business must understand the essence of technical networking and, conversely, information management must understand the business. From an organizational point of view, the strategies and processes that can be implemented by means of networking applications are closely linked up with a great many other processes and strategies. In the Riverwood International example, a project for reorganizing the sales process affected the processes of distribution, inventory management, production planning, production, maintenance, procurement, controlling and accounts payable. The integration of these processes and the associated strategies, organizational structures, such as departments and above all human resources, take up a good deal of management time. Examples are the definition of new processes (procurement or sales) and/or strategic business areas (product/market mix), the coordination of marketing, sales, production and inventory strategies or communication of the solution to the partners affected. While information management can encourage networking projects and make major contributions to their success, the most effective dimensions of a network must, however, be evolved by the business for the business.

13.3.5 Nucleus and Rapid Diffusion: 'Grow by Chunking'

The quality and success of many networking projects will depend on the number of networked partners [cf. Shaprio/Varian 1999, 173]. Such projects must set themselves the prime goal of fast growth in the number of users. Examples of how to achieve rapid diffusion are provided by Netscape, Hotmail or Compaq. In the initial phase they would make their software, services or hardware available free of charge and thus generate a fast growing customer base [cf. Kelly 1998, 50]. In order to accelerate growth, they would design services that operate according to the rules of increasing economies of scale [cf. Arthur 1990], i.e. marginal return and customer benefits tend to grow as the customer base expands.[4]

In addition to coordinated marketing strategies and the requirement for reciprocity, this goal is targeted in particular by the nucleus approach which addresses the design of 'nuclei' that are conducive to rapid growth.[5]

13.3.6 Standards and System Integration as a 'Conditio Sine Qua Non'

By providing external access to what were previously internal functions and information, EC solutions ultimately go a long way towards achieving the vision of the extended enterprise (cf. [Ashkenas et al. 1995], [Wigand et al. 1997]). Examples of such information are inventory levels, delivery dates, special terms of sale or order status which can be called up by external partners. Internal ERP/legacy systems, such as production planning systems, finance systems or order management systems, are responsible for this information. For this reason, networking applications can never be isolated solutions. It is far more appropriate to see them as a new front end to existing systems which outsources functionality to partners and makes new functionality possible. They process the information provided by other information systems and pass it on to partners without any human intervention. This leads to important requirements which the data and their standardization and/or integration will have to satisfy:

- All the information which a business unit wants to make available to its partners must be known to the business unit. This is contingent on a properly functioning internal organization and/or the internal integration of the information systems. The *integration* of new applications with internal and external information systems represents the greatest challenge for networking projects. The standards applied at the process and information system level play a major role in integration.

- Networking applications place a new and disproportionately greater emphasis on interorganizational process standards. Networking calls for the various

---

[4] Further hints on the rapid diffusion of EC solutions are provided by [Kelly 1998, 47]. The most important of these are 'touch as many nets as you can', 'maximize the opportunities of others', 'don't pamper with commodities; let them flow' and 'avoid proprietary systems'.

[5] 'Grow by Chunking' is one of the nine principles for managing complex adaptive systems (cf. [Kelly 1995, 469], [Stüttgen 1999]).

processes of various independent business units to be synchronized. Today, business units operate individual processes with a wide range of information systems and data models with different business semantics. A purchasing process, for instance, has to be synchronized with the supplier's sales process, the credit card institution's payment transaction process, the authentication process of the trusted third party and various processes within the business unit itself (authorization, accounts, etc.).

- Networking also builds on information standards. Dun & Bradstreet's SPSC standard for product categories (standard product & service codes), for example, prescribes a uniform metastructure for product catalogs. This standard thus helps to consolidate the catalogs of different manufacturers in a multi-vendor catalog. Further examples are standards for catalog interchange formats (CIF), access protocols (lightweight directory access), authorization (RSA procedures), payment transactions (OTP), security (SSL, IPSec, PPTP, Socks5, RSA, X.509), method calls (API), protocols (HTTP) and formats (XML) (e.g. [Dolmetsch et al. 1999], [Scheller et al. 1994, 20], [Neuburger 1994, 22]). For many companies, the main emphasis is on harmonizing and homogenizing master data, e.g. reorganizing the master data for products, customers and outline agreements.

13.4 Conclusions

Establishing networkability is a necessity for achieving and sustaining competitive advantage. It combines enhanced and individualized relationships with increased efficiency and flexibility. Since Business Networking inherently relies on sophisticated IT, aligning business and technological requirements is of foremost importance. Thus, BNS, which sustain networkability, are critical for the success of networked organizational entities. Evidence also shows that BNS require the participation of a critical mass (cf. Chap. 2.2.3) of partners. Therefore, the main issues of this Chapter were how to ensure the participation of partners and how to align business and IT issues.

Three types of BNS were presented and illustrated in three case studies. To offer the desired customer value and efficiencies the BNS have to be configured and tailored to the relationships. Partner profiling was presented as a successful technique to reach these goals. Profiles provide a transparent view of the current partner situation and form the basis for broad and systematic partner integration. As customer profiles, they are valuable marketing and customer retention tools. Especially, the modular design of coordination outputs and standard relationships reduced the time for setting up new relationships. In providing a technique for collecting information on partners, processes and systems partner profiling supported the alignment of business and IT issues.

All case studies dealt with how to convince business partners to use the new form of coordination. Creating win-win situations was a technique used to attain a buy-in from the stakeholders. Costs and benefits were calculated on the basis of quick wins that were derived from a first pilot implementation. As the Commtech case suggests, this is a major success factor for data sharing systems, such as EDI, and an important element in explaining the adoption lag of inter-business systems.

Both techniques, partner profiling and creating win-win situations, yielded valuable results for the design of application architectures in internal and external environments. Therefore, they should be an integral element in the management of Business Networking projects [cf. IMG 1998a].

14 Towards a Method for Business Networking

Rainer Alt, Robert Betts, Karl Maria Grünauer, Roland Klüber,
Karl-Heinz Schelhas

14.1 Challenges of Making Business Networking Happen 266
    14.1.1 Relevance of a Method for Business Networking 266
    14.1.2 Existing Approaches and Requirements 266
    14.1.3 Benefits of an Engineering Approach 268
    14.1.4 Focus and Procedure Model of the Method 270

14.2 Case I: eProcurement at Deutsche Telekom AG 272
    14.2.1 Business Context of Deutsche Telekom AG 272
    14.2.2 Options for Organizing Procurement 272
    14.2.3 Steps Undertaken at Deutsche Telekom 274

14.3 Case II: Supply Chain Management at Riverwood
    International 275
    14.3.1 Supply Chain Scenario at Riverwood International 275
    14.3.2 Steps Undertaken at Riverwood International 277

14.4 Towards a Method for Business Networking 280
    14.4.1 Design Areas of a Method for Business Networking 281
    14.4.2 Meta Model 282
    14.4.3 Role Model 283
    14.4.4 Procedure Model and Techniques 283

14.5 Conclusions and Outlook 286

14.1   Challenges of Making Business Networking Happen

14.1.1   Relevance of a Method for Business Networking

Translating the key success factors developed in Chapter 13 into implemented processes and applications represents a major challenge. In order to reach Business Networking goals, such as improved customer care or reduced inventories, business partners have to be convinced, business processes among the partners have to be agreed upon, and the strategic and process scenario has to be translated into enabling IT applications. Some of the specific questions which arose in the various cases discussed in previous chapters are:

• What is a proven sequence for proceeding in a Business Networking project? What are the major steps and what are suitable techniques for ensuring quick and successful implementation?

• Which networking scenario (cf. Chap. 3.3) and strategy (cf. Chap. 4) meets our goals? What is the return on investment of this solution?

• Are partners needed to realize the solution? How is the participation of future users ensured and how are partner relationships organized

• What applications are chosen and how can they be integrated into existing system landscapes? What are the implications of the networking solution for the overall application and service architecture?

Methods have proven helpful to address these issues systematically, to take advantage of the experience gained in other projects, and to ensure the proper documentation of project activities. Although a variety of methods are available from consultants, system providers and in the literature, these only cover specific areas of Business Networking. There is still an obvious need to integrate all aspects, from choosing the right Business Networking strategy to the execution of local projects. This chapter gives an overview of the method that was developed between 1998 and 2000 in cooperation with the eight partner companies of CC iBN (cf. Chap. 1). An example for applying the method and integration into SAP's ASAP for APO 2.0a method is given in Chapter 15.

14.1.2   Existing Approaches and Requirements

In the first place, a method for Business Networking has to take into account the specifics of inter-business relationships. The main areas are all aspects associated with cooperation, the extended supply chain and new (electronic) services. Existing methods emerged primarily from the three areas shown in Table 14-1: cooperation management, process (re-)design, and implementation of Business Networking systems. However, these methods present shortcomings in three respects:

- They *focus on a specific level* of the Business Engineering model, i.e. they emphasize either the strategy, process or systems level. They do not provide guidance from the Business Networking strategy through to the implementation of a Business Networking system. For example, the methods for cooperation management offer valuable insights into setting up and managing cooperations, but do not address the selection, configuration, and implementation of systems supporting these relationships.

- They frequently have only a *low level of formalization*. Systematic methods require a meta model, a procedure model, techniques, a role model, as well as result documents. Many methods, especially in strategy development and cooperation management, include only a procedure model and some techniques. Structured documentation of the result is often lacking, despite the fact that these documents form an important input for system implementation.

- They do not provide *support for networking processes*. The networking processes described in previous chapters (cf. Chaps. 3.3.1 and 4.3) consist of supply chain management, customer relationship management and the like. Existing methods are either generalized (e.g. BPR methods) or focus on designing particular networking processes (e.g. supply chain methods)

The goal of this Chapter is to present an initial outline of a method for Business Networking. The following requirements can be noted:

- The method should provide support for cooperation-intensive projects in the design, measurement, and implementation of cooperation processes,

- It should include new business models (cf. Chap. 2), potentials of electronic processes (e.g. EC, SCM), as well as IT systems and eServices,

- It should include knowledge of existing methods and follow the design principles of method engineering [cf. Gutzwiller 1994].

Strengths	Weaknesses	Examples
Methods for Cooperation Management		
• Propose examples of models for establishing and managing cooperations • Often include political and social aspects	• Lack advice on specific types of cooperations and the role of IT • Inadequate specificity concerning business processes	[Doz/Hamel 1998], [Gomez-Casseres 1996], [Håkansson/Snehota 1995], [Chisholm 1998], [Sydow 1992]
Methods for Business Process (Re-)Design		
• Generalized and applicable to a variety of industries • Methods for supply chain management (SCM) include specific supply chain knowledge	• Inadequate extended supply chain focus and knowledge of cooperations • SCM methods neglect other processes, e.g. customer relationship processes	[Davenport 1993], see overview in [Hess/Brecht 1995] [Bowersox/Closs 1996, 523], [Christopher 1998, 48]
Methods for IS Implementation		
• Include vital specifics for implementing Business Networking systems (e.g. SCM systems, EC systems)	• Methods are vendor and/or tool-specific and are weak at the strategy and process levels	[SAP 1999b], [IMG 1998b], [Manugistics 1998], [i2 1997], [Syncra 1998]

Table 14-1: Overview of Existing Methods in Business Networking

14.1.3 Benefits of an Engineering Approach

Method engineering is an approach developed by Gutzwiller/Heym (cf. [Gutzwiller 1994], [Heym/Österle 1993]) to ensure the systematic development of methods. It has been used in the definition of various methods which are being used successfully in practice. Methods based on method engineering principles consist of five building blocks (see Figure 14-1):

- The *procedure model* contains the recommended sequence of all top-level activities. For example, a method for business process redesign may start with a preliminary analysis, continue with macro-design and finish with micro-design [cf. IMG 1997].

- *Techniques* describe how one or more results can be achieved. For example, a technique to measure supply chain performance includes the steps that have to be undertaken as well as various metrics, and provides hints on how to complete result documents. Tools, such as the ARIS Toolset [cf. Scheer 1995], may support the application of techniques.

- *Result documents* are produced for the documentation of results and represent an important input for the specification of IT requirements. A result document for analyzing as-is processes, for example, would be a process network.

- *Roles* describe who is participating in a project at a certain stage. These are determined by the decisions which have to be taken and the knowledge required to complete the result documents.

- The *meta model* contains the main objects of design and the relationships between these objects. For example, a method for business process redesign would specify that processes produce outputs and consist of activities.

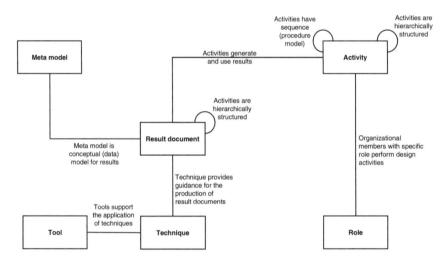

Figure 14-1: Elements of Method Engineering [cf. Gutzwiller 1994, 13]

Besides helping to structure a project, methods are used to facilitate training and (self-)learning. In providing a common language they improve communication between people with heterogeneous backgrounds. Another advantage is that formalization enables knowledge transfer, i.e. example result documents elaborated in one project can be used in another similar project. Experience has shown that these benefits are apt to lead to improvements in terms of hard (time, cost, quality) and soft (flexibility and knowledge) factors.

14.1.4 Focus and Procedure Model of the Method

Prior to developing and applying a method, clarity is required concerning the method's application area. Following the projects within CC iBN, the method focuses on cooperation projects. In the organization literature, cooperations are characterized as hybrids between markets and hierarchies [cf. Fleisch 2000, 90; Wigand et al. 1997]. They may be defined as a set of organizational units (OU) which perform coordinated activities and pursue common goals [cf. Grochla 1972, 3]. Based on these criteria, the method should be applicable in projects which:

- require the design of long-term relationships between two OUs,

- involve relationships with key customers and suppliers,

- include transactions with medium frequency and information breadth[1].

Attribute	Hierarchy	Cooperation	Market
Purpose	Central planning and control	Pursue common goals	Market transparency and dynamic pricing
Vertical integration	High – Production factors belong to one company	Medium – Production factors are jointly owned by partners	None – Decentralized ownership of production factors
Specificity of resources (e.g. IS)	High – Investment in resources are company-specific and not transferable to partners	Medium – Resources are partner-specific, but may be adapted to new partners with medium additional investments	Low – Resources are not specific and can be used all with all business partners
Trust required	Low	Medium - high	Low
Transactions	Long relationships – high in repetition and information breadth	Medium to long relationships – medium in repetition and information breadth	Short relationships – low in repetition and information breadth
Legal framework	Hierarchical control mechanisms and long-term contracts	Mutual engagement based on medium to long-term contracts	Individual contracts for each transaction

Table 14-2: Profile of Cooperations [cf. Alstyne 1997; Fleisch 2000, 92f]

The Business Networking method assumes that cooperations not only have common characteristics but are also similar in their implementation. This procedure

---

[1] The breadth of information describes the variety of exchanged information, e.g. not only transaction information, such as price, volume, article description, but also planning data and the like.

model was obtained in several partner projects and distinguishes the four top-level activities 'analyze, design, plan/implement' (see Figure 14-2):

- *Analysis of cooperation potentials.* First, an analysis is undertaken to determine the area(s) with the highest returns for Business Networking. Often, a quick preliminary study of 2-3 weeks is conducted for this purpose. The result of this phase is a cooperation concept which is presented to top management.

- *Design and evaluation of scenarios.* Based on a cooperation concept, the specific design alternatives are developed and evaluated. This phase is performed jointly with the cooperation partner and leads to a cooperation contract.

- *Planning and implementation of pilot projects.* Based on the cooperation contract, individual projects are carried out (e.g. process reengineering, EC or APS implementation). This phase links with the implementation methods of system vendors (e.g. SAP's ASAP).

- *Continuation.* Depending on the success of the pilot projects (and other criteria) it will be decided how the pilot solution is to be continued. Possible decisions are (1) roll out the solution to other OUs, (2) discontinue the pilot, and/or (3) pursue other cooperation projects.

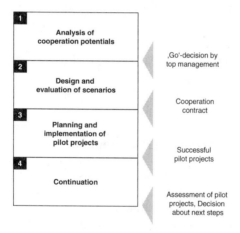

Figure 14-2: Procedure Model of the Business Networking Method

In order to provide some insight into the individual phases, two cases will be described. These cases are (1) the introduction of a buy-side electronic commerce system (cf. Chap. 4.3.1) at Deutsche Telekom, and (2) the design of a supply chain solution at Riverwood International (cf. Chap. 5).

14.2   Case I: eProcurement at Deutsche Telekom AG

14.2.1   Business Context of Deutsche Telekom AG

Deutsche Telekom AG (Telekom) is a formerly state-owned telecommunications company that was converted into a stock corporation on January 1, 1995 and went public in November 1996. In 1999, Telekom's revenues amounted to Euro 35.5 billion with a net income of Euro 1.9 billion. The major part of their revenue stems from the national full service telecommunication business with 172,000 employees (1999). This included 46.5 million telephone lines in the area of fixed lines and 13.3 million ISDN basic channels at the end of 1999, which is more ISDN lines than the USA and Japan together. Furthermore, Telekom is a major cellular provider with 9.1 million customers in his digital GSM-net, Europe's biggest online and Internet service provider and serves 17.8 million customers with its cable TV infrastructure [cf. DTAG 1999].

The transformation process from a vertically integrated monopolist toward a worldwide active competitive organization involved major changes in all dimensions. This has partly been enforced by deregulation and liberalization in the European telecommunications market since January 1, 1998. Another major driver is the convergence of the media, telecommunications and IT. These developments have significant implications on Telekom's future core competencies, existing process efficiencies as well as internal and external partner relationships. Starting with the new corporate strategy in 1998, the procurement of indirect materials was to be redesigned to reap the potentials of Business Networking.

14.2.2   Options for Organizing Procurement

As explained earlier (cf. Chap. 10), indirect goods encompass MRO goods, office materials and other C-parts. The electronic procurement process for these goods (eProcurement) has the following characteristics: goods are not planned, large numbers of what tend to be standardized, low-value products, many users, catalog-based purchases, and authorization processes [cf. Killen & Associates 1997].

In general, the procurement process for indirect products consists of a strategic and an operational component (see Figure 14-3). *Strategic procurement* includes customer and supplier management and deals with the selection, contracting and evaluation of partners, i.e. suppliers of indirect goods as well as content and catalog management services. Although this process has a strong knowledge component it relies on (operational) transaction data. For example, information about the performance of partners serves as a basis for negotiating prices as well as for communicating win-win situations. *Operational procurement* consists of four elements (see Figure 14-3):

- The electronic product catalogs offered by MRO material suppliers,

- Desktop purchasing systems (DPS) permit end-users to purchase indirect goods directly via an Internet browser. They offer process and workflow functionality, system administration and the integration into ERP systems (cf. Chap. 10.3).

- Content and catalog management services. Content management merges multiple (supplier) catalogs and catalog management provides the platform for catalogs. They are shown separately in Figure 14-3 to emphasize the fact that these functionalities are evolving into individual business segments.

- Services for logistics and payment perform the settlement of transactions.

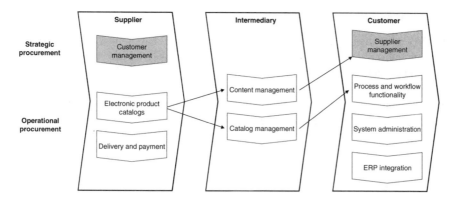

Figure 14-3: Elements of the eProcurement Process

Each of the eProcurement segments is an area where companies have to decide on how to establish or access the required resources. This involves strategic decisions as to which activities are insourced and which outsourced as well as where closer cooperation with partners is necessary. For example, catalog and content management could be outsourced, whereas relationships with suppliers (which offer the catalogs) will involve closer cooperation. Designing workflows and ERP integration is done internally. However, a company could also choose to adopt a more active strategy and offer content or catalog management services to other players as well.

14.2.3 Steps Undertaken at Deutsche Telekom

1. Analysis of Cooperation Potentials

Among the first steps in the Telekom project was the definition of potential areas for Business Networking. The main strategic options for initiating a Business Networking project were discussed in workshops on the basis of best practice examples. One of the areas which was examined in greater detail was the procurement process for indirect goods and services. This decision was based on a high-level scoring model derived from a market, resource and strategy analysis that included soft and hard factors. The analysis of networking potentials showed that eProcurement was an area with high potentials since the process was characterized by time-consuming individual, paper-based requests, many exceptions, and only little IT support. This situation led to a costly and non-transparent process, which offered a high potential for the introduction of an eProcurement solution.

2. Design and Evaluation of Scenarios

Based on the management decision to go ahead with eProcurement, a joint project team involving the IT and procurement departments was set up. A project portfolio showed that similar projects already existed within the Telekom group. After analyzing these projects and best practices from US companies [cf. Dolmetsch 1999], scenarios were detailed on how to organize eProcurement. The main options in respect of possible service providers for the partner-oriented part of the process were:

- *Procurement via an external service*, i.e. outsourcing of the eProcurement process to a service provider, such as GE TPN.

- *Establish an internal service*, i.e. an internal shared service for eProcurement which is offered to all Telekom subsidiaries.

- *Offer the service on the market*, i.e. extend the internal service to external business partners, thus establishing a new business segment.

Using various evaluation criteria, such as strategic fit, impact on strategic flexibility, knowledge and risk, initial investments, and operational benefits, a decision was made in favor of one or more feasible scenarios. Since a market survey did not yield any operative solution providers for catalog and content management in Germany, Telekom decided to establish an internal service.

Scenario design involves the specification of the process network for the selected scenario as well as the decision in respect of external partners. Discussions were held with software providers that led to several DPS and service provider solutions, two of which are being considered in more detail for pilot implementations. Based on some critical requirements, such as the customizing effort necessary to adapt the systems to the Telekom processes as well as integration into Telekom's existing SAP R/2 systems, Commerce One was selected as provider of the eProcurement system.

3. Planning and Implementation of Pilot Projects

Following the decision in favor of a specific process and application scenario, detailed planning for the project is now ongoing. This includes the application architecture, standards for data and communication protocols, business bus (cf. Chap. 2.3.4) configuration etc., as well as activities to coordinate the implementation projects.

4. Continuation

Once an internal procurement service is established, this could be extended in a second step. One strategy already being discussed is to become an external eService provider for catalog and content management offered by a Telekom subsidiary (see Figure 14-4). This would provide new sources of revenue by exploiting the buying power, high number of transactions, brand name, critical mass and the IT infrastructure of Telekom. By enhancing the existing service, an external service can be established which continues Business Networking at Telekom.

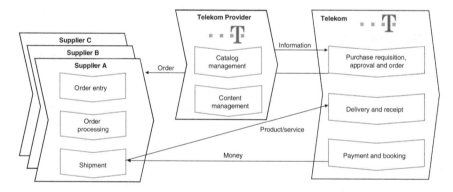

Figure 14-4: eProcurement Scenario at Deutsche Telekom

14.3 Case II: Supply Chain Management at Riverwood International

14.3.1 Supply Chain Scenario at Riverwood International

As explained in Chapter 5, Riverwood International is a leading provider of paperboard and packaging solutions. As part of a restructuring effort, the company reengineered their supply chain applications landscape. With the migration from existing ERP legacy applications to an integrated SAP R/3 system, Riverwood's supply chain execution processes are supported more efficiently.

The introduction of SAP's advanced planning system (APS), known as advanced planner and optimizer (APO), now enables Riverwood to implement inter-company planning processes, such as vendor-managed inventory (VMI). VMI is a supply chain strategy that helps a company to collaborate with its customers to gather individual demand forecasts and synchronizes forecasts with local produc-tion plans to achieve greater flexibility in the planning and manufacturing process (cf. Chap. 4.3.2).

In an initial step, the company set up a VMI) pilot project with Universal Packag-ing (Universal). The pilot project includes some five Riverwood plants and distri-bution centers, plus ten Universal locations in New England, and will be imple-mented for selected products at the end of the third quarter 1999.

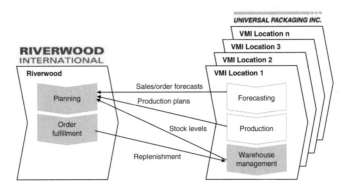

Figure 14-5: VMI between Riverwood and Universal

In order to obtain an accurate demand signal, Riverwood is willing to insource some stock management tasks that have traditionally been in the hands of Univer-sal (see Figure 14-5). The warehouses at Universal's plants and distribution cen-ters are automatically replenished by Riverwood. This means that product replen-ishment and purchase order creation will become the responsibility of Riverwood and will be based on actual and forecasted demand. Therefore, Riverwood has to be able to consider Universal inventory levels and demand forecasts during their planning process. The VMI scenario involves the following key activities:

- *Data assembly.* The primary data driver for VMI programs is warehouse withdrawal data from Universal's distribution centers (VMI locations).

- *Forecasting.* The primary forecasting effort is based on withdrawals from Universal's plants/distribution centers. Order forecasting is controlled by Riv-erwood and uses agreed-upon inventory targets and transportation cost objectives. Universal is responsible for providing Riverwood with their production plans.

- *Order generation.* The Riverwood SAP R/3 system generates purchase orders which are driven by the replenishment pull on Universal's VMI locations. Since Riverwood controls the process, Universal receives priority service when shortages occur.

- *Order fulfillment:* Riverwood fills products primarily out of inventory (make-to-stock). However, in some cases a make-to-order fulfillment occurs.

The VMI scenario was conceived on the assumption that it would create a win-win situation between Riverwood and Universal. Benefits for both partners are shown in Table 14-3.

Benefits for Riverwood (Vendor)	Benefits for Universal (Customer)
Broader view of the inventories and supply chain activities gives Riverwood better information for planning inventory deployment and production.	Universal shifts the administrative burden for inventory replenishment of selected products (VMI products) at their local warehouse back to the vendor.
Riverwood achieves greater flexibility in the planning and manufacturing process.	Universal has lower supply chain costs through the outsourcing of the order management process; delayed transference of ownership means reduced working capital costs.
Riverwood can be more customer-specific in its planning and is able to plan at a higher level of detail.	Universal gets guaranteed fulfillment of demand and 'available-to-promise' service for VMI products.
Benefits for Both Parties	
Shorter lead times for the entire replenishment process.	
Overall improvement of asset utilization through a decrease in total inventory days of supply.	

Table 14-3: Benefits of VMI for Riverwood and Universal

14.3.2 Steps Undertaken at Riverwood International

1. Analysis of Cooperation Potentials

At Riverwood, supply chain management (SCM) revealed high potentials for Business Networking. After checking the networkability it became clear that proper visibility of stock levels in all warehouse locations was an essential prerequisite for proceeding with the project. Riverwood set the focus on inventory management with downstream supply chain partners. As a customer requirement which had already been articulated, VMI was chosen from SCM best practices, such as collaborative planning, forecasting and replenishment (CPFR)).

Important elements of this first phase were a high-level sketch of as-is supply chain processes and the IS architecture, as well as the scoping of the project in terms of products, supply chain partners and geographical locations. This led to a first cooperation concept, which also included detailed and mutually agreed performance targets for the future cooperation between the pilot customer Universal and Riverwood. The first phase terminated with the forming of an inter-company team.

2. Design and Evaluation of Scenarios

Riverwood identified two macro-scenarios for realizing VMI, which are based upon two different architecture alternatives:

- Setting up and maintaining a VMI module of SAP's APO with interfaces to Riverwood's SAP R/3 ERP system and Universal's ERP legacy application.

- Usage of an existing VMI service provided by an external provider [cf. Durlacher 1999], such as IBM's continuous replenishment service [cf. IBM 1998].

In order to increase flexibility in tailoring VMI solutions to the requirements of specific customers and include Riverwood's very specific needs in the area of production planning and scheduling, Riverwood decided to set up their own VMI module.

3. Planning and Implementation of Pilot Projects

For this scenario a detailed picture of the process network was elaborated and its impact on resources and operations assessed. An example of the micro process design is shown in Figure 14-6. It distinguishes between VMI planning and VMI execution:

VMI planning starts with the weekly transfer of production plans and sales forecasts from Universal to Riverwood. This data is provided by Universal's legacy ERP system[2] and will be used by the demand planning module of Riverwood's APS to generate demand plans. After the release of the demand plan to the supply network planning module (SNP) the APS will consider constraints in the produc-

---

[2] In the current process design, there are no plans for an electronic link between Universal's ERP application and Riverwood's APS. Instead, Universal's VMI planner uses a Web gateway to the so-called 'demand planning book' within Riverwood's APS for manual data entry.

tion and distribution network[3] and release production orders via the ERP to the MRP II planning system.

VMI execution starts with checking the availability (ATP) and detailed scheduling in the MRP II system. The order is then confirmed, trim optimization performed and the product produced. At the Universal site, goods issued are captured with a barcode reader. This information is used by Riverwood's ERP to track product withdrawal and calculate on-hand inventory at Universal's warehouse. If stocks should fall below a certain level, an order is automatically generated by River-wood's ERP, the VMI products shipped and an invoice issued.

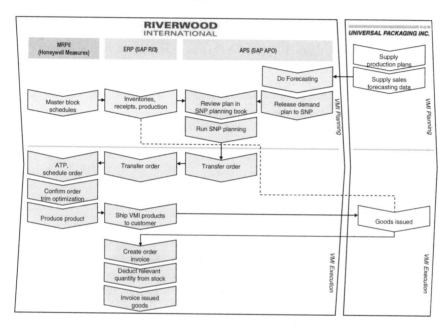

Figure 14-6: Process Design for VMI at Riverwood

To ensure a successful implementation of VMI, Riverwood designed a project portfolio which includes eight different local projects (see Table 14-4). Part A of the project portfolio deals with four internal Riverwood projects. Part B addresses customer-oriented projects and details the plan to support VMI customers with a service package that fully enables outsourcing of warehouse management for selected VMI products. This package will contain customized modules, which means that Riverwood will perform or coordinate four internal customer projects.

---

[3] Examples are master block schedules for production capacity, inventory levels, transportation capacity and order lead times.

Project Portfolio Part A: Internal Riverwood Projects	
1.	One APS project for setting up and customizing the demand and supply network planning modules in the SAP APO application.
2.	One master data (MD) project for setting up the unidirectional transfer of ERP master data (e.g. product master, bill of material (BOM), customer locations, units of measurement) to the APS system.
3.	One core interface project to ensure the bilateral exchange of transactional data (orders) between the ERP and APS system. Order types include production, transportation, replenishment and consignment orders.
4.	One project for the development of the customer service package modules.
Project Portfolio Part B: Modules of the Customer Service Package	
1.	Business process redesign (BPR) module in order to enable customers to support Riverwood's VMI process standard.
2.	Infrastructure module which will include ready-to-run clients for forecast data entry in the demand planning book and barcode scanners to track warehouse withdrawal.
3.	Internet service provider (ISP) module to ensure data transmission from local VMI locations according to Riverwood's security standards.
4.	On-site training courses.

Table 14-4: Riverwood Project Portfolio

4. Continuation

Potential areas for enhancing Business Networking have been discussed to leverage Riverwood's ERP and APS investments. Riverwood is planning to become an eService provider, offering a collaborative planning eService scenario for the US paperboard industry and using portals, such as mySAP.com to customers as the platform for their service. This continuation of the VMI solution will start with the successful implementation of the VMI pilot.

14.4   Towards a Method for Business Networking

Both cases presented above reflect different scenarios in Business Networking. The Telekom case focused on buy-side EC, whereas the Riverwood case emphasized SCM. In the following chapter, the structure of a method will be developed which provides techniques that are applicable to all Business Networking strategies (cf. Chap. 4). The key features of the method are:

- The consistent usage of aspects relevant to cooperation at the strategy, process and IS levels (cf. Chap. 14.4.1), and

- The usage of method engineering which comprises a meta model, a role model, a procedure model and techniques (cf. Chaps. 14.4.2 to 14.4.4) plus various result documents (shown in method application in Chapter 15).

14.4.1 Design Areas of a Method for Business Networking

The advantage of the Business Networking method is that it can start from existing and established approaches in business engineering. As shown in the left columns of Figure 14-7, business engineering "structures the organization, data and function dimensions at the business strategy, process and information systems levels." [Österle 1995, 29]. The method for Business Networking proposes three cooperation-specific enhancements:

- *Metrics.* Besides well-known process metrics, such as quality, time, cost, and flexibility, the method also includes measurements for cooperation processes. These build on the construct of networkability and include the efficiency of setting up relationships with a new OU, the implementation of an EDI link to a new OU, and the like.

- *Cooperation management.* Although Business Networking is IT-enabled, Business Networking projects are not primarily technical projects and require substantial cooperation management skills. This includes selecting and convincing business partners, generating trust, defining win-win situations and cooperation contracts, conflict management, initiating pilot projects, setting up project teams, cooperation controlling procedures etc.

- *Networking.* Business Networking builds on a new business model as outlined in Chapter 2.3.4. On the strategy level this includes new cooperation models, on the process level new forms of electronic coordination (e.g. multi-vendor product catalogs, supply chain scenarios), and on the systems level the use of eServices (cf. Chap. 2.3.5) and the design of the business bus.

The method's systematic approach involves successively elaborating and refining the content of the three dimensions. In the case of cooperation management, for example, the structure of the initial cooperation concept is retained when drawing up the cooperation contract - additional details are merely added. The cooperation contract in turn serves as the basis for cooperation controlling. In the same way, initial assessments of networkability are successively refined into concrete and quantitative indicators.

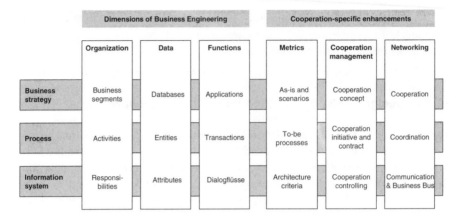

Figure 14-7: Dimensions of Business Engineering and Cooperation-specific Enhancements

14.4.2 Meta Model

According to [Brenner 1995, 11], a meta model is the conceptual data model of the results of a method and represents the constituent parts of the major design results of a method. Its purpose is to ensure consistency, providing a rapid overview of description and design areas and the terminology employed. The terms and their interrelationships are explained for each level (business strategy, process, IS). Figure 14-8 shows the meta model at the strategy level.

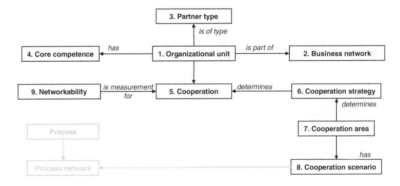

Figure 14-8: Meta Model at the Strategy Level

14.4.3 Role Model

The assignment of activities to ultimate units of responsibility is referred to as the role model. Roles are assumed by a business unit or individual employees, and involve tasks, competencies and responsibilities. The role model starts off by distinguishing the familiar roles of the people concerned: moderator, decision-maker, responsible and supporter.

In addition to inwardly oriented BPR methods, cooperation projects require a role model which includes the roles of the cooperation partners. The method assumes that an initiator has a cooperation idea and successively concretizes it (see Table 14-5). The first step towards concretization takes place in the initiator's own company with an assessment of the cooperation idea (or vision), along with its scope, benefits and consequences. The decision whether to go ahead with a concrete cooperation project in collaboration with one or more pilot partners is then made on the basis of this assessment. The experience systematically collected from the pilot partner project is the prerequisite for winning several partners and/or for a roll-out.

Roles at	Organizational Level		
Employee Level	Project initiator (PI)	Pilot partner (PP)	Partner (P)
Moderator (M)			
Decision maker (D)			
Responsible (R)			
Supporter (U)			

Table 14-5: Role model of the Business Networking Method

14.4.4 Procedure Model and Techniques

[Heinen 1991, 311] states that procedure models define the temporal, logical sequence of steps in a problem-solving process. The four phases of the Business Networking method (cf. Chap. 17.1.4) have already been used in the case studies. The goals and results of each phase are achieved by means of techniques which consist of a detailed procedure and result documents. The 11 techniques in total (see Figure 14-9) are explained below.

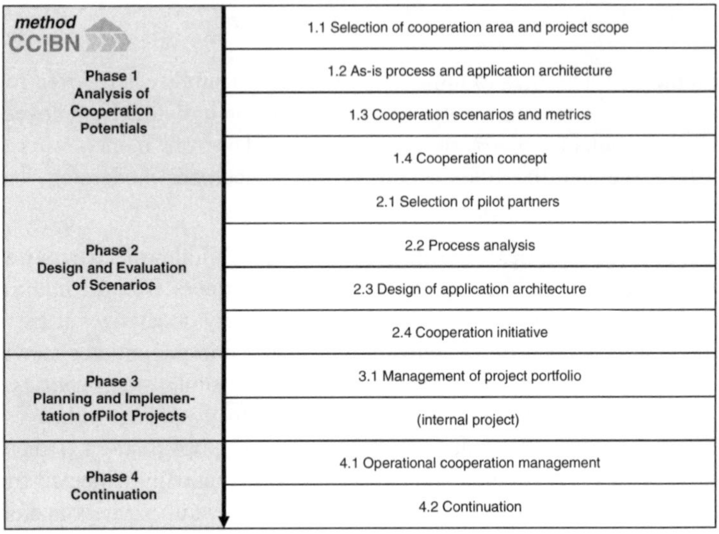

method CCiBN ⟫⟫ Phase 1 Analysis of Cooperation Potentials	1.1 Selection of cooperation area and project scope
	1.2 As-is process and application architecture
	1.3 Cooperation scenarios and metrics
	1.4 Cooperation concept
Phase 2 Design and Evaluation of Scenarios	2.1 Selection of pilot partners
	2.2 Process analysis
	2.3 Design of application architecture
	2.4 Cooperation initiative
Phase 3 Planning and Implementation ofPilot Projects	3.1 Management of project portfolio
	(internal project)
Phase 4 Continuation	4.1 Operational cooperation management
	4.2 Continuation

Figure 14-9: Phases and Techniques of the Business Networking Method

Phase 1: Analysis of Cooperation Potentials

1.1   Selection of cooperation area and project scope. The areas in which cooperation is to take place are specified. The starting point is the cooperation goals and the cooperation road map which shows possible areas of cooperation. A performance analysis is carried out for assessment purposes, and the project initiator determines the relevant dimensions of the project and the composition of the project team.

1.2   As-is process and application architecture. The as-is business, process and application network is modeled, taking into account the defined project scope. As-is analysis is the prerequisite for the design and implementation of optimized structures and processes.

1.3   Goals, potentials and architecture of the to-be process network. Cooperation scenarios, consisting of the business, process and application network, are developed and evaluated according to the extent to which they meet the goals.

1.4   Cooperation concept. The main result document is the cooperation concept which is presented to the potential pilot partners at the beginning of the second phase (technique 1.2) and corresponds to a letter of intent. In order to achieve this result, the project initiator defines partner profiles, draws up a rough assessment of benefit categories (win-win situation) and selects the preferred type of partner.

Phase 2: Design and Evaluation of Scenarios

2.1 Pilot partner selection. The initiator selects the partners for the pilot project. The objective is to identify partners who have an interest in a quick win. The technique also includes team-building activities.

2.2 Process analysis. The focus is on defining the to-be process network. This involves selecting the strategic alignment and the basic processes. The objective is to develop the best suited process scenarios for which a standard software application already exists; i.e. the idea is not to develop a a 'best case scenario' but one which can best be depicted in applications.

2.3 Design of application architecture. The definitive choice of applications and eServices is made for the best suited application / eService scenario. The scenario is analyzed to identify any shortcomings with regard to the processes modeled. This is followed by an analysis to determine how these gaps can be filled in terms of IS.

2.4 Cooperation initiative. This technique completes the cooperation contract in respect of common goals, obligations and resource deployment. The objective is to bring together the results obtained prior to implementation and, in particular, to review cost and benefit elements.

Phase 3: Planning and Implementation of Pilot Projects

3.1 Management of the project portfolio. The inter-organizational activities required to achieve goals in respect of deadlines, costs and target fulfillment levels have to be coordinated. The methodological support for project realization is not part of the Business Networking method; this is where the specific approaches of the project initiator, the pilot partners and the software manufacturer (e.g. ASAP for APO) come in.

(Execution of internal partner projects). Executes defined projects and monitors the delivery of results. It is not an integral element of the Business Networking method.

Phase 4: Continuation

4.1 Establish operational cooperation management. The objective is ensure that the cooperation runs smoothly and that the cooperation goals are actually fulfilled.

4.2 Continuation decision. A final review of the pilot project is performed and the success of the project communicated to the decision-makers. In addition, a 'business case' is drawn up to gain (roll out) partners and the success of the cooperation is marketed at the inter-organizational level. Finally, a decision is made on how to proceed, i.e. roll-out to other partners or follow on with a new cooperation project.

Although the method proposes an ideal sequence of activities, we are aware that certain projects require modifications. For this reason, each technique contains a clear description of the required inputs. This permits lower starting points, parallel activities, cycles and the like.

14.5   Conclusions and Outlook

Due to their specific characteristics, Business Networking or cooperation projects require additional steps and competencies in project work and procedure. Although a variety of methods are available, these methods present significant shortcomings since they either focus only on strategic aspects, do not include knowledge of networking processes, or else provide only a low level of formalization. The advantages of a method for Business Networking are that it:

- Provides an *integrative framework* that includes all activities relevant to analyzing, designing, planning/implementing and continuing Business Networking projects. It offers a structured path from (strategic) analysis and conceptualization to implementation. Strengths of existing methods can be integrated.

- Facilitates *inter-organizational project management* by providing a common procedure model, using understandable techniques and result documents as well as role descriptions. This helps to structure a shared project plan, to determine which tasks have to be performed and to decide who should be involved at which stage of the project. Problems arising from different corporate cultures, languages and systems can be avoided.

- Addresses *critical success factors* relevant to Business Networking. As Chapter 13 has shown, the success of Business Networking projects is often determined by non-technical, i.e. organizational and political, factors. Examples are creating win-win situations, homogenization of master data and the like.

- Supports *knowledge management* by transferring knowledge relating to prior and ongoing projects. It includes success factors and best practices as well as critical configuration and implementation know-how. Besides helping to provide direct benefits for project management, the method improves employee training. In doing so, it increases the flexibility and responsiveness of an organization to cope with future networking challenges.

- Helps to improve a company's *networkability*. Networkability is an integral part of the method and is addressed in each phase, i.e. within potentials analysis, scenario design, and the planning/implementation phase.

As described in Chapter 2, the information age presents a variety of challenges to management. The implications and opportunities are dynamic and the method for

Business Networking represents a solid foundation for tackling these challenges in a systematic way. We see two areas in which the method can be extended:

- *Interaction with knowledge management.* The increasing volume of electronic transactions handled via Business Networking systems presents an important source for extracting information about customers. The integration of trans-action-oriented and relationship-oriented Business Networking systems will provide new perspectives for creating tailored and efficient customer service.

- *Development of eServices.* Electronic services (cf. Chap. 2.3.5) will be an important part of Business Networking in the future. How eServices can be developed or how they can be integrated at a business, process and information systems level are questions to be addressed in further development of the method.

- *Electronic marketplaces.* In comparison with long-term supply chain projects, cooperation with business partners by means of eMarkets is frequently of a short-term nature. Extending the method to include techniques which also cover systems of this kind represents another direction in which the method might be developed.

15 Application of the Business Networking Method at SAP

Christian Reichmayr, Rainer Alt, Thomas Reiss, Andreas Pfadenhauer

15.1 Distinction Between Business Networking Strategies 290
    15.1.1 Overview..290
    15.1.2 Interaction of Strategies From the Customer Perspective 290

15.2 A Method for Implementing Supply Chain Modules.......................292
    15.2.1 Goals of the Method...292
    15.2.2 Business Networking Systems and Methods of SAP...............292
    15.2.3 Accelerated SAP (ASAP) Roadmap 293
    15.2.4 Strategic Blueprint of ASAP for APO 2.0a 294

15.3 Reference Case for the Strategic Blueprint: Woodbridge, Int.............295

15.4 Conclusions and Next Steps..302

15.1 Distinction Between Business Networking Strategies

15.1.1 Overview

Chapter 4 describes different Business Networking strategies based on three levels of the Business Engineering Model. In reality these strategies do not normally appear in their original form. Existing strategies, IT applications and their functionalities tend to mix them. Examples of this fact are businesses that:

- Use 'outsourcing', 'insourcing' or 'virtual organizing' in parallel according to their business processes. For example, a corporation runs a virtual organization in procurement, operates insourcing in sales by taking over an eMarket and outsources all fulfillment activities.

- Realize integrated electronic transactions. In the long-term it makes no sense to inform customers about new products, prices, specific product information, availabilities, etc. without giving them the chance to order. And without a selection of products and more or less individual negotiation no physical supply chain can be triggered and no order entry occurs.

- Use different Business Networking systems at the same time. For example, decentralized eProcurement applications and eMarkets are used in parallel for procurement, and process portals support the entire customer needs on the sell side.

Therefore, businesses need to consider different strategies at the same time. A structured approach, such as the Business Networking Method described in Chapter 14, helps to speed up projects and to coordinate dependencies between different projects. Chap. 15.2 suggests how the method can be used to implement Business Networking strategies with standard software components.

15.1.2 Interaction of Strategies From the Customer Perspective

Electronic commerce (EC), supply chain management (SCM) and customer relationship management (CRM) are complementary strategies that focus on different areas of support for the customer process. Successful solutions integrate these strategies in a manner which allows the customer to fulfill his various needs without changing the medium or channel, i.e. 'Amazon' (cf. Chap. 3.2.2) or 'ETA Online Shop (cf. Chap. 6.3). When it comes to developing such solutions and designing a Business Network, however, a clear differentiation of the processes is important in order to define:

- which applications and/or functionalities should be used for what,

- where to store (master) data, and

- what interfaces between applications are necessary, which data are to be exchanged etc.

As described in Chapter 4, these strategies focus on different core processes: EC
on 'Information', 'Contracting' and 'Settlement', SCM on 'Plan', 'Source',
'Make' and 'Deliver', and CRM on 'Customer selection', 'Customer acquisition'
and 'Customer retention'. From a customer perspective, only the outcome of these
strategies is relevant, i.e. the maximum support of the customer process (cf. Chap.
2.3.6). As Figure 15-1 shows, customer portals1 provide support by profiling and
obtaining advance information on solving the problem of how to dispose of used
goods. Thus, a method has to provide support when identifying the customer segments, the elements of the customer process as well as the functionalities and
other properties at the application level. Methods provided by application providers, such as SAP, therefore need to support not only the implementation and configuration process but also the strategy and process levels.

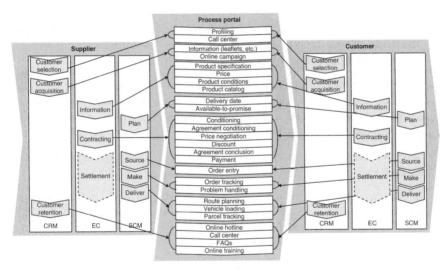

Figure 15-1: Process Portal and Business Networking Processes

---

[1] Portals are Internet-based systems that integrate content, services and functionalities in order to
     offer a personalized 'window' for the user.

15.2 A Method for Implementing Supply Chain Modules

15.2.1 Goals of the Method

In order to attain Business Networking goals, such as the simple and fast exchange of transactions, increased customer care or reduced inventories, business partners have to be convinced about new ideas, new business processes among them and new (information) systems. For implementation to be successful, a variety of decisions will have to be taken at the strategy, process and systems levels. Business Networking projects require a procedure completely different from that of traditional ERP implementations because:

- The goals of all business partners have to be taken into consideration in order to establish win-win-situations and reach critical mass (cf. Chap. 2.2.3) both on the supplier and customer sides. Goals might be, for example, a 30% improvement in service level, a 20% reduction in cycle time or a 60% reduction in inventory level.

- Different scenarios have to be evaluated in order to find the appropriate configuration of the supply chain solution, i.e. a vendor-managed inventory (VMI) or continuous replenishment strategy (cf. Chap. 4.3.2).

- A solution which offers full customer support needs to integrate multiple modules, e.g. eProcurement (cf. Chap. 10.2), advanced planning systems (cf. Chap. 9.4), and services, e.g. electronic billing & payment systems, which may be from different vendors.

- Inter-organizational processes (e.g. a VMI process) and exchanged information needs to be coordinated between business partners.

These elements are typically not included in existing implementation methods from software vendors or consulting companies. However, they are a must if the potentials of Business Networking systems are to be exhausted.

15.2.2 Business Networking Systems and Methods of SAP

One successful example that takes the above mentioned points into consideration is SAP AG, headquartered in Walldorf, Germany. SAP AG made a turnover that exceeded   5 billion in 1999 with 20,975 employees worldwide (8,912 in Germany) [cf. SAP 1999b]. SAP provides solutions for all strategies and components of Business Networking – from traditional ERP, such as financials, human resources, product life cycle management, to newer areas such as business intelligence, SCM, CRM and EC, and finally to the mySAP.com workplace and marketplace. To support the implementation of these products, SAP provides a method called Accelerated SAP (ASAP) which consists of a procedure model, project-specific knowledge (project management, change management, risk analysis, review), tools (implementation assistant, Q&A database, etc.) and services (training, documentation, support, etc.).

The increasing level of networking between components and between business partners means that methodologies of the past need to be enhanced in order to cater for the needs of inter-business networking. At SAP, the first step in this direction has been the introduction of 'Global ASAP', a solution including a methodology for implementing multiple SAP systems within a company or corporation. ASAP solutions for APO, BBP and CRM will include component-specific views of eBusiness strategy, with part of the methodology helping to evaluate business alternatives for cross-company processes, and link the evaluation to the specific component's functionality. Some inter-organizational processes supported by APO, BBP and CRM involve all three components, for example procurement between BBP and CRM in the future as part of a supply chain planned by APO. For these processes it is important that a common language exists to describe them, i.e. we need to avoid having a supply chain-type description, a procurement-based description and a CRM-based description.

15.2.3 Accelerated SAP (ASAP) Roadmap

Traditionally, ASAP has concentrated on the ERP solutions provided by SAP AG. With the advent of mySAP.com components, such as APO (Advanced Planner and Optimizer) for SCM, BBP (Business-to-Business Procurement) for eProcurement and CRM (Customer Relationship Management) for CRM, ASAP methodology has been and still is being enhanced to include Business Networking aspects in the project preparation and business blueprint steps. The ASAP method goes beyond simply explaining how to configure SAP systems and aims to look at the big picture, giving customers and partners a roadmap for a complete project. The 'roadmap' consists of the following steps (see Figure 15-2):

1. *Project preparation* (project planning, project organization, project standards),

2. *Business blueprint* (organization structure of the enterprise, business processes of the enterprise),

3. *Realization* (baseline configuration, configuration and integration testing, conversions, interfaces, enhancements, reports, and user documentation),

4. *Final preparation* (go-live plan, end-user training, system administration, conversions), and

5. *Go-live and support* (system support and system optimization).

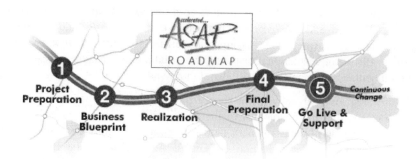

Figure 15-2: Roadmap of the ASAP Method

The second step, the business blueprint, is where a customer's business strategy is analyzed and matched to SAP's solutions. In particular this means analyzing and defining the companies' eBusiness strategy as it relates to the particular mySAP.com component, for example collaborative planning with APO. This part of the business blueprint is called the strategic blueprint and will be the topic of this Chapter.

15.2.4   Strategic Blueprint of ASAP for APO 2.0a

The 'strategic blueprint' is part of the business blueprint within ASAP for APO 2.0a, which focuses on supply chain collaboration scenarios. It consists of the following steps and work packages:

- *Enterprise Vision Definition.* The starting point for defining a Business Networking project is an overall vision. The problems of the as-is situation trigger the need for various analyses such as competitor analyses, best practices, stakeholders, etc. The main goal is to find out the real problems and to create a vision to set up the project.

- *Supply Chain Goals and Performance.* Detailed goals have to be developed for the underlying supply chain processes. This also includes expressive metrics to measure changes over as-is performance.

- *Identify Supply Chain Partners.* Successful collaboration between business partners first needs goals in respect of how the collaboration can be defined, started and maintained. Then collaboration scenarios have to be developed and collaboration partners defined in order to put the scenarios into action.

- *Elaborate Win-Win Situation with Supply Chain Partners.* The main goal is to clarify the collaboration scenarios together with the collaboration partners. The focus must be set on developing win-win situations for all partners concerned.

- *Supply Chain Landscape Considerations.* Commonly agreed strategic goals and a clear picture of specific success factors and potentials must form the basis for defining the to-be business architecture and processes, and implementing projects.

The Business Networking Method (cf. Chap. 14) has been fully integrated into the overall ASAP APO 2.0a method. But it was needed to adapt titles and subtitles to the established ASAP terminology. However, the first three ASAP steps roughly reflect the first phase in the BN method, and the last two ASAP steps the second phase of the BN method.

15.3 Reference Case for the Strategic Blueprint: Woodbridge, Int.

The Woodbridge case is fictitious and was developed in order to provide a general and neutral example which would explain the use of the Business Networking method. It represents the project experience gained within the CC iBN (cf. Chap. 1), which formed the basis for the development of the Business Networking method. In this case, EC elements have been included that are not part of ASAP APO 2.0a.

Woodbridge, Int., located in Seattle, Washington, is a long-established, international manufacturer of cardboard, aluminum and plastic packaging materials. The main customer in the USA is Walters Best in Richmond, Kentucky. Walters Best produces different types of pasta that are packaged with plastics from Woodbridge. Walters Best sells the pasta to its end-customers, i.e. supermarkets, wholesalers, etc. Woodbridge has its own car pool to deliver the materials to Walters Best distribution center.

Enterprise Vision Definition

Over the last two years Woodbridge ran into financial difficulties for the first time. The reasons for this, as shown by internal analyses, were a new competitive situation, rising costs and quality demands. Management's first reaction was to perform various analyses, i.e. potentials and risks, stakeholder, as-is customer, market and portfolio analyses, etc. It was then decided to define new cooperation concepts, open up new markets in South America and increase the level of customer service.

In order to improve external relationships it was decided to improve forecasting capabilities. In the past, it was not possible to exchange future demand figures electronically with business partners and no advanced planning system was in place to calculate different production plans. Customer demand was exchanged by telephone on a monthly basis only. Problems arising from this were:

- poor production capacity utilization,

- high inventory stock levels at Woodbridge and Walters Best,

- no flexible reaction to changing demands, i.e. special offers, postponements, etc.

The results of all analyses revealed weaknesses in logistics and warehousing. The as-is situations of the following three result documents were established: business architecture, process architecture and IS architecture. The as-is business architecture shows a geographic overview of all linked business units, i.e. warehouses, plants, distribution centers, wholesalers, and, of course, end-customers (see Figure 15-3)

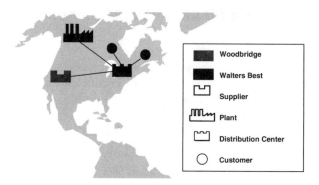

Figure 15-3: As-Is Business Architecture

The process architecture consists of a macro and a micro level similar to established BPR methods [cf. Österle 1995, 49]. The as-is process architecture describes all flows of information, goods and funds that are exchanged between business units (see Figure 15-4). The as-is process architecture at a more detailed (micro) level describes the main processes of the business units and their inputs and outputs within an activity chain diagram (see Figure 15-5).

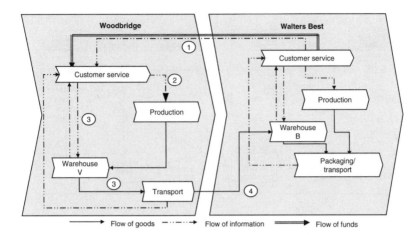

Figure 15-4: As-Is Process Architecture - Macro

At the beginning of the project the customer service from Walters Best ordered plastic materials from the Woodbridge customer service by telephone (1). Woodbridge produced an account of these orders along with past trends (2), and delivered plastics from warehouse V to warehouse B (3 & 4).

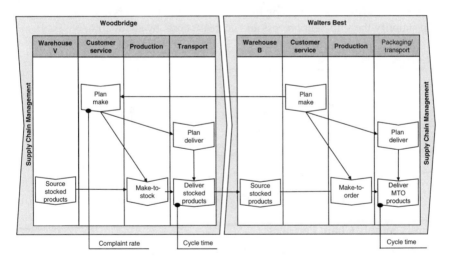

Figure 15-5: As-Is Process Architecture - Micro

As indicated in Figure 15-5 and Figure 15-6, there was neither an integrated planning function for the complete supply chain and future demands, nor an EC-solution to facilitate data exchange. Both enterprises only used ERP systems to plan their internal production (plan-make), delivery (plan-deliver), etc.

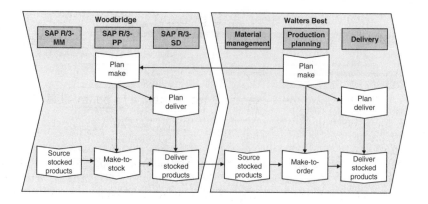

Figure 15-6: As-Is IS Architecture

Supply Chain Goals and Performance

For the purpose of developing efficient collaboration scenarios, Woodbridge decided to consider benchmarking databases and best practices in the sector, such as Riverwood International (see Figure 15-7). As a result, a VMI scenario was established to solve the problems in production and warehousing. An eService scenario was developed to solve the problems in shipment. The VMI scenario was to help decrease the costs of warehousing by about 40%, and the eService scenario was to help simplify the shipment process and decrease costs by about 20%.

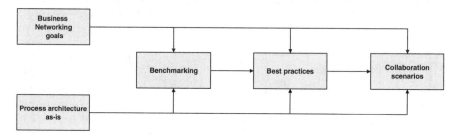

Figure 15-7: Developing Collaboration Scenarios

Identify Supply Chain Partners

Woodbridge analyzed the market in South America and selected three corporations with which they considered collaboration to be a viable proposition: Wheat Ind., Brewers Finest and Delta Choc.[2] Walters Best and these new corporations signed a preliminary collaboration agreement. Walters Best was defined as the

---

[2] Wheat, Ind. produces cereal products, Brewers Finest is a large brewery and Delta Choc. produces various sweets.

pilot partner and the others as partners for the continuation of the project when the pilot was rolled out.

Elaborate Win-Win Situation with Supply Chain Partners

Woodbridge and its partners held various workshops in order to obtain a clear picture of how the benefits could be shared within the collaboration scenario, i.e. the win-win situation. The overall collaboration principles, performance and collaboration goals were also defined. This included, for example, how to deal with conflicts, trust building and management, behavior in relation to competitors and collaboration processes. Finally, the main performance indicators for the scenario were fixed.

Scenario	Process	Metric	As-is Value
VMI	Make-to-Stock	Capacity utilization	40%
VMI	Make-to-Stock	Unit cost	USD 1 Mio.
eService	Deliver Stocked Products	Order fulfillment cycle time	5 days
eService	Plan Deliver	Order management cost per ton of plastic	USD 15,000

Table 15-1: Metrics of Scenarios at the Start of the Project

Supply Chain Landscape Considerations

The to-be business architecture shows the pilot project and the continuation partners, all warehouses, distribution centers, plants, etc. (see Figure 15-8).

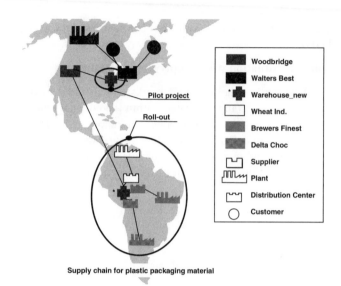

Supply chain for plastic packaging material

Figure 15-8: To-Be Business Architecture

While the responsibilities of the various customer services remained unchanged, Warehouse V and the new Warehouse B are now managed by Woodbridge. They are responsible for product availabilities and stock level optimization. Transport has been completely outsourced to a new partner, eLogistics (see Figure 15-9).

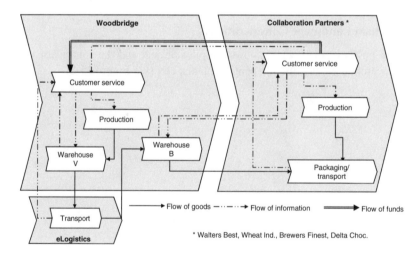

Figure 15-9: To-Be Process Architecture - Macro

These facts are again depicted in Figure 15-10: 'Source Stocked Product' now belongs to Woodbridge and 'Plan Deliver' and 'Deliver Stocked Products' to eLogistics. For the interaction with eLogistics an EC solution was established to facilitate requests for required capacities, availabilities and status information by developing two new processes: 'Inform MTO Service' and 'Contract MTO Service'[3].

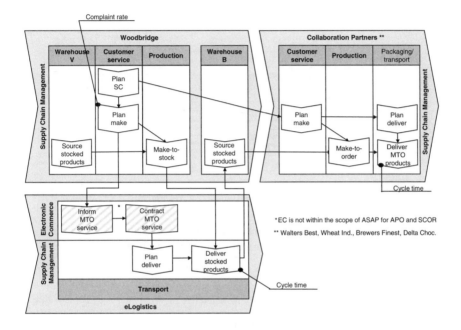

Figure 15-10: To-Be Process Architecture - Micro

To manage the new warehouses and continuous forecasting, Woodbridge implemented an Advanced Planning System (APS) that has various interfaces to the core ERP systems of Woodbridge and partners. On the other hand, Woodbridge uses an electronic catalog system from eLogistics that shows availabilities and conditions of transporters (see Figure 15-11) as well as the status of parcels to be delivered to partners and to Woodbridge itself via the Internet.

---

[3] EC processes do not fall within the scope of ASAP for APO but are seen as an important further development within SAP's method family.

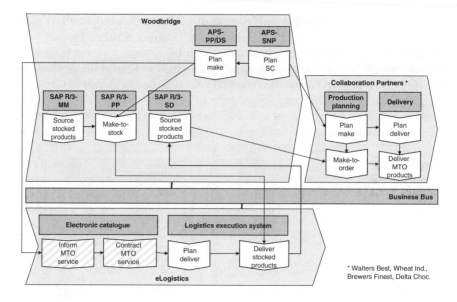

Figure 15-11: To-Be Application Architecture

At the end of the project a final evaluation of the main goals was conducted. As Table 15-2 shows, the project led to significant reductions in all core metrics.

Scenario	Process	Metric	As-is Value
VMI	Make-to-Stock	Capacity utilization	85%
VMI	Make-to-Stock	Unit cost	USD 560,000
eService	Deliver Stocked Products	Order fulfillment cycle time	1.5 days
eService	Plan Deliver	Order management cost per ton of plastic	USD 8,500

Table 15-2: Metrics of the Scenarios at the End of the Project

15.4   Conclusions and Next Steps

Customer-oriented solutions integrate multiple Business Networking strategies and systems. In many cases systems for eProcurement or EC are implemented, which neglect (1) strategy and process issues and/or (2) the interrelationships with

other strategies. We believe that in the future, the differences between implementing processes between systems or components within a company and implementing inter-organizational processes across company borders will shrink. This
has important implications for application providers, such as SAP. As Figure
15-12 shows, in some companies all the components will belong to the company;
in other cases, many components will belong to different companies. Collaboration will make the building of virtual companies much easier, at least for certain
areas; the building blocks are collaboration scenarios. An Internet trader, for example, might have a CRM system, outsource HR and look to partners for manufacturing and logistics. In other words, he defines and implements collaboration
scenarios with his partners, thus creating a virtual company.

Figure 15-12: mySAP.com[4] Components

In order to provide a methodology for implementing mySAP.com, we need to
build on a common language for describing cross-component business processes,
be they within a company or between different business partners. Once a common
language is defined, we can set about joining Global ASAP methodologies with
eBusiness methodologies for APO, BBP and CRM in order to arrive at a methodology for implementing eBusiness solutions across multiple SAP components, be
they Intranet, Internet or both.

The authors were involved in producing ASAP for APO 2.0A, and are currently
working on the definition of a common language for describing cross-component
business processes. The interaction of SCM and EC as shown in the Woodbridge
case represents a first approach to this problem.

---

[4] With mySAP.com any of the above components could be running in systems owned by one company, or owned by collaborating partner companies. LES stands for Logistics Execution (Transport
and Shipping), MES for Manufacturing Execution, HR for Human Resources, FI for Financial Accounting and Controlling, PLM for Product Life Cycle Management, BW for Business Information
Warehouse, and SEM for Strategic Enterprise Management.

16 Architecture Planning for Global Networked Enterprises

Sven Pohland, Elgar Fleisch

16.1 Introduction 306
    16.1.1 Challenge of Architecture Planning 306
    16.1.2 Goals of Architecture Planning 307

16.2 Business Architecture 309
    16.2.1 Organization Profile 309
    16.2.2 Process Architecture 311

16.3 Application Architecture 313
    16.3.1 Distribution Concepts in Packaged Software 313
    16.3.2 Integration Areas at the Application Level 313
    16.3.3 Structure of Application Architecture 314

16.4 Methodological Procedure 316
    16.4.1 Existing Approaches 316
    16.4.2 Deficits of Existing Methods 318
    16.4.3 Proposed Method 318

16.5 Conclusions and Outlook 321

16.1   Introduction

16.1.1   Challenge of Architecture Planning

An international chemicals group decides to introduce the packaged software SAP R/3 throughout the organization. This decision will affect eight divisions, 200 legally independent companies and some 150 different countries. Initial implementations were based on individual companies within the group. However, an investigation of the global supply chain revealed a lack of consistency in core processes. This investigation made it clear that future implementations will have to be coordinated throughout the group. The first question to be clarified is the significance which the legal entities, divisions and regions are to have for the group in the future and the dependencies which will result. The integration requirements can then be derived from this analysis of the business relationships involved.

Alliances in the airline industry are another example. The corporations concerned share a common strategy: the customer should receive the same level of service throughout. However, as soon as the customer contacts one of the airlines, the limitations of cooperation become apparent: double check-in for connecting flights or no means of reserving seats through the partner airline. In some cases the processes are coordinated, e.g. through the presence of ground staff from both airlines at the check-in. This is not the case with the architecture of the information systems however. Depending on the cooperation depth and the existing applications, the question is whether concurrent use of check-in systems would be useful or whether a common application should be used.

These examples show typical questions facing large corporations. Business strategies are developed and translated into processes. However, they bear no relationship with the architecture of the information systems, despite the fact that a suitable architecture provides the basis for huge cost savings. In a study for an international electronics corporation it was proven that up to USD 1.1 billion could be saved through the use of synergies [cf. Fleisch 1998]. In the available literature on the subject, authors also underline the necessity for organization and information system to be calibrated: "The information system must be designed so that the information system architecture[1] and the organization structure are homologous" [Wall 1996, 76]. [Jagoda 1999, 4] also stresses the integration of business strategy and information systems: "On the one hand, because data processing can be expected to lead to the creation of new business fields. On the other hand, because

---

[1]   For the purposes of this Chapter, a target application architecture is understood to be the totality of all applications, requirements and concepts which a business should possess in three to five years' time (cf. [Schwarze 1998, 128] and [Brenner 1996, 354]).

the efficient and effective use of information and communication systems is imperative for certain strategic realignments".

Businesses are becoming increasingly decentralized [cf. Wigand et al. 1997, 199]. Geographical divisions and organizational splits are a reflection of this development [cf. Österle/Fleisch 1996, 8]. The aim is to combine the advantages of the small business with those of large corporations. These changes imply new inter-organizational business processes and thus new demands on the information systems. Packaged software must allow the business to be split into smaller units and at the same time provide for the integration of distributed business units. This Chapter considers structures within large corporations with a special focus on the distributed use of business management, transaction-oriented packaged software (ERP systems). The following critical success factors have been derived as driving forces for designing application architectures:

- The application architecture must be planned at the strategic level,

- Cross-organization business management relationships must be transparent when planning the architecture,

- Business architecture and application architecture must be matched, and

- Coordination is essential in the case of a distributed concept and implementation of business management packaged software.

16.1.2 Goals of Architecture Planning

Up to now, manufacturers of packaged software have adopted the approach of depicting a business in precisely one system. A coordinated approach to combining systems to form a network of systems (referred to as 'distributed systems') improves the support for business networks. The task is to find a suitable application architecture. At present, the application landscape reflects a functional, formal organization structure. The 'owner', usually a specialist area, is responsible for implementations. There is a lack of perspective on cross-organizational questions, such as e.g. centralization, harmonization or at least coordination of customer information, one of the core problems in the cases mentioned at the beginning of this Chapter. There is also a lack of transparency with regard to the consequences of not integrating or failing to adequately integrate processes which extend beyond an individual area. The consequences include the following:

- Reintegration involves high costs, e.g. as a result of the interface complexity required to integrate isolated solutions.

- Avoidable costs are generated through duplication within the company, e.g. similar implementation tasks.

- Inadequate structuring of the architecture results in a high level of application complexity, which in turn increases the complexity of interfaces, for example, when parts of the architecture migrate.

- Integrated packaged software concepts do not fully exploit potential, e.g. there may be no cross-system reporting facility despite worldwide product responsibility.

The following graphic shows possible cost savings where application architecture planning is driven by business management considerations. Here our approach is based on the concept of total cost of ownership (TCO)[2]: We consider all the costs incurred in the life cycle of an ERP system.

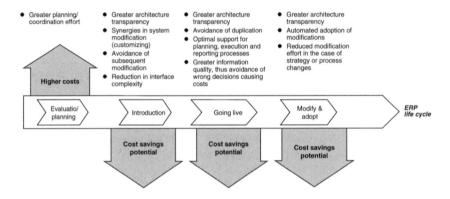

Figure 16-1: Cost Savings in the ERP System Life Cycle

Although a distribution project initially means higher costs for planning and coordinating the implementation, major cost savings can be realized in subsequent phases of the ERP Life Cycle (implementation, going live plus modifications and adoption). The most important source of savings is the utilization of synergies in the planning and implementation phases. Lower investments for interface programming and system maintenance should also be mentioned in this context.

When planning application architectures, benefits which are not immediately quantifiable, such as increasing the level of service, are also a major issue in addition to cost savings. The following can be said in respect of benefits [cf. QED 1985, 4]:

- Concepts embedded in the software are optimally utilized,

- The complexity of the application architecture is reduced,

---

[2] For an explanation of the relationship between TCO and other approaches to cost analysis [cf. Pottholf 1998, 8].

- The involvement of top management and users in the design process is guaranteed,

- The use of cross-system processes becomes possible, and

- The global supply chain becomes transparent.

16.2   Business Architecture

The aim of analyzing the business network is to identify areas of the company with a high integration requirement from a business management point of view. For this purpose we document subsystems in the company which we refer to as 'Business Clusters'. A wide range of concepts are used in business management theory: integration areas are identified by terms, such as the formation of 'subsystems' [Schmidt 1991, 70], 'moduls' [Wigand et al. 1997, 199] or the 'manufacturing segments' [Wildemann 1994]. Existing approaches can be applied to the question of business architecture with certain limitations [cf. Rolf 1998, 261].

16.2.1   Organization Profile

The starting point for architectural considerations is usually the formal structure of the organization, where the basic principles of organizational distribution start to become visible. Product responsibility, functional separation, the significance of various customer groups or regional structures assist in the appraisal of company structures. However, there are clear differences between formal organizational structure and the structure which is of relevance to the architecture. An organizational structure has usually grown historically and is characterized by tradition, departmental thinking and functional alignment. The application architecture must be oriented towards the company's medium and long-term structure and not its present setup. Otherwise there will be a discrepancy between business and application architecture as a result of what are often relatively long implementation phases. We introduce what we call an 'organization profile' in order to characterize the company. This comprises three aspects: dimensions showing possible structuring criteria, the permanency and topology of the company representing the underlying conditions for the architectural design.

Dimensions

We use the clustering dimensions shown in Figure 16-2 to delimit the integration areas. The individual dimensions represent idealized, typical characteristics which are not without overlap. In most cases, for example, an organization unit also represents an individual area of responsibility. Conversely, however, not every area of responsibility necessarily corresponds to an organization unit.

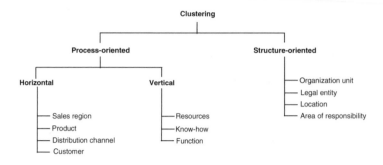

Figure 16-2: Dimension Tree

Dimensions are used to identify areas along them, which are largely independent of one another. In other words, there are few dependencies to be found along these dimensions. Here we speak of 'rated breaking points'. One example is the dimension 'product' in the case of corporations with a particularly heterogeneous product range, such as Mitsubishi, which produces video recorders as well as automobiles. Another example is the concept of a purely financial holding company where the individual companies (dimension 'legal entity') play an important role.

Yet another example is Henkel: traditionally, the corporation tends to be organized on a decentralized basis. As the corporation developed - frequently through acquisitions - the affiliated companies in the group enjoyed extensive freedom. The corporation now wants to increase the responsibility for business areas. This means shifting the focus from the affiliated companies (dimension 'legal entity') to the business areas which are structured according to product groups (dimension 'product', referred to as 'business' at Henkel). IBM is a further example: this corporation gave up its regional orientation (dimension 'region') in favor of a global approach with distribution and product responsibility (dimensions 'distribution channel' and 'product'). The ultimate goal is to achieve uniform customer care across the globe.

Permanency

Figure 16-3: Permanency of the Organization

The criterion of permanency of the organization is defined by the opposing poles of 'Palaces' and 'Tents' after [Gomez/Zimmermann 1993]. An efficiency-oriented organization strives for a strict division of labor in order to exploit rationalization and cost savings potential, while an organization geared towards effectiveness sets up flexible structures to ensure rapid striking power when it comes to implementing strategies. We also introduce the time horizon: at one end of the scale there is the organization established in advance for an indefinite period of time, at the other, structures designed to fulfil tasks over a limited time span. An application example is the telecommunications sector: since liberalization of the market the previously state-run organizations ('palaces') have shown a realignment towards flexible businesses with the capacity to offer short-term responses ('tents').

Topology

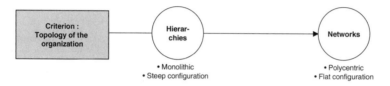

Figure 16-4: Topology of the Organization

The criterion of topology is defined by the opposing poles of 'hierarchies' and 'networks' after [Gomez/Zimmermann 1993]. The topology expresses the degree of centralization of an organization: traditional corporations with a pronounced hierarchy and a leader at the top are termed 'hierarchies', as opposed to 'networks' which are characterized by a small number of hierarchical levels and a high level of decentralization. The two extremes are to be found in the chemical industry: some corporations place the focus on highly independent business areas (e.g. in the Hoechst corporation), others present themselves as a single entity throughout the group (e.g. the Bayer corporation).

16.2.2 Process Architecture

For the analysis and visualization of business networks we rely on proven techniques. Flow charts [cf. Hess 1996, 140] are used for visualizing processes and communication charts [cf. Grochla 1982, 313] for documenting dependencies. By and large, the size and complexity of the corporations looked at here do not permit a detailed description of all processes. Analysis has to focus on core processes with high granularity plus cross-organizational process dependencies. A process architecture is derived from strategic statements. The findings are depicted in rules for process structures. When documenting the process architecture the following aspects are considered: the assignment of processes to organizational areas, the demonstration of dependencies between processes and the categorization of processes.

SAP R/3 reference processes, for example, or processes specific to the corporation can serve as the basis for the processes architecture. The processes are assigned to organization units and/or business areas. At this point it is important to use processes which apply throughout the business or corporation. Process categorization describes the dependencies between the processes of different business areas. The characterization performed will have a major influence on system distribution.

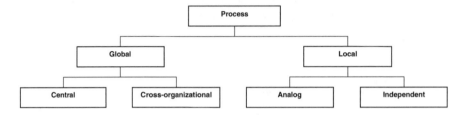

Figure 16-5: Process Categories

These categories indicate whether a process is 'global' or 'local'. A global process will always affect several business areas. Here we distinguish between global cross-organizational processes (the process runs in several areas of the corporation) and global central (the process is executed at one point in the corporation for various areas). Local processes run within an area of the corporation and do not lead to immediate dependencies with other areas. At the same time there are local analog processes which run similarly in various areas while local independent processes are not coordinated within an area.

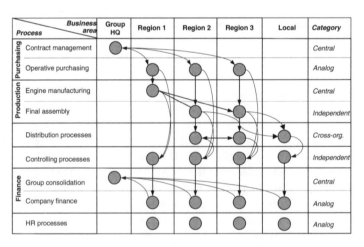

Figure 16-6: Example of Process Distribution[3]

---

[3]   The table reflects the simplified visualization of an international automobile manufacturer.

A few central processes are characteristic, usually group consolidation and group procurement. Many central processes are subsumed under the term 'shared services' [cf. Schuurmans/Stoller 1998]. Operative purchasing activities in the various business units are usually standardized within the framework of group procurement, i.e. they are analog processes. Production processes are mostly local independent due to heterogeneous product structures, distribution processes differ according to region and distribution channel, but seldom according to product.

16.3   Application Architecture

16.3.1   Distribution Concepts in Packaged Software

Distributed businesses are modeled by looking at the relationship between distributed and integrated information systems. The concept behind integrated systems is to depict the entire corporation in precisely one information system. A major question here is the distribution concepts supported by the software. Investigations [Kranz 1997] have shown that while it is possible to find examples of packaged software distribution, such as the application link enabling (ALE) concepts from SAP AG, all manufacturers place the main emphasis on the isolated implementation of software packages. All manufacturers offer integration mechanisms at the technical level. However, these technical solutions do not generally include support for business management distribution at the conception level. Here we understand a system to mean software components with strong interdependencies and which typically access a common database. A system is thus a logically integrated software package. In this Chapter we look at distribution in the logical sense, rather than adopting the more technically oriented view of distribution[4]: here we understand distributed systems to be several integrated systems which exchange data.

16.3.2   Integration Areas at the Application Level

It is not possible to depict corporations of unlimited size and complexity in an integrated system. There are a large number of restrictions at the technical level. Typical restrictions are multilingual capability, multicurrency capability, performance or failsafe operation. At the same time there are organizational restrictions,

---

[4]   Although a common understanding is usually assumed in the relevant literature, discrepancies are found on further reading. [Turowski 1997] gives an overview of various interpretations of system distribution in the technical sense.

such as the chances of pushing through an integrated solution or an unacceptably high level of project complexity.

In view of such limitations on distribution it is necessary to strike a balance between what is desirable in terms of business management and what is feasible in terms of applications. Application clusters are 'feasible business clusters'. The requirement for integration at the information system level can be derived from the intensity of business management dependencies. A high cooperation intensity favors a high level of linkage at the technical level. Conversely, if the level of exchange is low, a solution without system support might be useful. The diagram below assigns various integration possibilities to their respective integration depths. In extreme cases we can talk of 'integration by user' (low integration depth) or an integrated system (with a high integration depth).

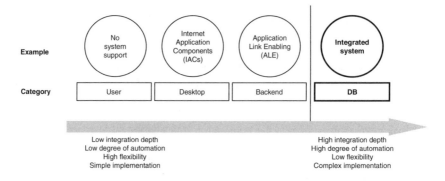

Figure 16-7: Integration Depth

We start off by assuming the highest possible level of integration. In our minds we depict all the functions of a business in precisely one system on a 'virtual megaserver'. Other requirements in terms of integration depth may arise from the business management constellation. For collaboration in project-like conditions it may be useful to merely opt for a desktop integration. Other integration possibilities will be excluded by the underlying business management environment. Integration with the ALE concept from SAP AG, for example, is only realistic in the case of a long-term business relationship with partners in view of the high coordination effort involved. Business clusters are checked for feasibility and adapted as necessary on the basis of the desired integration depth in business management terms and the above mentioned applications-related and technical factors.

16.3.3 Structure of Application Architecture

Figure 16-8 illustrates an application architecture by way of example. It shows the worldwide use of SAP R/3 in the case of the automobile manufacturer (cf. Chap.

16.2.2). The diagrams will vary depending on the modeling possibilities of the application types. However, functionality and data are always assigned to business areas.

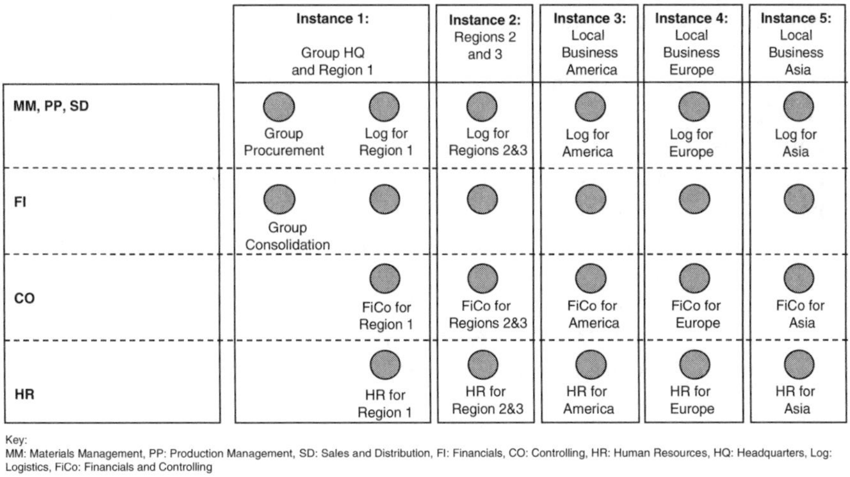

	Instance 1: Group HQ and Region 1		Instance 2: Regions 2 and 3	Instance 3: Local Business America	Instance 4: Local Business Europe	Instance 5: Local Business Asia
MM, PP, SD	Group Procurement	Log for Region 1	Log for Regions 2&3	Log for America	Log for Europe	Log for Asia
FI	Group Consolidation					
CO		FiCo for Region 1	FiCo for Regions 2&3	FiCo for America	FiCo for Europe	FiCo for Asia
HR		HR for Region 1	HR for Region 2&3	HR for America	HR for Europe	HR for Asia

Key:
MM: Materials Management, PP: Production Management, SD: Sales and Distribution, FI: Financials, CO: Controlling, HR: Human Resources, HQ: Headquarters, Log: Logistics, FiCo: Financials and Controlling

Figure 16-8: Example of an Application Architecture[5]

It is typical to form a central cluster or system to which central or cross-organizational functionality and central data are assigned. In this example, functionality to implement group procurement and group consolidation is depicted at group level. In order to make this possible, certain business objects, such as material, customer, supplier, standard chart of accounts or contract, have to be standardized throughout the organization and centrally coordinated. In most cases a central master data server will be the solution, but a central directory with distributed data storage is also conceivable. In cases where only certain elements are exchanged between systems rather than complete data records, we talk about a 'reduction'. In addition, it is important to visualize which data records are valid for the complete organization and which are only relevant for specific areas of the organization (referred to as 'filters'). It is conceivable, for example, that only certain procurement materials will be relevant for each product group and therefore only certain data records will be transferred.

---

[5]   Note that this is a simplified view without integration relationships.

16.4   Methodological Procedure

16.4.1 Existing Approaches

In organization theory we find approaches to the analysis and design of organizations. While the terminology employed by the various approaches to the formation of subsystems may differ, the basic intention is the same, i.e. to identify areas in an organization which are closely linked to one another. Another focus for methodology is the implementation of processes in information systems. Some approaches go from statements on business strategy via processes and on to application architecture. These are to be found e.g. in Strategic Information System Planning (SISP) [Riedl 1991], in St. Gallen Information System Management [Österle et al. 1993]. The table below gives aspects of existing methodological approaches which were of particular relevance for the development of the PROMET eBN[6] method.

Approach	Aspects Relevant to a Distribution Method
Subsystem Formation (cf. [Wildemann 1994], [Osterloh/Frost 1998, 139], [Wigand et al. 1997, 199])	Identification of business management integration areas within the framework of segmentation / modularization of organizations.
Implementation Methods (cf. [Lozinsky 1998, 70], [Arnold 1998], [Scheruhn 1997], [Buck-Emden 1998, 305], [Ullmann 1997]	Conventional projects for the implementation of packaged software are based on the assumption that it is possible to depict all processes in precisely one integrated application system. These are nevertheless far-reaching methods which build on the concept of the relevant software.
Calibration of Business and Information Strategy (cf. [Kreikebaum 1997, 208], [Norman 1992], [Parker et al. 1988, 79], [Wall 1996], [QED 1985], [Wexelblat/Srinivasan 1999, 266])	The process of comparing business and information system strategies aims to achieve a better understanding of the business requirements and to ensure that application architecture planning is business-driven. The idea is to help the method user in deriving an architecture with 'design recommendations'. A positive feature is that it investigates the interplay between long-range and operative planning. The concept of 'Business / IS plans linkage' thus attempts to combine various approaches to information system planning, using proven methods. Linkage activities make it possible to calibrate business and IS planning.

---

[6] PROMET is the acronym for project method and is a registered trademark of IMG AG. eBN stands for electronic Business Networking.

Strategic Information Systems Planning (SISP) (cf. [Pruijm 1990], [Kruse 1987], [Martin 1989], [Nüttgens 1995, 30])	The approaches to strategic information system planning presented here are on the whole comprehensive concepts based on a business-driven approach. These approaches incorporate various levels and views of the relevant questions. Attempts to combine business strategy and information system planning are always positive. However, the proposed procedure cannot be used in large corporations as common planning does not exist, the main emphasis being instead on coordinating distributed activities.
St. Gallen Information System Management (cf. [Österle et al. 1993], [Hilbers 1989])	The approach proposed by the St. Gallen Information System Management concept is based on the idea of a large, decentralized corporation. This corresponds to the reality in most large organizations. An important point is the fact that decentralized organizations do not have a detailed, cross-organizational information system architecture. A positive feature is the formation of integration areas for structuring such organizations, also the structuring of various forms of realization.
Business System Planning (BSP) (cf. [Pruijm 1990, 64], [Martiny/Klotz 1990, 94], [Heinrich 1992, 290], [Brenner 1994, 101])	This involves a far-reaching, proven procedure where cross-organizational information systems are planned from the top down and implemented from the bottom up. A cross-organizational team comprising managers, representatives of the specialist departments and IS specialists is formed to structure statements regarding business strategy and processes. Company processes and classes of data are grouped together in matrices to form larger system areas. Origin and use of data are documented and dependencies shown.
Information System Study (ISS) (cf. [Neu 1991, 147], [Pruijm 1990, 64]	A characteristic feature here is the heavy involvement of qualified managers and/or decision-makers. There is a focus on ensuring an orientation towards optimal data flow based on data use.
System Development (cf. [Becker 1998], [Gutzwiller 1994], [Scheer 1990b, 403], [Nüttgens 1995, 19], [Lehner et al. 1991], [Winter 1998, 6])	Within the framework of system development, the importance of a flexible procedural model has become paramount. The top-down approach has also proved to be advantageous for the issue of distribution. Clearly defined phase completion is again of central importance, particularly in the case of the waterfall model. However, in the case of more recent analyses – based on packaged software – there is a big difference in the granularity applied: "Up until now we were dealing with micro-structures in the software; now it's the turn of the macro-structure which can extend to complete application components" [Bues 1994, 185].

Table 16-1: Existing Approaches to Architecture Planning

16.4.2 Deficits of Existing Methods

At the present time there is no procedure which covers the question of distribution all the way through from the corporate strategy level to the application architecture. What is required is not a complex method for planning the architecture but a coordination framework for implementation projects in individual business areas.

With all the approaches looked at – with the exception of the implementation methods – ERP packaged software plays a secondary role. The question of distribution is increasingly moving away from the detailed, step-by-step development of applications in favor of the conceptual approach, i.e. towards a distribution of integrated systems. Approaches, such as the BSP, analyze and distribute functionality and data at a detailed level. However, as distribution is now largely based on packaged software, the focus is on the optimal use of existing IS concepts, rather than on the technical solution.

This becomes evident in the case of the Information System Study, for example. The real challenges become somewhat obscured against the background of a more quantitative approach with automated information processing. The analysis neglects a business-driven, revolutionary view in favor of the wishes of decision-makers and/or users. Political aspects, which are of particular significance in the case of change processes in large corporations, can be introduced into the evaluation without critical analysis, thus preventing massive realignments. Against the background of ERP standard solutions, the analysis appears to be too detailed and as a result misses the real questions, such as the degree of centralization or structuring dimensions.

Up to now, methods have placed the emphasis on an isolated analysis of individual business areas [cf. Schwarzer 1994, 363]. One deficit is to be found in the way in which the coordination between business areas is considered. This becomes particularly clear with the classic approach of business process redesign in the context of implementation methods: the design emphasis is on the optimized operation of a process, such as order processing. Dependencies between processes, on the other hand, hardly enter into the analysis as ought to be the case when considering the overall optimization of a large area.

16.4.3 Proposed Method

The PROMET eBN method is used to implement strategies in a distributed process and system environment. For this purpose, the requirements at the organizational level are calibrated with the possible solutions at the technical level: cross-organizational business processes lead to a distributed requirement for functionality and data. A methodologically sound decision determines whether the required functionality and data should be provided by one or more systems. The implementation of business networks calls for a calibrated set of tools which:

- allow the depiction of global, regional and local processes as well as reporting structures in systems, thus ensuring the transparency of the global supply chain,

- set forth the conceptual steps for engineering an application architecture which will be workable in the long term,

- support the standardization of processes and the data on which they are based,

- lead to the selection of the right integration technologies and concepts and

- result in practicable migration planning including project portfolio.

The aim of this method is:

- to develop a common understanding of strategy and global processes,

- to find a suitable process and application architecture,

- to support consistent implementation planning for the architecture solutions found as well as

- to secure the coordination of the resulting distributed projects.

The structure of PROMET eBN is oriented towards the method engineering approach. The procedure corresponds with the basic idea behind business system planning: we start off with a business-driven top-down approach which is then realized bottom-up in one or more implementation projects. Figure 16-9 shows the procedural model which we subsequently adapt to suit the concrete point of departure and the task of the specific project. In the case of PROMET eBN we distinguish between the four phases of *set-up, business architecture, application architecture* and d*istributed implementation*. The set-up phase ensures that the architecture project is properly situated within the organization and also that it is run by the right people. The tasks of analyzing the business architecture and deriving the requirements which the application architecture will need to meet (referred to as 'architecture drivers') are dealt with in the second phase (business architecture). The development of technical application drivers and their implementation in the form of an application architecture takes place in the third phase (application architecture). Preparations for implementing the architecture are then covered in the final phase (distributed implementation). Some of the core techniques belonging to this method are outlined below.

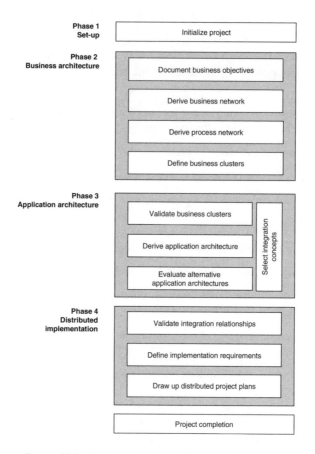

Figure 16-9: Procedural Model of PROMET eBN V2.0

Analyzing the Business Network (Phase 2)

The process architecture is derived from the business strategies. Process design is performed at global, regional or local level. The clustering of processes, the establishment of reporting requirements and the classification of existing organization units are all factors which will influence the application architecture.

Deriving the Architecture Requirements (Phase 2)

An initial distribution hypothesis is documented by business clustering. These business clusters can be formed on the basis of various dimensions. We document the requirements, which the application architecture must meet from a business management point of view. An initial distribution hypothesis represents the completion of the second phase and the starting point for the third phase.

Engineering the Application Architecture (Phase 3)

In addition to the requirements derived from the business network and from application restrictions, the integration concepts are the most important factors influencing the application architecture. Documentation of the application architecture takes the form of instances, their integration relationships as well as a migration strategy [cf. Barak 1997]. We document and evaluate possible distributions on the basis of the business drivers established in Phase 2.

Managing the Distributed Implementation (Phase 4)

The migration objects from the business network and the application architecture are calibrated with the existing project portfolio. Standardization activities, the use of group templates and system development are defined. The resulting project portfolio also includes a cost/benefits analysis which shows the profitability of the cross-project and cross-organizational approach. Clear specifications for future projects are outlined in the final stage of the project. An architecture project based on PROMET eBN typically results in several implementation projects which are coordinated through the use of suitable predefined settings. This avoids duplication and creates the right conditions for a high integration depth.

16.5   Conclusions and Outlook

The method presented supports the critical success factors outlined at the beginning of this Chapter: the documentation of strategic considerations, the visualization of the business network and the analysis of the process network provide a clear picture of cross-organizational business management relationships. The clear formulation of the requirements to be met by the application architecture from a business management point of view aids the subsequent calibration of business and application architecture.

The methodological planning of the application architecture and the requirements derived for the implementation projects support the coordinated introduction of distributed systems. This planning of the application architecture must have the support of the corporation's top management. The documentation of results and the transparency of the issues involved can be helpful when planning the architecture. The application architecture will only ensure the proper interaction between business network and application architecture if planned at the strategic level.

However, there is one central question which cannot be resolved by methodology: while 'soft facts', i.e. restrictions at the political and personal level, can be supported by the methodology, this is no replacement for the personal commitment of the project team and huge support from the corporation's top management. The creation of architecture teams incorporating both IS and specialist departments is also significant. A 'business sponsor' must be found at corporate level in order to ensure that business-driven architectures can actually be implemented. In addition to this sponsor, people in positions of responsibility who are committed to the process are needed at the decentralized level.

This Chapter has shown the potential provided by cross-organizational planning. However, the risk of overregulation should also be borne in mind. If constraints are too narrow they will limit the flexibility of business areas unnecessarily and make it difficult to realize innovative solutions. It is therefore important to aim for a planning framework based on the principle of 'as much as necessary and as little as possible'.

17 Business Networking - Summary and Outlook

Rainer Alt, Elgar Fleisch, Hubert Österle

17.1 Bottom Line of Business Networking 324
    17.1.1 Improving Business Efficiency and Creating New
           Opportunities 324
    17.1.2 Goals of Business Networking 325
    17.1.3 Changing Face of Business Networking Systems 326
    17.1.4 Model of Business Networking 327

17.2 Next Steps in Business Networking 328
    17.2.1 Advent of Process Portals and eServices 328
    17.2.2 Networking Smart Appliances and Real-Life Assets 330

17.1   Bottom Line of Business Networking

17.1.1 Improving Business Efficiency and Creating New Opportunities

This book has described Business Networking as one of the seven trends companies have to address in order to remain competitive (cf. Chap. 2.3). Its relevance is growing and many brick-and-mortar companies are investing substantially in Business Networking (or eBusiness) projects. Established companies, such as Bayer, Deutsche Post, DaimlerChrysler or Deutsche Telekom are being transformed: new organizational units are being formed for eBusiness, traditional channels for procurement, marketing and sales redesigned, and new 'eCompanies' (co-) founded (e.g. Covisint by DaimlerChrysler, CheMatch by Bayer or emaro by Deutsche Bank and SAP. The goals behind these developments are twofold:

- *Increased process efficiencies.* Business Networking is an efficient strategy for improving the interaction with customers and suppliers. A large number of the eMarkets (e.g. e2open, Covisint, Globalnetexchange, Chemconnect) have been founded in order to reduce the costs of the procurement process by using a common standard. IBM provides an illustration of the cost-saving potential: although increased electronic sales brought savings of USD 1 billion in 1999, this only corresponds to 17% of IBM's total turnover. In comparison, Dell handles 50% of its turnover via the Net [cf. Sager 2000]. Another example of the cost-saving potential is the EC solution at ETA SA (cf. Chap. 6) which achieved a tenfold reduction in handling costs.

- *New business opportunities.* Business Networking can support companies in developing innovative business models and new opportunities in the market. This mainly refers to new intermediaries, such as Amazon, Dell, Market-Site.net or the Ariba network (cf. Chaps. 3 and 4.2). An example described in more detail was the supply chain integration center that Riverwood is planning to develop from their VMI solution (cf. Chap. 5.7) or the procurement service offered by Deutsche Telekom (cf. Chap. 14.2).

These two areas differ in nature. Efficiency improvements tend to be the result of inside-out action. The implementation of an EDI system was logical after an internal process optimization project, and the electronic procurement marketplaces are logical once a certain number of organizations have decided to pool their procurement volume. However, new business opportunities tend to materialize largely as a result of outside-in action. The Internet has given birth to a large number of companies that discovered a specific customer need and then established internal operations to meet that need. This is a phenomenon that also explains why back-end integration is often found to be lacking in young Internet companies. Achieving a trade-off between both approaches – quick time-to-market on the one hand and providing a convincing, stable and efficient solution on the other – represents one of the core challenges.

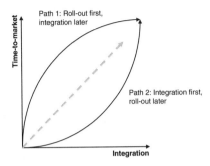

Figure 17-1: Development Strategies for Business Networking Solutions

17.1.2 Goals of Business Networking

Throughout this book it was our aim to show that Business Networking goes beyond a simple EC or SCM strategy and beyond the technological implementation of some Internet system. Three aspects are summarized below:

- *Business Networking supports business goals.* Process improvements and new business opportunities have direct impact on a company's strategy and future competitiveness. Assessing networkability and developing Business Networking strategies is a top management task that cannot be delegated to line management, the IT department, or a consultant.

- *Business Networking integrates strategies.* The popular strategies of EC, SCM, and CRM are all addressing inter-business relationships (cf. Chap. 4). Business Networking provides an integrated picture of these strategies and recognizes, for example, that each EC solution also requires an SCM solution. Thus, Business Networking overcomes the isolated view of individual strategies and helps in extending existing solutions (e.g. an EC solution with a CRM component).

- *Business Networking aims for successful implementations.* The success factors identified in this book (cf. Chaps. 6 and 13) are mostly organizational (e.g. homogenized master data, alignment with marketing strategy) and political (e.g. creating win-win situations) in nature. They show that Business Networking is a technology-enabled, but not a technological concept. Applying the levels of business engineering, i.e. strategy, process and systems, to Business Networking (cf. Chap. 3.5.1) ensures the alignment of technological, organizational and technological factors. This approach has been pursued in the methodological considerations in Chapters 14, 15 and 16.

All three aspects shape the nature of Business Networking. Evidently, they are not all new, and certain elements have already been available for some time. The strength of Business Networking is that it presents a logically consistent overall framework for developing inter-business relationships which includes these aspects.

17.1.3 Changing Face of Business Networking Systems

One of the objects of this book was to develop a model that addresses the major developments in Business Networking and elaborates logic building blocks for networked companies. We are aware of the fact that this can only be a snapshot of one particular development path. Although other technological or management trends may be just looming on the horizon, we have found substantial evidence of this path. The main drivers in Business Networking which we can see at this stage are:

- *Increasing standardization.* Various initiatives have been launched to standardize data (e.g. CXML, RosettaNet, Uddi, Bolero) and processes (e.g. CPFR, OBI) for Business Networking (cf. Chap. 2.3). These standards tend to increase inter-organizational connectivity and reduce the transaction costs involved in Business Networking.

- *Interaction of networking strategies.* A large number of companies have implemented initial Business Networking solutions. These solutions often focus on one particular networking strategy (cf. Chap. 4.3), for instance an EC solution for selling products. In coming years, we expect to see these solutions being enhanced by elements of other networking strategies, such as CRM or SCM, a factor liable to foster a convergence of networking strategies.

- *Increased business volume.* Projections forecast a significant growth in Internet users for the next few years. This implies that businesses will increasingly move onto the Internet. Forrester Research, for instance, believes that business-to-business EC will grow from USD 43 billion in 1998 to USD 2,700 billion in 2004 [Stepanek 2000, EB 26]. However, forecast revenues for Internet-based commerce only give a poor indication of usage or value creation on the Web. Therefore, we rely on the Internet host count which is carried out twice a year. These figures indicate that the number of potential business partners rose from 16 million hosts in July 1996 to 72 million in January 2000 [ISC 2000].

- *1:n develops to n:m.* In view of the growing Internet business volume and the potentials for information-based services, many of the existing Business Networking systems will evolve from 1:n to n:m systems with electronic markets becoming a reality in many industries (cf. Chaps. 1.1.2 and 2.2.7). Since critical mass determines the benefit of these systems [cf. Klein 1996], early movers will enjoy a clear advantage.

17.1.4 Model of Business Networking

The Business Networking model reflects the major principles of networked enterprises or Internet businesses. We believe that, regardless of the size and the industrial environment in which a company acts, networked enterprises will be the dominating organizational form in the information age. They build on four building blocks that have been proposed throughout this book:

- *Networked processes.* At the core of every Business Networking solution are the supported business processes (procurement, sales etc.) which stretch across several business partners. Networked processes need to be agreed upon by all partners or, ideally, are standardized within a certain business community (e.g. the chemical industry). In this book we have discussed networking scenarios (cf. Chap. 3.3) and networking strategies (cf. Chap. 4.3).

- *Business bus.* The availability of a standardized infrastructure for Business Networking is a critical necessity. As described in Chapters 2.3.4 and 3.4, the business bus consists mainly of standards, and provides middleware functionality. Important actors that shape the business bus are market-leading vendors (e.g. SAP, Microsoft) and standardization organizations/consortia (e.g. RosettaNet, Uddi, Bolero).

- *Electronic services (eServices).* In the same way as the ethernet bus provides access to services, such as printer or file services, in a local area network (LAN) the business bus will allow connection to eServices. These 'small' standardized services are available on the Internet and will be included in portals and eMarkets. Various eServices have been described in the previous chapters (cf. Chaps. 2.3.5 and 3.4.1).

- *Service integrator.* In the same way that eService providers have appeared as new players in Business Networking, customer-orientation will lead to new intermediaries. These service integrators have also been referred to as 'infomediaries' [Hagel/Armstrong 1997] and derive their value from supporting the customer process (e.g. Avnet Marshall, cf. Chaps. 2.3.6 and 3.2.3), managing customer information (cf. Chap. 7) and the like.

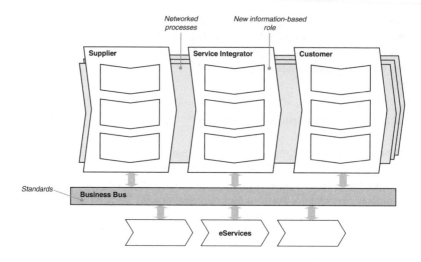

Figure 17-2: Building Blocks of the Business Networking Model

17.2 Next Steps in Business Networking

17.2.1 Advent of Process Portals and eServices

The development towards n:m systems implies that Business Networking solutions have the potential to generate revenues on their own. The most prominent example is already a classic and comes from American Airlines. Initially, their Sabre reservation system was implemented to manage the allocation of seats internally. It was extended step by step to become an eMarket for services in tourism with airline tickets from American being only one product among others. Sabre has been spun off from American Airlines as an independent business which also provides the Travelocity website (cf. Chap. 7.1). Comparable developments are now occurring in many other industries as well. We see two critical aspects which both require a thorough analysis of existing core competencies and the future market position as explained in Chapter 4.2:

- *Positioning as eServices.* Companies have to decide whether their Business Networking solutions have the potential to become eServices in their own right. Being part of the infrastructure offers the opportunity to provide services to a large number of portals and eMarkets (since many eServices are not industry-specific) and to collect fees with every transaction effected via the portal / eMarket.

- *Positioning as process portal.* As discussed in Chapter 2.3.6, there is little doubt that customer loyalty and customer-orientation will determine the success of Business Networking solutions. Today, many solutions are still product and not customer-oriented. We expect to see process portals which integrate multiple eMarkets and other portals depending on specific customer segments. Multi-market and multi-portal management will become an important topic in the years to come.

Portals and eMarkets are the third wave in Business Networking. The linking of distributed ERP solutions was the first phase in Business Networking. It was followed by the second phase which spawned such Business Networking systems as EC or SCM (cf. Chap. 13.2). Internet-based portals and platforms, such as mySAP.com, represent the third phase. The challenge for information management is to come up with solutions for integrating these three worlds. Important aspects are the distribution of master data and the distribution of functionality between the various systems.

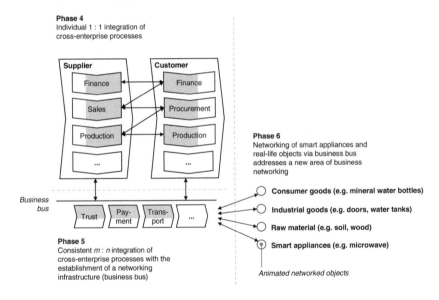

Figure 17-3: Types of Systems in Business Networking[1]

---

[1]   See Figure 1-1 in Chapter 1.1.2.

17.2.2 Networking Smart Appliances and Real-Life Assets

The increasing miniaturization of information processing and communication devices has been described as one of the major trends in Chapter 2.3.3. In the future we expect smart appliances to make profound inroads into Business Networking. Smart appliances [cf. Thiesse/Österle 2000] and animated real-life assets, such as consumer goods (e.g. mineral water bottles, textiles), industrial goods (e.g. doors, water tanks) and raw materials (e.g. soil, water) and the like open up new perspectives (see Figure 17-3). These embedded networked processors are very small and simple IT devices. Due to the vast volume produced, their cost is negligible. Elements of such networking between real-life assets have been described by [Kelly 1998] who termed them 'jelly beans'. He gave some idea of the type and scope of developments that will mark the next 5 to 10 years in Business Networking.

> *"A tiny chip [jelly bean] plastered inside a water tank on an Australian ranch transmits only the telegraphic 2-bit message of whether the tank is FULL or NOT. A chip attached to the ear of each steer on the same ranch beams out his location in GPS numbers; [...] 'I'm here, I'm here' it tells the rancher's log book.[...] The chip in the gate at the end of the rancher's road communicates only a single word, reporting when it was last opened: 'Tuesday'."*
> [Kelly 1998, 12]

After networking people via telephone or fax, information systems via EDI or the Internet we started networking processes and organizations. We are now heading towards connecting real-life assets with other real-life assets, people, processes and information systems. And we are thus addressing the next generation of the networked economy by pushing the possibilities and the potentials of networks beyond the confines of today's imagination.

List of Abbreviations

ADSL	Asymmetric Digital Subscriber Line
ALE	Application Link Enabling
API	Application Programming Interface
APO	Advanced Planner and Optimizer
APS	Advanced Planning and Scheduling
ASAP	Accelerated SAP
ATP	Available-To-Promise
BAPI	Business Application Programming Interface
BN	Business Networking
BNS	Business Networking System
BPR	Business Process Redesign
CAD	Computer Aided Design
CDMA	Code Division Multiple Access
CIO	Chief Information Officer
CPFR	Collaborative Planning, Forecasting, and Replenishment
CRLC	Customer Resource Life Cycle
CRM	Customer Relationship Management
cXML	Commerce Extended Markup Language
DPS	Desktop Purchasing System
DVD	Digital Versatile Disk
DW	Data Warehouse
EAI	Enterprise Application Integration
EAN	European Article Number
EC	Electronic Commerce
ECC	Electronic Commerce Conference
ECIS	European Conference on Information Systems
ECR	Efficient Consumer Response
EDI	Electronic Data Interchange

EDIFACT	Electronic Data Interchange for Administration, Commerce and Trade
ER	Efficient Replenishment
ERP	Enterprise Resource Planning
EU	European Union
GPS	Global Positioning System
GSM	Global System for Mobile Communication
HICSS	Hawaii International Conference on Systems Sciences
HSG	University of St. Gallen
HTML	Hypertext Markup Language
HTTP	Hypertext Transfer Protocol
IBN	Inter-Business Networking
ICS	Information and Communication System
ISO/OSI	International Organization for Standardization / Open Systems Interconnection
IS	Information System
IT	Information Technology
IWI-HSG	Insitute for Information Management at University of St. Gallen
JIT	Just in Time
LAN	Local Area Network
MPEG	Motion Picture Expert Group
MRO	Maintenance, Repair and Operations
MRP I	Material Requirements Planning
MRP II	Manufacturing Resource Planning
MSC	Multi-Supplier Catalog
PDA	Personal Digital Assistant
POS	Point of Sale
PND	Process Network Design
PPC	Production Planning and Control
QR	Quick Response
R&D	Research and Development
RWI	Riverwood International

SC	Supply Chain
SCM	Supply Chain Management
SCOR	Supply Chain Operations Reference-model
SGML	Standard Generalized Markup Language
SMS	Short Message Service
SMTP	Simple Mail Transfer Protocol
TCP/IP	Transmission Control Protocol / Internet Protocol
TQM	Total Quality Management
UPnP	Universal Plug and Play
UMTS	Universal Mobile Telecommunication System
VMI	Vendor Managed Inventory
VR	Vendor Replenishment
WAN	Wide Area Network
WAP	Wireless Access Protocol
WFMS	Workflow Management System
WWW	World Wide Web
XML	Extended Markup Language
Y2K	Year 2000

Glossary

Advanced Planning and Scheduling (APS)	Advanced planning is the process of balancing materials and plant resources to best meet customer demand while achieving business goals. [AMR 1999] Advanced scheduling is the process of precise sequencing of all material and plant resources, at an operation level, over the near term time horizon, (typically less than a month) to best meet customer demand. [AMR 1999]
Advanced Planning and Scheduling System (APS system)	Advanced planning and scheduling systems are real-time systems for production planning and scheduling ($\Rightarrow$ *Advanced planning and scheduling*). In contrast to MRP II ($\Rightarrow$ *Manufacturing resource planning*) APS systems synchronize material and capacity planning simultaneously and against restricted available capacity.
Application Architecture	An application architecture consists of single technical components (applications) of a company-wide information system as well as the connections (interfaces) between these components. [Huber et al. 2000, 34]
Assemble-to-Order	Assemble-to-order is a logistics concept which is related to the order penetration point, the point along the space and time axes in the supply chain, at which a previously manufactured product is assembled to a specific order. [Klaus/Krieger 1998, 367]
Available-to-Promise (ATP)	Available-to-promise is a supply chain management concept ($\Rightarrow$ *supply chain management*) whose objective is to provide the customer with reliable information about product availability and delivery time at the time of the customer's order. [Klaus/Krieger 1998, 31]

Business Model	A business model allows managers to identify real options and to assess the consequences of their decisions. It provides a clear concept on mission, structure, processes, revenues, as well as legal and technological issues.
Business Networking	Business Networking is management of relationships among internal and external business units. It includes process optimization as well as the development of innovative information age strategies.
Business Networking Systems (BNS)	Business Networking systems are systems that support the coordination ($\Rightarrow$ *Coordination*) among business units. They invariably involve more than one organizational unit and often integrate business partners (customers, suppliers etc.) with a company's information infrastructure. Prominent examples are systems for electronic commerce ($\Rightarrow$ *Electronic commerce systems*) and supply chain management ($\Rightarrow$ *Supply chain management systems*). (cf. Chap. 13.2.1)
Category Management (CM)	Category management is a cooperative, customer-oriented management system in retail which is part of ECR ($\Rightarrow$ *Efficient consumer response*). CM stands for the planning and controlling of product groups as strategic business units instead of the traditional division in brands (manufacturers) and departments (retailers). [Klaus/Krieger 1998, 59]
Continuous Replenishment (CRP)	Continuous replenishment is a special form of ER ($\Rightarrow$ *Efficient replenishment*) with the goal to reduce stock by stabilizing the flow of goods between manufacturer and retailer with EDI ($\Rightarrow$ *Electronic data interchange*). [Klaus/Krieger 1998, 67]

Cooperation	Cooperations are connections of companies or business units in which the fulfillment of similar, delegated part activities of the members are coordinated. [Grochla 1972, 3]
Coordination	Coordination is managing dependencies between activities. [Malone/Crowston 1994, 90]
Collaborative Planning Forecasting and Replenishment (CPFR)	Collaborative planning, forecasting and replenishment is a concept that allows collaborative processes across the supply chain through dynamic information sharing between different partner companies or business units. [CPFR 1999]
Core Competence	A core competence is a competence a company performs best and has four characteristics: (1) It provides potential access to a wide variety of markets. (2) It should make a significant contribution to the perceived customer benefits. (3) It should be difficult for competitors to imitate, and (4) it should not wear out. [Hamel/Prahalad 1990]
Crossdocking	Crossdocking is a distribution strategy designed to improve the handling of goods (mostly finished goods on pallets) through the avoidance of stockkeeping. [Klaus/Krieger 1998, 71]
Customer Relationship Management (CRM)	Customer relationship management means increasing revenues and profitability by coordinating, consolidating and integrating all points of contact that enterprises have with their customers, employees, partners and suppliers to integrate sales, marketing, customer service, enterprise resource planning and virtual sales office. [ECCS 1999]

Customer Resource Life Cycle (CRLC)	The customer resource life cycle is the sequence of tasks for which the customer needs the services of a supplier. [Ives/Learmonth 1984]
Cycle Time	The cycle time is the amount of time from when a product or service is ordered until it is received by the customer. [SCC 2000]
Desktop Purchasing System (DPS)	A DPS is a buy-side electronic commerce system (⇒ *Electronic commerce system*) which supports the procurement process of indirect goods and services.
Efficient Consumer Response (ECR)	Efficient Consumer Response is a strategic management concept designed to optimize the supply chain between manufacturers and retailers through demand-oriented (pull) control. [Klaus/Krieger 1998, 93], [ECR 1999]
Efficient Replenishment (ER)	Efficient replenishment is a general logistics concept which refers to the co-operation between manufacturer and retailer with the goal to establish an efficient flow of goods. [Klaus/Krieger 1998, 99]
Electronic Commerce (EC)	Electronic commerce is the electronic support of all economical value-adding activities, i.e. procurement, production and distribution. EC involves activities in information, contracting, settlement and order entry (not R&D and production). (cf. Chap. 6.2.2)
Electronic Commerce Systems	Electronic commerce systems support the EC-phases of information, contracting, settlement and order entry (⇒ *Electronic commerce*) and can be divided into three categories: Sell-side or eSales systems (1:n), buy-side or eProcurement systems (n:1), and trading systems (n:m). (cf. Chap. 3)

Electronic Data Interchange (EDI)	EDI means computer-to-computer communication of structured business messages in agreed-on standard codes and formats. [Keen/Ballance 1997]
Electronic Market (eMarket)	An electronic market(place) represents a virtual place where multiple buyers and sellers conduct online transactions via market coordination mechanisms (cf. [Segev et al. 1999, 138], [Schmid 1993, 468]).
Electronic Procurement (eProcurement)	eProcurement stands for the procurement of indirect/MRO-goods ($\Rightarrow$ Maintenance, repair and operations) via electronic commerce systems ($\Rightarrow$ *Electronic commerce systems*). [Dolmetsch et al. 1999]
Electronic Service (eService)	eServices are Internet-based applications which are offered as individual products to customers. They derive their value from information and may include physical elements and/or other eServices. [Alt/Österle 2000]
Enterprise Resource Planning System ERP System	An enterprise resource planning system is an integrated collection of software programs which ties together all of an enterprise's various functions – i.e. human resources, finance, manufacturing, sales, etc. on the basis of an integrated data model. Such software also provides functions for the analysis of this data to plan production, forecast sales, analyze quality, and so on. [Peoplesoft 1999]

Extended Markup Language (XML)	XML is a markup language for documents containing structured information. Structured information contains both content (words, pictures, etc.) and some indication of what role that content plays (for example, content in a section heading has a different meaning from content in a footnote which means something different than content in a figure). The XML specification defines a standard way to add markup to documents.
Global Sourcing	Global sourcing is a procurement strategy whose goal is to search for a supplier for each procurement object on a worldwide basis ($\Rightarrow$ *Single Sourcing*). [Klaus/Krieger 1998, 154]
Information Technology (IT)	Information Technology includes the entirety of all hardware and software that serves to support information processing and communication. [Stickel et al. 1997, 351]
Information System (IS)	An information system consists of a coordinated arrangement of personnel, organizational and technical elements that serve to coordinate the exchange of used and created goods in the value-creation process with suppliers and customers as well as to supply the value activities with demand-oriented information. [Pfohl 1997, 7]
Integration	Integration means the networking of human resources, their tasks and the information and communication technology used. A distinction can be made between the object of integration (e.g. data integration, function integration, process integration, etc.), the direction of integration (horizontal or vertical), and the scope of integration (intraorganizational and interorganizational). [Mertens 1997, 2]

Insourcing	Insourcing is a strategy that uses in-house and/or outside resources to perform new activities and services that relate to the existing core competencies of a company ($\Rightarrow$ *Core competence*).
Just-in-Time (JIT)	Just-in-Time is a logistics concept designed to synchronize production and the procurement of goods needed for the production process. JIT requires other concepts like TQM ($\Rightarrow$ Total quality management), production smoothing, standardization of products and processes, automation of processes (e.g. quality check), Kaizen, etc. [Klaus/Krieger 1998, 205]
Logistics	Logistics provides a single logic to guide the process of planning, allocating and controlling financial and human resources committed to physical distribution, manufacturing support and purchasing operations. [Bowersox/Closs 1996, 3]
Method	A method is a structured procedure consisting of the components design activities, techniques, tools, results, roles, and meta model. [Gutzwiller 1994, 13]
Maintenance, Repair and Operations (MRO) Goods	MRO goods are goods that are not directly compounded with the end product or, in the case of retail, are not directly sold to the end consumer. [Grieco 1997, 1]
Manufacturing Resource Planning (MRP II)	MRP II is a concept for computerized production planning and control (PPC). MRP II is based on a four level planning hierarchy consisting of program planning, rough-cut planning, detailed planning, and control that are proceeded through in a sequential order. [Klaus/Krieger 1998, 343]

Mass Customization	Mass customization means the endeavor of many companies to offer adjusted products or services arising from individual, specific customer needs without sacrificing the efficiency of industrial mass production. [Klaus/Krieger 1998, 344]
Material Requirements Planning (MRP I)	MRP I is a concept for the computerized determination of requirements, procurement, storage, and the staging of material needed for manufacturing. In contrast to MRP II (⇒ *Manufacturing resource planning*) it is based on the assumption of unlimited plant capacity. [Klaus/Krieger 1998, 343]
Networkability	Networkability is the ability to cooperate internally as well as externally. It refers to the time and cost efficiency of establishing relationships with business partners. (cf. Chap. 1)
Outsourcing	Outsourcing is a management strategy by which an organization outsources major, non-core functions to specialized, efficient service providers. [Outsourcing Institute 1999]
Portal	Portals can be defined as web-based, personalized and integrated systems which offer access to applications, content and services.
Postponement	Postponement is a logistics concept for the optimization of stockkeeping by delaying decisions until unfailing information for forecasts is available. It is possible to differentiate between value-adding postponement (assembly or form postponement) and logistical postponement. The first term refers to decisions about the specification of the product (e.g. customer-specific assembly) whereas the second term refers to distribution logistics. [Klaus/Krieger 1998, 380]

Process Portal	Process portals are portals ($\Rightarrow$ *Portal*) which support the entire Customer Resource Life Cycle ($\Rightarrow$ *Customer Resource Life Cycle*) and offers a personalized view specific customer segments.
Quick Response (QR)	Quick response is a cooperational logistics concept based on EDI-order systems. By the use of barcoded products (e.g. EAN) QR aims at accelerating reactions to guarantee general product availability. [Klaus/Krieger 1998, 397]
Single Sourcing	Single sourcing is a procurement strategy whose goal is to procure all commodities and goods from one single supplier ($\Rightarrow$ *Global Sourcing*). [Klaus/Krieger 1998, 414]
Supply Chain	A supply chain is a network of organizations that are involved, through upstream and downstream linkages, in different processes and activities that produce value in the form of products and services in the hands of the ultimate customer. [Christopher 1998, 15]
Supply Chain Management (SCM)	Supply chain management means the delivery of enhanced customer and economic values through the synchronized management of the flow of physical goods, associated information and financial information from sourcing through consumption. [Klaus/Krieger 1998, 434]
Supply Chain Management System	$\Rightarrow$ *Advanced planning and scheduling system (APSS)*
Template	Templates are concepts or models for the standardization of processes, functions, and data that are capable of being implemented in a physical information system. A template's purpose is to integrate different information systems on a semantic level. (cf. Chap. 11.2.1)

Total Quality Management (TQM)	Total quality management is a management strategy that consistently integrates quality orientation into the whole structure and workflow of a company by using the methods and techniques of quality management. [Klaus/Krieger 1998, 452]
Value Chain	The value chain is a model describing a company as a flow of value-adding activities (primary activities) like inbound logistics, operation, outbound logistics and customer service and its support activities like firm infrastructure, human resource management, technology development and procurement which support the primary activities. [Porter 1985, 37]
Vendor Managed Inventory (VMI)	Vendor managed inventory means that a company's inventory in terms of inventory volume and readiness for delivery is managed by a supplier on the company's business premises. [Klaus/Krieger 1998, 483]
Virtual Community	A virtual community is an IT enabled community, which has a distinctive focus, the capacity to integrate content and communication, appreciates member-generated content, provides access to competing publishers and vendors, and is commercially oriented. [Hagel/Armstrong 1997, 8]
Virtual Organizing	Virtual organizing is an organization strategy in which a collection of legal entities, institutions, or individuals join forces on a short–term basis for a specific mission. Each member contributes his or her core competencies ($\Rightarrow$ *Core competence*) relevant to the mission and all partners act as a single entity via-à-vis a third party. Typically no formal management bureaucracy is established, and instead co-ordination ($\Rightarrow$ *Coordination*) is realized through information and communication systems. [Arnold et al. 1995, 10]

References

[Aberdeen Group 1998]
Aberdeen Group, Internet Procurement Automation: Separating the EC Wheat from the Chaff, 11 (1998) 6

[Aberdeen Group 1999]
Aberdeen Group, Internet Procurement Automation Looks Like a Winner, Market Viewpoint, 12 (1999) 1

[Absatzwirtschaft 1995]
Absatzwirtschaft (Ed.), Begriffsdefinitionen aus der Handels- und Absatzwirtschaft, 4th Ed., Köln, 1995

[Adam/Yesha 1996]
Adam, N.R., Yesha, Y., Electronic Commerce: in: Adam, N.R., Yesha, Y. (Eds.), Electronic Commerce: Current Research Issues and Applications, Springer, Berlin etc., 1996, pp. 5-12

[ADP 1999]
ADP, ADP in Figures, http://www.adp.com, 20.4.1999

[AFB 1999]
AFB Software GmbH, Autokatalog - der Autokauf im Internet, in: http://www.afb.de, 20.6.1999

[Alpar et al. 1998]
Alpar, P., Grob, H.L., Weimann, P., Winter, R., Unternehmensorientierte Wirtschaftsinformatik: eine Einführung in die Strategie und Realisation erfolgreicher IuK-Systeme, Vieweg, Braunschweig/Wiesbaden, 1998

[Alstyne 1997]
Alstyne, M.V., The State of Network Organization, A Survey in Three Frameworks, in: Journal of Organizational Computing, 7 (1997) 3, http://www.mit.edu/people/marshall/Abstracts.html#anchorNWOrg

[Alt et al. 1999]
Alt, R., Österle, H., Reichmayr, C., Zurmühlen, R., Business Networking in The Swatch Group, in: Electronic Markets, 9 (1999) 3, pp. 169-173

[Alt/Klein 1999]
Alt, R., Klein, S., Lessons in Electronic Commerce: The Case of Electronic Transportation Markets, in: Failure & Lessons Learned in Information Technology Management, 3 (1999) 3, pp. 81-93

[Alt et al. 2000]

Alt, R., Fleisch, E., Werle, O., The Concept of Networkability - How to Make Companies Competitive in Business Networks, in: Hansen, H.R., Bichler, M., Mahrer, H. (Eds.), Proceedings of the 8th ECIS, Vol. 1, Vienna University of Economics, Vienna, 2000, pp. 405-411

[Alt/Österle 2000]

Alt, R., Österle, H., E-Services als neue Herausforderung im Business Networking, in: Information Management & Consulting, 15 (2000) 2, pp. 63-67

[Alt/Schmid 2000]

Alt, R., Schmid, B., Electronic Commerce und Logistik: Perspektiven durch zwei sich wechselseitig ergänzende Konzepte, in: Zeitschrift für Betriebswirtschaft, 70 (2000) 1, pp. 75-99

[Amazon 1999]

Amazon.com, About Amazon.com: Company Information, www.amazon.com, 6.4.1999

[AMR 1997]

AMR Research, Internet Enabled Indirect Procurement: A Low Risk/High Return Project?, White Paper, Boston, July 1997

[AMR 1998]

AMR Research, AMR Research Predicts ERP Market Will Reach $ 52 Billion by 2002, http://www.amrresearch.com/press/980806.htm, 6.8.1998

[AMR 1999]

AMR Research, 1999 Supply Chain Strategies Outlook, in: AMR Research SCS Report, January 1999

[Andrade/Chapman 1998]

Andrade, K., Chapman, R.B., Insourcing After the Outsourcing: MIS Survival Guide, Amacom, New York, 1998

[Ante/Weintraub 2000]

Ante, S.E., Weintraub, A., Why B2B Is a Scary Place to Be, in: Business Week, September 11, 2000, pp. 36-37

[Ariba 1998a]

Ariba Technologies, The Ariba ORMS: Operating Resource Management for the Enterprise, Product White Paper, Sunnyvale, March 1998

[Ariba 1998b]

Ariba Technologies, Catalog Interchange Format (CIF), 2.1 Specification, Technical White Paper, Sunnyvale, April 1998

[Arnold 1998]

Arnold, B., Projektbeschleuniger haben noch Lücken, in: Computerwoche Focus, Nr. 4/98, 21. August 1998, pp. 16-19

[Arnold et al. 1995]
Arnold, O., Faisst, W., Haertling, M., Sieber, P., Virtuelle Unternehmen als Unternehmenstyp der Zukunft?, in: HMD 32 (1995) 185, pp. 8-23

[Arthur 1989]
Arthur, W.B., Competing Technologies, Increasing Returns and Lock-In by Historical Small Events, in: Economic Journal, 99 (1989), pp. 116-131

[Arthur 1990]
Arthur, W.B., Positive Feedback in the Economy, in: Scientific American, February 1990, pp. 92-99

[Ashkenas et al. 1995]
Ashkenas, R., Ulrich, D., Jick, T., Kerr, S., The Boundaryless Organization: Breaking the Chains of Organizational Structure, Jossey-Bass Publishers, San Francisco, 1995

[Association 1999]
The Association of Support Professionals, The Ten Best Web Support Sites 1999, http://www.asponline.com/awards.html, 13.8.1999

[Austin et al. 1997]
Austin, T.A., Lee, H.L., Kopczak, L., Unlocking the Supply Chain's Hidden Value: A Lesson from the PC Industry, Andersen Consulting, Stanford University, Northwestern University, San Francisco, 1997

[Avnet Marshall 1999]
Avnet Marshall, About Avnet Marshall, http://www.marshall.com/dynamic/html/marshall/about/marabout.htm, 6.4.1999

[Bach/Österle 1999]
Bach, V., Österle, H., Wissensmanagement - Eine unternehmerische Perspektive, in: [Bach et al. 1999]

[Bach et al. 1999]
Bach, V., Österle, H., Vogler, P. (Eds.), Business Knowledge Management: Praxiserfahrungen mit Intranet-basierten Lösungen, Springer, Berlin etc., 1999

[Bach/Österle 2000]
Bach, V., Österle, H. (Eds.), Customer Relationship Management in der Praxis: Wege zu kundenzentrierten Lösungen, Springer, Berlin etc., 2000

[Bach et al. 2000]
Bach, V., Österle, H., Vogler, P. (Eds.), Business Knowledge Management: Prozessorientierte Lösungen zwischen Knowledge Portal und Kompetenzmanagement, Springer, Berlin etc., 2000

[Barak 1997]
Barak, V., Systemmigration: Strategien für die Informatik, Wiesbaden, Deutscher Universitäts-Verlag, 1997

[Barling/Stark 1998]
Barling, B., Stark, H., Business-to-Business Electronic Commerce: Opening the Market, Ovum Ltd., Burlington, London, Southbank, 1998

[Barth 1993]
Barth, K., Betriebswirtschaftslehre des Handels, 2nd Ed., Wiesbaden, 1993

[Battelle 1998]
Battelle Institute, Battelle Forecasts Technology's Top 10 Challenges and Opportunities for 2007, www.battelle.org/pr/Drivers2.htm, 7.1998

[Becker 1998]
Becker, M., Umsetzung betrieblicher Prozesse: Methode, Fallbeispiele, Workflow-Technologie, Dissertation, Institute of Information Management, University of St. Gallen, Difo-Druck, Bamberg, 1998

[Becker/Geimer 1999]
Becker, T., Geimer, H., Prozeßgestaltung und Leistungsmessung: wesentliche Bausteine für eine Weltklasse Supply Chain, in: HMD, 36 (1999) 207, pp. 25-34

[Becker/Schütte 1996]
Becker, J., Schütte, R., Handelsinformationssysteme, Verlag Moderne Industrie, Landsberg/Lech, 1996

[Belz et al. 1997]
Belz, C., Schuh, G., Gross, S.A., Reinecke, S., Erfolgreiche Leistungssysteme in der Industrie - Industrie als Dienstleister, in: Fachbuch für Marketing, Verlag Thexis, St. Gallen, 1997, pp. 14-107

[Benchmarking Partners 1997]
Benchmarking Partners, Supply Chain Planning and Scheduling: The Market Leaders, in: Value Chain Strategies, June 1997, pp. 1-73

[Benjamin et al. 1990]
Benjamin, R.J., DeLong, D.W., Scott Morton, M.S., Electronic Data Interchange: How Much Competitive Advantage?, in: Long Range Planning, 23 (1990) 1, pp. 29-40

[Benz 1999]
Benz, R., Entwurf geschäftseinheitsübergreifender Prozeßnetzwerke, Dissertation, Institute of Information Management, University of St. Gallen, 1999

[Benz et al. 1999]
Benz, R., Fleisch, E., Grünauer, K.M., Österle, H., Zurmühlen, R., Entwurf von Prozessnetzwerken am Beispiel von zwei Business Networking-Projekten der Swatch Group, in: Scheer, A.-W., Nüttgens, M. (Eds.), Electronic Business Engineering, Physica-Verlag, Heidelberg, 1999, pp. 309-329

[Berners-Lee 1999]
Berners-Lee, T., Weaving the Web: The Original Design and Ultimate Destiny of the World Wide Web by Its Inventor, HarperCollins, San Francisco, 1999

[Bermudez/Girard 1997]
Bermudez, J., Girard, G., The Report on Supply Chain Management: i2 versus Manugistics, AMR Research, 1997

[Bermudez/Richardson 1999]
Bermudez, J., Richardson, B., The SAP Advisor: SAP APO Is Not Ready for Everyone, AMR Research, 1999

[Bill 1998]
Bill, A., Saying Volumes About a Maturing Market, in: Electronic Buyer´s News, 28.9.1998, p. 51

[Blaupunkt 1999]
Blaupunkt, Das Blaupunkt Extr@Net, Product Brochure, 1999

[Bleicher 1995]
Bleicher, K., Konzept Integriertes Management, Campus, Frankfurt/New York, 1995

[Bleicher 1996]
Bleicher, K., Neue Arbeits- und Organisationsformen - Der Weg zum virtuellen Unternehmen, in: Office Management, 1-2 (1996), pp. 10-15

[Blodget/McCabe 2000]
Blodget, H., McCabe, E., The B2B Market Maker Book, Merill Lynch, New York, 2000

[Bothe 1998]
Bothe, M., IT-Integration in der Supply Chain als strategische Herausforderung, in: Information, Management & Consulting, 13 (1998) 3, pp. 33-35

[Boutellier et al. 1999]
Boutellier, R., Gassmann, O., von Zedtwitz, M., Managing Global Innovation: Uncovering the Secrets of Future Competiveness, Springer, Berlin etc., 1999

[Bowersox/Closs 1996]
Bowersox, D.J., Closs, D.J., Logistical Management: The Integrated Supply Chain Process, McGraw-Hill, New York etc., 1996

[Bradley/Nolan 1998]
Bradley, S.P., Nolan, R.L, Sense and Respond, Harvard Business School Press, Boston, 1998

[Braun 1996]
Braun, S., Die Prozeßkostenrechnung: Ein fortschrittliches Kostenrechnungssystem?, Sternenfels, Berlin, 1996

[Brecht et al. 1998]
Brecht, L., Legner, C., Muschter, S., Österle, H., Prozeßführung mit nichtfinanziellen Führungsgrößen, Konzept und Erfahrungen, in: Controlling, 10 (1998) 5, pp. 286-294

[Brenner 1994]
Brenner, W., Grundzüge des Informationsmanagements, Springer, Berlin etc., 1994

[Brenner 1995]

Brenner, C., Techniken und Metamodell des Business Engineering, Institute of Information Management, University of St. Gallen, 1995

[Brenner 1996]

Brenner, W., Informationsmanagement, in: Thommen, J.-P. (Ed.), Betriebswirtschafts-lehre, 4th Ed., Versus, Zürich, 1996

[Brousseau 1994]

Brousseau, E., EDI and Inter-firm Relationships: Toward a Standardization of Coordination Processes?, in: Information Economics and Policy, 6 (1994), pp. 319-347

[Buck-Emden 1998]

Buck-Emden, R., Die Technologie des SAP-Systemes: Basis für betriebswirtschaftliche Anwendungen, 4th Ed., Addison Wesley Longman, Bonn etc., 1998

[Bues 1994]

Bues, M., Offene Systeme, Strategien, Konzepte und Techniken für das Informations-management, Springer, Berlin etc., 1994

[Burrows/Reinhardt 1999]

Burrows, P., Reinhardt, A., Beyond the PC, in: Business Week, March 8, 1999, pp. 36-42

[Burt 1999]

Burt, T., Ford to Farm Out Key Final Assembly Jobs to Contractors, Outsourcing Move in Brazil Could Signal Change in Carmaker´s Core Activities, in: Financial Times, August 4 1999, p. 1

[Buxmann 1996]

Buxmann, P., Standardisierung betrieblicher Informationssysteme, Gabler, Wiesbaden, 1996

[Byrne 1998]

Byrne, J.A., The Corporation of the Future, in: Business Week, Special Ed. September 1998, The 21st Century Economy, McGraw-Hill, New York, 1998

[Cannon 1993]

Cannon, E., EDI Guide: A Step by Step Approach, Van Nostrand Reinhold, New York, 1993

[Cargill 1989]

Cargill, C.F., Information Technology Standardization: Theory, Process, and Organization, Digital Press, Bedford, 1989

[Caves et al. 1990]

Caves, R.E., Frankel, J.A., Jones, R.W., World Trade and Payments, 5th Ed., Scott, Foresman and Company, Glenview, 1990

[Checkland 1991]
Checkland, P., From Framework Through Experience to Learning: The Essential Nature of Action Research, in: Nissen, H.E., Klein, H.K., Information Systems Research, Elsevier, Amsterdam, 1991

[Checkland 1997]
Checkland, P., Rhetoric and Reality in Contracting: Research In and On the NHS, Contracting for Health, Oxford University Press, London, 1997

[Checkland/Holwell 1998]
Checkland, P., Holwell, S., Action Research: Its Nature and Validity, in: Systemic Practice and Action Research, 11 (1998) 1, pp. 9-21

[Chesher/Kaura 1998]
Chesher, M., Kaura, R., Electronic Commerce and Business Communications, Springer, Berlin etc., 1998

[Chisholm 1998]
Chisholm, R.F., Developing Network Organizations: Learning from Practice and Theory, Addison Wesley Longman, Bonn etc., 1998

[Choi et al. 1997]
Choi, S.Y., Stahl, D.O., Whinston, A.B., The Economics of Electronic Commerce, Macmillan, Indianapolis, 1997

[Christiaanse et al. 1996]
Christiaanse, E., Been, J., Van Diepen, T., Factors Determining the Failure of Global Systems in the Air Cargo Community, in: Proceedings of the 29th HICSS, IEEE Computer Society Press, Los Alamitos, 1996, pp. 418-429

[Christopher 1998]
Christopher, M., Logistics and Supply Chain Management: Strategies for Reducing Costs and Improving Services, 2nd Ed., Financial Times/Pitman Publishing, London, 1998

[Christopher/McDonald 1995]
Christoper, M., McDonald, M., Marketing, MacMillan, Houndmills etc., 1995

[Clark 1999]
Clark, R., The Willingness of Net-Consumers to Pay: A Lack-of-Progress Report, in: Klein, S., Gricar, J., Pucihar, A. (Eds.), Proceedings of the 12th ECC, Moderna organizacija, Kranj, 1999, pp. 270-286

[Clemons/Reddi 1993]
Clemons, E.K., Reddi, S.P., Some Propositions Regarding the Role of Information Technology in the Organization of Economic Activity, in: Nunamaker, J.F., Sprague, R.H. (Eds.), Proceedings of the 26th HICSS, IEEE Computer Society Press, Los Alamitos, 1993, pp. 809-818

[Cole et al. 1999]

Cole, S.J., Woodring, S.D., Gatoff, J., Chun, H., The Apps Market: 1998 - 2003, The Forrester Report, April 1999

[Collis/Montgomery 1995]

Collis, D.J., Montgomery, C.A., Competing on Resources: Strategy in the 1990s, in: Harvard Business Review, 73 (1995) 4, pp. 118-128

[Commerce One 1999a]

Commerce One Inc., Commerce One Transactive Content Management, Whitepaper, 1999

[Commerce One 1999b]

Commerce One Inc., Enabling the Business-to-Business Trading Web Using MarketSite 3.0 Open Marketplace Platform, Whitepaper, 1999

[CPFR 1999]

The Collaborative Planning, Forecasting and Replenishment Committee, http://www.cpfr.org/Intro.html, 30.7.1999

[Crowston 1994a]

Crowston, K., Electronic Communication and New Organizational Forms: A Coordination Theory Approach, MIT, Center for Coordination Science, Technical Report 175, 1994, ccs.mit.edu/papers/CCSWP175.html, 25.3.1999

[Crowston 1994b]

Crowston, K., A Taxonomy of Organizational Dependencies and Coordination Mechanisms, Technical Report 174, MIT, Center for Coordination Science, 1994, ccs.mit.edu/papersCCSWP174.html, 19.7.1999

[Davenport 1993]

Davenport, T.H., Process Innovation: Reengineering Work Through Information Technology, Harvard Business School Press, Boston, 1993

[Davenport/Prusak 1998]

Davenport, T.H., Prusak, L., Working Knowledge - How Organizations Manage What They Know, Harvard Business School Press, Boston (MA), 1998

[Davidow/Malone 1992]

Davidow, W.H., Malone, M.S., The Virtual Corporation: Structuring and Revitalizing the Corporation for the 21st Century, Harperbusiness, New York 1992

[Davis/Meyer 1998]

Davis, S., Meyer, C., We're Already Surrounded by Them... What Happens When They Team up?, in: Forbes, 161 (1.6.1998) 11, p. 74

[DeCovny 1998]

DeCovny, S., Electronic Commerce Comes of Age, in: Journal of Business Strategy, 19 (1998) 6, pp. 38-44

[Dell 1999]
Dell, The Dell Story, http://www.dell.com, 4.9.1999

[Delphi 1997]
Delphi Consulting Group, Delphi on Knowledge Management, Boston (MA), 1997, http://www.delphigroup.com/pubs/sample/KM-HIGHLIGHT-1997-11.PDF, 1.4.1999

[DeSanctis/Monge 1998]
DeSanctis, G., Monge, P., Communication Processes for Virtual Organizations, in: Journal of Computer-Mediated Communications, 3 (1998) 4, http://www.ascusc.org/jcmc/vol3/issue4/desanctis.html, 5.8.1999

[Deutsche Post 1999]
Deutsche Post AG, http://www.postag.de/postag/news/new9903/ne990308.html, 25.5.1999

[Diamond 1999]
Diamond Multimedia Systems, Inc., http://www.diamondmm.com, 25.6.1999

[Dolmetsch et al. 1999]
Dolmetsch, R., Fleisch, E., Österle, H., Desktop-Purchasing: I-Net-Technologien in der Beschaffung, in: HMD, 36 (1998) 206, pp. 77-89

[Dolmetsch 1999]
Dolmetsch, R., Desktop Purchasing, IP-Netzwerkapplikationen in der Beschaffung, Dissertation, Institute of Information Management, University of St. Gallen, Difo-Druck, Bamberg, 1999

[Downes/Mui 1998]
Downes, L., Mui, C., Unleashing the Killer App: Digital Strategies for Market Dominances, Harvard Business School Press, Boston (MA), 1998

[Doz/Hamel 1998]
Doz, Y.L., Hamel, G., Alliance Advantage: The Art of Creating Value Through Partnering, Harvard Business School Press, Boston, 1998

[DTAG 1999]
Company Portrait, http://www.dtag.de/english/company/profile/index.htm, 25.5.1999

[Dubois/Carmel 1994]
Dubois, F.L., Carmel, E., Information Technology and Leadtime Management in International Manufacturing Operations, in: Deans, P.C., Karwan, K.R (Eds.), Global Information Systems and Technology: Focus on the Organization and its Functional Areas, Idea Group, Harrisburg, 1994, pp.279-293

[Dun & Bradstreet 1998]
Dun & Bradstreet Corp., SPSC Standard Product & Service Codes, Draft Version, Scottdale, 1998

[Durlacher 1999]

Durlacher Research, Application Service Providers, London, 1999

[ECCS 1999]

ECCS: CRM Definitions - Defining Customer Relationship Marketing and Management, http://www.eccs.uk.com/crmdefinitions/define.asp, 27.7.1999

[ECR 1999]

Efficient Consumer Response Initiative Canada, What is ECR?, http://www.ecr.ca/en/index.html, 30.6.1999

[Ellram 1991]

Ellram, L.M., Supply Chain Management: The Industrial Organization Perspective, in: International Journal of Physical Distribution and Logistics Management, 21 (1991) 1, pp. 13-21

[El Sawy et al. 1999]

El Sawy, O.A., Malhotra, A., Gosain, S., Young, K.M., IT-intensive Value Innovation in the Electronic Economy: Insights from Marshall Industries, in: MIS Quarterly, 23 (1999) 3

[Enslow 1999]

Enslow, B., Supply Chain Planning Magic Quadrant Update 2Q99, Research Note Markets 2 April 1999, Gartner Group, 1999

[Eppler et al. 1999]

Eppler, M., Seifried, P., Röpnack, A., Improving Knowledge Intensive Processes Through an Enterprise Knowledge Medium, in: Managing Organizational Knowledge for Strategic Advantage: The Key Role of Information Technology and Personnel, SIGCPR 1999 Conference, New Orleans, 1999

[Evan 1976]

Evan, W.M., Interorganizational Relations, Penguin, Harmondsworth, 1976

[Falk/Wolf 1992]

Falk, B., Wolf, J., Handelsbetriebslehre, 11th Ed., Moderne Industrie, Landsberg/ Lech, 1992

[Faucheux 1997]

Faucheux, C., How Virtual Organizing is Transforming Management Science, in: Communications of the ACM, 40 (1997) 9, pp. 50-55

[FedEx 1999]

Federal Express Corporation, FedEx and AvantGo to Provide Hand-held Device Users with Package Tracking Information, http://www.fedex.com/us/about/pressreleases/pressrelease051099.html, 8.7.1999

[Fine 1998]

Fine, C.H., Clockspeed, Perseus Books, New York, 1998

[FIR-RWTH 1999]
FIR-RWTH, Marktspiegel Supply Chain Management Software, Forschungsinstitut für Rationalisierung, Technical University of Aachen, June 1999

[Fleisch 1998]
Fleisch, E., Instance Strategy at Commtech Ltd., Working Paper, Institute of Information Management, University of St. Gallen, 1998

[Fleisch/Wintersteiger 1999]
Fleisch, E., Wintersteiger, W., Business Networking and Software Quality Management, in: Proceedings of the 6th ECIS, Vienna, 1999, pp. 56-70

[Fleisch 2000]
Fleisch, E., Koordination in Netzwerkunternehmen - Prozeßorientierung als Gestaltungsprinzip bei der Vernetzung von Unternehmen, Postdoctoral Thesis, Institute of Information Management, University of St. Gallen, 2000

[Forrester 1998]
Forrester Research, U.S. On-line Business Trade Will Soar To $1.3 Trillion By 2003, http://www.forrester.com/Press/Releases/Standard/ 0,1184,121,00.html, 12.1998

[Fritsche 1999]
Fritsche, B., Advanced Planning and Scheduling (APS): Die Zukunft von PPS und Supply Chain, in: Logistik heute, 21 (1999) 5, pp. 50-56

[Fröschel 1999]
Fröschel, F., Vom IuK-Outsourcing zum Business Process Outsourcing, in: Wirtschaftsinformatik, 41 (1999) 5, pp. 458-460

[Gartner Group 1998a]
GartnerGroup, Advanced Technologies: Key to Supply Chain Excellence, Gartner Group Monthly Research Review, 1 April 1998

[Gartner Group 1998b]
Gartner Group, The Industry Trends Scenario: Delivering Business Value Through IT, Gartner Group, April 1998

[Gartner Group 1998c]
Gartner Group, Transition Challenges: The CIO's Perspective, Gartner Group, April 1998

[GartnerGroup 2000]
GartnerGroup, E-Business Resource Center, Gartner Group, http://gartner6.gartnerweb.com/public/static/home/ggebiz.html, 13.3.2000

[Gassmann 1997]
Gassmann, O., Management transnationaler Forschungs- und Entwicklungsprojekte: Eine empirische Untersuchung von Potentialen und Gestaltungskonzepten transnationaler F&E-Projekte in industriellen Großunternehmen, Difo-Druck, Bamberg, 1997

[Gebauer et al. 1998]

Gebauer, J., Beam, C., Segev, A., Procurement in the Internet Age - Current Practices and Emerging Trends (Results From a Field Study), Fisher Center Working Paper 98-WP-1033, University of California, Berkeley, 1998

[Giaglis et al. 1999]

Giaglis, G., Klein, S., O´Keefe, R., Disintermediation, Reintermediation, or Cybermediation? The Future of Intermediaries in Electronic Marketplaces, in: Klein, S., Gricar, J., Novak, J. (Eds.), Proceedings of the 12th ECC, Moderna organizacija, Kranj, 1999, pp. 389 - 407

[Ginsburg et al. 1999]

Ginsburg, M., Gebauer, J., Segev, A., Multi-Vendor Electronic Catalogs to Support Procurement: Current Practice and Future Directions, in: Klein, S. Gricar, J., Pucihar, A. (Eds.), Proceedings of the 12th ECC, Moderna organizacija, Kranj, 1999, pp. 331-345

[Goldratt/Cox 1995]

Goldratt, E., Cox, J., The Goal: Excellence in Manufacturing, 2nd Ed., McGraw-Hill, London etc., 1995

[Gomes 1999]

Gomes, L, Linking Your PC to a Stereo Is a Ticket to CD Carousel, in: The Wall Street Journal Europe, July 30-31, 1999, p. 5

[Gomez-Casseres 1996]

Gomes-Casseres, B., The Alliance Revolution: The New Shape of Business Rivalry, Harvard University Press, Cambridge, 1996

[Gomez/Zimmermann 1993]

Gomez, P., Zimmermann, T., Unternehmensorganisation: Profile, Dynamik, Methodik, St. Galler Management-Konzept, 2nd Ed., Campus, Frankfurt etc., 1993

[GPS 1997]

GPS, GPS Software Atlas: Generalplan Industrieunternehmen, GPS Gesellschaft zur Prüfung von Software, Ulm, 1997

[Gray/Reuter 1993]

Gray, J., Reuter, A., Transaction Processing - Concepts and Techniques, San Mateo, 1993

[Grieco 1997]

Grieco, P., MRO-Purchasing, PT Publications, West Palm Beach, 1997

[Grochla 1972]

Grochla, E., Die Kooperation von Unternehmungen aus organisationstheoretischer Sicht, in: Böttcher, E., Theorie und Praxis der Kooperation, Tübingen, 1972, pp. 1-18

[Grochla 1982]

Grochla, E., Grundlagen der organisatorischen Gestaltung, Poeschel, Stuttgart, 1982

[Gronau 1997]
Gronau, N., Management von Produktion und Logistik mit SAP R/3, 2nd Ed., Oldenbourg, München etc., 1997

[Gutzwiller 1994]
Gutzwiller, T.A., Das CC RIM-Referenzmodell für den Entwurf von betrieblichen, transaktionsorientierten Informationssystemen, Physica, Heidelberg, 1994

[Hagel/Armstrong 1997]
Hagel, J., Armstrong, A.G., Net Gain: Expanding Markets Through Virtual Communities, Harvard Business School Press, Boston (MA), 1997

[Hagel/Singer 1999]
Hagel, J., Singer, M., Net Worth: Shaping Markets When Customers Make the Rules, Harvard Business School Press, Boston, 1999

[Håkansson/Snehota 1995]
Håkansson, H., Snehota, I., Developing Relationships in Business Networks, Routledge, London etc., 1995

[Hamel/Prahalad 1990]
Hamel, G., Prahalad, C.K., TheCore Competence of the Corporation, in: Havard Business Review, (1990) 2, S. 79-91

[Hamel/Prahalad 1994]
Hamel, G., Prahalad, C.K., Competing for the Future, Harvard Business School Press, Boston, 1994

[Hamm/Stepanek 1999]
Hamm, S., Stepanek, M., From Reengineering to E-Engineering, in: Business Week, e.biz, March 22, 1999, pp. EB 14-18

[Handfield/Nichols 1998]
Handfield, R., Nichols, Jr., Introduction to Supply Chain Management, Prentice Hall, Upper Saddle River (NJ), 1998

[Hankason 1999]
Hankason, B., Supply Chain Management: Where Today's Business Compete, in: Anderson, D.L., Lee, H., Herbold, B. (Eds.), Achieving Supply Chain Excellence through Technology, Montgomery Research, Inc., San Francisco, 1999

[Hantusch et al 1997]
Hantusch, T., Matzke, B., Pérez, M., SAP R/3 im Internet, Addison Wesley Longman, Bonn etc., 1997

[Hartman 1997]
Hartman, C., Sales Force, in: FastCompany, 9 (1997), pp. 134

[Hartman et al. 2000]
Hartman, A., Sifonis, J., Kador, J., Net Ready - Strategies for Success in the E-conomy, McGraw-Hill, New York, 2000

[Hedberg et al. 1997]
Hedberg, B., Dahlgren, G., Hansson, J., Olve, N.-G., Virtual Organizations and Beyond: Discover Imaginary Systems, Wiley & Sons, Chichester, 1997

[Heinen 1991]
Heinen, E., Industriebetriebslehre: Entscheidungen im Industriebetrieb, 9th Ed., Gabler, Wiesbaden, 1991

[Heinrich 1992]
Heinrich, L.J., Informationsmanagement: Planung, Überwachung und Steuerung der Informations-Infrastruktur, 4th Ed., Oldenburg, München etc., 1992

[van Heijst et al. 1996]
van Heijst, G., van der Spek, R., Kruizinga, E., Organizing Corporate Memories, in: 10th Knowledge Acquisition for Knowledge-Based Systems, Workshop, Banff, 1996

[Hess 1996]
Hess, T., Entwurf betrieblicher Prozesse: Grundlagen – Bestehende Methoden – Neue Ansätze, Gabler, Wiesbaden, 1996

[Hess/Brecht 1995]
Hess, T., Brecht, L., State of the Art des Business Process Redesign, Gabler, Wiesbaden, 1995

[Hess/Schumann 1999]
Hess, T., Schumann, M., Medienunternehmen im digitalen Zeitalter: Neue Technologien - Neue Märkte - Neue Geschäftsansätze, Gabler, Wiesbaden, 1999

[Hewlett Packard 1998]
Hewlett Packard, Trust Bank Trusts HP NetServers to Support Expansion, http://www.microsoft.hp.com/trustbank.htm, 30.7.1999

[Heym/Österle 1993]
Heym, M., Österle, H., Computer-Aided Methodology Engineering, in: Information and Software Technology, 35 (1993) 6, pp. 345-354

[Hiemenz 1998]
Hiemenz, C., Potentiale nutzen - Durchgängiges Supply Chain Management erhöht die Wertschöpfung, in: Information Management & Consulting, 13 (1998) 3, pp. 56-59

[Hilb 1997]
Hilb, M., Management der Human-Ressourcen in virtuellen Organisationen, in: [Müller-Stewens 1997]

[Hilbers 1989]

Hilbers, K., Informationssystem-Architekturen: Zielsetzung, Bestandteile, Erfolgsfaktoren, Information Management 2000, Working Paper, Institute of Information Management, University of St. Gallen, 1989

[Hinterhuber 1992]

Hinterhuber, H.H., Strategische Unternehmensführung, Part 1: Strategisches Denken, 5th Ed., de Gruyter, New York, 1992

[van Hoek/Weken 1997]

van Hoel, R., Weken, H., How Modular Production Can Contribute to Integration in Inbound and Outbound Logistics, in: Proceedings of the Logistics Research Network Conference, University of Huddersfield, 16.-17. September 1997

[Hof 2000]

Hof, R.D., E-Marketplaces Face a Bloodbath, in: Business Week, e.biz, April 3, 2000, p. 72

[Hofer 1999]

Hofer, J., Computec geht in den USA in die Offensive, in: Handelsblatt, 03.08.1999, p. 22

[Hofmann/Killer 1996]

Hofmann, M., Killer, B., Interoperability Between and Within Enterprises, Whitepaper SAP AG, Walldorf, 1995

[Hofman/Rockart 1994]

Hofman, J.D., Rockart, J.F., Application Templates: Faster, Better, and Cheaper Systems, in: Sloan Management Review, 36 (1994) 1, pp. 49-60.

[Hoovers 1999a]

Hoovers, Key Performance Indicators of Amazon.com, www.hoovers.com, 1999

[Hoovers 1999b]

Hoovers, Key Performance Indicators of UBS, www.hoovers.com, 1999

[Huber et al. 2000]

Huber, T., Alt, R., Österle, H., Templates as Instruments for the Standardization of ERP Systems, in: Proceedings of the 33rd HICSS, IEEE Computer Society Press, Hawaii, 2000

[Hübner 2000]

Hübner, K., Virtueller Marktplatz der Möglichkeiten, Bayer Report April 2000, Bayer AG, Leverkusen, 2000

[Hwang et al. 1998]

Hwang, D., Hause, K., Kaldor, S., IDC's Forecast of the Worldwide Information Appliance Market, 1997-2002, Report #17437, International Data Corporation, Framingham (MA), 1998

[IBM 1998]

IBM Corporation, Continuous Replenishment Service, http://www.disu.ibm.com/discrp.htm, 5.8.1998

[IBM 2000]

IBM, The Application Framework for e-Business, www.ibm.com, 13.3.2000

[i2 1997]

i2, Rhythm - An Overview, i2 Technologies, Irving, 1997

[IMG 1997]

IMG AG, PROMET-BPR: Method for Business Process Redesign, Release 2.0., St. Gallen, 1997

[IMG 1998a]

IMG AG, PROMET eBN: Method for electronic Business Networking, St. Gallen, 1998

[IMG 1998b]

IMG AG, PROMET SSW: Method for the Implementation of Standard Application Software Packages, Release 3.0, St. Gallen, 1998

[IML-FHG 1999]

IML-FHG, Marktstudie Planungssysteme für SCM, SCM-CTC am Frauenhofer-Institut für Materialfluß und Logistik, Dortmund, May 1999

[Intel 1998]

Intel Corporation, Dynamic E-procurement, White Paper, Santa Clara, 1998

[Intersearch 1998]

Intersearch Corp., National Purchasing Organizations User Group Survey, Palo Alto 1998

[iPlanet 2000]

iPlanet E-Commerce Solutions, Netscape ECXpert, White Paper, Mountain View, http://www.iplanet.com/products/ecommerce/ecxpert/whitepaper.html, 18.9.2000

[ISC 2000]

Internet Software Consortium, Internet Domain Survey, http://www.isc.org, 01.2000

[Ives/Learmonth 1984]

Ives, B., Learmonth, G.P., The Information System as a Competitive Weapon, in: Communications of the ACM, 27 (1984) 12, pp. 1193-1201

[Jagoda 1999]

Jagoda, F., Business und IT integriert betrachten, in: Computerwoche Extra, Nr. 1, 19.2.1999, pp. 4-12

[Jarillo 1993]

Jarillo, J.C., Strategic Networks, Creating the Borderless Organization, Butterworth-Heinemann, Oxford, 1993

[Jimenez-Martinez/Polo-Redondo 1998]
Jimenez-Martinez, J., Polo-Redondo, Y, International Diffusion of a New Tool: The Case of Electronic Data Interchange (EDI) in the Retailing Sector, in: Research Policy 26 (1998), pp. 811-827

[Jones 1998]
Jones, D.H., The New Logistics: Shaping the New Economy, in: Tapscott, D., Lowy, A., Ticoll, D. (Eds.), Blueprint of the Digital Economy: Creating Wealth in the Area of E-Business, McGraw-Hill, New York etc., 1998, pp. 221-235

[Jonsson 1998]
Jonsson, D., The Changing Requirements of Inter-Company Messaging, GE Information Services, Rockville etc., 1998

[Kaiser et al. 1998]
Kaiser, T.M., Beck, D., Österle, H., I-NET Enabled Customer Focus - The Case of LGT Bank in Liechtenstein, Working Paper, Institute of Information Management, University of St. Gallen, 1998

[Kalakota/Robinson 1999]
Kalakota, R., Robinson, M., E-Business: Roadmap for Success, Addison Wesley, Massachusetts etc., 1999

[Kalakota/Winston 1997]
Kalakota, R., Winston, A.B., Electronic Commerce: A Manager's Guide, Addison Wesley Longman, Mexico City, 1997

[Keen/Ballance 1997]
Keen, P., Ballance, C., On-Line Profits: A Managers Guide to Electronic Commerce, Harvard Business School Press, Boston, 1997

[Keenan 2000]
Keenan, V., Internet Exchange 2000 – B2X Emerges as New Industry to Service Exchange Transactions, Keenan Vision Inc., San Francisco 2000

[Kelly 1995]
Kelly, K., Out of Control: The New Biology of Machines, Social Systems and the Economic World, 2nd Ed., Addison Wesley Longman, Harlow, 1995

[Kelly 1998]
Kelly, K., New Rules for the New Economy, Viking Penguin, New York, 1998

[Kilger 1998]
Kilger, C., Optimierung der Supply Chain durch Advanced Planning Systems, in: Information Management & Consulting, 13 (1998) 3, pp. 49-55

[Killen & Associates 1997]
Killen & Associates, Operating Resources Management: How Enterprises Can Make Money by Reducing ORM Costs, White Paper, Palo Alto, 1997

[Klaus/Krieger 1998]

Klaus, P., Krieger, W. (Eds.), Gabler-Lexikon Logistik: Management logistischer Netzwerke und Flüsse, Gabler, Wiesbaden, 1998

[Klein 1996]

Klein, S., Interorganisationssysteme und Unternehmensnetzwerke, Deutscher Universitäts-Verlag, Wiesbaden, 1996

[Klein 1999]

Klein, S., Preisorientierte Geschäftsmodelle auf dem WWW, in: Pförtsch, H. (Ed.), Living Web - Erfolgreiche Anwendungen im Internet, Campus, Frankfurt/New York, 1999

[Kling et al. 1999]

Kling, R., Kraemer, K.L., Allen, J.P., Bakos, Y., Gurbaxani, V., Elliott, M., Transforming Coordination: The Promise and Problems of Information Technology in Coordination, in: Malone, T., Olson, G., Smith, J.B. (Eds.), Coordination Theory and Collaboration Technology, Lawrence Erlbaum, Mahwah (NJ), 1999, www.slis.indiana.edu/kling/pubs/CTCT97B.htm, 5.7.1999

[Klueber et al. 1999]

Klueber, R., Alt, R., Oesterle, H., Emerging Electronic Services for Virtual Organizations - Concepts and Framework, in: Proceedings of the Workshop on Organizational Virtualness and Electronic Commerce, Simowa, Zürich, 1999, pp. 183-204

[Körner/Zimmermann 1999]

Körner, V., Zimmermann, H.-D., Management of Customer Relationship in Business Media: Motivation for a New Approach, in: Klein, S., Gricar, J., Pucihar, A. (Eds.), Global Networked Organizations, Proceedings of the 12th ECC, Moderna organizacija, Kranj, 1999, pp. 453-468

[Koppelmann 1996]

Koppelmann, U., Outsourcing, Schäffer-Poeschel, Stuttgart, 1996

[Korzeniowski 1998]

Korzeniowski, P., Navigating the Net Without a PC, TechWeb, http://www.techweb.com:3040/wire/story/TWB19980629S0006, 29.6.1998

[KPMG 1998]

KPMG, The Power of Knowledge, London, http://www.kpmg.co.uk/uk/services/manage/powknow/powknow.pdf, 29.6.1998

[Kranz 1997]

Kranz, P., Verteilungskonzepte von Standardsoftware, Thesis, Institute of Information Management, University of St. Gallen, 1997

[Kreikebaum 1997]

Kreikebaum, H., Strategische Unternehmensplanung, 6th Ed., Kohlhammer, Stuttgart etc., 1997

[Kris 1998]
Kris, A., The Global Connection to Shared Services, http://www.akris.com, 23.1.1999

[Kruse 1987]
Kruse, H.F., Die Gestaltung und Durchführung der strategischen Informations-systemplanung, Dissertation, University of Freiburg/Switzerland, Freiburg, 1987

[Kubicek 1992]
Kubicek, H., The Organization Gap in Large-Scale EDI Systems, in: Streng, R.J., Eker-ing, C.F., van Heck, E., Schultz, J.F.H. (Eds.): Scientific Research on EDI 'Bringing Worlds Together', Samsom, Amsterdam, 1992, pp. 11-41

[Kühn 1999]
Kühn, M., Collaborative Planning, Whitepaper SAP AG, SAPPHIRE '99, Nice, 1999

[Kühn/Grandke 1997]
Kühn, F., Grandke, R., Kundennutzen in der Leistungserstellung verankern, in: Hirzel, Leder & Partner (Eds.), Fokussiertes Business Design, Gabler, Wiesbaden, 1997, pp. 133-148

[Kuper/Billington 2000]
Kuper, A., Billington, C., Real Options for Doing Business at Internet Speed, The IT Journal, Mountainview, 2000

[Kuri 1999]
Kuri, J., Soft Machine, in: c't, 6/99, pp. 154-159

[Laaper 1998]
Laaper, B., Procurement Reengineering, PT Publications, West Palm Beach, 1998

[Lacity/Hirschheim 1995]
Lacity, M.C., Hirschheim, R., Beyond the Information Systems Outsourcing Band-wagon: The Insourcing Response, Ed., Wiley, Chichester etc.,1995

[Lane 1998]
Lane, R.J., The Computing Model for the Information Age, in: Tapscott, D., Lowy, A., Ticoll, D. (Eds.), Blueprint of the Digital Economy, McGraw-Hill, New York, pp. 239-259

[Lapide 1998]
Lapide, L., Supply Chain Planning Optimization: Just the Facts, in: The AMR Report on Supply Chain Management, Mai 1998

[Laszlo 1997]
Laszlo, E., Laszlo, C., Management-Wissen der 3. Art, Gabler, Wiesbaden, 1997

[Lee et al. 1997]
Lee, H., Padmanabhan, V., Whang, S., The Bullwhip Effect in Supply Chains, in: Sloan Management Review, 38 (1997) 1, pp. 93-102

[Lehmann 1996]
  Lehmann, F., Machine-Negotiated, Ontology-Based EDI (Electronic Data Interchange), in: Adam, N.R., Yesha, Y. (Eds.): Electronic Commerce: Current Research Issues and Applications, Springer, Berlin etc., 1996, pp. 27-45

[Lehner et al. 1991]
  Lehner, F., Auer-Rizzi, W., Bauer, R., Breit, R., Lehner, J.M., Reber, G., Organisationslehre für Wirtschaftsinformatiker, Hanser, München etc., 1991

[Lerchenmüller 1998]
  Lerchenmüller, M., Handelbetriebslehre, 3rd Ed., Friedrich Kiehl, Ludwigshafen, 1998

[Linthicum 2000]
  Linthicum, D.S., Enterprise Application Integration, Addison Wesley Longman, Reading (MA) etc., 2000

[Lozinsky 1998]
  Lozinsky, S., Enterprise-wide Software Solutions: Integration Strategies and Practices, Addison Wesley Longman, Harlow, 1998

[Malik 1999]
  Malik, O., Virtual Stationary, in: Forbes, Nr. 4/14, http://www.forbes.com/tool/html/99/apr/0414/featb.htm#top, 6.4.1999

[Malone et al. 1987]
  Malone, T.W., Yates, J., Benjamin, R.I., Electronic Markets and Electronic Hierarchies, in: Communication of the ACM, 30 (1987) 6, pp. 484-497

[Malone 1988]
  Malone, T.W., What is Coordination Theory?, Working Paper, MIT, Sloan School of Management, Cambridge (MA), 1988, pp. 89-167

[Malone/Crowston 1994]
  Malone, T.W., Crowston, K., The Interdisciplinary Study of Coordination, in: ACM Computing Surveys, 26 (1994) 1, pp. 87-119

[Malone/Rockart 1991]
  Malone, T.W., Rockart, J.F., Computers, Networks, and the Corporation, in: Scientific American, 91 (1991) 9, pp. 92-99

[Manugistics 1998]
  Manugistics, Manugistics Announces Results Delivery Process: New Methodology Uniquely Focuses on Delivering Client Results, Press Release, 1.6.1998

[Margherito 1998]
  Margherito, The Emerging Digital Economy, U.S. Department of Commerce, Washington, 1998

[Marks 1996]
Marks, S., EDI-Purchasing, The Electronic Gateway to the Future, PT Publications, West Palm Beach, 1996

[Martin 1989]
Martin, J., Information Engineering, Prentice Hall, Englewood Cliffs, 1989

[Martin et al. 1995]
Martin, J., Kavanagh Chapman, K., Leben, J., Enterprise Networking: Datalink Subnetworks, Prentice Hall, Englewood Cliffs, 1995

[Martiny/Klotz 1990]
Martiny, L., Klotz, M., Strategisches Informationsmanagement: Bedeutung und organisatorische Umsetzung, 2nd Ed., Oldenburg, München etc., 1990

[Meffert 1998]
Meffert, H., Marketing, Gabler, Wiesbaden, 1998

[Mertens 1997]
Mertens, P., Integrierte Informationsverarbeitung, Band 1: Administrations- und Dispositionssysteme in der Industrie, Gabler, Wiesbaden, 1997

[Mertens et al. 1998]
Mertens, P., Griese, J., Ehrenberg, D. (Eds.), Virtuelle Unternehmen und Informationsverarbeitung, Springer, Berlin etc., 1998

[Merz 1996]
Merz, M., Elektronische Märkte im Internet, Thomson Publishing, Bonn, 1996

[Metagroup 1997]
Metagroup, Enterprise Architecture Strategies: 'Best Practices' of Adaptive Systems, Metagroup, Stamford, 1997

[Metagroup 1998]
Metagroup, Enterprise Architecture Strategies: Adaptive Systems, The Role of Enterprisewide Technical Architecture, Metagroup, Stamford, 1998

[MGFS 2000]
MGFS, Fundamentals, Media General Financial Services, http://quicken.excite.com/investments/stats/?defview=TABLE&symbol=ITWO+MANU+SAP+JDEC, 18.8.2000

[Microsoft 1999a]
Microsoft Corporation, Open Applications Group and Microsoft Announce First Pilot Project To Migrate Industry Standard to BizTalk Framework Specifications, http://www.microsoft.com/presspass/press/1999/Jul99/OAGpr.htm, 21.7.1999

[Microsoft 1999b]
Microsoft Corporation, Summary to: Gates, B., Business @ the Speed of Thought, Using a Digital Nervous System, Warner Books, New York, 1999, http://www.speed-of-thought.com/looking/chapter.html, 18.8.1999

[Migros 1999]

Migros, Zahlen und Fakten, http://www.migros.ch, 19.4.1999

[Miller-Williams 1998]

Miller-Williams, Inc., 1998 Customer Value Report, September 21st 1998, http://www.i2.com/value/valueprop/value_report.pdf, 1.7.1999

[Millett 1997]

Millett, S., Battelle Forecasts, http://battelle.org/pr/drivers2.htm, 10.3.1997

[Moss-Kanter 1989]

Moss-Kanter, R., Becoming PALs: Pooling, Allying, and Linking Across Companies, in: The Academy of Management Executive, 3 (1989) 3, pp. 183-193

[Müller-Hagedorn 1998]

Müller-Hagedorn, L., Der Handel, Kohlhammer, Stuttgart, 1998

[Müller-Stewens 1997]

Müller-Stewens, G. (Ed.), Virtualisierung von Organisationen, Verlag Neue Zürcher Zeitung, Schäffer-Poeschel, Zürich, 1997

[Murray/Myers 1997]

Murray, P., Myers, A., The Facts About Knowledge, Information Strategy, September, 1997, http://www.info-strategy.com/knowsur1, 1.4.1999

[Muther 1998]

Muther, A., Electronic Customer Care: Die Anbieter-Kundenbeziehung im Informationszeitalter, Springer, Berlin etc., 1998

[Naisbitt 1994]

Naisbitt, J., Megatrends 2000 - Ten New Directions for the 1990s, Avon, New York, 1994

[Negroponte 1995]

Negroponte, N.P., Being Digital, Knopf, New York, 1995

[Netscape 1998]

Netscape, Netscape BuyerXpert - An Internet Commerce Application for Enterprise Purchasing, Product Whitepaper, Mountain View, 1998, http://www.netscape.com/commapps/expert/buyerx_data.html

[Neu 1991]

Neu, P., Strategische Informationssystem-Planung, Springer, Berlin etc., 1991

[Neuburger 1994]

Neuburger, R., Electronic Data Interchange: Einsatzmöglichkeiten und ökonomische Auswirkungen, Gabler, Wiesbaden, 1994

[Nolan/Croson 1995]

Nolan, R.C., Croson, D.C., Creative Destruction: A Six Stage Process for Transforming the Organization, Harvard Business School Press, Boston, Massachusetts, 1995

[Nonaka/Takeuchi 1995]

Nonaka, I., Takeuchi, H., The Knowledge-creating Company, Oxford University Press, Oxford, 1995

[Norman 1992]

Norman, D., Why Information Strategies Fail, in: Brown, E. (Ed.), Creating a Business-based IT Strategy, Chapman & Hall, London, 1992

[Norman 1999]

Norman, D., The Invisible Computer, The MIT Press, Cambridge (MA)/London, 1999

[Nüttgens 1995]

Nüttgens, M., Koordiniert-dezentrales Informationsmanagement: Rahmenkonzept, Ko-ordinationsmodelle, Werkzeug-Shell, Gabler, Wiesbaden, 1995

[OBI 1998]

The OBI Consortium, Open Buying on the Internet (OBI) Technical Specifications - Release V1.1, http://www.openbuy.org/obi/library.html, 4.6.1998

[OECD 1996]

OECD, ICT Standardization in the New Global Context, OECD Working Paper No. 75, Paris, 1996

[OrderZone 1999]

OrderZone, About Us: What We Offer, http://www.orderzone.com/7972620944/sim/about/get/AboutFS.html, 15.7.1999

[Orths 1995]

Orths, H., Von der Kundenorientierung zum Supply Management, Gabler, Wiesbaden, 1995

[Österle et al. 1993]

Österle, H., Brenner, W., Hilbers, K., Total Information Systems Management: A European Approach, Wiley & Sons, Chichester, 1993

[Österle 1995]

Österle, H., Business in the Information Age: Heading for New Processes, Springer, Berlin etc., 1995

[Österle/Fleisch 1996]

Österle, H., Fleisch, E., Auf der Suche nach Rezepten für den Unternehmenserfolg, Das Geschäftsmodell des Informationszeitalters, in: SAP INFO 10/96, pp. 8-11

[Österle/Muther 1998]

Österle, H., Muther, A., Electronic Customer Care - Neue Wege zum Kunden, in: Wirtschaftsinformatik, 40 (1998) 2, pp. 105-113

[Osterloh/Frost 1998]

Osterloh, M., Frost, J., Prozessmanagement als Kernkompetenz: wie Sie Business Reengineering strategisch nutzen können, 2nd Ed., Gabler, Wiesbaden, 1998

[Outsourcing Institute 1999]

The Outsourcing Institute, Survey of Current and Potential Outsourcing, http://www.outsourcing.com/howandwhy/surveyresults/index.hat, 10.7.1998

[Parker et al. 1988]

Parker, M.M., Benson, R.J., Trainor, H.E., Information Economics: Linking Business Performance to Information Technology, Prentice Hall, Englewood Cliffs, 1988

[Peoplesoft 1999]

Peoplesoft Glossary, http://www.peoplesoft.com/en/utilities/glossary/ glossary_e_en.html, 1.7.1999

[Peppers/Rogers 1997]

Peppers, D., Rogers, M., Enterprise One to One: Tools for Competing in the Interactive Age, Currency/Doubleday, New York (NY), 1997

[Pfohl 1994]

Pfohl, H.-C., Logistikmanagement, Springer, Berlin etc., 1994

[Pfohl 1997]

Pfohl, H.-C., Gestaltung von Informationen und Informationssystemen in der Logistik-kette, in: Pfohl, H.-C., Informationsfluß in der Logistikkette – EDI – Prozeßgestaltung – Vernetzung, Erich Schmidt Verlag, Berlin, 1997, pp. 5-45

[Pirron et al. 1998]

Pirron, J., Reisch, O., Kulow, B., Hezel, H., Werkzeuge der Zukunft, in: Logistik heute, 20 (1998) 11, pp. 60-69

[Pirron et al. 1999]

Pirron, J., Kulow, B., Hellingrath, B., Laakmann, F., Marktübersicht SCM-Software: Gut, daß wir verglichen haben, in: Logistik heute, 21 (1999) 3, pp. 69-76

[Ploenzke 2000]

CSC Ploenzke AG, Critical Issues of Information Systems Management, http://www.cscploenzke.de/index.cfm?MenuLevel=5&Type=DocTyp&ServiceID=/de/P ress/20000310_d_criticalissues.cfm, 10.3.2000

[Plummer/Smith 2000]

Plummer, D., Smith, D., E-Services: Are They Really the Next 'E'?, Gartner Group, http://gartner6.gartnerweb.com/public/static/hotc/hc0086767.html, 14.03.2000

[Porter 1985]

Porter, M.E., Competitive Advantage: Creating and Sustaining Superior Performance, The Free Press, New York, 1985

[Porter 1992a]

Porter, M.E., Competitive Strategy: Techniques for Analyzing Industries and Competi-tors, The Free Press, New York, 1992

[Porter 1992b]

Porter, M.E., Wettbewerbsstrategie: Methoden zur Analyse von Branchen und Konkurrenten, 7th Ed., Campus Verlag, Frankfurt/Main etc., 1992

[Porter 1996]

Porter, M.E., What Is Strategy?, in: Harvard Business Review, 74 (1996) 6, pp. 61-78

[Pottholf 1998]

Pottholf, I., Kosten und Nutzen der Informationsverarbeitung: Analyse und Beurteilung von Investitionsentscheidungen, Gabler, Wiesbaden, 1998

[Prahalad/Hamel 1990]

Prahalad, C.K., Hamel, G., The Core Competence of the Corporation, in: Harvard Business Review, 68 (1990) 3, pp. 79-91

[Preisig 1999]

Preisig, A., $10 Mio per Day in Less than 2 Years, in: Institute of Information Management, University of St. Gallen (Ed.), Research Report Business Engineering, University of St. Gallen, Luzern, 1999

[Probst et al. 1999]

Probst, G., Raub, S., Romhardt, K., Wissen managen - Wie Unternehmen ihre wertvollste Ressource optimal nutzen, 3rd Ed., Gabler, Wiesbaden, 1999

[Prockl 1998]

Prockl, G., Supply Chain Software, in: [Klaus/Krieger 1998]

[Pruijm 1990]

Pruijm, R.A.M., Corporate Strategy and Strategic Information Systems, Erasmus Universiteit Rotterdam, Samson BedrijfsInformatie, Alphen / R., 1990

[QED 1985]

QED, Strategic and Operational Planning for Information Systems, The Chanticotechnical Management Series, QED Information Sciences, Inc., Wellesley, 1985

[Raffeé 1993]

Raffeé, H., Gegenstand, Methoden und Konzepte der Betriebswirtschaftslehre, in: Bitz, M. Dellmann, K., Domsch, M., Egner, H. (Eds.), Vahlens Kompendium der Betrieswirtschaftslehre, Vahlen, München, pp. 1-46

[Reichwald et al. 1998]

Reichwald, R., Moeslein, K., Sachenbacher, H., Englberger, H., Oldenburg, S., Telekooperation: Verteilte Arbeits- und Organisationsformen, Springer, Berlin etc., 1998

[Reiter 1999]

Reiter, C.: Toolbasierte Referenzmodellierung – State-of-the-Art und Entwicklungstrends, in: Becker, J., Rosemann, M., Schütte, R. (Eds.), Referenzmodellierung, Physica, Heidelberg, 1999, pp. 45-68

[Reve 1990]
Reve, T., The Firm as a Nexus of Internal and External Contracts, in: Aoki, M., Gustafsson, B., Williamson, O. (Eds.), The Firm as a Nexus of Treaties, Sage, London, 1990, pp. 133-161

[Riedl 1991]
Riedl, R., Strategische Planung von Informationssystemen, Methode zur Entwicklung von langfristigen Konzepten für die Informationsverarbeitung, Physica, Heidelberg, 1991

[Riehm 1997]
Riehm, R., Integration von heterogenen Applikationen, Difo-Druck, Bamberg, 1997

[Riggs/Robbins 1998]
Rigggs, D.A., Robbins, S.L., The Executive's Guide to Supply Chain Management: Building Supply Chain Thinking into All Business Processes, Amacon, New York etc., 1998

[Rodin 1999]
Rodin, R., Hartmann, C., Free, Perfect, and Now, Connecting to the Three Insatiable Customer Demands: A CEO´s True Story, Simon & Schuster, New York, 1999

[Rolf 1998]
Rolf, A., Herausforderungen für die Wirtschaftsinformatik, in: Informatik-Spektrum, 21 (1998) 5, pp. 259-264

[Ruigrok et al. 1999]
Ruigrok, W., Pettigrew, A., Peck, S., Wittington, R., Corporate Restructuring and New Forms of Organizing: Evidence from Europe, in: Management International Review, 39 (1999) 2, pp. 41 - 64

[Sachs et al. 2000]
Sachs, M., Dan, A., Nguyen, T., Kearney, R., Shaikh, H., Dias, D., Executable Trading-Partner Agreements in Electronic Commerce, IBM T.J. Watson Research Center, New York, 2000

[Sager 2000]
Sager, I., Big Blue Gets Wired, in: Business Week, e.biz, April 3, 2000, pp. EB 56-58

[Sägesser 1999]
Sägesser, R., Outsourcing-Partnerschaften und unternehmensweite Business Excellence, in: HMD, 36 (1998) 206, pp. 19-29

[SAP 1998a]
SAP AG, Prozeßmodell, http://www.sap.com, 1998

[SAP 1998b]
SAP AG, SAP Business-to-Business Procurement, Whitepaper, Walldorf, http://www.sap.com, 1998

[SAP 1998c]
SAP AG, Advanced Planner & Optimizer, Product Whitepaper, Walldorf, 1998

[SAP 1999a]
SAP AG, SAP APO Installation Overview, Walldorf, 1999

[SAP 1999b]
SAP AG, Global ASAP, Version 1.0, CD-ROM, Juni 1999

[Sawyer 1998]
Sawyer, J., Europe's Internet Growth, Forrester Research, Cambridge (MA), 1998

[SCC 2000]
SCOR Metrics Level 1 Primer, White Paper, Supply Chain Council (SCC), http://www.supply-chain.org/members/html/wpaper.cfm, 18.10.2000

[Schary/Skjott-Larsen 1995]
Schary, P., Skjott-Larsen, T., Managing the Global Supply Chain, Copenhagen Studies in Economies and Management, Handelshojskolens Forlag, Kopenhagen, 1995

[Scheckenbach 1997]
Scheckenbach, R., Semantische Geschäftsprozeßintegration, Deutscher Universitäts-Verlag, Wiesbaden, 1997

[Scheer 1990a]
Scheer, A.-W., CIM - Computer Integrated Manufacturing: Towards the Factory of the Future, Springer, Berlin etc., 1990

[Scheer 1990b]
Scheer, A.-W., Modellierung betriebswirtschaftlicher Informationssysteme, in: Wirtschaftsinformatik, 31 (1990) 5, pp. 403-421

[Scheer 1995]
Scheer, A.-W., ARIS - Business Process Frameworks, Springer, Berlin etc., 1995

[Scheer 1998]
Scheer, A.-W., Supply Chain Management: ein unabsehbar weiter Markt, in: Information, Management & Consulting, 13 (1998) 3, pp. 3

[Schelle 1989]
Schelle, H., Kostenplanung und -kontrolle: ein Überblick, in: Reschke, H., Schelle, H., Schnopp, R. (Eds.), Handbuch Projektmanagement, TÜV Rheinland, Köln, 1989

[Scheller et al. 1994]
Scheller, M., Boden, K.P., Geenen, A., Kampermann, J., Internet: Werkzeuge und Dienste, Springer, Berlin etc., 1994

[Scheruhn 1997]
Scheruhn, H.-J., Einführung betrieblicher Anwendungssysteme, in: Klockhaus, E., Scheruhn, H.-J. (Eds.), Modellbasierte Einführung betrieblicher Anwendungssoftware, Gabler, Wiesbaden, 1997

[Schmid 1993]

Schmid, B., Elektronische Märkte, in: Wirtschaftsinformatik, 35 (1993) 5, pp. 465-480

[Schmid 1997]

Schmid, B., IKT als Träger einer neuen Industriellen Revolution, in: Schuh, G., Wiendahl, H.P. (Eds.), Komplexität und Agilität, Berlin, Heidelberg, Springer, pp. 103-117

[Schmid/Lindemann 1998]

Schmid, B., Lindemann, M., Elements of a Reference Model for Electronic Markets, in: Blanning, R.W., King, D.R. (Eds.), Proceedings of the 31st HICSS, Vol. IV, 1998, pp. 193-201

[Schmid et al. 1998]

Schmid, B., Selz, D., Sing, R. (Eds.), EM-Electronic Markets, Special Issue on Electronic Contracting, 8 (1998) 3

[Schmidt 1991]

Schmidt, G., Methoden und Techniken der Organisation, Band 1, Der Organisator, 9th Ed., Schmidt, Gießen, 1991

[Schnedl/Schweizer 1999]

Schnedl, W., Schweizer, M., Dynamische IT-Organisationen im nächsten Millenium, Thesis MBA-NDU, St. Gallen, 1999

[Schnitzler 1999]

Schnitzler, L., Aus der Portokasse, in: Wirtschaftswoche, No. 21, 20.5.1999, pp. 62-66

[Schögel et al. 1999]

Schögel, M., Birkhofer, B., Tomczak, T., Kooperative Leistungssysteme: Eigenschaften, Herausforderungen und Lösungsansätze, in: Thexis, 3(1999), pp. 10-16

[Scholz 1997]

Scholz, C., Strategische Organisation - Prinzipien zur Vitalisierung und Virtualisierung, Moderne Industrie, Landsberg/Lech, 1997

[Schuurmans/Stoller 1998]

Schuurmans, L., Stoller, C., Der Shared Service Center Trend, in: io management, 67 (1998) 6, pp. 37-41

[Schwarze 1998]

Schwarze, J., Informationsmanagement: Planung, Steuerung, Koordination und Kontrolle der Informationsversorgung im Unternehmen, Studienbücher Wirtschaftsinformatik, Herne, Berlin, 1998

[Schwarzer 1994]

Schwarzer, B., Prozessorientiertes Informationsmanagement in multinationalen Unternehmen: Eine empirische Untersuchung in der Pharmaindustrie, Gabler, Wiesbaden, 1994

[Schwede 1999]
Schwede, S., Nur im Doppelpack erfolgreich, in: Computerwoche, Nr. 11, 1999

[SCOR 1998]
Supply Chain Operations Reference-model (SCOR), Version 3, Supply Chain Council, Pittsburgh, PA, September 1998

[Segev et al. 1999]
Segev, A., Gebauer, J., Färber, F., Internet-based Electronic Markets, in: Electronic Markets, 9 (1999) 3. pp. 138-146

[Shaprio/Varian 1999]
Shaprio, C., Varian, H.R., Information Rules: A Strategic Guide to the Network Economy, Harvard Business School Press, Boston, 1999

[Shum 1997]
Shum, S.B., Representing Hard-to-Formalise Contextualised, Multidisciplinary Organisational Knowledge, AAAI Spring Symposium on Artificial Intelligence in Knowledge Management, Palo Alto, 1997

[Siebel 1996]
Siebel, T., Malone, M., Virtual Selling – Going Beyond the Automated Sales Force to Achieve Total Sales Quality, The Free Press, New York, 1996

[Simchi-Levi et al. 2000]
Simchi-Levi, D., Kaminsky, P., Simchi-Levi, E., Designing and Managing the Supply Chain: Concepts, Strategies, and Case Studies, Irwin/McGraw-Hill, Boston, 2000

[Skyrme/Abidon 1997]
Skyrme, D.J., Amidon, D., Creating the Knowledge-based Business, Business Intelligence Ltd., Wimbledon, 1997

[Skyway 1999]
Skyway, Supply Chain and Transportation Services, Santa Cruz, http://www.skyway. com, 10.7.1999

[Smith 1776]
Smith, A., An Inquiry Into the Nature and Causes of the Wealth of Nations, Strahan and Cadell, London, 1776

[Snow et al. 1992]
Snow, C., Miles, R., Coleman, H., Managing 21st Century Network Organization, in: Organizational Dynamics, 20 (1992) 3, pp. 5-20

[van der Spek/Spijkervet 1997]
van der Spek, R., Spijkervet, A., Knowledge Management: Dealing Intelligently with Knowledge, in: Liebowitz, J., Wilcox, L.C. (Eds.), Knowledge Management and its Integrative Elements, CRC Press, Boca Raton, 1997, pp. 31-59

[Steier et al. 1997]
Steier, D., Huffman, S., Kalish, D., Beyond Full-text Search: AI-based Technology to Support the Knowledge Cycle, in: AAAI Spring Symposium Artificial Intelligence in Knowledge Management, Palo Alto, 1997

[Stein 1997]
Stein, J., On Building and Leveraging Competences Across Organizational Borders: A Socio-cognitive Framework, in: Heene, A., Sanchez, R. (Eds.), Competence-based Strategic Management, Wiley & Sons, Chichester, 1997, pp. 267-284

[Stender/Schulz-Klein 1998]
Stender, M., Schulz-Klein, E., Internetbasierte Vertriebsinformationssysteme - Perspektiven moderner Informationssysteme für den Einsatz in Marketing, Vertrieb und Service, Fraunhofer IRM, Stuttgart, 1998

[Stepanek 2000]
Stepanek, M., Are You Web Smart?, in: Business Week, e.biz, September 18, 2000, pp. EB 24-26

[Stewart 1997]
Stewart, T.A., Intellectual Capital - The New Wealth of Organizations, Doubleday, New York, 1997

[Stickel et al. 1997]
Stickel, E., Groffmann, H.-D., Rau, K.-H., Gabler Wirtschaftsinformatik-Lexikon, Gabler, Wiesbaden, 1997

[Strack-Zimmermann 1998]
Strack-Zimmermann, H., E-Commerce Transaktionen mit SAP R/3, Presentation at the University of St. Gallen, 1.12.1998

[Strauss 1998]
Strauss, H., The Future of the Web, Intelligent Devices, and Education, Princeton University, http://webware.princeton.edu/howard/slides/future/, 1.6.1998

[Stüttgen 1999]
Stüttgen, M., Strategien der Komplexitätsbewältigung in Unternehmen: Ein transdisziplinärer Bezugsrahmen, Haupt, Bern, 1999

[Supply Chain Council 1998]
Supply Chain Council and the Supply Chain Operations Reference-model (SCOR), http://www.supply-chain.org, 1998

[Sydow 1992]
Sydow, J., Strategische Netzwerke, Gabler, Wiesbaden, 1992

[Syncra 1998]
Syncra Software Inc., QuickWin: Guide to Trading Partner Collaboration, 1998

[Szyperski/Klein 1993]
Szyperski, N., Klein, S., Informationslogistik und virtuelle Organisationen: Die Wechselwirkung von Informationslogistik und Netzwerkmodellen der Unternehmung, in: Die Betriebswirtschaft DBW, 53 (1993) 2, pp. 187-208

[Tapscott 1995]
Tapscott, D., The Digital Economy, McGraw-Hill, New York, 1995

[Teufel et al. 1999]
Teufel, T., Röhricht, J., Willems, P., SAP R/3 Prozeßanalyse mit Knowledge Maps: Von einem beschleunigten Business Engineering zum organisatorischen Wissensmanagement, Addison Wesley Longman, München, 1999

[Thiesse/Österle 2000]
Thiesse, F., Österle, H., Connected Smart Appliances: Intelligente Gebrauchsgegenstände erweitern die Möglichkeiten des Internets, in: io management, 69 (2000) 9, pp. 70-77

[Tibbetts 1995]
Tibbetts, K., Enterprise Architectures: A Comparison of Vendor Initiatives, IBM, http://www.software.ibm.com/openblue/kx95/cover.htm, 2.9.1998

[Turowski 1997]
Turowski, K., Flexible Verteilung von PPS-Systemen: Methodik Planungsobjektbasierter Softwareentwicklung, Gabler, Wiesbaden, 1997

[Ullmann 1997]
Ullmann, W., Orgwaregestützte Einführung von Triton/Baan IV, in: Klockhaus, E., Scheruhn, H.J. (Eds.), Modellbasierte Einführung betrieblicher Anwendungssoftware, Gabler, Wiesbaden, 1997

[Ulrich 1984]
Ulrich, H., Management, Haupt, Bern, 1984

[Varian 1994]
Varian, H.R., The Information Economy: The Economics of the Internet, Information Goods, Intellectual Property and Related Issues, http://www.sims.berkeley.edu/resources/infoecon/, 1.2.1999

[Venkatraman 1991]
Venkatraman, N., IT-induced Business Reconfiguration, in: Scott Morton, M.S. (Ed.), The Corporation of the 1990's: Information Technology and Organizational Transformation, Mc Graw Hill, New York, pp. 122-158

[Venkatraman/Henderson 1998]
Venkatraman, N., Henderson, J.C., Real Strategies for Virtual Organizing, in: Sloan Management Review, 40 (1998) 1, pp. 33-48

[VICS 1998]
VICS - Voluntary Interindustry Commerce Standards, CPFR Collaborative Planning, Forecasting, and Replenishment, Voluntary Guidelines, http://www.vics.org, 1998

[Walker 1994]
Walker, M., Quick Response: The Road to Lean Logistics, in: Cooper, J. (Ed.), Logistics and Distribution Planning: Strategies for Management, Kogan Page, London 1994, pp. 207-219

[Wall 1996]
Wall, F., Organisation und betriebliche Informationssysteme: Elemente einer Konstruktionstheorie, Gabler, Wiesbaden, 1996

[Ware/Degoey 1998]
Ware, J., Degoey, P., Knowledge Work and Information Technology, Working Paper #98-WP-1028, Fisher Center for Management and Information Technology, University of California, Berkeley, 1998

[Westkämper/Wildemann 1993]
Westkämper, E, Wildemann, H., Make or Buy & Insourcing, Transfer-Centrum für Produktions-Logistik und Technologie-Management München, Technische Universität München, 1993

[Wexelblat/Srinivasan 1999]
Wexelblat, R.L., Srinivasan, N., Planning for Information Technology in a Federated Organization, in: Information & Management, 35 (1999) 5, pp. 265-282

[Wigand 1997]
Wigand, R.T., Electronic Commerce: Definition, Theory, and Context, in: The Information Society, (1997) 13, pp.1-16

[Wigand et al. 1997]
Wigand, R.T., Picot, A., Reichwald, R., Information, Organization and Management, Wiley & Sons, Chichester, 1997

[Wildemann 1994]
Wildemann, H., Die modulare Fabrik: Kundennahe Produktion durch Fertigungssegmentierung, TCW-Transfer-Centrum GmbH, München, 1994

[Williamson 1985]
Williamson, O.E., The Economic Institutions of Capitalism: Firms, Markets, Relational Contracting, The Free Press, New York, 1985

[Williamson 1989]
Williamson, O.E., Transaction Cost Economics, in: Schmalensee, R., Willig, R.D. (Eds.), Handbook of Industrial Organization, Elsevier Science Publishing, Amsterdam, 1989, pp. 135-182

[Williamson 1991]

Williamson, O.E., Comparative Economic Organization: The Analysis of Discrete Structural Alternatives, in: Administrative Science Quarterly, (1991) 36, pp. 269-296

[Winter 1991]

Winter, R., Mehrstufige Produktionsplanung in Abstraktionshierachien auf der Basis relationaler Informationsstrukturen, Springer, Berlin et. al., 1991

[Winter 1998]

Winter, R., Informationsableitung in betrieblichen Anwendungssystemen, Vieweg, Braunschweig etc., 1998

[Zbornik 1996]

Zbornik, S., Elektronische Märkte, elektronische Hierarchien und elektronische Netzwerke, Universitäts-Verlag Konstanz, Konstanz, 1996

[Zerdick et al. 1999]

Zerdick, A., Picot, A., Schrape, K., Artopé, A., Goldhammer, K., Lange, U.T., Vierkant, E., López-Escobar, E., Silverstone, R., Die Internet-Ökonomie: Strategien für die digitale Wirtschaft, European Communication Council Report, Springer, Berlin etc., 1999

Index

A

Accelerated SAP
  (ASAP) 48, 217,
  266, 293, 294
Account
  Management 58,
  147
Action Research
  Guidelines 10
Adaptec 104, 105
Adapters 198, 236,
  240, 241
Adoption 206, 209,
  250, 251, 255, 264
ADP 38, 167, 171
Advanced Planner
  and Optimizer
  (APO) 118, 172,
  189, 253, 276, 293
Advanced Planning
  and Scheduling
  (APS) 170, 171,
  172, 176, 335
Advanced Planning
  and Scheduling
  (APS) System
  181, 183, 185,
  253, 276, 292,
  295, 335
AFB Software 97
After-market 97,
  103
After-sales 99, 100,
  102, 107, 108,
  109, 115, 156,
  167, 172
Agents 125
Alignment 130
Alliances 20, 156,
  199

Altavista 101
Amazon.com 3, 59,
  164, 212
Amoco 38, 231
AOL 40, 61, 95
Application
  Architecture 155,
  157, 164, 166,
  170, 200, 266,
  305, 313, 314,
  321, 335
Application Link
  Enabling (ALE)
  253, 313, 314
Application
  Programming
  Interface (API)
  39, 201, 202, 207,
  208, 263
Application-to-
  Application (A2A)
  236, 240, 241, 242
Approval 163, 196,
  219
Archiving 150, 172
Ariba 40, 64, 65, 66,
  97, 101, 117, 198,
  199, 201, 206, 209
Arpanet 214
Artificial Intelligence
  28
Assembler 125, 147,
  156
Assemble-to-Order
  335
Asset Management
  73, 177
Asymmetric Digital
  Subscriber Line
  (ADSL) 34, 40

Atomicy,
  Consistency,
  Isolation,
  Durability (ACID)
  244
Atomistic 107
Auction 37, 84, 99,
  110, 122, 128,
  200, 202, 231,
  234, 235, 237,
  239, 240, 244,
  245, 253
Authentication 245,
  263
Authorization 200,
  203, 204, 219,
  221, 263
Authorization
  Workflow 203
AutoBild 30, 46, 97,
  98
AutoByTel 46
Automation 86, 149,
  150
Automotive Sector
  4, 18, 36, 47, 95,
  97, 158, 189, 220,
  230, 235, 254
Available-to-Promise
  (ATP) 123, 184,
  186, 259, 335
Aventis 235
Avnet Marshall 47,
  49, 61, 107

B

Baan 187, 194, 207,
  212, 214, 252
Backbone 117
Backlogs 103
Backoffice 107, 139

Banks 18, 65, 93, 107, 139, 140
BASF 231
Basic Standards 245
Batch Processing 181, 183
Bayer 12
BBC 33
Benchmarking 190
Benefits 105, 118, 127, 130, 177, 209, 225, 231, 232, 239, 260, 268
Best-of-breed 26
Beverage Industry 114
Bidding 231, 237, 239, 244, 245
Billing 102, 163, 181, 189
BizTalk 39, 40
Blancpain 124
Blaupunkt 103, 109
Bloomberg 33
Bluetooth 34
BMEcat 233
Boeing 29
Bolero 4
Book Industry 59
Bosch 12, 103, 216, 217, 220, 221, 222
Branding 21, 124, 125, 127, 130, 133, 256
Break-even 209
British Petroleum (BP) 38, 231
Broadband 34, 75
Broker 160
Browser 127, 129, 199, 200, 201, 202
BSI 213
Bullwhip Effect 254

Bundling 82, 106, 203, 208
Bureaucracy 197
Business Application Programming Interface (BAPI) 39, 40, 208
Business Bus 4, 39, 40, 118, 160, 233, 244, 246
Business Concept 87
Business Engineering 11, 19, 138, 253
Business Engineering Model 267, 290
Business Forecasting 182
Business Guidelines 171
Business Knowledge Management (BKM) 138
Business Model 19, 84, 95, 117, 119, 156, 157, 159, 160, 161, 162, 163, 164, 173, 230, 236, 267, 336
Business Network 84, 96, 119, 124, 131, 152, 180, 253, 255, 260, 261
Business Network Redesign (BNR) 12
Business Network Structure 114
Business Networking 1, 2, 36, 111, 336
Business Networking Benefit 115

Business Networking Cases 57, 129
Business Networking Development 4
Business Networking Framework 6
Business Networking Goals 266, 325
Business Networking Infrastructure 118
Business Networking Method 244, 265, 267, 268, 270, 280, 289
Business Networking Model 37, 41, 119, 232, 234, 239, 243, 327, 328
Business Networking Phases 2
Business Networking Process 291
Business Networking Project 264
Business Networking Requirements 221, 255
Business Networking Services 44
Business Networking Solution 156
Business Networking Strategies 89, 90, 99, 100, 109, 122, 133, 266, 290
Business Networking System (BNS) 2, 118, 194, 230, 249, 250, 251, 253, 254, 292, 326, 336
Business Networking Vision 113, 114

Business Process 69,
    75, 142, 144, 145,
    150, 239
Business Process
    Redesign (BPR)
    5, 27, 71, 143,
    163, 180, 194,
    267, 268
Business
    Relationship 70,
    78, 80, 81, 82,
    258, 259, 266
Business Strategy
    252
Business-to-Business
    (B2B) 22, 47, 63,
    97, 101, 109, 124,
    133, 189, 250, 293
Business-to-
    Consumer (B2C)
    101, 189, 204
BuyerXpert 66, 199
Buying Process 152
Buy-side Electronic
    Commerce
    (eProcurement)
    37, 40, 102, 122,
    206, 271, 272, 338
BuySite 66, 199

C

Call Center
    Management 147
Capacity Planning
    105, 106
Capacity
    Requirements
    Planning (CRP)
    182, 183
CAPS 187
Car Dealer 20
Cargo 251
CarPoint 46
Case Study 124, 139

Cash-to-cash 115
Catalog 65, 97, 107,
    129, 200, 201, 237
Catalog Interchange
    Format (CIF) 198,
    206, 263
Catalogic 238
Category
    Management
    (CM) 336
CC iBN 11, 12, 220,
    266, 270
Celanese 231
Centralization 75,
    76, 77, 86, 95,
    106, 123, 127,
    128, 142, 157,
    161, 195, 196,
    197, 203, 217,
    220, 227, 240
Certina 124
Change Management
    23, 260
Charles Schwab 30
ChemConnect 230,
    231
Chemical Industry
    230, 231
Chemplorer 231
Chevron 206, 209
Chief Executive
    Officer (CEO) 45,
    76
Chief Information
    Officer (CIO) 68,
    224, 251
Cisco 37, 38, 47, 90,
    122, 129, 130,
    156, 209
ClickPlastics 237
Client-server 252
Code Division
    Multiple Access
    (CDMA) 34

Collaboration 20,
    24, 44, 186, 189,
    190, 191, 243, 254
Collaborative
    Planning
    Forecasting and
    Replenishment
    (CPFR) 39, 82,
    189, 191, 233,
    278, 337
Commerce Extended
    Markup Language
    (cXML) 39, 233,
    242, 245
Commerce Network
    199
CommerceXpert
    199
Commodity 200,
    203
Common Coding
    System (CCS)
    205
Commtech 67, 256,
    257, 258, 259,
    261, 264
Communication
    Model 214, 215,
    232
Communication
    Protocol 200, 241
Communication
    Standards 80, 82,
    83, 215, 232, 244
Communication
    Technology 103,
    109, 220
Community 50, 56,
    62, 76, 101, 102,
    107, 110, 128,
    133, 158, 212,
    213, 216, 220,
    250, 251
Compaq 47, 90, 262

Competence Center
11, 12, 13, 138
Complaint
Management 109,
128
Componentization
18, 164, 170, 171,
185, 201
CompoNET 237,
238
Computer Aided
Design (CAD)
167, 230, 237
Computer Aided
Software
Engineering
(CASE) 217
Computer Integrated
Logistics (CIL)
101
Computer Integrated
Manufacturing
(CIM) 176, 191
Computerization 3,
75
Concerto 90
Configuration 200,
219, 220, 226,
236, 240, 241, 267
Configurator 150
Conflict
Management
System 80
Consors 48
Construction Method
158
Content and Catalog
Management 64,
198, 201, 273
Content Management
199, 200, 204, 206
Continuous
Replenishment
(CRP) 106, 336

Contract
Management 146
Convergence 127,
158, 250
Conversation Model
244
Cooperation 5, 41,
66, 95, 98, 108,
109, 114, 118,
232, 234, 268,
270, 274, 277,
281, 284, 337
Coordination 4, 70,
71, 72, 117, 147,
183, 195, 231,
252, 256, 270,
307, 337
Coordination
Technology 72
Core Competence
36, 90, 91, 92, 93,
94, 96, 97, 98,
113, 141, 156,
272, 328, 337,
341, 344
Corporate
Management 24
Cost/benefit 79, 133
Critical Mass 20, 50,
116, 231, 251,
263, 292, 327
Critical Success
Factor 129
Crossdocking 106,
337
Culture 77, 79
Customer Buying
Cycle 148
Customer Centricity
45, 48, 136, 163
Customer
Management 191
Customer
Orientation 83,

107, 124, 136,
139, 164, 179
Customer Process
24
Customer Process
Support 45, 49
Customer Profiling
152
Customer
Relationship 107,
114, 125, 128,
136, 152, 257, 270
Customer
Relationship
Management
(CRM) 57, 59, 61,
62, 72, 99, 107,
109, 135, 143,
163, 170, 172, 337
Customer
Relationship
Management
(CRM) Model
144
Customer
Relationship
Management
(CRM) Processes
147
Customer Resource
Life Cycle
(CRLC) 338
Customer Value 136
Customization 26,
74, 82, 83, 100,
105, 107, 114,
172, 217, 219,
221, 222, 233
Cycle Time 338

D

DaimlerChrysler 13,
36, 95, 231
Danzas 46, 94

Data Communication 39
Data Model 263
Data Standards 82, 245
Data Warehouse 52, 149, 150, 164, 168, 170, 172, 173, 186, 252
Database Management System (DMS) 26, 43
DCA/DIA 214
Debis 18
Decentralization 67, 117, 168, 227
Decision Support System (DSS) 170, 184
DECNet 214
Dell 57
Delphi 144
Demand Management 182, 190
Demand Planning 90, 106, 167, 186
Desktop Purchasing 167, 198
Desktop Purchasing System (DPS) 63, 194, 197, 198, 199, 200, 201, 202, 203, 204, 205, 207, 208, 209, 230, 338
Deutsche Telekom 12, 272
Diamond Multimedia Systems 90, 91
Diffusion 133, 212, 214, 233, 251, 261, 262

Digital Versatile Disc (DVD) 42
Digitalization 32, 33, 82, 163
Disintegration 2
Distribution 124, 125, 161
Distribution Channel 250
Distribution Network 125, 126, 186
Distribution Planning 186
Distribution Requirements Planning (DRP) 182
Document Interchange 245
Document Management 150, 168
Document Management System (DMS) 149
DOMA 190
Drill-down 212, 259
Dun & Bradstreet 94, 205, 215, 216, 263

E

Eastman 231
eBusiness 56, 230, 234, 240, 246, 252
eCash 101, 118
eClass 232, 233
Ecology 119
ECXpert 199
EDI Platform 163
EDIINT 200

Education News and Entertainment Network 62
Efficient Consumer Response (ECR) 172, 338
Efficient Replenishment (ER) 338
Electronic Business Process Optimization (eBPO) 189
Electronic Commerce (EC) 99, 101, 102, 109, 121, 124, 132, 151, 193, 256, 338
Electronic Commerce (EC) System 72, 199, 252, 338
Electronic Commerce Network (ECN) 206
Electronic Data Interchange (EDI) 65, 163, 214, 250, 339
Electronic Data Interchange for Administration, Commerce and Trade (EDIFACT) 39, 166, 215
Electronic Market (eMarket) 22, 63, 93, 229, 230, 231, 234, 246, 251, 255, 329, 339
Electronic Payment (ePayment) 204

Electronic Platform
91
Electronic
Procurement
(eProcurement)
230, 232, 293, 339
Electronic Service
(eService) 24, 43,
75, 163, 229, 328,
339
eLink 236, 240, 241,
242
emagine 13
eMail 44, 151, 160,
203, 208
Enabler 2, 212, 250,
260
Enba 95, 96
Enterprise
Application
Integration (EAI)
75, 236
Enterprise Resource
Management 25
Enterprise Resource
Planning (ERP)
24, 116, 123, 163,
170, 180, 194,
207, 216, 217,
230, 253, 254
Enterprise Resource
Planning (ERP)
Modules 123
Enterprise Resource
Planning (ERP)
System 73, 212,
339
ERP@Web 80
eSpeak 230
e-Steel 37
ETA SA 12, 124,
129, 256, 324
eTrade 37, 48
Euro-Log 106

European Article
Number (EAN)
215, 232
Excite 61
Executive
Information
System (EIS) 167,
170, 172, 173
Experian 30
Expertise Network
161
Extended Supply
Chain 104, 250,
256, 257, 266
Extr@Net 103

F

F. Hoffmann-La
Roche 12
FAQs 110, 128
FDX Corporation 76
FedEx 33, 35, 46,
106
File Transfer
Protocol (FTP)
214
Filter 151, 241
Final Assembly
Scheduling (FAS)
182
Finance 25, 48, 94,
95, 98, 101, 104,
129, 140, 161,
167, 200, 212,
220, 226, 227,
232, 253, 254
Finance System 262
Financial Indicator
141
Financial
Management 51
Financial Planning
182

Financial Process
172
Finite Capacity
Planning (FCP)
190
Flexibility 81, 98,
108, 112, 165,
178, 233, 236
Flow Perspective
104
Food and Drug
Administration
(FDA) 163
Ford 36, 231
Forecast 104, 114,
183, 186, 189,
227, 235, 250,
254, 257
Framework 77, 78,
91, 97, 138, 204,
236, 270
Freight 97, 186
Frequency 101, 116,
125, 156, 194,
200, 204, 205,
207, 208, 217,
242, 254, 267, 270
Front-office 137
Fulfillment 90, 102,
115, 130, 151,
171, 173, 177,
244, 255

G

Gateway 84
GEIS 200, 206, 216
Generic SCOR
Process 131, 176
Getzner Textil 24
Global Positioning
System (GPS) 3,
24, 32, 34, 70
Global Sourcing
106, 340, 343

Globalization 18,
    113, 139, 156,
    157, 165, 225
Goals 77, 83, 90, 92,
    100, 115, 141,
    263, 266, 270
Governance 117,
    227, 250, 254
Government 159
Grainger 102, 103,
    109
Granularity 56
Grenley Stewart
    Resources (GSR)
    33
Groupware 29, 142,
    172
GSM-net 32, 34

H

Harbinger 18, 65,
    164, 200, 206
Harmonization 85,
    257, 260, 263
Health Care 158,
    159, 161, 162, 163
Heineken 165
Helpdesk 63, 236,
    240
Henkel 12
Heterogeneity 30,
    99, 143, 151, 164,
    166, 171, 172,
    186, 212, 213,
    244, 269
Hewlett-Packard 12,
    90, 93, 230
Hierarchical
    Network 261
Hierarchy 56, 83,
    93, 95, 101, 132,
    201, 202, 205,
    228, 244, 254, 270

High-tech Sector
    188
HiServ 12, 235
Homogeneity 81,
    126, 128
HotMail 44
Hybrid 93, 270
Hypertext Markup
    Language
    (HTML) 39, 166,
    200, 212
Hypertext Transfer
    Protocol (HTTP)
    245, 263

I

I2 Technologies
    117, 123, 164,
    172, 187, 188,
    189, 253
IBM 213, 214, 230,
    243, 244
Implementation 97,
    110, 118, 127,
    129, 139, 157,
    200, 212, 216, 233
Implementation
    Guide 218
Implicit Knowledge
    29, 31
Incentive 71, 130,
    133, 227
Indirect Goods 63,
    65, 193, 194, 195,
    197, 200
Individualization 32,
    76, 128, 140, 206,
    233
I-Net-Logistics 230
Information Age 17,
    160, 164
Information
    Management 12,
    100, 114, 124,

138, 220, 255,
    256, 257, 261
Information System
    (IS) 71, 80, 142,
    146, 153, 175,
    207, 208, 235, 340
Information
    Technology (IT)
    3, 77, 100, 151,
    157, 165, 176,
    191, 250, 268, 340
Infrastructure 40,
    73, 118, 150, 230
Inquiry 98, 112,
    195, 240, 256
Inside-out 201
Insourcing 92, 94,
    96, 97, 98, 109,
    290, 341
Institutional
    Economy 4
Insurance 98, 162
Integration 71, 112,
    113, 124, 165,
    181, 207, 215,
    230, 232, 234,
    250, 340
Integration Service
    43, 230, 246
Integrator 37, 38,
    106
Integrity 118, 129,
    225
Intel 38, 197
Intelligence 151,
    163, 255
Interaction 102, 110,
    123, 172, 184,
    214, 243, 244,
    246, 255
Interchange 125,
    127, 129, 130,
    198, 250, 263

Inter-company 79,
    252
Interconnectivity
    212, 214
Interface 108, 118,
    140, 158, 163,
    164, 194, 198,
    200, 201, 202,
    212, 230, 233,
    236, 241, 246
Interface Standards
    230
Intermediary 37, 38,
    39, 47, 114, 204,
    205, 232, 233, 239
Intermediation 22,
    131, 201, 203, 253
Internal Network 83,
    84, 85, 93, 161
Internet 2, 34, 39,
    86, 90, 95, 97,
    103, 112, 136,
    151, 152, 156,
    161, 163, 166,
    172, 189, 190,
    191, 194, 197,
    199, 208, 214,
    231, 233, 236,
    258, 259
Internet Age 19
Internet Application
    136
Internet Banking 18,
    93
Internet Protocol (IP)
    214
Internet Standards
    212
Internet Technology
    252
Interoperability 104
Inter-organizational
    71, 73, 74, 81, 82,
    93, 131, 165, 176,

179, 183, 184,
    190, 215, 250,
    251, 252, 254, 262
Intershop 253
Intranet 29, 107,
    156, 200
Intranet Application
    139
Intranet Technology
    252
Intra-organizational
    73, 74, 178, 180,
    252
Inventory Level 38,
    105, 117, 208,
    262, 276, 292
Inventory
    Management 38,
    97, 167, 171, 261
Invoicing 96, 102,
    105, 180, 195,
    203, 215
IS/IT Domain 165
IS/IT Level 157
IS/IT Project 165,
    173, 208
IS/IT View 159
ISO/OSI Model 214,
    215
IT Industry 164
IT Infrastructure 232
IT Outsourcing 94
IT Planning 252
IT Platform 96, 241

J

JD Edwards 187,
    188, 190
Just-in-Time (JIT)
    341

K

Key Performance
    Indicator 18, 23,
    24, 30, 51
Key Success Factor
    247, 249, 255
Killer Application
    40
Knowledge Category
    148
Knowledge
    Exchange 81
Knowledge Flow
    145
Knowledge
    Infrastructure
    145, 150
Knowledge
    Management
    (KM) 24, 28, 138,
    141, 142, 143,
    144, 152, 163,
    170, 172
Knowledge
    Management
    Model 29
Knowledge
    Measurement
    145, 151
Knowledge
    Repository 149,
    151
Knowledge Roles
    151
Knowledge Service
    236
Knowledge Structure
    148, 151
Knowledge Transfer
    269
Knowledge Value
    Measurement 31
Knowledge Work
    143

L

Life Cycle Planning 106
Local Area Network (LAN) 166
Localization 179, 186, 218, 219, 222, 225, 226, 227, 266
Logistics 38, 76, 90, 94, 101, 104, 105, 106, 114, 116, 122, 129, 202, 208, 230, 232, 235, 256, 341
Logistics Network 176
Logistics Service 61
Loyalty 62, 114, 115, 142, 143

M

Macro Process 145
Macrodesign 268
Made-to-Order 131
Maintenance, Repair and Operations (MRO) 65, 97, 102, 194, 197, 237, 341
Make-or-Buy 106, 168
Make-to-Order 106
Make-to-Stock 106
Management Skills 53
Management Trends 157, 250
Manufacturing Resource Planning (MRP II) 176, 181, 182, 183, 184, 194, 341

Manugistics 117, 123, 164, 172, 187, 188, 189, 253, 268
Market Capitalization 18
Market Orientation 78
Market Power 109
Market Research 98, 139, 140, 148, 172
Market Segment 81, 94, 102, 146
Market Services 18, 160
Market Share 50
Marketing 94, 99, 107, 122, 130, 132, 133, 137, 142, 145, 146, 150, 152, 159, 161, 172, 261, 262, 263
Marketing Process 107
MarketSite.net 63
Mass Customization 342
Master Data Management 73, 129, 130, 164, 170, 171, 173
Master Data Standards 215
Master Production Scheduling (MPS) 182
Mastercard 209
Material Planning 186
Material Requirements Planning (MRP I) 176, 181, 182, 342

Materials Management 25, 122, 194
Measurement 18, 52, 79, 83, 84, 91, 94, 115, 122, 132, 139, 141, 151, 191, 232, 237, 267, 268
Mental Model 10
Merger 18, 95, 163, 165, 230, 235
Message Brokering 245
Messaging 43, 166, 190, 241, 242
Meta Model 201, 206, 263, 267, 269, 282
Meta Network 199
Metadata 64
Method 341
Method Engineering 220, 267, 268, 269, 281, 319
Methodology 11
Metrics 115, 131, 133, 268
Micro Compact Car (MCC) 36
Microdesign 268
Micropayments 75
Microprocesses 117
Microsoft 39, 40, 168, 199, 213
Middleware 34, 39, 189, 235, 236, 241, 242, 243
Migration Planning 53
Migros 66
Miniaturization 32
MLP 42

Mobile
  Communication
  34
Modeling 131
Modularity 26, 71,
  80, 82, 83, 84, 97,
  233, 259, 263
Module 164, 167,
  176, 180, 181,
  185, 186, 189,
  190, 250
Monitoring 80, 107,
  112, 128, 146,
  151, 164, 232,
  244, 245
Motion Picture
  Expert Group
  (MPEG) 35
MP3 35, 90
MQSeries 244
MRO Procurement
  37, 40, 82, 97,
  194, 197
Multi-channel 152
Multidimensional
  Management 53
Multi-eMarket
  Integration 235
Multimedia 90, 205,
  237
Multi-mode Access
  32
Multinational 166,
  212, 217, 219,
  225, 227
Multi-protocol 97,
  237
Multitude 200
Multi-vendor
  Product Catalog
  38, 39, 40, 84,
  101, 109, 198,
  200, 201, 202,

205, 206, 207,
  237, 263
MySap.com 40, 65,
  78, 230

N

Negotiation 112,
  123, 200, 201,
  202, 206, 208,
  216, 244
Netscape 66, 117,
  197, 198, 199, 262
Network Design 71
Network
  Management 252
Network Partner 70,
  78
Network Provider
  118
Network Topology
  83
Networkability 5,
  22, 42, 77, 78, 79,
  80, 81, 83, 84, 86,
  342
Networked
  Appliance 32
Networked Economy
  2, 162, 250
Networked
  Enterprise 2, 55,
  75, 76, 77, 84, 85,
  86, 305
Networked
  Enterprise Model
  56, 57, 75, 76, 84,
  85, 86
Networked
  Organization 93
New Economy 2,
  234
New Market 20, 98
Newsgroup 63

Newtron 234, 235,
  237, 238, 239,
  241, 242, 245
Niche Market 44
Numerix 187, 188,
  190

O

OBI 82, 200, 245
Object 70, 76, 80,
  83, 166, 213
Omega 124
One-stop 49
One-to-One
  Marketing 20
Online Bookshop
  42, 59
Online Buying
  Center 102
Online Pharmacy
  162
Online Service
  System 62
Open Application
  Group Integration
  Specification
  (OAGIS) 39
Open Application
  Group Middleware
  Api Standard
  (OAMAS) 39
Operating Resource
  Management
  System (ORMS)
  66, 97, 199
Oracle 40, 194, 198,
  207, 252
Order 102, 104, 112,
  123, 126, 128, 156
Order Management
  90
Order Management
  System 262

Order Processing
108
Order Tracking 60
OrderZone 102
Organization 70, 75,
79, 196, 253, 270
Organization
Strategy 92, 98
Organization Theory
4, 93
Outside-in 200
Outsourcing 22, 44,
77, 80, 90, 91, 92,
93, 94, 97, 99,
113, 114, 118,
165, 208, 230,
232, 233, 236,
246, 262, 290, 342

P

PalmPilot 33
Partner Management
115, 259
Partnering 2, 19, 20,
56, 79, 92, 98, 99,
108, 117, 131,
230, 259, 270
PartnerNet 107
Pay-back 44
Payment 74, 80,
101, 102, 114,
127, 129, 133,
160, 204, 257,
261, 263
Payment Process
123
PayNet 101
Payroll 38, 44, 73,
97, 99, 118, 167,
171
Peoplesoft 187, 212
Performance 70, 73,
94, 102, 104, 106,
115, 123, 125,

129, 131, 132,
133, 138, 151,
156, 180, 186,
188, 206, 216,
220, 233, 255
Performance
Indicator 53, 204,
299
Personal Digital
Assistant (PDA)
33, 34
Personalization 78,
158, 204
Pervasive 166, 216
Pfizer 163
Pharmaceutical
Industry 36, 155,
159, 160, 161,
162, 225, 235
Phase Model 101,
142
Pilot 127, 132, 198,
202, 208, 216,
227, 264
PlanetRx 162
Planning 106, 114,
146, 212, 253, 261
Planning Data 84,
116, 181, 254, 257
Planning Horizon
179
Planning Process
124, 131, 176,
178, 179
Planning System
180, 181, 190
Planning Tool 117,
176
Plant Management
224
Platform Provider
236
Point of Sale (POS)
106

PointCast 30, 40
Policy 156
Portable Device 90
Portal 30, 43, 342
Portfolio 139, 173
Portfolio
Management 53,
147
Postponement 82,
342
Potential 71, 78, 85,
92, 104, 105, 113,
122, 124, 125,
130, 132, 163,
189, 191, 194,
208, 209, 246,
254, 267
Pragmatic 82, 143,
215, 216, 232,
245, 246
Pragmatic Standards
76
Pre-sales 107
Pricing 104, 129,
270
Procedure 73, 76,
102, 117, 124,
133, 140, 190,
202, 208, 218,
222, 245, 260,
263, 267
Procedure Model
133, 220, 268,
270, 283, 320
Process 107, 108,
123, 124, 144,
178, 196
Process Efficiency
22
Process Integration
83
Process Knowledge
254

Process
  Measurement 52
Process Model 70,
  99, 145
Process Network 36,
  40, 85, 131, 132,
  269
Process Optimization
  27
Process Performance
  136
Process Portal 291,
  328, 343
Process Standards
  27, 83, 215, 245,
  280
Process-orientation
  6, 10, 76, 144,
  176, 212
Procurement 81,
  102, 231, 232, 272
Product and Sales
  Planning (PSP)
  182
Product Centricity
  136
Product Data
  Management 167
Product Life Cycle
  Management 189
Product Management
  139, 140, 147
Product-centered 45,
  136
Product-driven 139
Production 25, 104,
  177, 181
Production Activity
  Control (PAC)
  182
Production and
  Distribution
  Planning 38

Production and Sales
  Planning (PSP)
  182
Production Planning
  106, 167, 178,
  182, 186, 188,
  194, 262
Productivity 177
Profitability 74, 107,
  159, 186
Project Method 86
Project Planning 145
Proprietary Network
  166
Protocols 236, 242,
  263
Prototype 240
PublishingXpert 199
Purchase Order 181,
  194, 200, 240
Purchase Requisition
  65, 196, 197, 200,
  202, 203, 204, 207
Purchasing and
  Material
  Management 38
Purchasing Process
  200

Q

Quality Management
  149
Quasi-externalization
  93
Quasi-internalization
  93
Quick Response
  (QR) 106, 343
Quotation 76, 180,
  196, 240

R

Rado 124
Real-life Assets 330
Real-time 26, 34,
  61, 64, 82, 98,
  105, 163, 186,
  201, 207, 208,
  212, 254
Receipt 160, 176,
  203
Reciprocity 81, 133,
  260, 262
Recoverability 11
Redesign 72, 80,
  101, 124, 133,
  136, 138, 194,
  250, 256, 268, 269
Reference Model
  138, 144, 145,
  148, 208
Regionalization 159
Relationship
  Management 72,
  74, 77, 81, 85, 86,
  110
Relationship
  Marketing 142,
  143
Reliability 124, 208
Renault 231
Reorganization 261,
  263
Repository 137, 148,
  216
Requests for Bid
  (RFB) 231, 234,
  235, 237, 239, 240
Requests for
  Quotation (RFQ)
  202
Requirements
  Planning 167, 189

Research &
  Development
  (R&D) 104, 161,
  162, 163
Research Method 11
Resource
  Requirements
  Planning (RRP)
  182
Resource-based 93
Resource-oriented
  141
Responsiveness 189
Retailer 51, 104,
  112, 131, 176,
  178, 183
Retention 143, 238,
  263
Return on Assets
  (ROA) 176, 177,
  178, 179, 183
Return on
  Investment (ROI)
  112, 116, 198
Reverse Engineering
  3
Rhythm 187, 188
RIO Music Player
  90, 91
Riverwood
  International
  (RWI) 12, 81,
  111, 256, 275, 278
Road-pricing 32
Role Model 283
Roll-out 132, 218,
  219, 222, 224
RosettaNet 39, 233,
  242, 245
Rough Cut Capacity
  Planning (RCRP)
  182
Royal Nedlloyd 94
RSA 245, 263

S

SABRE 41
Sales Force
  Automation (SFA)
  150, 163, 171, 173
Sales Force
  Management 147
Sales Planning 147
Sales Process 107,
  139
SAP AG 12, 13, 25,
  40, 48, 62, 107,
  189, 289
SAP Business
  Warehouse 168
SAP Business-to-
  Business (B2B)
  66
SAP R/2 117
SAP R/3 25, 63, 65,
  117, 118, 189,
  194, 205, 207,
  208, 212, 217,
  218, 220, 221,
  224, 225, 239
SAP R/3 FI 167,
  226
SAP R/3 MM 167,
  180, 226, 237,
  240, 241
SAP R/3 PP 167,
  226
SAP R/3 SD 167,
  180, 226, 237, 240
SCOR Processes
  185, 186
Secure Sockets
  Layer (SSL) 245,
  263
Security 118, 130,
  158, 199, 233,
  242, 243, 245, 263
SellerXpert 199

Sell-side Electronic
  Commerce
  (eSales) 37, 40,
  102, 103, 122, 338
Semantic 40, 82,
  208, 215, 216,
  217, 232, 233,
  244, 245, 246,
  257, 263
Semantic Standards
  76, 217, 232, 233
Serlog 65
Service Architecture
  266
Service Integrator
  46, 48, 49, 327
Service Planning
  147
Service Provider 35
Shareholder Value
  23, 51
ShareNet 163
Shipment 90, 102,
  110, 116, 129,
  176, 186, 258, 259
Short Message
  Service (SMS) 32
Siebel 18, 27, 40,
  137, 138, 150,
  164, 172
Simple Mail Transfer
  Protocol (SMTP)
  166, 214, 245
Simultaneous
  Planning 184
Single Sourcing 343
Single-Point-of-
  Contact 184
Skills 23, 191
Smart Appliances
  24, 32, 330
SmartMoney 48
SNA 214

Stakeholder 264,
  294, 295
Stakeholder Value
  51
Standard Application
  233
Standard Generalized
  Markup Language
  (SGML) 39
Standard Product and
  Services Code
  (SPSC) 205, 206,
  263
Standardization 83,
  166, 168, 211,
  213, 215, 245,
  257, 260
Standards 28, 64,
  75, 76, 86, 166,
  170, 213, 255, 262
Start-up 18, 95, 198,
  238
Stock Management
  180
Stock Value 95
Stockkeeping 82,
  125
Strategic Blueprint
  165, 173
Strategic
  Management 91,
  132
Strategic Network
  93
Strategic Planning
  185
Strategy 77, 91, 124,
  136, 141, 236,
  253, 267
Sub-processes 24,
  145, 186, 230
Sun Microsystems
  199

Supplier 74, 112,
  176, 195, 231
Supplier
  Management 102
Supplier Network
  84, 161
Supplier
  Relationship 123,
  194, 270
Supply Chain 24,
  112, 122, 172,
  176, 343
Supply Chain Assets
  115, 176, 179
Supply Chain Costs
  177
Supply Chain
  Efficiency 105
Supply Chain
  Integration 81,
  113, 118
Supply Chain
  Management
  (SCM) 57, 59, 61,
  72, 99, 100, 104,
  111, 121, 124,
  131, 203, 252,
  267, 343
Supply Chain
  Management
  (SCM) Method
  268
Supply Chain
  Management
  (SCM) System
  175, 180
Supply Chain Model
  105
Supply Chain
  Modules 292
Supply Chain
  Network 36, 106,
  132, 253

Supply Chain
  Operations
  Reference-model
  (SCOR) 70, 99,
  105, 131, 176, 179
Supply Chain
  Performance 130,
  268
Supply Chain
  Planning (SCP)
  75, 123, 186, 250
Supply Chain
  Potential 113
Supply Chain
  Process 24, 106,
  257
Supply Chain
  Pyramid 177
Supply Chain
  Scenario 105, 275
Swatch 121, 124,
  125, 127, 132, 256
Synchronization
  131, 179, 185,
  186, 207, 263
Synergies 68, 139,
  246
Syntax 215, 232,
  233, 245, 257

T

Taiwan
  Semiconductor
  Manufacturing
  Company (TSMC)
  104, 105
Telecommunication
  95, 237
Telematics 103
Template 82, 211,
  217, 218, 219,
  220, 221, 222,
  224, 225, 226,
  227, 228, 343

Template Handbook
216, 218, 219,
220, 221, 222,
223, 227
Template Method
219
Tenders 200, 202
Threshold Value
116, 117
ThyssenKrupp 235
Time Management
147
TIScover 29, 48
Tissot 124
Tobit 18
Total Cost of
Ownership (TCO)
308
Total Quality
Management
(TQM) 344
Tourism Industry 36
TPN Register 200,
206
Trade-off 122, 184
Trading Partner
Agreement (TPA)
244
Trading Platform
102, 129, 234, 235
Traffic 103
Transaction 73, 99,
133, 163, 180,
201, 252
Transaction
Management 199
Transaction
Perspective 101
Transaction Process
263
Transaction
Standards 245
Transformation 2, 3,
4, 18, 101, 137,

156, 157, 159,
241, 254
Transformation
Management 53
Transmission
Control Protocol
(TCP) 214
Transmission
Control
Protocol/Internet
Protocol (TCP/IP)
39, 166, 212, 244,
245
Transparency 80,
130, 208, 228, 263
Transportation
Planning 186
Travelocity 48, 136,
137
Trends 23, 113, 114,
136, 139, 140,
157, 159, 162,
164, 172, 176,
187, 188, 191,
230, 231
Triaton 230, 234,
235, 236, 237,
238, 239, 240,
241, 245, 246

U

UBS 38, 65
UN 205, 206
UN/SPSC 205, 206
Universal Mobile
Telecommunica-
tion Standard
(UMTS) 34
Upstream 100, 172,
184
User Guide 218
User-friendliness
158, 190, 198

V

Value Chain 344
Value Management
51
Value-added 164,
177, 188
Value-added Service
50, 142
Vantive 172
Vendor Managed
Inventory (VMI)
26, 106, 117, 172,
256, 259, 276, 344
Viagra 163
Virtual Community
18, 48, 344
Virtual Organizing
90, 92, 95, 96, 97,
98, 290, 344
Virtualization 83,
157
VISA 209
Vision 2, 157
Voicemail 32

W

Wal-Mart 106, 164
Warehouse
Management 90,
104, 114, 116,
132, 161
Wholesaler 131, 176
Wide Area Network
(WAN) 166
Windows CE 34
Win-Win Situation
78, 105, 112, 119,
130, 133, 238,
256, 260, 264
Wireless Access
Protocol (WAP)
34

Workflow
  Functionality 201
Workflow
  Management
  System (WFMS)
  151, 172, 198, 215
Workforce 116, 188
Work-in-progress
  105

Workplace 158, 202
WWW 149, 203,
  237

X

XML 39, 166, 200,
  263, 340

XML-related
  Standards 233

Y

Y2K 18, 27, 252
Yahoo! 18, 30, 37,
  40, 61, 101

Authors

Alt, Rainer Dr.	Project Manager of Competence Center Business Networking, Institute of Information Management, University of St. Gallen, Switzerland
Bach, Volker Dr.	Project Manager of Competence Center Business Knowledge Management, Institute of Information Management, University of St. Gallen, Switzerland
Barak, Vladimir Dr.	Head of IM/IT Coordination EMEA, Pharma Informatics, F. Hoffmann-La Roche Ltd., Basel, Switzerland
Betts, Robert	Internet Integration Practice Executive, IBM Global Services, USA
Dolmetsch, Ralph Dr.	Project Leader eProcurement Business Processes, Corporate Supply Management, SAir Group, Zürich, Switzerland
Fleisch, Elgar Dr. PD	Vice Director, Institute of Information Management, University of St. Gallen, Switzerland
Grünauer, Karl Maria	Consulting Manager, Information Management Group (IMG) AG, Arlesheim, Switzerland
Huber, Thomas Dr.	IM/IT Coordination EMEA, Pharma Informatics, F. Hoffmann-La Roche Ltd., Basel, Switzerland
Kaltenmorgen, Norbert	Service Unit Software & Solutions, HiServ Hightech International Services GmbH, A Company of ThyssenKrupp Information Services, Frankfurt, Germany
Klüber, Roland	Business Development Manager, E-Business / Conextrade, Swisscom AG, Zürich, Switzerland
Lehmann, Günter	Department Manager SAP Coordination, IT Division, Robert Bosch GmbH, Stuttgart, Germany

Österle, Hubert Prof. Dr.	Professor and Director of the Institute of Information Management at the University of St. Gallen, Partner of Information Management Group (IMG AG), St. Gallen, Switzerland
Pfadenhauer, Andreas	Product Manager, SAP AG, Walldorf, Germany
Pohland, Sven Dr.	Vice President, Practice Portal Builder, Information Management Group (IMG) AG, St. Gallen, Switzerland
Puschmann, Thomas	Research Assistant in the Competence Center Business Networking, Institute of Information Management, University of St. Gallen, Switzerland
Reichmayr, Christian	Research Assistant in the Competence Center Business Networking, Institute of Information Management, University of St. Gallen, Switzerland
Reiss, Thomas Dr.	Vice President, CRM Component Integration, SAP AG, Walldorf, Germany
Schelhas, Karl-Heinz	SAP Management, Groupwide Overall Planning for Information Systems, Information and Innovation Management, Deutsche Telekom AG, Bonn, Germany
Schulze, Jens Dr.	Consultant, Customer Relationship Management and Enterprise Application Integration, Lufthansa Systems AG, Norderstedt, Germany
Thiesse, Frederic	Research Assistant in the Competence Center Business Knowledge Management, Institute of Information Management, University of St. Gallen, Switzerland
Zurmühlen, Rudolf Dr.	Head of Customer Service, ETA SA Fabriques d'Ebauches, Grenchen, Switzerland

Questionnaire for Networkability Assessment

Networkability is the ability to cooperate internally and externally. Organizations and/or their dimensions are networkable if they can be integrated into other networks quickly and economically, e.g. if they can establish stable customer relationships quickly and economically. Networkability refers to the dimensions:

(a) Products/services (output),

(b) Business processes,

(c) Employees and managers,

(d) Information systems,

(e) Organization structure and

(f) Organization culture.

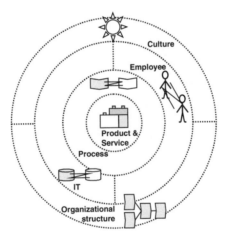

Dimensions of Networkability According to [Fleisch 2000]

The Task

Evaluate and discuss your networkability, i.e. that of your organization. The following questions are designed to help you with evaluation and discussion:

Question	No					Yes
	0	1	2	3	4	5
Networkability of a Product						
The product/service can be adapted to customer requirements quickly and easily (individualization)	❏	❏	❏	❏	❏	❏
The product (e.g. component) can be integrated into a larger output system quickly and easily (e.g. higher ranking component).	❏	❏	❏	❏	❏	❏
The product is a constituent part of numerous other output systems	❏	❏	❏	❏	❏	❏
Products are largely standardized	❏	❏	❏	❏	❏	❏
Products are largely modularized	❏	❏	❏	❏	❏	❏
Products are informatized as far as possible	❏	❏	❏	❏	❏	❏
Networkability of Processes						
The customer resource life cycle is known	❏	❏	❏	❏	❏	❏
I know my processes. They are transparent.	❏	❏	❏	❏	❏	❏
My processes comply with generally accepted standards	❏	❏	❏	❏	❏	❏
My processes are scalable in terms of quantity with a reasonable level of effort	❏	❏	❏	❏	❏	❏
My processes are scalable in terms of content with a reasonable level of effort	❏	❏	❏	❏	❏	❏

Question	No					Yes
	0	**1**	**2**	**3**	**4**	**5**
My innovation process is now consistently networked with the processes of the partners involved	❏	❏	❏	❏	❏	❏
My customer relationship process is now consistently networked with my customers' processes	❏	❏	❏	❏	❏	❏
My supply chain management process is now consistently networked with my customers' processes	❏	❏	❏	❏	❏	❏
My organization development process is now consistently networked with my customers' processes	❏	❏	❏	❏	❏	❏
I would consider the outsourcing of further support processes to be straightforward.	❏	❏	❏	❏	❏	❏
Networkability of an Employee						
Able to obtain and select external information	❏	❏	❏	❏	❏	❏
Identifies with own company; is able to recognize contributions to a company's market success without being told	❏	❏	❏	❏	❏	❏
Cooperates with other teams and/or business units, especially with a view to fulfilling customer requirements	❏	❏	❏	❏	❏	❏
Establishes contacts to external teams	❏	❏	❏	❏	❏	❏
Capable of self-motivation, self-discipline and self-control	❏	❏	❏	❏	❏	❏
Independently identifies problems, opportunities and alternatives; makes decisions	❏	❏	❏	❏	❏	❏

Question	No					Yes
	0	1	2	3	4	5
Able to innovate; bring about improvements in the work process	❏	❏	❏	❏	❏	❏
Able to manage distance to the company	❏	❏	❏	❏	❏	❏
Possesses communication skills; able to listen and to put the message across	❏	❏	❏	❏	❏	❏
Networkability of a Manager						
Maintains personal networks	❏	❏	❏	❏	❏	❏
Looks for and passes on information inside and outside the network	❏	❏	❏	❏	❏	❏
Represents the companies in the network	❏	❏	❏	❏	❏	❏
Networks with experts	❏	❏	❏	❏	❏	❏
Ability to build trust: demonstrates trust, shares values, acknowledges, sympathizes, shows sensitivity and willingness to take risks	❏	❏	❏	❏	❏	❏
Ability to empower employees: delegates responsibility and control, puts together effective teams, supports problem-solving processes	❏	❏	❏	❏	❏	❏
Enables employees to exercise self-management	❏	❏	❏	❏	❏	❏
Generates and implements strategic visions	❏	❏	❏	❏	❏	❏
Ability to organize processes of change: understands human reactions to change, implements change	❏	❏	❏	❏	❏	❏
Communication skills: rapidly assimilates condensed information, writes clearly, speaks convincingly and listens effectively	❏	❏	❏	❏	❏	❏

Question	No					Yes
	0	1	2	3	4	5
Political skills: negotiates, solves conflicts, establishes consensus	❏	❏	❏	❏	❏	❏
Motivating skills: is familiar with the cognitive and behavioral aspects of motivation and how to use them	❏	❏	❏	❏	❏	❏
Networkability of Information Systems						
All "relevant" information is accessible resp. externalized	❏	❏	❏	❏	❏	❏
The way in which all "relevant" information is stored is transparent	❏	❏	❏	❏	❏	❏
The semantics of externalized information is generally understandable	❏	❏	❏	❏	❏	❏
Network partners have "simple" access to information	❏	❏	❏	❏	❏	❏
Access for network partners can be set up quickly and economically (standardized and well-conceived)	❏	❏	❏	❏	❏	❏
It is possible to provide differentiated access for network partners	❏	❏	❏	❏	❏	❏
The relevant communication standards are known and have been taken into account	❏	❏	❏	❏	❏	❏
Capability for providing real-time information (integration with internal processing systems)	❏	❏	❏	❏	❏	❏
Information is available 24 hours a day	❏	❏	❏	❏	❏	❏

Question	No					Yes
	0	1	2	3	4	5
Networkability of Organization Structures						
The networking of my business unit is the concern of top management	❏	❏	❏	❏	❏	❏
Today, my business unit consistently participates in internal networks	❏	❏	❏	❏	❏	❏
The structures for internal networking are in place	❏	❏	❏	❏	❏	❏
Today, my business unit consistently participates in stable networks	❏	❏	❏	❏	❏	❏
Today, my business unit consistently participates in dynamic networks	❏	❏	❏	❏	❏	❏
The position of my business unit is clearly formulated (core competence per network)	❏	❏	❏	❏	❏	❏
My business unit takes a leap of faith in respect of network partners. We already have experience with the process of building trust.	❏	❏	❏	❏	❏	❏
The benefits of networking are transparent and are communicated	❏	❏	❏	❏	❏	❏
Organization development is oriented towards networking	❏	❏	❏	❏	❏	❏
My business unit lives out the rules of the "networked economy". The rules are known to all.	❏	❏	❏	❏	❏	❏
Processes for winning, developing, assessing and rewarding network partners are in place	❏	❏	❏	❏	❏	❏
The position of "networking manager" is filled	❏	❏	❏	❏	❏	❏

Question	No					Yes
	0	**1**	**2**	**3**	**4**	**5**
Networkability of Organization Cultures						
There is a clear understanding of the organization's purpose and its self-image is shared by all managers and employees	❑	❑	❑	❑	❑	❑
Information is used consciously as a tool for building trust	❑	❑	❑	❑	❑	❑
Trust within the organization and in relationship to network partners is highly developed	❑	❑	❑	❑	❑	❑
The values and standards lived out within the organization match those practiced outwardly	❑	❑	❑	❑	❑	❑
The willingness to take risks on the part of individuals and/or subsystems is highly developed and supported by stable agreements	❑	❑	❑	❑	❑	❑
Clear agreements with 100% commitment are the basis for decentralized, intelligent powers to act and make decisions	❑	❑	❑	❑	❑	❑
Deviations from agreements are actively taken up by the partners concerned and discussed on the basis of concrete proposals for a solution.	❑	❑	❑	❑	❑	❑
There are rituals for accepting responsibility when mistakes happen and a culture of learning from mistakes is well established (disillusionment = the end of an illusion)	❑	❑	❑	❑	❑	❑
Compensation between partners is not limited to money. There is a shared, basic attitude towards compensation.	❑	❑	❑	❑	❑	❑

Druck: Strauss Offsetdruck, Mörlenbach
Verarbeitung: Schäffer, Grünstadt